⊚Harden's

In association with **RÉMY MARTIN**
FINE CHAMPAGNE COGNAC
The Heart of Cognac

UK Restaurant Guide
2010

"Restaurant lovers bible" Daily Mail

Survey-driven reviews of over 1850
restaurants, pubs and cafés

The appreciation of excellence

Few business partnerships last as long as the co-operation between Rémy Martin and Harden's. This is based on many things, but particularly on authenticity, integrity and reliability, which are important to both of us.

Harden's derives its authenticity from its annual nationwide survey of restaurant-goers, leading to the creation of the UK's definitive democratic restaurant guides. For Rémy Martin, it comes from three centuries of tradition, its origins in the heart of Cognac and the unique know-how of the cellar-master.

The Heart of Cognac

Since 1724, Rémy Martin – the only large cognac house still in family ownership – has produced cognacs of exceptional quality and taste. Alone, it sources 100% of its grapes from the very 'heart of Cognac'. The "heart" has its own official designation: 'Appellation Fine Champagne Contrôllée'. "Fine Champagne" indicates a blend of cognac from the two best areas in the centre of the Cognac region, Grande Champagne (at least half the blend) and Petite Champagne.

Champagne lends its name to these two Cognac areas because, like the famous sparkling wine region, the soil is chalky. Over 80% of all the Fine Champagne cognac produced in this designated area is used in Rémy Martin Fine Champagne cognacs.

The result is three main characteristics which distinguish Rémy Martin: the harmony between the complex aromas and the sweetness of the flavours; the elegant richness of the aromas and palate; and the supreme length of the finish.

This is why we believe that Rémy Martin captures the very heart of Cognac and it is this unswerving dedication to quality over nearly three centuries that has led Rémy Martin to become the worldwide leader in the most premium of cognacs.

The Centaur

The Sagittarius Centaur – a symbol of the alliance of man and nature – was adopted by the Rémy Martin family in 1870. Not only is Sagittarius the star sign of Rémy Martin's founding father, Paul-Émile Rémy Martin, but it is also representative of many of the values that the family upholds – courage, energy, audacity and generosity.

Artist and Artisan

The role of the cellar master commands huge respect. It demands a special combination of skills: knowledgeable viticultualist, skilled wine maker, master blender, and expert taster, all whilst never losing sight of the house style. Thanks to the skilled craftsmanship of generations of cellar masters, Rémy Martin has been able to anticipate the evolution of consumer tastes and adapt and innovate accordingly.

Spirit for Life

Much more than a digestif, Rémy Martin has a cognac to suit every mood and occasion from celebrations to moments of solace. Throw out the rule book: aperitif, digestif, cocktail or frozen, Rémy Martin captures the spirit for living.

Rémy Martin V.S.O.P

This is the world's favourite V.S.O.P (Very Superior Old Pale) cognac and the benchmark by which all other V.S.O.P's are measured. Rémy Martin V.S.O.P shows near perfect balance of the three cornerstones of great cognac: floral, fruity and spice. Blended from over 240 eaux-de-vie, the result is a wonderfully balanced and smooth V.S.O.P.

Much more than simply a traditional digestif, the versatility of Rémy Martin V.S.O.P means it is perfect for many occasions. Why not try the recent trend from the US and impress friends by pulling a bottle out of the freezer and serving it chilled? Traditionally served at room temperature, freezing the cognac gives it a different dimension. The superior aromatic intensity which is characteristic of Rémy Martin V.S.O.P intensifies and concentrates to create an entirely new delicious drink with a smooth, richer viscosity. Every serve has a powerful depth of flavour creating a fuller, rounder taste and works particularly well with smoked fish such as salmon.

The pleasure of Rémy Martin V.S.O.P can make any moment special.

Coeur de Cognac

Through expert blending, Rémy Martin has created a fruit-driven and succulent spirit – Coeur de Cognac. Fresher and lighter than traditional cognacs, the predominant flavours are of apricot, honey and vanilla. The first taste is like biting into a succulent, juicy apricot whilst the nose bursts with ripe summer fruits and the palate is rich and soft – without the fiery finish usually associated with spirits.

Coeur de Cognac is intended for sheer drinking pleasure to be enjoyed anytime, anywhere. Try it with an ice cube or two which will help to reveal all its complex flavours and make an ideal aperitif.

Developed with people who appreciate fine food and dining in mind, it is a natural accompaniment to fruity deserts like apricot tart or petit fours such as macaroons or fruit jellies.

Rémy Martin XO

Sophisticated and beautifully balanced, Rémy Martin XO
Excellence (Extra Old) combines aromatic richness and
complexity with a wonderful velvety texture. The nose yields
hints of jasmine, ripe fig and candied orange and the palate
shows notes of cinnamon and freshly baked brioche.

Rémy Martin XO is aged for up to 37 years in Limousin oak cask
to achieve its maturity and balance.

XO is a wonderful digestif and the perfect partner to rich
hazelnut and cinnamon desserts. Rémy Martin XO truly is the
taste of extravagance.

Enjoying Rémy Martin

Not only are Rémy Martin Fine Champagne cognacs the ideal choice to round off a wonderful meal, but Rémy Martin can also be enjoyed as a long drink before dinner or as the perfect accompaniment to fine food.

Centaur Spice

A refreshing long drink, combining Rémy Martin V.S.O.P with a hint of orange and bitters, lengthened with ginger ale. A simple but stunning drink – ideal for dinner parties.

Method:

Fill a glass with ice

Add 2 dashes of Angostura bitters

Twist a sliver of orange peel over ice and drop into glass

Add a shot of Rémy Martin V.S.O.P

Top with ginger ale

Gently stir

French Mojito

50 ml of Remy Martin VSOP

Half of a lime

4 small cane sugar cubes (white or brown)

10 mints leafs

Crushed ice

Soda water

Method: build in a high ball glass

Muddle (mash) the mint, lime and sugar together.

Then fill your glass with crushed ice

Pour the cognac and stir gently

Topped up with a splash of soda water

Garnish with a mint sprig

RÉMY MARTIN
FINE CHAMPAGNE COGNAC

The Heart of Cognac

2010 Rémy Martin Restaurant Awards

2010 sees a new structure to the Restaurant Rémys. The Rémy Martin VSOP Award for the Best-Rated Newcomer remains the industry's most coveted recognition of up and coming restaurants and Rémy Martin is once again proud to be associated with the development of such a dynamic category.

Rémy Martin XO Excellence Award for Best All-Round Restaurant – London

Winner

Marcus Wareing at The Berkeley

Famously once number two to England's most prominent chef, Marcus Wareing has got off to a roaring start trading under his own name. Formerly called Pétrus (and part of the Gordon Ramsay empire), the restaurant at this grand Knightsbridge hotel – always of very high quality – has upped its already very skillful game now it has Marcus's name over the door. The year 2010 will present an amusing challenge. A new restaurant called Pétrus will be opened by Marcus's former boss, just a few hundred yards away. As London's leading hands-on chef-patron, however, Marcus faces the challenge with equanimity.

Runners Up
Chez Bruce
Le Gavroche
The Ledbury
La Trompette

New to the line up is the Coeur de Cognac Award for Best Dessert – a much overlooked, yet sublime aspect to a complete dining experience. Also new is the Rémy Martin XO Excellence Award for the Best All-Round Restaurant. This award is the result of painstaking analysis of the survey results to identify the true crème de la crème in the UK's ever more competitive restaurant world.

Rémy Martin XO Excellence Award for Best All-Round Restaurant – Rest of UK

Winner

Mr Underhills

 This restaurant-with-rooms, on the bank of the River Terne in Ludlow, has been a fixture of the 'Ludlow phenomenon' for a dozen years. This year has seen the ratings reporters award – always impressive – rise to exceptional levels, making this the best all-round restaurant across the board. Husband-and-wife team Chris and Judy Bradley have created a welcoming and unpretentious atmosphere in the airy dining room which looks over a bright courtyard. The food has been praised for being expertly cooked and beautifully presented, the highlight being the seven-course market menu of the day, with an emphasis on locally-sourced ingredients. The food is complemented by an excellent range of reasonably-priced wines.

Runners Up
Gidleigh Park, Chagford
Manoir aux Quat' Saisons, Great Milton
Waterside Inn, Bray
Northcote, Langho

RÉMY MARTIN
FINE CHAMPAGNE COGNAC

The Heart of Cognac

Coeur de Cognac Award for
Best Dessert – London

Winner

Marcus Wareing at the Berkeley
(Custard tart)

As a native Lancastrian – and having won recognition as London's top chef – it's particularly appropriate that Marcus Wareing should also carry off the prize for that most essential course in British cuisine: pudding. Marcus's skill for creating food that's both flawlessly presented and big on taste are showcased perfectly in his desserts. His best and this year's winner, his famed custard tart, owes much to his upbringing, having been the favourite dish of both his mother and grandmother.

Runners Up
The Ivy *(Iced berries with hot white chocolate sauce)*
Chez Bruce *(Cheeseboard)*
The Wolseley *(Victoria sandwich)*
L'Atelier de Joel Robuchon *(Le chocolat tendance)*

Coeur de Cognac Award for Best Dessert – Rest of UK

Winner

Lucy's on a Plate

Given the Lake District's renown for tea and cakes, Lucy Nicholson's acclaimed Ambleside venture is a fitting first winner of the Coeur de Cognac Best Dessert award. Starting with a specialist grocers in 1989, her empire has grown over the years to encompass a wine bar and outside caterering business. It's her café, though – which started life as tea rooms – that's still best known. Menus change daily, but what stays constant is the popularity of the homemade puddings: so much so that the restaurant runs a special 'Up the Duff Pudding Night' every month, when nothing but 'afters' is served.

Runners Up
J Bakers Bistro Moderne, York
Sportsman, Whitstable
Hambleton Hall, Hambleton
Waterside Inn, Bray

Rémy Martin VSOP Award for
Best Rated Newcomer – London

Winner

Murano

Although Angela Hartnett achieved fame in her time at the Connaught, it's at her latest Mayfair venture – part of the Gordon Ramsay group – that her cuisine has fully come into its own. The room is bright and comfortable, enlivened by impeccable service. Her Italian roots are clearly evident on her menu, although the style of the simple yet elegant cuisine is probably best characterised as modern European. With Murano, Angela has accomplished an extremely unusual achievement: winning the respect not only of her customers but also the esteem of her fellow chefs, in what remains a famously male-dominated world.

Runners Up
Min Jiang
Bull & Last
Soseki
Trishna

Rémy Martin VSOP Award for Best Rated Newcomer – Rest of UK

Winner

Wedgwood

Scots-born chef, Paul Wedgwood, returned from running the kitchen of a restaurant in the Lake District to put his name over the door of this Old Town venture in August 2007. Right on the Royal Mile – and run with his partner Lisa Channon – it combines contemporary looks with enthusiastic service and a relaxed atmosphere. Having just 48 covers allows for the couple's personal style and attention to detail to shine through. This is most evident in the excellent-value cuisine – putting the emphasis on locally sourced and foraged ingredients – and a carefully chosen wine list.

Runners Up
The Fish House, Chilgrove
Turners, Birmingham
Vatika, Southampton
Sams of Brighton, Brighton

Put us in your pocket!

Coming soon to your iPhone or BlackBerry

Be the first to know! register at www.hardens.com/pda/launch

© **Harden's Limited 2009**

British Library Cataloguing-in-Publication data: a catalogue record for this book is available from the British Library.

Underlying UK map images ©MAPS IN MINUTES™/Collins Bartholomew (2008).

Printed in Italy by Rotolito Lombarda

Research assistants: Hannah Hodges, Sarah Ashpole, Lidia Fessahazion, Gregg Patton, Sean Noel de Souza, Elyse Quinn

Content Manager: Alexandra Woodward

Harden's Limited
14 Buckingham Street
London WC2N 6DF

The views expressed in the editorial section of this guide are exclusively those of Harden's Limited

Would restaurateurs (and PRs) please address communications to 'Editorial' at the above address, or ideally by email to: editorial@hardens.com

CONTENTS

J Sheekey 100

Babur 42

RATINGS & PRICES

We see little point in traditional rating systems, which generally tell you nothing more than that expensive restaurants are 'better' than cheap ones, as they use costlier ingredients and attempt more ambitious dishes. You probably knew that already. Our system assumes that, as prices rise, so do diners' expectations.

£ Price
The cost of a three-course dinner for one person.
We include half a bottle of house wine, coffee and service (or a 10% tip if there is no service charge).

Food
The following symbols indicate that, *in comparison with other restaurants in the same price-bracket*, the cooking at the establishment is:

 Exceptional

Very good

Some restaurants are worth a mention but, for some reason (typically low feedback) we do not think a rating is appropriate. These are indicated as follows:

Tip

 A top choice for both eating and sleeping

We also have a category for places which attract a notably high proportion of adverse comment:

Disappointing

Ambience
Restaurants which provide a setting which is very charming, stylish or 'buzzy' are indicated as follows:

Particularly atmospheric

Restaurant Rémy awards
A Restaurant Rémy symbol signifies this year's winners – see front colour section

Small print

Telephone number – All numbers in the London section are (020) numbers.
Details – the following information is given where relevant:
Directions – to help you find the establishment.
Website – if applicable.
Last orders time – at dinner (Sun may be up to 90 mins earlier).
Opening hours – unless otherwise stated, restaurants are open for lunch and dinner seven days a week.
Credit and debit cards – unless otherwise stated, Mastercard, Visa, Amex and Maestro are accepted.
Dress – where appropriate, the management's preferences concerning patrons' dress are given.
Children – if we know of a specified minimum age for children, we note this.
Accommodation – if an establishment has rooms, we list how many and the minimum price for a double.

FROM THE EDITORS

To an extent we believe to be unique, this guide is written 'from the bottom up'. That is to say, its composition reflects the restaurants, pubs and cafés which people across the country – as represented by our diverse reporter base – talk about. It does not, therefore, concentrate on hotel restaurants (as does one of the major 'independent' guides whose publisher also does big business in paid-for hotel inspections). Nor does it 'overweight' European cuisines. Most restaurants in this country fall in the category usually called 'ethnic', but most guidebooks would lead you to think that such places are generally unworthy of serious commentary. It seems to us that this approach is positively wrong-headed in a country where the diversity of restaurant types is one of the most notable (and positive) features.

The effects of London's restaurant revolution of the '90s are now apparent across the whole of the UK. Most major conurbations, for example, now have several ambitious restaurants good enough to be of note to visitors. The areas that are still truly 'culinary deserts' are becoming both smaller and more dispersed. Much as this is to be applauded, it does not make our task any easier, and we are keenly aware – as any honest publisher must acknowledge – that all guide books are imperfect. There will be deserving places missing, and opinions will be repeated that the passing of time has rendered redundant. However, we believe that our system – involving the careful processing of tens of thousands of reports – is the best available.

We are very grateful to each of our thousands of reporters, without whose input this guide could simply not have been written. Many of our reporters express views about a number of restaurants at some length, knowing full well that – given the concise format of the guide – we can seemingly never 'do justice' to their observations. We must assume that they do so in the confidence that the short – and we hope snappy – summaries we produce are as fair and as well-informed as possible. You, the reader, must judge – restaurant guides are not works of literature, and should be assessed on the basis of utility. This is a case where the proof of the pudding really is in the eating.

Given the growing scale of our task, we are particularly grateful for the continuing support we have received from Rémy Martin Fine Champagne Cognac in the publication of this guide. With their help, this is now well on the way to becoming the most comprehensive – as well as the most democratic and diverse – guide available to the restaurants of the UK.

All restaurant guides are the subject of continual revision. This is especially true when the restaurant scene is undergoing a period of rapid change, as at present. **Please help us to make the next edition even more comprehensive and accurate: sign up to join the survey by following the instructions overleaf.**

Richard Harden   **Peter Harden**

How This Book Is Organised

This guide begins in London, which, in recognition of the scale and diversity of its restaurant scene, has an extensive introduction and indexes, as well as its own maps. Thereafter, the guide is organised strictly alphabetically, without regard to national divisions – Ballater, Beaumaris, Belfast and Birmingham appear together under 'B'.

For cities and larger towns, you should therefore be able to turn straight to the relevant section. Cities which have significant numbers of restaurants also have a brief introductory overview, as well as entries for the restaurants themselves.

In less densely populated areas, you will generally find it easiest to start with the map of the relevant area at the back of the book, which will guide you to the appropriate place names.

How This Book Is Researched

This book is the result of a research effort involving thousands of 'reporters'. These are 'ordinary' members of the public who share with us summary reviews of the best and the worst of their annual dining experiences. This year, more than 8,000 people gave us over 85,000 reviews in total.

The density of the feedback on London (where many of the top places attract several hundred reviews each) is such that the ratings for the restaurants in the capital included in this edition are almost exclusively statistical in derivation. We have, as it happens, visited almost all the restaurants in the London section, anonymously, and at our own expense, but we use our personal experiences only to inform the standpoint from which to interpret the consensus opinion.

In the case of the more commented-upon restaurants away from the capital, we have adopted an approach very similar to London. In the case of less-visited provincial establishments, however, the interpretation of survey results owes as much to art as it does to science.

In our experience, smaller establishments are – for better or worse – generally quite consistent, and we have therefore felt able to place a relatively high level of confidence in a lower level of commentary. Conservatism on our part, however, may have led to some smaller places being underrated compared to their more visited peers.

How You Can Join The Survey

Register on our mailing list at www.hardens.com and you will be invited, in the spring of 2010, to participate in our next survey. **If you take part you will, on publication, receive a complimentary copy of Harden's Restaurant Guide 2011.**

LONDON
INTRODUCTION &
SURVEY RESULTS

LONDON INTRODUCTION

What makes London special?
This question would once have been easy to answer: London was the opposite of Paris. There you could eat one cuisine only – albeit in all its various regional glories – supremely well. London, like New York, was a city where nothing was done especially well, but at least the scene was cosmopolitan.

Well, London's cosmopolitanism has not gone away, and standards continue to improve across the board, but there are now at least two specialities of particular note. The first, chronologically speaking, was the cuisine of the Indian subcontinent, which is offered in London in greater variety, within a small geographical area, than anywhere else in the world. And the more recent speciality is…British cuisine! London is now the only city where you can consistently eat well in a varied idiom which is clearly British!

Which is London's best restaurant?
It's getting more and more difficult to say, because the old rules – which boiled down to French is Best – seem ever more inappropriate today. But let's stick with the traditional 'haute cuisine' definition. If you want the whole high-falutin' Gallic dining experience, the top all-rounder – no question – is *Marcus Wareing at the Berkeley*. In a rather more traditional style, London's original post-war grand restaurant, *Le Gavroche*, still has a lot going for it.

In a very superior second tier are a number of restaurants which have maintained very high quality for a good number of years, including *Pied à Terre,* the *Square* and the *Capital Hotel.* (and, heading up the reserves, the *Greenhouse*). A recent opening which is beginning to knock on the door of the front rank – and which offers a bit of grand hotel bling thrown in – is *The Landau. (*With that exception, and *Marcus Wareing*, London's hotels offer little truly top-end dining.)

What about something a little more reasonably priced?
For top-flight French culinary experiences just below the top tier, price-wise, *Roussillon* (Pimlico) and *Morgan M* (Islington) are the two places most worth seeking out. If you'd like to check out a member of the group associated with worldwide TV star Gordon Ramsay, by far the best group restaurant of the moment is the excellent new *Murano* (Mayfair).

Notting Hill's *The Ledbury* also rates mention. It's part of a fine group of restaurants that have in common the 'hidden' guiding hand of restaurateur Nigel Platts-Martin – this includes not just 'London's Favourite Restaurant', *Chez Bruce* (Wandsworth), but also *La Trompette* (Chiswick) and the *Glasshouse* (Kew), as well as the aforementioned Square.

What about some really good suggestions in the heart of the West End?
It used to be difficult to recommend places to dine well in the West End at reasonable cost, but the position has improved

hugely in recent years. Names particularly to consider include *Arbutus*, *Giaconda Dining Room*, *Galvin Bistro de Luxe* and *Wild Honey*. If you're happy to eat in tapas style, add to this list such recent arrivals as *Barrafina*, *Bocca di Lupo*, *Dehesa*, *Sheekey's Oyster Bar* and *Terroirs*.

If you want a little more comfort and style, as well as pretty good food you're unlikely to go far wrong at the discreet *Caprice* (just behind the Ritz), or its siblings *J Sheekey* (hidden-away in Theatreland) and *Scott's* (a celebrity magnet on one of the grandest streets in Mayfair). These last are hardly bargain suggestions, but they do offer all-round value. For pure theatre, a visitor looking for that sort of style should probably try to eat at the *Wolseley* – the nation's 'grand café', by the Ritz – at some point:

Covent Garden is a tricky area, rich in tourist traps, but is now the unlikely home of a restaurant that's beginning to approach 'destination' status – *Clos Maggiore*.

And for the best of British?
As we hinted above, British food has only very recently emerged from a sort of tourist ghetto. If it's the grand end of that market you're looking for, seek out the Roast Beef of Olde England at *Simpson's-on-the-Strand*. Less impressive in scale, but much better, is nearby *Rules* – a beautiful old-timer, where game is the culinary speciality.

That, though, is not the sort of cooking, – often offal-rich and rediscovering historical dishes – that's making British one of the most fashionable cuisines in town. The pioneer establishment of the new-wave Brits – which for so long seemed to be crying in the wilderness – was *St John*. Over the last few years, however, the trend – often mixed in with 'gastropub' cooking in many people's minds – has become mainstream. Restaurants proper which may be said to be strongly influenced by the style include *Magdalen*, *Great Queen Street*, *Hereford Road* and *St John Bread & Wine*. It will probably also feature at the new Heston Blumenthal restaurant to open at the swanky Mandarin Oriental hotel in 2010. But a lot of this sort of cooking is taking place in gastropubs…

What are gastropubs?
These are essentially bistros in the premises of former pubs. They come in a variety of styles. What many people think of as the original gastropub (*The Eagle*, 1991) still looks very much like a pub with a food counter. At the other end of the scale, however, the 'pub' element is almost redundant, and the business is really just a restaurant housed in premises that happen once to have been a pub.

Few of the best gastropubs are particularly central. The reasonably handy location of the *Anchor & Hope*, on the South Bank, is no doubt part of the reason for its crazy popularity. Hammersmith and its environs, for some reason, have a particular concentration, with the *Anglesea Arms* the stand-out

27

performer there. Two new stars are the *Bull & Last* (Kentish Town) and *Harwood Arms* (Fulham).

Isn't London supposed to be a top place for curry?

London, as noted above, has a reasonable claim to being the world's top Indian restaurant city. Leading lights such as *Rasoi, Amaya, The Painted Heron, Benares* and *Zaika* are pushing back the frontiers, but – perfectly reasonably – charge the same as their European equivalents. What's more exciting in terms of value are the many Indian restaurants where you can eat much more cheaply than you could eat European. Two top names in the East End are almost legendary 'value' experiences – the *Lahore Kebab House* and *New Tayyabs*.

Any tips to beat the crunch?

●The top tip, already noted, is to lunch not dine. If you're a visitor, you'll find that it's better for your wallet, as well as your digestion, to have your main meal in the middle of the day. In the centre of town, it's one of the best ways you can be sure of eating 'properly' at reasonable cost.

●Think ethnic – for a food 'experience' at modest cost, you'll still generally be better off going Indian, Thai, Chinese or Vietnamese (to choose four of the most obvious cuisines) than French, English or Italian. The days when there was any sort of assumption that ethnic restaurants were – in terms of comfort, service and décor – in any way inferior to European ones is long gone.

●Try to avoid the West End. That's not to say that, armed with this book, you shouldn't be able to eat well in the heart of things, but you'll almost certainly do better in value terms outside the Circle line. Many of the best and cheapest restaurants in this guide are easily accessible by tube. Use the maps at the back of this book to identify restaurants near tube stations on a line that's handy for you.

●If you must dine in the West End, try to find either pre-theatre (generally before 7.30 pm) or post-theatre (generally after 10 pm) menus. You will generally save at least the cost of a cinema ticket, compared to dining à la carte. Many of the more upmarket restaurants in Theatreland do such deals.

●Use this book! Don't take pot luck, when you can benefit from the pre-digested views of thousands of other diners-out. Choose a place with a 1 or 2 for food, and you're very likely to eat much better than if you walk in somewhere on spec' – this is good advice anywhere, but is most particularly so in the West End. Once you have decided that you want to eat within a particular area, use the Area Overviews (starting on p280) to identify the restaurants that are offering top value.

●Visit our website, www.hardens.com, for the latest reviews, and restaurant news.

SURVEY MOST MENTIONED

These are the restaurants which were most frequently mentioned by reporters. (Last year's position is given in brackets.) An asterisk* indicates the first appearance in the list of a recently-opened restaurant.

1   J Sheekey (1)
2   Chez Bruce (2)
3   Scott's (7)
4   The Wolseley (3)
5   Marcus Wareing at the Berkeley (8)
6   Hakkasan (4)
7   Bleeding Heart (6)
8   Le Gavroche (9)
9= Gordon Ramsay (5)
9= Galvin Bistrot de Luxe (15)

Chez Bruce

11 Le Caprice (16)
12=The Ivy (10)
12=La Poule au Pot (11)
14 Andrew Edmunds (17)
15 La Trompette (12)
16 The Cinnamon Club (-)
17 Arbutus (13)
18=Zuma (18)
18=maze (28)
20 Oxo Tower (14)

Yauatcha

21 Gordon Ramsay at Claridge's (20)
22 L'Atelier de Joel Robuchon (30)
23 Yauatcha (21)
24 Clos Maggiore (-)
25 The Square (19)
26 Benares (26)
27 The Anchor & Hope (22)
28 St John (38)
29 Wild Honey (23)
30 The River Café (33)

Cinnamon Club

31 The Ledbury (35)
32 Locanda Locatelli (25)
33 Le Café Anglais (29)
34 Amaya (34)
35 Corrigan's Mayfair*
36=The Don (36)
36=Bocca Di Lupo*
38 New Tayyabs (-)
39 Moro (32)
40 Murano*

Amaya

LONDON - HIGHEST RATINGS

These are the restaurants which received the best average food ratings (excluding establishments with a small or notably local following).

Where the most common types of cuisine are concerned, we present the results in two price-brackets. For less common cuisines, we list the top three, regardless of price.

British, Modern

£45 and over	**Under £45**
1 Chez Bruce	1 Tom Ilic
2 Lamberts	2 Harwood Arms
3 The Glasshouse	3 Market
4 The Landau	4 Palmerston
5 Trinity	5 Anglesea Arms, W6

French

£45 and over	**Under £45**
1 Morgan M	1 Upstairs Bar
2 Marcus Wareing	2 Brula
3 The Ledbury	3 Terroirs
4 La Trompette	4 Giaconda Dining Rooms
5 Roussillon	5 Cellar Gascon

Italian/Mediterranean

£45 and over	**Under £45**
1 Assaggi	1 Salt Yard
2 Murano	2 Dehesa
3 Latium	3 Ristorante Semplice
4 Tentazioni	4 Bocca Di Lupo
5 Oliveto	5 500

Indian

£45 and over	**Under £45**
1 Amaya	1 Rasa N16
2 Rasoi	2 New Tayyabs
3 Zaika	3 Ragam
4 The Painted Heron	4 Lahore Kebab House
5 Cinnamon Kitchen	5 Babur

Chinese

£45 and over
1. Hunan
2. Yauatcha
3. Hakkasan
4. Min Jiang
5. Princess Garden

Under £45
1. Mandarin Kitchen
2. Dragon Castle
3. Haozhan
4. Goldfish
5. Harbour City

Japanese

£45 and over
1. Zuma
2. Roka
3. Umu
4. Nobu
5. Nobu Berkeley

Under £45
1. Sushi-Say
2. Dinings
3. Jin Kichi
4. Café Japan
5. Pham Sushi

British, Traditional
1. Scott's
2. St John Bread & Wine
3. The Anchor & Hope

Vegetarian
1. Roussillon
2. Mildreds
3. The Gate

Burgers, etc
1. Lucky Seven
2. Haché
3. Ground

Pizza
1. Franco Manca
2. Oliveto
3. The Oak

Fish & Chips
1. Nautilus
2. Golden Hind
3. Fish Club

Thai
1. Sukho Thai Cuisine
2. Esarn Kheaw
3. Addie's Thai Café

Fusion
1. The Providores
2. Champor-Champor
3. Village East

Fish & Seafood
1. One-O-One
2. Mandarin Kitchen
3. J Sheekey

Greek
1. Vrisaki
2. Daphne
3. Lemonia

Spanish
1. Barrafina
2. Moro
3. El Faro

Turkish
1. Mangal Ocakbasi
2. Cyprus Mangal
3. Kazan

Lebanese
1. Chez Marcelle
2. Fakhreldine
3. Pasha

SURVEY - NOMINATIONS

Ranked by the number of reporters' votes.

Top gastronomic experience

The Square

1. Marcus Wareing at the Berkeley (3)
2. Chez Bruce (2)
3. Le Gavroche (4)
4. Gordon Ramsay (1)
5. La Trompette (5)
6. maze (9)
7. L'Atelier de Joel Robuchon (7)
8. The Ledbury (-)
9. The Square (-)
10. Murano*

Favourite

Le Caprice

1. Chez Bruce (1)
2. Le Caprice (2)
3. J Sheekey (3)
4= The Wolseley (5)
4= The Ivy (6)
6. La Trompette (4)
7. Galvin Bistrot de Luxe (9)
8. Scott's (-)
9. Moro (7)
10. St John (-)

Best for business

The Wolseley

1. The Wolseley (1)
2. Bleeding Heart (3)
3. The Don (2)
4. Coq d'Argent (6)
5. The Square (4)
6. L'Anima*
7. 1 Lombard Street (5)
8. Scott's (-)
9. Galvin Bistrot de Luxe (9)
10. St Alban (-)

Best for romance

La Poule au Pot

1. La Poule au Pot (1)
2. Andrew Edmunds (2)
3. Clos Maggiore (5)
4. Bleeding Heart (3)
5. Chez Bruce (4)
6. Le Caprice (6)
7. J Sheekey (10)
8. Marcus Wareing at the Berkeley (8)
9. Galvin at Windows (-)
10. Le Gavroche (-)

OPENINGS AND CLOSURES

Restaurants in bold are included in the London section of this guide – for the full selection, see Harden's London Restaurants 2010 (£11.99), available in all good bookshops.

Openings

Albion
Abeno *NW3*
Aqua Kyoto
Aqua Nueva
Arch One
Atari-Ya *NW4*
The Avalon
Ba Shan
Bar Trattoria Semplice
Il Baretto
The Bathhouse
Bocca Di Lupo
The Bolingbroke
La Bottega *SW7*
Brinkley's Kitchen
Brompton Bar & Grill
Brouge *TW2, TW9*
Bull & Last
Byron *W12*
The Cadogan Arms
Canteen *W1*
Caponata
Casa Brindisa
Cha Cha Moon *W2*
Chakalaka *W4*
The Chelsea Kitchen
Chilango *N1, EC4*
The Chippy
Coast
Comptoir Libanais *W1, W2, W12*
Corrigan's Mayfair
Côte *WC2, W8*
Daylesford Organics *W11*
Dean Street Townhouse & Dining Room
Dockmaster's House
Dotori
The Drapers Arms
The East Room
Eastside Inn
Ekachai *W1*
The Establishment *SW11*
Fat Boys *SW14*
The Fellow
Fire & Stone *W12*
500
Forman's
Gail's Bread *NW8*
Gallery Mess
Galvin La Chapelle
Garufa
Gilmour's
Goodman
Green's *EC3*

High Timber
Ibérica
Indali Lounge
Jamie's Italian
Keelung
The Kensington Wine Rooms
Kings Road Steakhouse & Grill
Lena
Lower East
Lutyens
The Luxe
Madsen
Marco Pierre White Steakhouse & Grill
The Meat & Wine Co
More
Mrs Marengos
No.20
Noto Kikuya
1001 Nights
Okawari *WC2*
Ooze *W12*
The Orange
Osteria Dell'Angolo
The Palm
The Pembroke
Pétrus
El Pirata de Tapas
Port of Manila
Portobello Ristorante Pizzeria
Princi
Le Provence
The Refinery
Le Relais de Venise L'Entrecôte *EC2*
The Restaurant at St Paul's
Rocca Di Papa
Roka
Rosa's
The Rose & Crown
Rossopomodoro *WC2*
Rotunda
The Roundhouse
Royal Wok
St Pancras Grand
Santo
Seasons Dining Room
Sophie's Steakhouse *WC2*
Soseki
Sushinho
The Swan & Edgar

Openings cont

A Taste Of McClements
Terroirs
tibits
Tierra Brindisa
Trishna
Tsunami *W1*
twotwentytwo
Ultimate Burger *W1*
Il Vaporetto
Viajante
Villandry Kitchen
Villiers Terrace
Vineria
Wahaca *W12, E14*
**Whitechapel Gallery
    Dining Room**
The Wine Theatre
Yalla Yalla
The Yellow House
Zeen

Closures

Aaya
Agni
Amato
L'Ambassade de L'Ile
Aperitivo
Aquasia
Arancia *two SE1 branches*
Bar Bourse
Barnes Grill
Bincho Yakitori *SE1*
Bodeguita del Medio
The Brackenbury
Brasserie St Quentin
Bush Bar & Grill
Caldesi
Drones
Eat & Two Veg *N10*
11 Abingdon Road
Eco *W4*
Franklins *SE11*
Freemasons

Giardinetto
Giusto
Greyhound at Battersea
Grille
Haiku
Iznik Kaftan
Lanes (East India House)
Levantine
Lilly's
Lindsay House
Made in China
Mimmo d'Ischia
Missouri Grill
Mosaico
Nanglo
Nosh
Notting Grill
Noto Kikuya
Osteria Stecca
Pacific Bar and Grill
Papageno
Passione
Philpotts Mezzaluna
Picasso's
Pick More Daisies
(Ciro's) Pizza Pomodoro *EC2*
Pomegranates
Rocket *SW15*
Rose & Crown
Rôtisserie Jules *W11*
Royal China Club *NW8*
San Carlo
Seabass *W2*
Singapura *EC3, EC4*
Snows on the Green
Spiga
Tatsuso
3 Monkeys
Tom's Place
Ubon
Vic Naylors
Vino Rosso
Yakitoria

LONDON DIRECTORY

A Cena TW1 £42
418 Richmond Rd   8288 0108

On "the wrong side of Richmond Bridge" (in St Margarets),
this "intimate" Italian has built an impressive following, thanks to its
"consistently good" food, "knowledgeable" staff and "lovely"
surroundings. / **Details:** www.acena.co.uk; 10 pm; closed Mon L & Sun D;
booking: max 6, Fri & Sat.

Abokado WC2 £15
160 Drury Ln   7242 5600   3–2D
"A brilliant alternative to the lunchtime sandwich"; this small oriental
take-away chain ("like Itsu but much better") is roundly praised for its
"fresh, delicious and inexpensive" fare, which includes some "excellent
sushi and wraps". / **Details:** www.abokado.com; 7.30 pm; closed Sat & Sun.

About Thyme SW1 £40
82 Wilton Rd   7821 7504   1–4B
Much improved in recent times, this "welcoming" Pimlico spot
is emerging as something of an unexpected "gem"; the Spanish/French
menu includes some "quite unusual" dishes, and the results are usually
"very good"; a tapas menu is a recent innovation.
/ **Details:** www.aboutthyme.co.uk; 11 pm.

Abu Zaad W12 £20
29 Uxbridge Rd   8749 5107   6–1C
"A small trip to Syria" is on offer to those who visit this "stalwart" café,
near Shepherd's Bush market... and at an "unbelievably cheap" price
too; "fab juices" and "first-class" mezze and kebabs.
/ **Details:** www.abuzaad.co.uk; 11 pm.

The Academy W11 £37
57 Princedale Rd   7221 0248   5–2A
"A great neighbourhood stand-by" in a "quiet backwater" of Holland
Park – this "traditional pub", with "separate conservatory dining area",
serves some "good-value" fare. / **Details:** www.academybar.com; 11 pm,
Sun 10.30 pm; no Amex.

Adams Café W12 £26
77 Askew Rd   8743 0572   6–1B
By day it's a regular greasy spoon, but at night this "fantastic", family-run
Shepherd's Bush "favourite" serves "delicious tajines and couscous" and
other "authentic" Tunisian dishes, with great "charm";
for modest corkage, you can BYO. / **Details:** www.adamscafe.co.uk; 11 pm;
closed Sun.

Addie's Thai Café SW5 £26 ⭐

121 Earl's Court Rd 7259 2620 4–2A
"Chock-full of oriental customers", this *"cramped and uncomfortable"* –
but *"very friendly"* – café, by Earl's Court tube, serves *"brilliant"* food
in *"true Bangkok style"*. / **Details:** www.addiesthai.co.uk; 11 pm; closed
Sat L & Sun L; no Amex.

Aglio e Olio SW10 £34

194 Fulham Rd 7351 0070 4–3B
A *"great Chelsea local"* that's *"packed to the rafters"* (and *"unbearably
noisy"*) – the food *"doesn't suffer from the popularity"*, though, and you
get *"perfect pasta"* in *"generous portions"*, and at *"excellent prices"* too.
/ **Details:** 11.30 pm.

Al-Waha W2 £33 ⭐

75 Westbourne Grove 7229 0806 5–1B
"Year after year", this *"quiet"* and unremarkable-looking Bayswater
Lebanese has proved itself *"unbelievably consistent"*, thanks to its
"extremely friendly" staff and its *"delightful"* food – *"rather like you find
in many other Middle Eastern restaurants, just better!"*
/ **Details:** www.alwaharestaurant.com; 11.30 pm; no Amex.

Alain Ducasse
Dorchester W1 £99

53 Park Ln 7629 8866 2–3A
"What is Michelin thinking, giving it two stars?" – *"massive hype meets
modest execution"*, at this *"disgracefully overpriced"* Mayfair
outpost of the mega-starry Parisian über-chef: the set lunch, though,
is undoubtedly a *"steal"*. / **Value tip:** set weekday L £65
(FP). **Details:** www.alainducasse-dorchester.com; 10 pm; closed Mon, Sat L & Sun;
jacket.

Alastair Little W1 £50

49 Frith St 7734 5183 3–2A
This *"café-like"* Soho site which was once at the forefront of the 'Modern
British' culinary revolution (as it was then called) was closed as this guide
went to press; we're told that a relaunch is planned. / **Value tip:** set pre
theatre £31 (FP). **Details:** 11.30 pm; closed Sun.

The Albemarle
Brown's Hotel W1d £72 Ⓐ

Albemarle St 7493 6020 2–3C
More *"classic"* in style than most hotel dining rooms nowadays,
this *"cosseting"* Mayfair chamber is a *"discreet setting for power
lunches"*, or *"comfortable"* fine dining; it inspires limited feedback,
however, suggesting its aim to become a sort of Savoy Grill II isn't quite
achieved yet… / **Details:** www.roccofortecollection.com; 10.30 pm.

Alisan HA9 £31 ⭐

The Junction, Engineers Way, Wembley 8903 3888

"Pretty amazing" dim sum justifies the trek to this *"oddly-located"* but
"friendly" restaurant, by Wembley Stadium; the *"lifeless"* setting, though,
has all the ambience of a *"school hall"*. / **Details:** www.alisan.co.uk; 11 pm,
Sat 11.30 pm, Sun 10.30 pm; closed Tue.

Amaya SW1 £57
Halkin Arc, 19 Motcomb St 7823 1166 4–1D

With its "eye-opening" cuisine (served "tapas"-style) and "striking" setting, this "brilliant" modern Indian, in Belgravia, is hard to beat; the staff can occasionally seem "aloof", but they're "very knowledgeable" too. / Details: www.realindianfood.com; 11.30 pm, Sun 10.30 pm.

Anarkali W6 £28
303-305 King St 8748 1760 6–2B
"I went here when I was a boy – now I take my own kids"; this Hammersmith stalwart has long been a local favourite for those in search of "British-traditional" Indian fare, despite dated-going-on-"dreary" décor; it's closed as we go to press, apparently for a refurb, but re-opening is promised soon. / Details: www.anarkalirestaurant.co.uk; midnight, Sun 11.30 pm.

The Anchor & Hope SE1 £35
36 The Cut 7928 9898
"Crazy-busy", this Waterloo legend is still the survey's No. 1 gastropub, thanks to its "exciting" and "hearty" cooking, from an "offal-centric" menu (with "shades of St John"); "it practically takes bare-knuckle fighting to get a table". / Details: 10.30 pm; closed Mon L & Sun D; no Amex; no booking.

Andrew Edmunds W1 £36
46 Lexington St 7437 5708 2–2D
"It's cramped and uncomfortable – I can't wait to go back!"; this "delightfully quirky" Soho townhouse is again voted "the most romantic spot in central London", thanks to its "gorgeous", candlelit, "Boho" ambience and its "cracking, fairly-priced wine list"; the food is "a decent support act". / Details: 10.30 pm; no Amex; booking: max 6.

Angelus W2 £61
4 Bathurst St 7402 0083 5–2D
A "magnificent wine list", "enthusiastic" service and "superb" cooking are finally beginning to win real acclaim for ex-Gavroche sommelier Thierry Tomasin's ambitious yearling – a "smart" Gallic pub-conversion, "tucked-away in a little cul-de-sac near Lancaster Gate". / Details: www.angelusrestaurant.co.uk; 11.30 pm.

The Anglesea Arms W6 £40
35 Wingate Rd 8749 1291 6–1B
This "lovely" (if "cramped") gastropub "classic", near Ravenscourt Park, "continues to delight" with its "inventive seasonal menu" ("amazing for such a tiny kitchen"); it's "better now you can book", and the "engaging" service is much-"improved" on a few years ago too. / Details: Tue-Sat 10.30 pm, Sun & Mon 10 pm; no Amex; no booking.

Anglo Asian Tandoori N16 £24
60-62 Stoke Newington Church St 7254 3633
A Stoke Newington veteran that's "still the best for a cheap 'n' cheerful curry", thanks not least to the "impeccable" service.
/ **Details:** www.angloasian.co.uk; 11.45 pm.

L'Anima EC2 £57
1 Snowden St 7422 7000 1–2B
Francesco Mazzei's "exceptional" cooking has helped make this Italian yearling "a breath of fresh air in the City"; with its "sophisticated" and "airy" décor, and its "exemplary" service, it continues to prove itself as "one of the best new openings of the last few years".
/ **Details:** www.lanima.co.uk; 11 pm; closed Sat L & Sun.

Annie's £42
162 Thames Rd, W4 8994 9080
36-38 White Hart Ln, SW13 8878 2020
"The lush and boudoir-ish décor is more important than the food", at these "wonderfully atmospheric" and "intimate" west London hangouts; burgers and brunches are recommended – otherwise the grub's "ordinary". / **Details:** www.anniesrestaurant.co.uk; 10 pm, Sat 10.30 pm.

Applebee's £38
4 Stoney St, SE1 7407 5777
17 Cambridge Pk, E11 8989 1977
"The highest-quality fish" and "fresh, simple seafood", served in "canteen-like settings" – the formula that's won wide-ranging acclaim for these "buzzy" operations in Borough Market and Wanstead; they're "perfect for lunch". / **Details:** www.applebeesfish.com; SE1 10.15 pm, Sun 5 pm; E11 11 pm; E11 closed Mon-Tue.

Apsleys
Lanesborough Hotel SW1 £85
1 Lanesborough Pl 7333 7254 4–1D
This "ostentatious" conservatory dining room, by Hyde Park Corner, has failed to make any waves in its first year of operation; even some fans concede its oddly "rustic" Italian food "isn't a wow", and critics just decry it as "fake", and "very poor value" too.
/ **Details:** www.apsleys.co.uk; 11 pm; booking: max 12.

aqua kyoto W1
240 Regent St 7478 0540 2–2C
An impressively large project on the top floor of the former Dickins & Jones store near Oxford Circus – this Hong Kong-backed late-2009 newcomer will include a sushi bar and a 'sumibiyaki 'charcoal grill; there will also be a bar, 'Aqua Spirit', and three outdoor terraces. /

aqua nueva W1
240 Regent St 7478 0540 2–2C
A late-2009 newcomer – sibling to Aqua Koto (see also) – specialising in 'contemporary northern Spanish cuisine'. /

Arbutus W1 £48
63-64 Frith St 7734 4545 3–2A

"If there were a category 'Best-Value Gourmet Food'",
this "sophisticated" (if "bland" and "cramped") Soho bistro might well
win it with its "creative" yet "ungimmicky" cuisine (and its "brilliant wines
by the 250ml carafe"); the set lunch, in particular, is "a staggeringly good
deal". / *Value tip:* set pre theatre £28
(FP). **Details:** www.arbutusrestaurant.co.uk; 10.45pm, Sun 9.30 pm.

Archipelago W1 £50
110 Whitfield St 7383 3346 1–1B

You're "not obliged to eat strange animals", if you visit this "bazaar
of Far East exotica", but it's all part of the "novelty" that makes this
"bonkers" Fitzrovian a big hit, especially for romance; of late, however,
the cooking has seemed less "weirdly wonderful" and more "gimmicky"
than before. / **Details:** www.archipelago-restaurant.co.uk; 10.30 pm; closed
Sat L & Sun.

Ark Fish E18 £36
142 Hermon Hill 8989 5345

"A real find in a gastronomic desert" – it's "well worth the wait" ("up to
an hour") for a table at this "fantastic" South Woodford chippy.
/ **Details:** www.arkfishrestaurant.co.uk; Tue-Thu 9.45 pm, Fri & Sat 10.15 pm,
Sun 8.45 pm; closed Mon; no Amex.

Asakusa NW1 £28
265 Eversholt St 7388 8533

"Still going strong after all these years"; this stalwart near Euston station
is "typically Japanese" – "a very basic-looking place", "full of oriental
customers", it serves "fresh sushi and sashimi, plus home-cooked
favourites", at "decent prices". / **Details:** 11.30 pm, Sat 11 pm; D only, closed
Sun; no Amex.

Asia de Cuba
St Martin's Lane Hotel WC2 £84
45 St Martin's Ln 7300 5588 3–4C

It's "still cool and buzzing", but this "loud" and "nightclubby" venue,
on the fringe of Covent Garden, seems all "style over substance"
nowadays; the "overpriced" Asian-Cuban sharing cuisine can
be "surprisingly poor", but it's the "obnoxious" service that really irks.
/ **Details:** www.stmartinslane.com; midnight, Thu-Sat 12.30 am, Sun 10.30 pm.

Assaggi W2 £58
39 Chepstow Pl 7792 5501 5–1B

It has a "bizarre location" – "a small, bright room over a Bayswater pub"
– but this "happy" venture is yet again rated London's best Italian,
thanks to Nino Sassu's "wonderful" but "unpretentious" cooking, and the
"entertaining and informative" service; NB "you need to book well
ahead". / **Details:** 11 pm; closed Sun; no Amex.

Les Associés N8 £37 Ⓐ
172 Park Rd 8348 8944

"Crouch End's finest!"; this "intimate" front-room operation continues to delight the neighbourhood with its "classic Gallic cooking" and its "friendly and informed" service. / Details: www.lesassocies.co.uk; 10 pm; Tue-Sat D only, closed Mon & Sun D.

Atari-Ya £16 ✪✪
20 James St, W1 7491 1178 2–1A
31 Vivian Ave, NW4 8202 2789

"Some of the best quality sushi outside of top restaurants" – "so cheap it makes you weep" – wins raves for this "amazing" Marylebone take-away ("there are a couple of tables, if you're early"), run by a leading firm of Japanese food importers; for greater comfort, head to their new sushi bar, in Hendon. / Details: www.atariya.co.uk; W1 8.30 pm, NW4 10 pm; NW4 closed Mon.

L'Atelier de Joel Robuchon WC2 £85 Ⓐ✪
13-15 West St 7010 8600 3–2B

Fans hail "sublime food from the world's best chef", at the "dark" and "sexy" Covent Garden outpost of M. Robuchon's global empire, where "exquisite" dishes are served tapas-style on "perched" seating, with the "magnificent drama" of an open kitchen (or more formally upstairs); the catch? – "nosebleeding" prices. / Value tip: set weekday L £48 (FP). Details: www.joel-robuchon.com; 11 pm; no trainers.

The Atlas SW6 £37 Ⓐ✪
16 Seagrave Rd 7385 9129 4–3A

A "benchmark for what a London local should be" – this "chilled" back-street boozer, near Earl's Court 2, offers a "breezy" and "constantly changing" Mediterranean menu, while all the time "managing to remain a pub"; "lovely, intimate garden". / Details: www.theatlaspub.co.uk; 10 pm; no booking.

Atma NW3 £40 ✪
106c Finchley Rd 7431 9487

"Interesting" Indian dishes are prepared with "genuine care" at this "quiet" and "sensibly-priced" Belsize Park "gem". / Value tip: set weekday L £26 (FP). Details: www.atmarestaurants.com; 11 pm; closed Mon.

Aubergine SW10 £92
11 Park Wk 7352 3449 4–3B

Even before the mid-2009 departure of William Drabble – the chef who succeed Gordon Ramsay on this Chelsea site almost a decade ago – this once-celebrated restaurant was drifting very badly; its prospective performance seems so uncertain that we can't see any point in awarding a rating. / Value tip: set weekday L £54 (FP). Details: www.auberginerestaurant.co.uk; 10.30 pm; closed Mon, Sat L & Sun D; no jeans or trainers.

Automat W1 £47
33 Dover St 7499 3033 2–3C

This "American-style diner", popular with Mayfair's "hedgies and Eurotrash", continues to divide opinion – fans "love everything about it" (especially the burgers and brunch), whereas critics think it's a "cheesy" place which "could try harder". / Details: www.automat-london.com; midnight, Sun 10 pm; closed Sat D & Sun D.

L'Autre Pied W1 £49

5-7 Blandford St 7486 9696 1–1A
"A worthy little sister to Pied à Terre", say fans of this year-old bistro, who laud its "adventurous" dishes (and "fabulous-value" set menus); the "cramped" Marylebone premises "have bad feng shui", though, and a few critics find the whole experience simply "overhyped". / Details: www.lautrepied.co.uk; 11 pm, Sun 9.30 pm.

L'Aventure NW8 £50

3 Blenheim Ter 7624 6232
"Just the spot for a romantic evening"; Catherine Parisot's "consummate neighbourhood French restaurant" in St John's Wood is "everyone's favourite", with "personal" service and "authentic" cuisine (plus, on sunny days, a "leafy" terrace); be prepared, though – "Madame occasionally 'loses it' with her staff". / Value tip: set weekday L £28 (FP). Details: 11 pm; closed Sat L & Sun.

Babur SE23 £35

119 Brockley Rise 8291 2400

For a "taste bud sensation", it's "worth the trip" to this "upmarket" but obscurely-located (Honor Oak Park) south London subcontinental, where the "unusual" cuisine has a huge fan club. / Details: www.babur.info; 11.30 pm.

Back to Basics W1 £45
21a Foley St 7436 2181 1–1B
It may look "cramped" and "rustic", but this Fitzrovia spot is a "top-class fish restaurant", where a "huge variety" of "inventive" dishes are realised to a "truly exceptional" standard; it's "excellent value" too, and on sunny days you can eat outside. / Details: www.backtobasics.uk.com; 10.30 pm; closed Sun.

Bam-Bou W1 £44
1 Percy St 7323 9130 1–1C
"A nice place to chill and be romanced"; this "dimly-lit" Fitzrovia townhouse – decorated in "chic", "French-colonial" style – not only offers a "buzzy" setting, but also "subtle" Franco-Vietnamese food of a "high standard", and "great cocktails" too. / Details: www.bam-bou.co.uk; 11 pm; closed Sat L & Sun; booking: max 6.

Bar Italia W1 £18
22 Frith St 7437 4520 3–2A
"Where else can you have such a good expresso, so late, while watching Soho's low-life drifting by?"; this "outstanding, traditional Italian bar" offers "London's best coffee" and "great people-watching" too, 24/7. / Details: www.baritaliasoho.com; open 24 hours, Sun 3 am; no booking.

Barrafina W1 £42 ✪✪✪
54 Frith St 7813 8016 3–2A

"The best tapas bar outside Spain!" – the Hart brothers' *"impeccable"* homage to Barcelona's 'Cal Pep' is pure genius; *"effervescent"* staff serve up *"exquisitely fresh and vibrant"* dishes to the lucky few (only 23 seats!) who have survived the *"long queue"*; *"you must get there early"*. / **Details:** www.barrafina.co.uk; 11 pm; no booking.

Barshu W1 £38 ✪
28 Frith St 7287 6688 3–3A
"Joltingly hot" dishes – *"the best Sichuan food in town"* – have made a big name for this *"amazing"* Soho corner spot, which was closed for much of 2009 after a fire; it should be back in business by the time you read this. / **Details:** www.bar-shu.co.uk; 11 pm.

Beirut Express £35 ✪
65 Old Brompton Rd, SW7 7591 0123 4–2B
112-114 Edgware Rd, W2 7724 2700 5–1D
"No-frills" and *"great-value"*, these Lebanese pit stops offer *"huge portions of tasty food"*. / **Details:** www.maroush.com; W2 2 am; SW7 midnight.

Bel Canto EC3 £73 Ⓐ
4 Minster Ct 7444 0004
"Brilliant opera-singing staff" lend a *"unique"* atmosphere to this City yearling; *"look out for half-price offers"*, though – otherwise its Gallic cuisine can seem *"a bit pricey"*. / **Details:** www.lebelcanto.co.uk; 11.30 pm; D only, closed Mon & Sun.

Bellamy's W1 £70
18-18a Bruton Pl 7491 2727 2–2B
"You know what you'll get", at this posh Mayfair mews brasserie – an *"über-smooth"* welcome, *"discreet"* service and *"clubby"* fare; the package is *"very, very expensive"* for what it is, though, and the uninitiated may find it *"underwhelming"*. / **Value tip:** set weekday L £51 (FP). **Details:** www.bellamysrestaurant.co.uk; 10.15 pm; closed Sat L & Sun.

Belvedere W8 £57 Ⓐ
Holland Pk, off Abbotsbury Rd 7602 1238 6–1D
Set in *"the prettiest park in London"*, this *"elegant"* Art Deco-styled fixture is unbeatable for a *"special occasion"*, or for *"romantic"* dining (and also for a *"fantastic-value Sunday lunch"*); *"the food is reliable and the service unquestionable, but don't expect culinary inspiration"*. / **Details:** www.belvedererestaurant.co.uk; 10 pm; closed Sun D.

Benares W1 £70
12 Berkeley Hs, Berkeley Sq   7629 8886   2–3B
"Modern Indian cuisine at its best" still wins very high acclaim for Atul Kochar's "slick" (if slightly "dull") first-floor Mayfair premises; a few reporters this year, however, found the food "not all it's cracked up to be" – is he starting to spend too much time on TV? / **Value tip:** set weekday L £41 (FP). **Details:** www.benaresrestaurant.co.uk; 10.30 pm; no trainers.

Benja W1 £45
17 Beak Street   7287 0555   2–2D
In the heart of the West End – but still often a "discovery" for reporters – this small but lavishly-furnished Soho townhouse Thai offers food that's somewhere between "good" and "excellent".
/ **Details:** www.benjarestaurant.com; 10.45 pm; closed Sun.

Bentley's W1 £60
11-15 Swallow St   7734 4756   2–3D
A "clubby" Mayfair seafood "classic" – revamped to good effect in recent times by Richard Corrigan – where the "casual" ground-floor oyster bar is often tipped in preference to the "stuffy" first-floor restaurant; opinions differ on whether service is "slick" or just "smug".
/ **Details:** www.bentleys.org; 10.30 pm; no jeans; booking: max 8.

Bento Cafe NW1 £30
9 Parkway   7482 3990
By Camden Town's celebrated Jazz Café, this "fun and buzzy" pit stop offers "fantastic budget sushi", plus a "mammoth" menu of "fairly adventurous" other dishes. / **Details:** bentocafe.co.uk; 10.15 pm, Fri & Sat 11 pm.

Bianco Nero W6 £40
206-208 Hammersmith Rd   8748 0212   6–2C
A "pleasingly weird" find, "opposite Hammersmith bus station" – thanks to its "crisp" monochrome design and "quality" cooking, this "classy" Italian is managing to make quite a go of its terrible location. / **Value tip:** set pre theatre £26 (FP). **Details:** www.bianconerorestaurants.com; 10 pm; closed Sat L & Sun.

Bibendum SW3 £67

81 Fulham Rd   7581 5817   4–2C
"Standards are up again", at this Brompton Cross "icon", whose "stunning" setting makes a particularly "lovely, light and airy" lunch location; service is "impeccable" too, the food is "sensitively prepared", and perusing the wine list is "like reading Hugh Johnson's World Atlas of Wine!" / **Details:** www.bibendum.co.uk; 11 pm, Sun 10.30 pm; booking: max 12 at L, 10 at D.

Bincho Yakitori W1 £31
16 Old Compton St   7287 9111   3–2A
This Soho yakitori (grilled skewer) restaurant seems a "likeable" enough place to most reporters ("as long as you like salt"); it's difficult, however, not to lament the closing of its infinitely more handsome South Bank sibling. / **Details:** www.bincho.co.uk; 11.30 pm, Sun 10.30 pm.

Blakes
Blakes Hotel SW7 £104
33 Roland Gdns 7370 6701 4–2B
This once famously louche and romantic South Kensington basement
attracts little comment nowadays (and has been reported
as "very quiet"); long-time supporters may still discern something
"special" in the atmosphere, and the eye-popping prices have
*an aphrodisiac quality all of their own. / **Details:** www.blakeshotels.com;*
11.30 pm.

Bleeding Heart EC1 £49
Bleeding Heart Yd, Greville St 7242 8238
"Hidden-away down a cobbled alley", near Holborn, this "historic"
warren – comprising a tavern, bistro and restaurant – remains one
of the best-liked places in town; with its "traditional Gallic" approach,
its "very intimate" nooks and its "epic" wine list, it manages to "cover all
*the bases, from business to romance". / **Details:** www.bleedingheart.co.uk;*
10.30 pm; closed Sun.

Blue Elephant SW6 £52
4-6 Fulham Broadway 7385 6595 4–4A
Tropical vegetation "transports you from Fulham to Phuket", at this
"Disneyesque" Thai extravaganza – one of the most "impressive"
restaurant interiors in town; but while this still pleases – even "enthralls"
– most reporters, neither food nor service are up to their
*past best standards. / **Details:** www.blueelephant.com; 11.30 pm,*
Sun 10.30 pm; closed Sat L (ex Stamford Bridge match days).

Blue Jade SW1 £31
44 Hugh St 7828 0321 1–4B
A tucked-away Pimlico Thai, where "really delightful" service is the
highlight; the food may be "predictable", but the overall experience
*is "a safe bet". / **Details:** 11 pm; closed Sat L & Sun.*

Bocca Di Lupo W1 £39
12 Archer St 7734 2223 2–2D
"Dazzling" Italian dishes – "regionally identified", and served "in 'tasting'
or 'full' portions" – have made this "vibey" and "fantastically friendly"
Soho newcomer a truly "exciting addition to London dining";
*"the best seats are at the chef's counter". / **Details:** www.boccadilupo.com;*
11 pm; booking: max 10.

Bombay Brasserie SW7 £73
Courtfield Close, Gloucester Rd 7370 4040 4–2B
After its "tragic" refurbishment ("'70s ballroom-meets-Novotel"),
this large South Kensington Indian looks unlikely to regain its former
"favourite" status any time soon; unless you go for the "excellent-value
*Sunday buffet", it can seem "grossly overpriced". / **Value tip:** set*
*weekday L £44 (FP). **Details:** www.bombaybrasserielondon.com; 11.30 pm.*

45

Bombay Palace W2 £44
50 Connaught St   7723 8855   5–1D

"Wonderfully fresh" and "subtly-spiced" Indian cooking (in "traditional" style) makes this Bayswater veteran a big "favourite" for its large fan club; service is "charming" too, but the setting is a "lost cause". / **Details:** www.bombay-palace.co.uk; 11.30 pm.

Il Bordello E1 £38
81 Wapping High St   7481 9950
"A miracle for Wapping" – this "bustling" and "squeezed-in" Italian has long been a firm favourite, thanks to its "huge portions" of "fresh and vibrant" fare (pizzas are "particularly excellent"); "the challenge is getting in". / **Details:** 11 pm; closed Sat L.

Boudin Blanc W1 £54
5 Trebeck St   7499 3292   2–4B
"Just the kind of place you expect to find in Paris"; this "charming" candlelit favourite, "tucked-away" in Shepherd Market, offers some "great classic dishes" (albeit with an occasional dose of "attitude"); "perfect" outside tables in summer. / **Value tip:** set weekday L £28 (FP). **Details:** www.boudinblanc.co.uk; 11 pm.

Brick Lane Beigel Bake E1 £ 6
159 Brick Ln   7729 0616   1–1C
"There's no better bagel either side of the Atlantic!" than at this 24/7 East End legend, where there's "always an eclectic mix of people queuing, especially after midnight"; most popular fillings: salt beef ("incredible"), or smoked salmon ("extraordinary"). / **Details:** open 24 hours; no credit cards; no booking.

Brilliant UB2 £35
72-76 Western Rd   8574 1928
Bollywood on the TV helps enliven the atmosphere at this large (and somewhat "odd and bright") Indian veteran, lost deep in the Southall suburbs; it's worth the trek if you're looking for a curry that's "the real McCoy". / **Details:** www.brilliantrestaurant.com; 11.30 pm, Fri & Sat midnight; closed Mon, Sat L & Sun L; booking: weekends only.

Brula TW1 £43
43 Crown Rd   8892 0602
This "quintessential" corner bistro, in St Margaret's, is "just the sort of place anyone would like to have on their street"; a number of reports speak of "recent improvements"… but it was already very good! / **Value tip:** set always available £26 (FP). **Details:** www.brula.co.uk; 10.30 pm; closed Sun D.

Brunello
Baglioni Hotel SW7 £70
60 Hyde Park Gate 7368 5900 4–1B
The Italian food can be "very good", but this self-conscious Kensington design hotel has a very small following among reporters; if you don't mind "hilarious" prices, though, check out the "extensive Italian wine list" . / Details: www.baglionihotellondon.com; 11 pm.

Buen Ayre E8 £42 ⭐
50 Broadway Mkt 7275 9900
*"Deepest Hackney masquerades convincingly as Buenos Aires", at this "cracking" 'parillada' (grill restaurant), which serves up "huge" and "perfectly-cooked" steaks at "bargain" prices.
/ Details: www.buenayre.co.uk; 10.30 pm; closed weekday L.*

Bull & Last NW5 £41 🅐⭐⭐
168 Highgate Rd 7267 3641
*"A true gastropub"; this "cracking" Kentish Town newcomer – with cooking "way beyond what you expect of a pub", and at very "decent" prices too – has been the best all-round opening of the year; the only real downside is that it can get "very noisy".
/ Details: www.thebullandlast.co.uk; 10 pm; no Amex.*

Busaba Eathai £29 🅐⭐
106-110 Wardour St, W1 7255 8686 2–2D
8-13 Bird St, W1 7518 8080 2–1A
22 Store St, WC1 7299 7900 1–1C
"Much better than Wagamama"; these "always-buzzing" communal Thais, stylishly "decked out with dark wood", serve up "fantastic", "fresh" and "fragrant" food (in particular "addictive calamari") at "canteen prices"; arrive early to avoid the "crazy" queue. / Details: 11 pm, Fri & Sat 11.30 pm, Sun 10 pm; W1 no booking; WC1 booking: min 10.

C&R Cafe £28 ⭐
3-4 Rupert Ct, W1 7434 1128 3–3A
52 Westbourne Grove, W2 7221 7979 5–1B
"It's well worth queuing for one of the cramped tables", say fans of this "hidden-away" Chinatown "gem" – a "proper, full-on, authentic Malaysian eating experience" offering "some of the best-value in the area"; the Bayswater sibling attracts limited attention. / Details: 11 pm.

The Cabin SW6 £39 🅐⭐
125 Dawes Rd 7385 8936

*In deepest Fulham – a bar/diner with an enthusiastic local following for its "great steaks", burgers and grills (and good brunches too).
/ Details: www.thecabinbarandgrill.co.uk; 10.30 pm; D only, ex Sun open L & D; no Amex.*

Café 209 SW6 £23
209 Munster Rd 7385 3625
Proprietress Joy "remains hilarious", at this "shabby" and "crammed-in" BYO Thai in deepest Fulham; "you go for her cheeriness, and the good-value food". / Details: 10.30 pm; D only, closed Sun, closed Dec; no Amex.

Le Café Anglais
Whiteley's W2 £52
8 Porchester Gdns 7221 1415 5–1C
Rowley Leigh's huge and "bright" Art Deco-style brasserie seems surprisingly "classy" for somewhere atop the Whiteleys shopping mall, in Bayswater; its "extensive" menu is generally "well executed" (especially the "remarkable hors d'oeuvres"), but service can be "haphazard". / Details: www.lecafeanglais.co.uk; 11.30 pm, Sun 10.30 pm.

Café du Marché EC1 £48
22 Charterhouse Sq 7608 1609
"You could be in France", at this "supremely consistent" stalwart, "tucked-away down an alley", near Smithfield Market; with its "excellent" rustic cooking, and its "fantastic" service, it suits both business or romance; "cool jazz piano" in the evenings. / Details: www.cafedumarche.co.uk; 10 pm; closed Sat L & Sun; no Amex.

Café Japan NW11 £30
626 Finchley Rd 8455 6854
"Fantastic" sushi – "fit for a connoisseur" – comes at prices that are "a steal" at this "very friendly" but "basic" Japanese stalwart, opposite Golder's Green station. / Details: www.cafejapan.co.uk; 10 pm; closed Mon & Tue; no Amex.

Café Spice Namaste E1 £40
16 Prescot St 7488 9242
"Cyrus Todiwala's innovative approach always yields some culinary surprises", at this "cheerful" and "slightly off-beat" stalwart on the eastern fringes of the City; service is notably "efficient and well-informed". / Details: www.cafespice.co.uk; 10.30 pm; closed Sat L & Sun.

Cambio de Tercio SW5 £48
163 Old Brompton Rd 7244 8970 4–2B
A "vibrant" setting, "daring" tapas and an "encyclopaedic" Spanish wine list win continuing acclaim for this Earl's Court bar; satisfaction slipped a bit this year, though, with occasional reports of "indifferent" service and food that "sometimes missed its mark". / Details: www.cambiodetercio.co.uk; 11.30 pm.

The Capital Restaurant
Capital Hotel SW3 £88
22-24 Basil St 7589 5171 4–1D
In culinary terms, this "hidden gem", by Harrods, has for many years been one of London's great Gallic dining rooms, thanks to the unstinting efforts of chef Eric Chavot; as this guide was going to press, however, news emerged on his departure. / Value tip: set weekday L £55 (FP). Details: www.capitalhotel.co.uk; 10 pm; no jeans or trainers.

Le Caprice SW1 £56
Arlington Hs, Arlington St   7629 2239   2–4C
This super-"smooth" '80s-style brasserie, behind the Ritz, remains the epitome of "effortless" sophistication, drawing a perennially "glamorous" crowd with its "utterly reliable" ("but not fancy") formula. / **Details:** *www.caprice-holdings.co.uk; midnight, Sun 11 pm.*

Caraffini SW1 £44
61-63 Lower Sloane St   7259 0235   4–2D
"Waiters who've been there for years" treat all guests "as regulars" at this "busy" Italian, near Sloane Square; foodwise it's pretty "reliable", but – especially on the ambience front – "some of the 'heart' has gone out of it in recent times". / **Details:** *www.caraffini.co.uk; 11.30 pm; closed Sun.*

Catch
Andaz Hotel EC2 £69
40 Liverpool St   7618 7200
Fans of this quite "classy"-looking City venue (deep in an hotel by Liverpool Street) praise its "very good fish"; the food often "misses", though, and other potential drawbacks include "mediocre" service, and noise-pollution from the adjoining bar. / **Details:** *www.andazdining.com; 10.15 pm; closed Sat & Sun.*

Cecconi's W1 £50
5a Burlington Gdns   7434 1500   2–3C
From breakfast on, Nick Jones's "smart" and "buzzy" Italian brasserie is a hub for Mayfair's "beau monde" (from "schmoozing PRs" to "hedge fund types"); the food is undoubtedly "pricey", but it's also "consistently good". / **Details:** *www.cecconis.co.uk; 1am, Sun midnight.*

Cellar Gascon EC1 £35
59 West Smithfield Rd   7600 7561
"There's always a decent glass of wine to be had", at this Smithfield budget spin-off from the nearby Club Gascon; it likewise features "unusual" tapas, but overall it's "not a patch on big brother". / **Details:** *www.cellargascon.com; midnight; closed Sat & Sun.*

Le Cercle SW1 £46
1 Wilbraham Pl   7901 9999   4–2D

"Exquisitely-presented, tiny French tapas" have carved a major reputation for this "dramatic" and "elegant" basement "gem", near Sloane Square – a sibling to Club Gascon; shoppers, don't miss the "terrific-value lunch"! / **Details:** *www.lecercle.co.uk; 11 pm; closed Mon & Sun.*

Champor-Champor SE1 £43
62 Weston St 7403 4600
"Out of the way, but worth finding!" – this *"unique"* venue, hidden-away near London Bridge, has *"a style all of its own"*, and offers *"poetically inventive"* Malay-fusion cuisine in an *"eccentric"* and *"magical"* setting; perhaps in the nature of the thing, however, the occasional doubter *"just can't see it"*. **/ Details:** www.champor-champor.com; 10.15 pm; D only, closed Sun.

The Chancery EC4 £48
9 Cursitor St 7831 4000
It may look "low-key", but this "minimalist" legal-land destination can be "perfect for a business lunch or dinner", thanks to its "original" cuisine and the generally "efficient" (but occasionally "slow") service. **/ Details:** www.thechancery.co.uk; 10.30 pm; closed Sat & Sun.

Chez Bruce SW17 £58
2 Bellevue Rd 8672 0114
"In a business fuelled by hype, exaggeration and celebrity", Bruce Poole's *"perfect neighbourhood place"*, by Wandsworth Common, *"quietly 'delivers' every time"*; for the fifth year it is London's Favourite Restaurant, thanks to its *"thoughtful"* staff, its *"refined"* yet *"unfussy"* cuisine and its *"lovely"* (if *"cramped"*) setting; *"exceptional"* wine too. **/ Value tip:** set Sun L £44 (FP). **Details:** www.chezbruce.co.uk; 10.30 pm; booking: max 6 at D.

Chez Liline N4 £36
101 Stroud Green Rd 7263 6550
Don't be put off by the "outdated" looks of this Finsbury Park "hidden gem"; chef Sylvain Hong (recently back at the stove) puts "an exotic Mauritian twist" on his "superb, inventive and original" dishes – some of the best fish in London. **/ Value tip:** set weekday L £22 (FP). **Details:** ww.chezliline.com; 11 pm; closed Mon.

Chez Marcelle W14 £27
34 Blythe Rd 7603 3241 6–1D
"Charming, control-freak Marcelle" personally oversees this Olympia institution, so service can sometimes be *"slow"* as a result; even so, it's an *"indisputably brilliant"* destination, with *"proper, home-cooked Lebanese food"* – a recent *"IKEA-style"* refit has *"dragged the décor into the '90s"* too! **/ Details:** 10 pm; closed Mon, Tue-Thu D only,Fri-Sun open L & D; no credit cards.

Chez Patrick W8 £43
7 Stratford Rd 7937 6388 4–2A
"Patrick, the charming and amusing owner" adds life to this Gallic venture in a quiet Kensington mews; a small but enthusiastic fan club praises its *"simple but exquisite"* fish and seafood.
/ Details: www.chezpatrickinlondon.co.uk; 11 pm; closed Sun D.

Chi Noodle & Wine Bar EC4 £24
5 New Bridge St 7353 2409
In the City, this "fabulous, family-run noodle bar" wins consistent applause for its "reliable" and "speedy" (but "relaxed") lunching possibilities. **/ Details:** www.chinoodle.com; 10.30 pm; closed Sat & Sun.

China Tang
Dorchester Hotel W1   **£75**
53 Park Ln   7629 9988   2–3A
"Silly prices" take the gloss off David Tang's *"sumptuous and breathtaking"* '30s-Shanghai-style Mayfair basement, and the *"average"* food and *"dismissive"* service don't help either – leave out the glitter-factor, and this place can feel like *"an overpriced theme park for people with too much money"*. / *Value tip:* set weekday L £37 (FP). **Details:** www.thedorchesterhotel.com; 11.30 pm.

Chisou W1   **£38**
4 Princes St   7629 3931   2–1C
It may look *"plain"*, but this Japanese café, near Oxford Circus, *"impresses"* reporters with its *"slick"* service of *"super fresh food"* – a *"reliable blend of conservative and innovative dishes"* (not least *"fantastic"* sushi and sashimi). / **Details:** www.chisou.co.uk; 10.30 pm; closed Sun.

Cho-San SW15   **£39**
292 Upper Richmond Rd   8788 9626
"Utterly delightful family service" adds to the *"really authentic"* spirit – *"just like being in Tokyo"* – of this Putney Japanese; it serves up *"excellent sushi and sashimi"* and *"good home cooking"*, at *"wonderful value-for-money prices"*. / **Details:** 10.30 pm; closed Mon; no Amex.

Chor Bizarre W1   **£43**
16 Albemarle St   7629 9802   2–3C
"Extravagant" décor helps create a *"fun"* atmosphere at this *"quirky"* Mayfair Indian; given its *"interesting"* and *"well-executed"* cuisine, it's perhaps surprising that it doesn't have a wider following. / **Details:** www.chorbizarre.com; 11.30 pm; closed Sun L.

Churchill Arms W8   **£22**
119 Kensington Church St   7792 1246   5–2B
Thai *"scoff"* as *"cheap-as-chips"* makes this *"life-affirming"* annexe to a pub near Notting Hill Gate a true *"perennial favourite"*; *"overcrowding is rife"*, however, and service *"quick but unsmiling"* – *"expect to be rushed"*. / **Details:** 10 pm; closed Sun D.

Chutney SW18   **£26**
11 Alma Rd   8870 4588
"Wonderful food, cooked with care" makes this *"cosy"* Wandsworth local *"a perfect place for a simple curry"*. / **Details:** www.chutneyrestaurant.co.uk; 11.30 pm; D only.

Chutney Mary SW10   **£52**
535 King's Rd   7351 3113   4–4B
With its *"beautiful, subtle and aromatic"* cuisine and its *"strikingly stylish"* décor, this Chelsea-fringe pioneer still offers a *"package which takes some beating"* – almost twenty years on, this is still *"one of the best Indians in London"*. / **Details:** www.realindianfood.com; 11.30 pm, Sun 10.30 pm; closed weekday L; booking: max 12.

Ciao Bella WC1 £31 Ⓐ
86-90 Lamb's Conduit St   7242 4119   1–1D
This "crammed" and "bustling" Bloomsbury stalwart is, for fans,
everything a "happy", "old-school" Italian should be, and "unbelievable
value" too; some reporters, though, sense that the always-"routine"
cooking has seemed positively "churned out" of late.
/ **Details:** www.ciaobellarestaurant.co.uk; 11.30 pm, Sun 10.30 pm.

The Cinnamon Club SW1 £62 Ⓐ⭐
Old Westminster Library, Great Smith St   7222 2555   1–4C
Westminster's old Library provides the "palatial" home for London's
grandest "nouvelle Indian"; even more impressive, though, is its
"stunning" and "delicate" cuisine – a "clever but unpretentious" take
on traditional dishes. / **Value tip:** set weekday L £41
(FP). **Details:** www.cinnamonclub.com; 10.45 pm; closed Sun; no trainers.

Cinnamon Kitchen EC2 £52 ⭐⭐
9 Devonshire Sq   7626 5000

"A real treat in the City"; the Cinnamon Club's lofty new "Manhattan-
style" offshoot, near Liverpool Street, looks set to rival its impressive
sibling, thanks to its "magical" Indian tapas dishes, its "glamorous" décor
and its overall "attention to detail". / **Value tip:** set weekday L £32
(FP). **Details:** www.cinnamon-kitchen.com; 10.30 pm, Sun 10 pm.

Cipriani W1 £75 ❌
25 Davies Street   7399 0500   2–2B
"Rude, arrogant, self-centred…", and that's just the customers!;
this "grossly self-important" Mayfair Italian serves up "bland"
("worst since Spaghetti House in 1970") and "overpriced" fare to a
"hilarious" crowd of "wannabe-hedgies and has-been celebs", at prices –
inevitably – that "only fools would pay". / **Details:** www.cipriani.com;
11.45 pm.

Clarke's W8 £56 ⭐
124 Kensington Church St   7221 9225   5–2B
While fans of Sally Clarke's Kensington stalwart say its Californian-
inspired cuisine is consistently "excellent", critics feel it has not been
as good "since they stopped the no-choice dinner" (which was a few
years ago); views on the ambience differ too – it's "romantic" or "staid",
to taste. / **Details:** www.sallyclarke.com; 10 pm; closed Sun; booking: max 14.

Clifton E1 £22 ⭐
1 Whitechapel Rd   7377 5533
"It hasn't failed me yet!" – this "deservedly busy" Brick Lane Bangladeshi
offers a "nicely varied regional menu", and "pleasant" service too.
/ **Details:** www.cliftonrestaurant.com; midnight, Sat & Sun 1am.

Clos Maggiore WC2 £45

33 King St 7379 9696 3–3C

*An "oasis" amidst Covent Garden's tourist tat that's beginning to make
quite a name for itself – this "magical" restaurant is of special note for
its "leafy" and "romantic" conservatory, and also its "mind-boggling"
(2000+ bins) wine list; amazingly, the food is "very competent" too,
and service "impeccable".* / **Value tip:** *set dinner £30*
(FP). **Details:** *www.closmaggiore.com; 10.45 pm, Sat 11.15 pm, Sun 10 pm; closed
Sat L.*

Club Gascon EC1 £62

57 West Smithfield 7796 0600

*With its "strongly flavoured and imaginative" tapas from SW France and
the Basque country, this foie-gras-fixated Smithfield fixture remains
on "brilliant" form; "unusual and well-chosen" regional wines add much
further interest.* / **Details:** *www.clubgascon.com; 10 pm, Fri & Sat 10.30 pm;
closed Sat L & Sun.*

The Collection SW3 £67

264 Brompton Rd 7225 1212 4–2C

*Approached via a catwalk, a large and Eurotrashy Brompton Cross bar
(with mezzanine restaurant), that's "so full of beautiful people you forget
about the food" – probably no bad thing.* / **Details:** *www.the-collection.co.uk;
midnight; D only, closed Sun.*

Le Colombier SW3 £48

145 Dovehouse St 7351 1155 4–2C

*"A wonderful feeling of France", "delicious classic fare", and "exemplary"
service help win high acclaim for this "smart but pricey" bistro,
by Chelsea Square.* / **Details:** *www.lecolombier-sw3.co.uk; 10.30 pm,
Sun 10 pm.*

Comptoir Gascon EC1 £46

63 Charterhouse St 7608 0851

*"Genuinely like a really good bistro in France", this "cute" but "cramped"
Smithfield spin-off from nearby Club Gascon offers "robust food with
minimal fuss", at "sensible prices"; by day, they do "wonderful coffee"
and "perfect pastries".* / **Details:** *www.comptoirgascon.com; 10 pm, Thu & Fri
11 pm; closed Mon & Sun.*

Il Convivio SW1 £55

143 Ebury St 7730 4099 1–4A

*Something of a "hidden gem"; this "bright and airy" Belgravia Italian
continues to win all-round acclaim for its "really accomplished" cooking
and "gracious" service.* / **Details:** *www.etruscarestaurants.com; 10.45 pm;
closed Sun.*

Coq d'Argent EC2 £58

1 Poultry 7395 5000

*With its "fantastic" terraces and roof gardens, this "unique" 6th-floor
D&D-group operation in the City is never going to be a budget
destination, but improved food and service have made it better value
of late; though it's mainly a business venue, of course, it can
be "surprisingly busy" at weekends too.* / **Details:** *www.coqdargent.co.uk;
9.45 pm; closed Sat L & Sun D.*

Corrigan's Mayfair W1 £60
28 Upper Grosvenor St 7499 9943 2–3A
Shame the amiable Richard Corrigan's smart Mayfair newcomer was
so "hyped" by his many friends in the media; some reporters do indeed
find "outstanding" results from his "rustic" British menu, but others are
"hugely disappointed" – given the build-up – to find no "wow-factor"
at all. / **Value tip:** set Sun L £44 (FP). **Details:** www.corrigansmayfair.com;
11 pm.

The Cow W2 £49
89 Westbourne Park Rd 7221 0021 5–1B
Tom Conran's "hip" faux-Irish pub is a Notting Hillbilly classic
(even though it's actually in Bayswater); downstairs, in the "packed" bar,
they serve "first-class" seafood and Guinness – upstairs, there's a "cosy"
room, where the style is more "gastronomic".
/ **Details:** www.thecowlondon.co.uk; 10.30 pm; closed weekday L; no Amex.

Crazy Bear W1 £56
26-28 Whitfield St 7631 0088 1–1C
With its "really sexy bar" and "cool" upstairs dining room, this Fitzrovia
spot is "definitely a place to impress a date", and the Thai/Chinese food
is "excellent" too (if progressively seeming rather "pricey" for what it is);
don't under any circumstances miss the "most bizarre" loos.
/ **Details:** www.crazybeargroup.co.uk; 10.30 pm; closed Sat L & Sun; no shorts.

Crazy Homies W2 £38
125 Westbourne Park Rd 7727 6771 5–1B
Tom Conran's "cramped" and "noisy" – but "thoroughly enjoyable" –
Bayswater hang-out has "quite a rough and authentic Mexican feel";
its "unfancy" and "affordable" scoff generally pleases, but the "slow and
forgetful" service does not. / **Details:** www.crazyhomieslondon.co.uk; closed
weekday L; no Amex.

Cyprus Mangal SW1 £25
45 Warwick Way 7828 5940 1–4B
"Leave at home any inhibitions about kebabs", if you visit this
"fine charcoal grill" behind a Pimlico take-away; its "cheerful" staff dish
up "the highest-quality Turkish grilled meat dishes", at "great-value"
prices. / **Details:** Sun-Thu midnight, Fri & Sat 1 am; no Amex.

Daphne NW1 £31
83 Bayham St 7267 7322
"You're made very welcome" at this "homely" taverna of long standing,
in Camden Town, which benefits from a "lovely roof terrace for the
summer"; the "good-value" food – featuring some "well-cooked" fish –
is a "cut above" most Greek places too. / **Details:** 11.30 pm; closed Sun;
no Amex.

Dean Street Townhouse & Dining Room W1
Dean St 3–2A
From Nick Jones's ever-trendy Soho House group, a new hotel and
members' club, to open in late-2009; expect the restaurant (open to all)
to become a place of the moment, even if precedent suggests that the
food will be no better than middle-of-the-road.
/ **Details:** www.deanstreettownhouse.com.

Defune W1 £35 ⭐⭐
34 George St   7935 8311   2–1A
The "Habitat-style" interior of this stalwart Marylebone Japanese has "little atmosphere" (and prices which are "through the roof"), but "it doesn't matter" – the sushi and sashimi are "just perfect", and service "flawless" too. / Details: 10.30 pm.

Dehesa W1 £40 🅐⭐
25 Ganton St   7494 4170   2–2C
With its "casual and elegant" style, "unbeatable central location" (off Carnaby Street) and "fabulous" Italian/Spanish tapas, this "bustling", if "slightly cramped", yearling may soon be even better-known that its brilliant elder brother, Salt Yard. / Details: www.dehesa.co.uk; 11 pm; closed Sun D; no booking.

Dinings W1 £34 ⭐⭐
22 Harcourt St   7723 0666
"A cheaper, tiny Nobu!"; Tomanari Chiba's "hard-to-find" two-year-old – in a "stark" Marylebone bunker – actually achieves even higher survey ratings than his former employers, thanks to his "divine" sushi (and "awesome" other dishes too); "book well ahead". / Details: 10.30 pm; closed Sat L & Sun L.

The Don EC4 £47 🅐⭐
20 St Swithin's Ln   7626 2606
"The best business restaurant in the City" – combining an "airy and civilised" upstairs, with an informal and "atmospheric" cellar – is quietly tucked-away near Bank; the cooking is "good verging on very good", backed up by a "cracking" wine list and "slick" service. / Details: www.thedonrestaurant.com; 10 pm; closed Sat & Sun; no trainers.

Donna Margherita SW11 £37 ⭐
183 Lavender Hill   7228 2660
"A great neighbourhood Italian", in Battersea, which serves up "fabulous thin crust pizzas" (plus "interesting daily specials"), and a "warm and friendly welcome every time". / Details: www.donna-margherita.com; 10.30 pm, Sat 11 pm; closed Mon, Tue-Fri D only, Sat & Sun open L & D.

Dorchester Grill
Dorchester Hotel W1 £83
53 Park Ln   7629 8888   2–3A
"Try to close your eyes" to the "tartan-riot" décor of this "bizarre"-looking Mayfair grill room; in fact, it's best to keep them closed all the way through until the "huge bill" arrives – given the "average" cooking, it can seem just as "hideous"! / Details: www.thedorchester.com; 11 pm, Sun 10.30 pm; no trainers.

Dragon Castle SE17 £30 🅐⭐⭐
114 Walworth Rd   7277 3388
"Worth a trip to Elephant & Castle" – this huge and "stylishly-decorated" Chinese is again hitting the "fabulous" standards which made it such a big hit when it opened two years ago; the top attraction is "dim sum better than anything in Chinatown", but the main menu is "wonderful" too. / Details: www.dragoncastle.eu; 11 pm, Fri 11.30 pm, Sun 10.30 pm.

The Drunken Monkey E1 £27
222 Shoreditch High St 7392 9606 1–1B

"Very fresh-tasting" dim sum "at bargain prices" maintains the appeal of this "fun" Shoreditch boozer; as the evening wears on, "a DJ adds to the vibe", and "you may need to shout to be heard".
/ ***Details:*** *www.thedrunkenmonkey.co.uk; midnight, Sun 11 pm; closed Sat L.*

The Duke of Wellington W1 £41
94a, Crawford St 7723 2790 2–3A
A "fine" make-over of a Marylebone inn wins acclaim for this "cramped" and "buzzy" yearling, whose cooking is "as good as you're likely to get in a pub which still looks like a pub". / ***Details:*** *www.thedukew1.co.uk; 10 pm, Sun 9 pm; Booking: max 25 in restaurant.*

The Duke's Head SW15 £34
8 Lower Richmond Rd 8788 2552
"The most amazing views of the Thames" are the highlight attraction of this "airy" dining room, which is located in a "pleasantly traditional" (but "child-friendly") landmark boozer, near Putney Bridge.
/ ***Details:*** *www.dukesheadputney.co.uk; 11 pm, Fri & Sat midnight.*

E&O W11 £45
14 Blenheim Cr 7229 5454 5–1A
"Beautiful people enjoy beautiful food", at Will Ricker's "sexy", softly-lit and always "buzzing" Notting Hill hang-out, where the "imaginative" cuisine of "Asian-fusion tapas" is as "awesome" as ever.
/ ***Details:*** *www.rickerrestaurants.com; 11 pm, Sun 10.30 pm; booking: max 6.*

The Eagle EC1 £25
159 Farringdon Rd 7837 1353
"The original, and still the best", claims a fan of this "ever-lively" Farringdon gastropub (London's first, 1992); that's overdoing it a bit nowadays, but the Mediterranean food is still "consistently good" (and getting a seat is still a "free-for-all"). / ***Details:*** *10.30 pm; closed Sun D; no Amex; no booking.*

The East Room EC2 £45
2a, Tabernacle St 847876 1–2A
The "chilled" dining room of a private club (open to non-members), just off Finsbury Square, featuring "awesome" funky décor (plus terrace), and "an interesting wine romp around the New World"; the "simple" food pleases too, but has rather a supporting role.
/ ***Details:*** *www.thstrm.com; 11 pm; closed Sat L & Sun D.*

Edokko WC1 £42
50 Red Lion St 7242 3490 1–1D
"No prizes for décor", at this rickety "slice of Japan", off Holborn, but – for "really good and authentic sushi" – it can be "outstanding".
/ **Details:** 10 pm, Sat 9.30 pm; closed Sat L & Sun.

Eight Over Eight SW3 £45
392 King's Rd 7349 9934 4–3B
A "fun" and "happening" Chelsea scene which serves up some "prime people-watching", to go with an "utterly delicious" menu of Asian-fusion tapas. / **Details:** www.rickerrestaurants.com; 11 pm, Sun 10.30 pm; closed Sun L.

Electric Brasserie W11 £39
191 Portobello Rd 7908 9696 5–1A
For weekend brunch, "it's a scrum waiting for a table", at this "fast-paced" Notting Hill hang-out; the attraction? – "classic, comfort food" served to a "super-trendy" crowd. / **Details:** www.the-electric.co.uk; 10.45 pm.

Emile's SW15 £37
96 Felsham Rd 8789 3323
Emile Fahy's "photographic memory for guests" helps draw much repeat custom to this "busy" bistro favourite, in the back streets of Putney; the menu offers "something for everyone" too (plus "superb" wines), at notably "competitive" prices. / **Details:** www.emilesrestaurant.co.uk; 11 pm; D only, closed Sun; no Amex.

The Engineer NW1 £43
65 Gloucester Ave 7722 0950
Despite ups and downs over the years, this "relaxed" gastropub linchpin of Primrose Hill life "remains a favourite", thanks to its "lovely" garden and "cosy" interior, and food that's "consistently good"; it's "a bit pricey", though, and service can be "sporadic". / **Details:** www.the-engineer.com; 11 pm, Sun 10.30 pm; no Amex.

Enoteca Turi SW15 £50
28 Putney High St 8785 4449
"Glorious" Italian cooking is but one of the attractions of the Turi family's "fabulous" and "friendly" stalwart, near Putney Bridge; top billing goes to the wine list – "an epic journey through the regions of Italy", with "gems at all price levels". / **Value tip:** set weekday L £30 (FP). **Details:** www.enotecaturi.com; 11 pm; closed Sun.

Eriki NW3 £37
4-6 Northways Pde, Finchley Rd 7722 0606
The location is "unexciting" and the décor "ordinary", but this Swiss Cottage Indian has won a formidable following, thanks to its "fantastic" service and its "sensational" cuisine – "better than Benares, and half the price!" / **Details:** www.eriki.co.uk; 10.30 pm; closed Sat L.

Esarn Kheaw W12 £27
314 Uxbridge Rd 8743 8930 6–1B
It certainly looks "unpromising", but this small Shepherd's Bush "treasure" has long offered "gorgeous", "simple" and "spicy" dishes that rank "among the very best Thai food in London"; "a little TLC on the décor", though, would do no harm. / **Details:** www.esarnkheaw.co.uk; 11 pm; closed Sat L & Sun L; no Amex.

Essenza W11 £52   A ⭐
210 Kensington Park Rd 7792 1066 5–1A
*Oddly little commented-on, given its fashionable Notting Hill location,
this small Italian restaurant is nevertheless unanimously hailed as a
"high-quality" destination, offering "great value for money". / **Value
tip:** set weekday L £31 (FP).* **Details:** *www.essenza.co.uk; 11.30 pm.*

Fabrizio EC1 £38   ⭐
30 Saint Cross St 7430 1503
*"It's a gem – shout it from the rooftops!"; fans of this "obscurely-located"
(and "under-reviewed") Farringdon café say it's "well worth a trip" for its
"charming" service and its "exceptional" Sicilian food.
/ **Details:** www.fabriziorestaurant.co.uk; 10 pm; closed Sat L & Sun.*

Fakhreldine W1 £54
85 Piccadilly 7493 3424 2–4C
*It may have "great views" over Green Park, but it's hard to recommend
this first-floor contemporary-look Lebanese, near the Ritz – the food can
seem "dull" and "pricey", and service "brusque" and "impatient";
see also 1001 Nights. / **Details:** www.fakhreldine.co.uk; midnight, Sun 11 pm.*

El Faro E14 £40   ⭐⭐
3 Turnberry Quay 7987 5511
*"Some of the best Spanish food in London!" – "not just tapas" either –
makes it worth tackling the "awkward" location of this "very friendly"
outfit, near Crossharbour DLR; it has a waterside position which "comes
into its own in summer". / **Details:** www.el-faro.co.uk; 11 pm; closed Sun D.*

Faulkner's E8 £30   ⭐
424-426 Kingsland Rd 7254 6152
*"Unbeatable" fish 'n' chips in "vast" portions wins continued acclaim
from (most) reporters on this celebrated Dalston veteran.
/ **Details:** 10 pm; no Amex; need 8+ to book.*

Fernandez & Wells £25
43 Lexington St, W1 7734 1546 2–2D
73 Beak St, W1 7287 8124 2–2D
*"Proof that a sandwich can be a memorable event!"; these "coolly
utilitarian" cafés dispense "simple" but "decadent" snacks, plus "juices
like nectar" and "coffee like no other"; "fab wine" too (Lexington).
/ **Details:** www.fernandezandwells.com; Lexington St 10 pm; Beak St 6 pm.*

Ffiona's W8 £45   A
51 Kensington Church St 7937 4152 4–1A
*"The food's OK", at this "cosy" candlelit Kensington bistro, "but you really
go for the atmosphere and to chat with Ffiona"; fall out with la patronne,
though – it can happen – and the party's over! / **Details:** www.ffionas.com;
11 pm, Sun 10 pm; D only, closed Mon; no Amex.*

Fifteen Dining Room N1 £85
15 Westland Pl 0871 330 1515 1–1A

*Jamie Oliver's charitable Hoxton Italian remains "way overpriced, 'cos of his name"; fans do say "the expense is worth it", citing "passionate food and service", but critics just find it just "too pricey for cooking by trainees", especially given the "dingy" and "soulless" basement setting. / **Details**: www.fifteenrestaurant.net; 9.30 pm; booking: max 6.*

54 Farringdon Road EC1 £35 ✪
54 Farringdon Rd 7336 0603
*An "out-of-the-way" Farringdon yearling which offers a slightly "strange" mix of Malay and European cuisine; the former is particularly "delicious", though, and service is notably "efficient".
/ **Details**: www.54farringdon.com; 11 pm; closed Sat L & Sun.*

Fig N1 £46 🅐✪
169 Hemingford Rd 7609 3009
*It may be "hidden-away in the leafy streets of Barnsbury", but this tiny "one-off" has won a big fan club with its "original", "Nordic-influenced" food, its "sweet" service, and its "casual" and "romantic" ambience.
/ **Details**: www.fig-restaurant.co.uk; 10.15 pm, Sun 9 pm; D only, closed Sun-Tue.*

La Figa E14 £36 ✪
45 Narrow St 7790 0077
*"Pizza and pasta in enormous portions" – and "sunny" service too – "draw in crowds" to this "well-run" Docklands Italian; it can get "loud".
/ **Details**: 11 pm, Sun 10.30 pm.*

Fino W1 £52 🅐✪
33 Charlotte St 7813 8010 1–1C
*"Impressive" tapas and a "terrific Spanish wine list" win continued acclaim for the Hart brothers' "always-buzzing" Fitzrovia venture, which manages to be "stylish, despite being in a basement".
/ **Details**: www.finorestaurant.com; 10.30 pm; closed Sat L & Sun; booking: max 12.*

First Floor W11 £42 🅐
186 Portobello Rd 7243 0072 5–1A
*If you're looking for "boho-chic" Notting Hill style, you won't do better than this "very dependable" and "romantic" local fixture (which features an "amazing" and "different'" party room).
/ **Details**: www.firstfloorportobello.co.uk; 11 pm; closed Mon & Sun D.*

Fish Club £32

189 St John's Hill, SW11   7978 7115
57 Clapham High St, SW4   7720 5853

"Making fish 'n' chips a gourmet treat"; these *"relaxed"* Clapham and Battersea concepts are a *"brilliant reinvention of the chippy for the 21st century"*, with everything *"cooked in varying styles, to order"; "for such sophisticated food"*, though, the eat-in space can seem a little *"primitive".* / **Details:** www.thefishclub.com; 10 pm, Sun 9 pm; SW4 closed Mon L, SW11 closed Mon.

Fish Hook W4 £47

6-8 Elliott Rd   8742 0766   6–2A
"Fantastically fresh fish and seafood" is cooked *"with confidence and flair"*, at Michael Nadra's very *"tightly-packed"* Chiswick fixture (where the top deal is the *"brilliant-value set lunch"*); service, however – which is generally *"charming"* – can sometimes be a *"let-down".* / **Value tip:** set weekday L £28 (FP). **Details:** www.fishhook.co.uk; 10.30 pm, Sun 10 pm.

5 Cavendish Square W1 £66

5 Cavendish Sq   7079 5000   2–1C
"Only go for the décor", to this showy bar/club/restaurant, in a massive Marylebone townhouse – it may be strong on *"grandeur"*, but service is *"lacklustre"*, and the food *"isn't worth half what they charge for it".* / **Value tip:** set weekday L £39 (FP). **Details:** www.no5ltd.com; 10 pm; closed Sat L & Sun D; no trainers.

Five Hot Chillies HA0 £23

875 Harrow Rd   8908 5900
"Freshly-cooked" curries and kebabs at *"fantastic prices"* make it worth braving the trip to this *"very friendly"*, if grotty-looking, Sudbury Indian, on a busy highway; *"BYO makes it even better value".*
/ **Details:** 11.30 pm; no Amex.

500 N19 £33

782 Holloway Rd   7272 3406
"There is life in Archway!"; this *"brave"* and *"simply-furnished"* Sicilian newcomer has brought *"a real spark of Mediterranean warmth"* to this unpicturesque corner of the capital; be warned, though – *"you'll need to book on any night of the week".* / **Details:** www.500restaurant.co.uk; 10 pm; closed Mon & Sun L.

The Flask N6 £34

77 Highgate West Hill   8348 7346
A *"superb"* location – *"quietly set in Highgate village with nice outside seating"* – ensures this lovely old inn is always *"busy"*; the food is *"varied"* and *"fresh"*, but ultimately a bit beside the point.
/ **Details:** 10 pm.

Flat White W1 £ 9

17 Berwick St 7734 0370 2–2D

*Coffee that's "so good it's illegal" is the – really – big deal at this "pokey" Kiwi-run bar, in a seamy part of Soho. / **Details:** www.flat-white.co.uk; L only; no credit cards.*

Foliage
Mandarin Oriental SW1 £87

66 Knightsbridge 7201 3723 4–1D

*With its "majestic views" (from the window tables) and "comfortable" interior, this park-side dining room put in a very decent showing under Chris Staines – his mid-2009 resignation, in anticipation of Heston Blumenthal's arrival at the hotel in 2010, doesn't augur particularly well for the restaurant's final months. / **Value tip:** set weekday L £52 (FP). **Details:** www.mandarinoriental.com; 10.15 pm; booking: max 6.*

Food for Thought WC2 £17

31 Neal St 7836 0239 3–2C

*The setting may be "rustic" and the chairs may be "wobbly", but this Covent Garden basement veggie is usually "insanely crowded" – well, there aren't many places where "you can buy an interesting and substantial lunch for well under a tenner"; BYO. / **Details:** 8 pm, Sun 5 pm; no credit cards; no booking.*

Forman's E3 £47

Stour Rd, Fish Island 8525 2365

*If you want to see the Olympic Stadium in construction, this lofty dining room – part of acclaimed smoked salmon producer, H Forman & Son's new-build smokery on the River Lea – is the place to be; it's nigh on impossible to find, but early reports – too few for a rating – are positive; all-English wine list. / **Details:** www.formans.co.uk; 11.30 pm; Sun-Wed closed D.*

(Fountain)
Fortnum & Mason W1 £50

181 Piccadilly 7734 8040 2–3D

*For a "delightful, quintessentially British breakfast", "ladies' lunch" or afternoon tea, the buttery at the grand "old-money" St James's grocery store offers "a quieter alternative to The Wolseley"... and one that's "improved since the recent make-over"; see also 1707. / **Details:** www.fortnumandmason.co.uk; 10.45 pm; closed Sun D; no booking at L.*

Four O Nine SW9 £46

409 Clapham Rd 7737 0722

*Entered "speakeasy-style", this "serene oasis" (above a Clapham pub) makes a "romantic" find, and one where the cooking is "above expectations"; of late, however, standards – particularly on the service front – have become more variable. / **Details:** www.fouronine.co.uk; 10.30 pm; D only, ex Sun open L & D.*

The Four Seasons W2 £27

84 Queensway 7229 4320 5–1C

*"The best crispy duck in the world" has long won renown for this "crowded" Bayswater veteran; it's a bit of "slum", though, and staff are "dismissive" going-on "rude" – "you should hear what they say about the customers in Cantonese!" / **Details:** 11 pm; no Amex.*

The Fox & Hounds SW11 £37

66 Latchmere Rd 7924 5483

"Battersea's number one"; this "brilliant" and "unfailing" gastropub attracts many compliments for its "inventive food" and "exceptional value". / **Details:** *www.thefoxandhoundspub.co.uk; 10 pm; closed Mon L, Tue, Wed & Thu.*

The Fox and Anchor EC1 £37

115 Charterhouse St 7250 1300

A "beautiful refurbishment" last year widened the appeal of this "wonderful" Victorian pub, in Smithfield; it still does its famous "gut-busting breakfasts, washed down with a pint of Guinness", but its "generous" (and not especially 'gastro') British cuisine makes a visit worthwhile at any time. / **Details:** *www.foxandanchor.co.uk; 10 pm; closed Sun.*

Franco Manca SW9 £14

Unit 4 Market Row 7738 3021

"If this isn't the best in England, tell me where is, and quickly!"; "hidden-away" in the heart of Brixton Market, this "taste of Naples" serves "simply perfect pizza" – "I've never tasted anything like it!" – at "extraordinary-value" prices. / **Details:** *www.francomanca.com; L only, closed Sun; no Amex.*

Frantoio SW10 £43

397 King's Rd 7352 4146 4–3B

"You can always be sure of a good reception", at this "brilliant local Italian" in World's End, which serves "traditional" food in a "genuine" style. / **Details:** *11.15 pm.*

Fresco W2 £16

25 Westbourne Grove 7221 2355 5–1C

"The best juices" are the star turn at this "efficient" Lebanese pit stop in Bayswater, which is also acclaimed for its "fantastic-value mezze" and falafel wraps that are a "must". / **Details:** *www.frescojuices.co.uk; 11 pm.*

La Fromagerie Café W1 £28

2-6 Moxon St 7935 0341 2–1A

"Beautiful" cheese isn't the sole attraction of eating in at Patricia Michaelson's fabled Marylebone store – it also does "excellent" salads and "great breakfasts and brunches"; recent expansion of the dining area seems to have improved standards generally.
/ **Details:** *www.lafromagerie.co.uk; 7.30 pm, Sat 7 pm, Sun 6 pm; L only; no booking.*

Fryer's Delight WC1 £10

19 Theobald's Rd 7405 4114 1–1D

A "classic old-school chippy", in Holborn, always of note for its "mouth-wateringly fresh fish 'n' chips". / **Details:** *11 pm; closed Sun; no credit cards; no booking.*

Fung Shing WC2 £36

15 Lisle St 7437 1539 3–3A

This Chinatown "stalwart" may be "shabby", but its cooking – while "not edgy, fusion or new" – is "more sophisticated than most"; highlights include "gorgeous seafood" and "superb specials".
/ **Details:** *www.fungshing.co.uk; 11.15 pm.*

Fuzzy's Grub   **£13**   ⭐

6 Crown Pas, SW1   7925 2791   2–4D
96 Tooley St, SE1   7089 7590
15 Basinghall St, Unit 1 Mason's Ave, EC2   7726 6771
56-57 Cornhill, EC3   7621 0444
58 Houndsditch, EC3   7929 1400
10 Well Ct, EC4   7236 8400
22 Carter Ln, EC4   7248 9795
62 Fleet St, EC4   7583 6060

*"A complete roast dinner in a sandwich!" – that's the proposition that
makes this (largely) take-away small chain "heaven" for traditionalists;
brace yourself for "interminable queues at peak times".*
/ **Details:** *www.fuzzysgrub.com; 3.30 pm-5 pm; no Amex; no booking.*

Galvin at Windows
Park Lane London Hilton Hotel W1   **£75**

22 Park Ln, 28th Floor   7208 4021   2–4A

*"Not just trading on its fantastic views", this 28th-floor Mayfair eyrie also
– to the surprise of some reporters – offers "rather good" food; needless
to say, though, you don't get anything like the same value you would
in the Galvin brothers' Marylebone HQ.* / **Value tip:** *set weekday L £42
(FP).* **Details:** *www.galvinatwindows.com; 11 pm; closed Sat L & Sun D;
no trainers.*

Galvin Bistrot de Luxe W1   **£45**

66 Baker St   7935 4007   1–1A

*"It would do Paris proud!"; the Galvin brothers' "smart" and
"very professional" Marylebone bistro has achieved an astonishing
following, and "never disappoints" with its "perfect" bourgeois cuisine;
"superb" wines too, many 'en carafe'.* / **Value tip:** *set dinner £29
(FP).* **Details:** *www.galvinrestaurants.com; 10.30 pm, Sun 9. 30 pm.*

Galvin La Chapelle E1

35 Spital Sq   1–2B
*The Galvin brothers have yet to put a foot seriously wrong, so there are
high hopes for this ambitious conversion of a Spitalfields chapel, set to
open in late-2009; it will include a range of dining options, and a bar.* /

Ganapati SE15   **£29**

38 Holly Grove   7277 2928
*"Far from the usual Identikit Indian", this "communal" but "lovely"
Peckham diner is "worth a trek", thanks to its "genuine", "ever-
changing" and "spice-scented" south Indian cuisine.*
/ **Details:** *www.ganapatirestaurant.com; 10.45 pm; closed Mon; no Amex.*

Garrison SE1 £43 **A**
99-101 Bermondsey St   7089 9355
This "happening" gastropub, near Bermondsey Antiques Market, remains extremely popular, thanks to the "cosy" and "laid-back" style of its "eclectically decorated" (and slightly "crushed") interior; "lovely" food – including "great" brunch fare – completes the formula.
/ **Details:** www.thegarrison.co.uk; 10 pm, Sun 9.30 pm.

The Gate W6 £39 ⭐
51 Queen Caroline St   8748 6932   6–2C
"They do amazing things with vegetables", at this "church hall"-style Hammersmith stalwart, long regarded as one of London's top meat-free destinations… although reports of some "heavy" meals of late signal a slight drift in overall satisfaction; pleasant summer terrace.
/ **Details:** www.thegate.tv; 10.45 pm; closed Sat L & Sun.

Le Gavroche W1 £112 **A**⭐
43 Upper Brook St   7408 0881   2–2A
Michel Roux's "clubby" Mayfair "old-stager" offers a "marvellous" and "indulgent" mix of "heavenly" ("so rich"!) "classic" cuisine, "exemplary" service and "mind-blowing" wine; even fans can find the formula "dated", though, and prices – apart from the "godsend" of a set lunch – are "flabbergasting". / **Value tip:** set weekday L £75
(FP). **Details:** www.le-gavroche.co.uk; 10.45 pm; closed Sat L & Sun; jacket required.

Geeta NW6 £18 ⭐
57-59 Willesden Ln   7624 1713
The staff, including the eponymous Geeta, are "always friendly", at this decrepit-looking Kilburn veteran; most reports applaud "outstanding" home-cooked south Indian dishes at "extraordinarily low prices"; BYO.
/ **Details:** 11 pm; no Amex.

The Giaconda Dining Room WC2 £35 ⭐
9 Denmark St   7240 3334   3–1A
In a "dingy" road in the shadow of Centre Point, Aussie chef Paul Merrony's "jammed" café "feels like a real find" (… unless you've read all the newspaper reviews, that is); its "lovely" staff serve up "proper" bistro dishes at "incredibly good-value" prices. / **Details:** www.giacondadining.com; 9.45 pm; closed Sat & Sun.

The Glasshouse TW9 £57 ⭐⭐
14 Station Pde   8940 6777

"Not quite as good as Chez Bruce… but nearly!" – the Kew sibling of London's Favourite Restaurant similarly offers "beautiful" cooking, "perfectly pitched" service, "spectacular" cheese and "interesting" wine in an "understated" (and "rather cramped") setting.
/ **Details:** www.glasshouserestaurant.co.uk; 10.30 pm.

Golden Hind W1 £20
73 Marylebone Ln   7486 3644   1–1A
"Head and shoulders, the best chippy in central London" – this *"tiny and bustling"* Marylebone café boasts not just *"perfect fish 'n' chips"* but also *"delightful"* service; BYO. / **Details:** 10 pm; closed Sat L & Sun.

Goldfish NW3 £39
82 Hampstead High St   7794 6666
"Interesting and delicious new-wave Chinese food" again wins more-than-local acclaim for this *"cramped but charming"* two-year-old, *"bang in the middle of Hampstead"*.
/ **Details:** www.goldfish-restaurant.co.uk; 10.30 pm, Sat & Sun 11 pm; no Amex.

Goodman W1 £53
26 Maddox St   7499 3776   2–2C
Bizarrely, it's Russian money which is behind *"the closest thing to a NY steakhouse London has to offer"* – a *"relentlessly masculine"* (but very welcoming) Mayfair newcomer serving *"a wide selection"* of *"superb"* USDA (and other) cuts. / **Value tip:** set weekday L £29 (FP). **Details:** www.goodmanrestaurants.com; 11 pm; closed Sun.

Gordon Ramsay SW3 £115
68-69 Royal Hospital Rd   7352 4441   4–3D
"Professional, but lacking soul"; esteem for GR's Chelsea HQ *"went down faster than the stock market"* this year; prices seem ever more *"stratospheric"*, but there's a growing feeling that this is just *"not a 3-Michelin-star experience"* – the expected *"excitement"* too often is absent… just like the man himself! / **Value tip:** set weekday L £65 (FP). **Details:** www.gordonramsay.com; 11 pm; closed Sat & Sun; no jeans or trainers; booking: max 8.

Gordon Ramsay at Claridge's
Claridge's Hotel W1 £93
55 Brook St   7499 0099   2–2B
"Claridges deserves better", say critics of this potentially *"lovely"* Art Deco Mayfair dining room; true, its (dwindling) fan club still says it's *"first-class"*, but too often the food's found to be *"not worth all (or any) of the hype"*, and to come at *"outrageous"* prices too. / **Value tip:** set weekday L £48 (FP). **Details:** www.gordonramsay.com; 11 pm; no jeans or trainers; booking: max 8.

Gordon's Wine Bar WC2 £24
47 Villiers St   7930 1408   3–4D
"Dark", *"dusty"* and *"Dickensian"*, this cellar wine bar, by Embankment tube, is just *"unbeatable"* for ambience, and the wine (and cheese) is pretty good too – otherwise, fare is *"basic"*; large, leafy terrace (recently enlarged), with barbecue. / **Details:** www.gordonswinebar.com; 11 pm, Sun 10 pm; no booking.

The Goring Hotel SW1 £68
15 Beeston Pl   7396 9000   1–4B
"The perfect place to take a great aunt", this *"wonderfully old-fashioned"* and very English family-run hotel is *"a haven of calm"*, near Victoria; with its *"splendid, airy dining room"* and *"discreet"* service, it's also great for business (and, inevitably, does an *"unbeatable breakfast"*). / **Value tip:** set weekday L £48 (FP). **Details:** www.goringhotel.com; 10 pm; closed Sat L.

Gourmet San E2 £15 ⭐⭐

261 Bethnal Green Rd   7613 1366   1–1D

"Don't be fooled by appearances" – the décor may be "terrible", but the quality of the "authentic" cuisine at this "brusque" East End Sichuanese "dive" is "amazing"; "expect to queue". / *Details: www.oldplace.co.uk; 11 pm; D only.*

The Gowlett SE15 £28 Ⓐ⭐

62 Gowlett Rd   7635 7048

"Unexpectedly good", "paper-thin" pizza is the particular draw to this "great little pub", in Peckham; "great ales" too.
/ *Details: www.thegowlett.com; 10.30 pm, Sun 9 pm.*

Great Queen Street WC2 £38 ⭐

32 Great Queen St   7242 0622   3–1D

"Real genius in combining simple ingredients" – to create "robust" and "seasonal" British menus – has won a vast following for this "buzzy" Covent Garden two-year-old; however, its "mock-frugal" style – "serving wine in tumblers", for example – irritates quite a few reporters.
/ *Details: 10.15 pm; closed Mon L & Sun D; no Amex.*

The Greenhouse W1 £90 Ⓐ

27a Hays Mews   7499 3331   2–3B

Now rivalling many better-known names, Marlon Abela's "discreet" Mayfair veteran is a "professional" operation, where Antonin Bonnet's "intricate and beautifully-executed" cooking is teamed up with "attentive" service and a "lovely" setting; the stand-out feature, however, is a wine list "like War & Peace". / *Details: www.greenhouserestaurant.co.uk; 10.30 pm; closed Sat L & Sun; booking: max 10.*

Grenadier SW1 £42 Ⓐ

18 Wilton Row   7235 3074   4–1D

A wonderful "olde worlde" pub, hidden-away in one of London's most picturesque mews, in Belgravia; its small dining room received few reports this year, but all of them complimentary; in the bar, the classic snack is a sausage and a Bloody Mary. / *Details: 9.30 pm, Sun 7.30 pm.*

Ground W4 £26 ⭐

219-221 Chiswick High Rd   8747 9113   6–2A

"Amazing burgers, with toppings both classic and unusual" still win a big fan club for this simple Chiswick outfit; its stellar ratings declined this year, however – ambience can be "lacklustre", and the food now "only narrowly beats the nearby GBK".
/ *Details: www.groundrestaurants.com; 10.30 pm.*

The Guinea Grill W1 £56 ⭐

30 Bruton Pl   7499 1210   2–3B

This "old-school" grill room, behind a Mayfair pub, may be "cramped" and "expensive", but it's "good at what it does" – "traditional British food", of the nature of "quality steaks" and "legendary pies".
/ *Details: www.theguinea.co.uk; 10.30 pm; closed Sat L & Sun; booking: max 10.*

The Gun E14 £43

27 Coldharbour   7515 5222

"A breath of fresh air, compared to the 'corporate' ventures of Canary Wharf", this "charming" and renowned Thames-side pub (with "great views of the O2") is especially good in summer (when attractions include a "Portuguese BBQ"); service can be "slow".
/ **Details:** www.thegundocklands.com; 10.30 pm, Sun 9.30 pm.

Gung-Ho NW6 £34

328-332 West End Ln   7794 1444
"A favourite for years", this "exemplary local Chinese", in West Hampstead, offers an appealing combination of "smart" décor, "genuinely warm" service and "above-average" cooking.
/ **Details:** www.stir-fry.co.uk; 11.30 pm; no Amex.

Haandi SW3 £35
7 Cheval Pl   7823 7373   4–1C
Hidden-away in a mews, just five minutes' walk from Harrods, this surprisingly "authentic" Indian is well worth knowing about for its "consistent" and "well-spiced" cuisine.
/ **Details:** www.haandi-restaurants.com; 11 pm, Fri-Sat 11.30 pm.

Haché £28

329-331 Fulham Rd, SW10   7823 3515   4–3B
24 Inverness St, NW1   7485 9100
"A cut-above GBK and Byron" – this "classy" (if "crowded") bistro-style mini-chain scores highly with reporters for its "wonderfully inventive" burgers (which are "properly cooked to order").
/ **Details:** www.hacheburgers.com; 10.30 pm, Sun 10 pm.

Hakkasan W1 £74

8 Hanway Pl   7927 7000   3–1A
"Hands down 'the daddy' of London's Chinese restaurants!" – this "so glam" West End basement's "sleek" looks and the "mouthwatering" quality of its cuisine have held up surprisingly well since founder Alan Yau sold out; prices remain "extortionate", though – for a 'value-visit', try weekend dim sum. / **Details:** www.hakkasan.com; 11.30 pm, Thu-Sat 12.30 am.

Haozhan W1 £37

8 Gerrard St   7434 3838   3–3A

This "stark" oriental yearling – with standards generally a "cut above" the Chinatown norm – is carving a strong reputation for "exciting" and "unusually creative" Chinese cuisine; service is atypically "friendly" too. / **Details:** www.haozhan.co.uk; 11.30 pm, Fri & Sat midnight, Sun 11 pm.

Harbour City W1 £29

46 Gerrard St   7439 7859   3–3B

"Always humming" at lunchtime, this Chinatown stalwart has a particular, and deserved, reputation for "great-value" dim sum. / **Details:** 11.30 pm, Fri & Sat midnight, Sun 10.

Harwood Arms SW6 £39

Walham Grove   7386 1847   4–3A

"Amazing game" ("cooked in exemplary style") is the highlight of the "seriously good" cooking at this backstreet Fulham local – "well and truly re-born under Brett Graham and Mike Robinson", it has quickly emerged as "one of the best gastropubs in town". / **Details:** www.harwoodarms.com; 9.30 pm, Fri & Sat 10 pm, Sun 9 pm.

Hélène Darroze
The Connaught Hotel W1 £102

Carlos Pl   7499 7070   2–3B

"Oh dear!"; with its "over-elaborate", "unbalanced" and "massively overpriced" cuisine, this outpost of the famous Parisienne chef has had a "dreadful" first year in its "plush" Mayfair home; service is "pretentious" and "haphazard" too – no wonder Michelin rushed to give the place a star! / **Value tip:** set weekday L £48 (FP). **Details:** www.the-connaught.co.uk; 10.30 pm; closed Mon, Sat & Sun; jacket & tie.

Hellenik W1 £36

30 Thayer St   7935 1257   1–1A

"Unchanging, reliable, extremely friendly" – this "civilised" Greek taverna maintains the virtues that first made it popular long before Marylebone became the trendy place it is today; "I always go back every 20 years, with no complaints!" / **Details:** 10.45 pm; closed Sun; no Amex.

Hereford Road W2 £40

3 Hereford Rd   7727 1144   5–1B

Tom Pemberton's "thoughtful" and "deliciously simple" British food is winning ever greater acclaim for this Bayswater yearling; the "minimal" interior can seem "underwhelming", but most reporters find it "pleasant" enough (the best seats being the booths at the front). / **Details:** www.herefordroad.org; 10.30 pm, Sun 10 pm.

Hibiscus W1 £85
29 Maddox St 7629 2999 2–2C

Claude Bosi's original Ludlow venture was so dazzling that it's hard not to feel "mildly let down" by its Mayfair reincarnation; the "elaborate" cuisine here shows "some flair" but too often "creates no excitement", and the "oh-so-safe" décor lends a pretty "soulless" air... all of which makes Michelin's award to it of two stars somewhat baffling! / *Value tip:* set weekday L £39 (FP). **Details:** www.hibiscusrestaurant.co.uk; 10 pm; closed Mon, Sat D & Sun.

High Road Brasserie W4 £48
162-166 Chiswick High Rd 8742 7474 6–2A

It's too "posy" for some tastes, but the Soho House group's "noisy" Chiswick outpost is certainly "very popular", not least with the glitterati of west London; the food is only "average", though, and service can get "stretched". / *Value tip:* set weekday L £24 (FP). **Details:** www.highroadhouse.co.uk; 11 pm, Fri & Sat midnight, Sun 10 pm.

Hilliard EC4 £27 ⭐⭐
26a Tudor St 7353 8150

A major "cut above your average casual City eatery" – this "cramped" diner, by the Temple, uses "superb" ingredients to produce "imaginative" sandwiches, salads and so on; it's "not cheap", but well "worth it". / **Details:** www.hilliardfood.co.uk; 6 pm; closed Sat & Sun; no booking.

Holly Bush NW3 £36 Ⓐ
22 Holly Mount 7435 2892

"Hidden-away in the back streets of Hampstead", a "superior old-style pub", with lots of "nooks and crannies", offering "decent" but "basic" fare. / **Details:** www.hollybushpub.com; 10 pm, Sun 9 pm; no Amex.

Homage
Waldorf Hilton WC2 £66
22 Aldwych 7759 4080 1–2D

Shame this "beautiful" and "ornate" – but rather hidden-away – Covent Garden dining room (once a ballroom) has never really 'taken off'... probably because it's "quite pricey" and "just not good enough, considering". / *Value tip:* set weekday L £39 (FP). **Details:** www.homagerestaurant.co.uk; 10.30 pm; closed Sat L & Sun L.

Hot Stuff SW8 £22 ⒶⒹⒹ
19 Wilcox Rd 7720 1480

"Appearances aren't everything"; this "shoe-box-sized" BYO caff, in a "dodgy-looking" Vauxhall street, "does not offer fine dining", but its "spicy and delicious" curries are "unbelievably cheap", and its "gregarious" service adds to the "welcoming" vibe. / **Details:** www.eathotstuff.com; 10 pm; closed Sun; no Amex.

The Hoxton Grille EC2 £41

81 Great Eastern St   7739 9111   1–1B

*This "oddly-located" eating place – part of the "combined reception/bar/kitchen/restaurant area" of a "hip" Hoxton hotel – was acquired by the Soho House group in mid-2009; it now boasts an all day 'American diner' menu and décor to match, but given all the recent changes, we've left it unrated. / **Details:** 11 pm.*

Hunan SW1 £48

51 Pimlico Rd   7730 5712   4–2D

*"Let Mr Peng order for you!" – "the food never stops coming" – and you'll enjoy an "utterly joyful" banquet at this "unparalleled" Pimlico stalwart; shame, though, that what's now – for cuisine – the survey's highest-rated Chinese is rather "cramped" and "claustrophobic". / **Details:** www.hunanlondon.com; 11 pm; closed Sun.*

Huong-Viet
An Viet House N1 £21

12-14 Englefield Rd   7249 0877

*"Hardly renovated since its days as public baths", this Vietnamese community hall in De Beauvoir Town converts at night into an "always-packed" canteen; "don't go in a hurry" – service is "often slow" – but you can have a "great, cheap BYO night out". / **Details:** www.huongviet.co.uk; 11 pm; closed Sun; no Amex.*

Ibérica W1 £40

195 Great Portland St   7636 8650   1–1B

*"Heavenly tapas" has won early-days plaudits for this "airy", contemporary newcomer, in the "soulless" environs of Great Portland Street tube; there's also a pricier upstairs, 'Caleya Ibérica'. / **Details:** www.ibericalondon.co.uk; midnight; no Amex.*

Ikeda W1 £75

30 Brook St   7629 2730   2–2B

*"My Japanese friend tells me this is the best sushi in London!"; this little-known Mayfair veteran has long been acclaimed for its "excellent" and "authentic" – "albeit expensive" – food; service is "engaging" too, but the setting is "austere". / **Details:** 10.30 pm; closed Sat L & Sun.*

Inaho W2 £33

4 Hereford Rd   7221 8495   5–1B

*Thanks to sushi that's amongst "the best in town", you "have to excuse the unbelievably bad service" at this tiny, "living room"-style Bayswater shack (where "you almost sit on top of your neighbour"). / **Details:** 11 pm; closed Sat L & Sun; no Amex or Maestro.*

Inamo W1 £34
134-136 Wardour St   7851 7051   2–1D
*"Yes, it's a gimmick" – "interactive" tables for ordering and entertainment – but, even if the Asian-fusion fare is "nothing special", reporters like this "fun" Soho yearling; "if your date's boring, you can always play battleships…" / **Details:** www.inamo-restaurant.com; midnight.*

L'Incontro SW1 £60
87 Pimlico Rd   7730 6327   4–2D
*An upmarket Pimlico Italian of long standing that rebranded briefly as 'Mauro for Santini' this year; in its new guise it inspired few reports and stood accused of mediocre "wannabe" standards – same as ever, then? / **Value tip:** set weekday L £34*
*(FP). **Details:** www.lincontro-restaurant.com; 11 pm; closed Mon L, Sat L & Sun.*

Indian Ocean SW17 £26
216 Trinity Rd   8672 7740
*"Busy every night", this "high-quality" Wandsworth operation remains a model local curry house. / **Details:** 11.30 pm.*

Indian Zing W6 £38
236 King St   8748 5959   6–2B

*"Out-zinging its rivals!"; Manoj Vasaikar's "cracking" modern Indian cuisine is building an impressive reputation for his "buzzy" but "unpretentious" establishment, "in a dreary stretch of Hammersmith"; service is notably "caring" and "professional" too.
/ **Details:** www.indianzing.co.uk; 10.30 pm.*

Inside SE10 £43
19 Greenwich South St   8265 5060
*"By far the best food in Greenwich" ("not a demanding accolade, admittedly") is to be had at this "good-value" local; even fans, though, may feel that the interior "could do with a bit of an upgrade". / **Value tip:** set weekday L £25 (FP). **Details:** www.insiderestaurant.co.uk; 10.30 pm, Fri-Sat 11pm; closed Mon & Sun D.*

Isarn N1 £35
119 Upper St   7424 5153
*"Islington's best Thai" is "a great local", with an "intimate" modern interior; it demonstrates "real attention to customer service", and its dishes are usually "beautifully presented". / **Details:** www.isarn.co.uk; 11 pm.*

Ishbilia SW1 £42
9 William St   7235 7788   4–1D
*A short walk from Harrods, this authentic Lebanese provides "attentive" service and "very good" food. / **Details:** www.ishbilia.com; 11.30 pm.*

Isola del Sole SW15 £38
16 Lacy Rd 8785 9962
"Earthy" and *"slightly unusual"* cuisine and *"obliging"* service win local praise for this *"cramped"* and *"buzzy"* Putney Sardinian. / **Value tip:** set weekday L £17 (FP). **Details:** www.isoladelsole.co.uk; 10.30 pm; closed Sun; no Amex.

The Ivy WC2 £60
1 West St 7836 4751 3–3B
It's *"not as starry, now the celebs have been siphoned off by the Ivy Club, next door"*, but this infamously hard-to-book Theatrelander is as *"buzzy"* as ever, and – for fans – still *"consistently fantastic"*; doubters, though, find realisation of the menu of *"comfort"* fare increasingly *"ordinary"*. / **Details:** www.the-ivy.co.uk; midnight; booking: max 6.

Jamie's Italian E14 £35
Churchill Place Mall
After a series of successful openings elsewhere, Jamie Oliver's Italian chain is set to reach the capital – well, Canary Wharf, anyway – around the publication date of this guide; a flagship branch follows in Covent Garden in mid-2010. / **Details:** www.jamiesitalian.com.

Jenny Lo's Tea House SW1 £27 ⭐
14 Eccleston St 7259 0399 1–4B
"Staff are always warm and welcoming", at this *"jam-packed"* and *"canteen-like"* Belgravia fixture, which serves *"zingy"* and *"comforting"* noodle dishes at *"great-value"* prices. / **Details:** www.jennylo.co.uk; 10 pm; closed Sat L & Sun; no credit cards; no booking.

Jin Kichi NW3 £38 ⭐⭐
73 Heath St 7794 6158
"Great" value, *"lovely"* people, *"lousy"* décor – that's the *"unchanging"* formula for the success of this *"cosy"* and *"crowded"* Hampstead Japanese; sushi and sashimi are *"excellent"*, but *"the yakitori (skewer) bar is the place to be"*. / **Details:** www.jinkichi.com; 11 pm, Sun 10 pm; closed Mon, Tue-Fri D only, Sat & Sun open L & D.

Joe Allen WC2 £42
13 Exeter St 7836 0651 3–3D
A *"famous haunt"* that's *"long traded on the incredible atmosphere of its virtually unmarked, dim and cavernous, basement location"*, just off the Strand; *"pre- or post-theatre, it's the place to be"*, but foodwise only the *"secret burger"* (famously *"off-menu"*) can really be recommended. / **Value tip:** set pre theatre £28 (FP). **Details:** www.joeallen.co.uk; 12.45 am, Sun 11.45 pm; booking: max 10 Fri & Sat.

Joy King Lau WC2 £27
3 Leicester St 7437 1132 3–3A
A Chinatown *"old favourite"* that *"may not be the snazziest place"*, but which offers *"most reliable"* cooking at *"thrifty"* prices; *"truly authentic dim sum"* completes a winning package. / **Details:** 11.30 pm.

Julie's W11 £56
135 Portland Rd   7229 8331   5–2A

With its "amazing" labyrinthine layout and lavish décor, this Holland Park veteran has a "magical" ambience, especially "for romantic trysts"; in other respects, it "lost the plot" a long time ago, but, a recent refurbishment has coincided with some "improvement" across the board. / **Details:** www.juliesrestaurant.com; 11 pm.

Kai Mayfair W1 £80
65 South Audley St   7493 8988   2–3A

Did that new Michelin star go straight to the head of this "über-posh" but "anodyne" Mayfair Chinese?; fans still say its cuisine's "beyond compare", but critics – for whom the food's "average" – now focus on its "outrageous" prices. / **Value tip:** set weekday L £51 (FP). **Details:** www.kaimayfair.com; 10.45 pm, Sun 10.15 pm.

Kastner & Ovens WC2 £10
52 Floral St   7836 2700   3–2D

We don't usually list take-aways, but this "hidden gem", beside the Royal Opera House, is of real note for its "brilliant lunch boxes" – "a bit more expensive than Pret, but worth every penny". / **Details:** L only, closed Sat & Sun; no credit cards; no booking.

Kastoori SW17 £28
188 Upper Tooting Rd   8767 7027

"Puris like little taste bombs" are amongst the "amazingly delicious" Gujarati/East African dishes that have made this extremely "friendly", family-run Tooting stalwart something of a south London legend... "even if the outside does look rather grungy". / **Details:** www.kastoorirestaurant.com; 10.30 pm; closed Mon L & Tue L; no Amex or Maestro; booking: max 12.

Kazan £38
93-94 Wilton Rd, SW1   7233 7100   1–4B
34-36 Houndsditch, EC3   7626 2222

"Good-quality Middle Eastern/Turkish cuisine" makes these "really lively" Pimlico and City "stand-bys" consistently popular – the former location, in a still surprisingly 'thin' part of inner London, is "a great find". / **Details:** www.kazan-restaurant.com; 10.45 pm; EC3 closed Sun.

Ken Lo's Memories SW1 £55
65-69 Ebury St   7730 7734   1–4B

"Consistency is the key", for the many long-term fans of this veteran Belgravia Chinese, for whom "it's not the cheapest, but it is the best" – of late, however, the odd disappointment has been reported. / **Details:** www.londonfinediningroup.com; 11 pm; closed Sun L.

Khan's W2 £20
13-15 Westbourne Grove   7727 5420   5–1C

For a "filling" curry at "bargain" prices, this cavernous Bayswater canteen has long been a "reliable" destination; no alcohol. / **Details:** www.khansrestaurant.com; 11.45 pm.

Kiku W1 £60
17 Half Moon St 7499 4208 2–4B
"Great-quality" Japanese cooking at "relatively affordable prices" wins consistent praise for this "rather sterile" and "canteen-like" fixture; the set lunch is – by Mayfair standards – a "bargain". / **Value tip:** set weekday L £27 (FP). **Details:** www.kikurestaurant.co.uk; 10.15 pm; closed Sun L.

Konditor & Cook £20
Curzon Soho, 99 Shaftesbury Ave, W1 7292 1684 3–3A
46 Gray's Inn Rd, WC1 7404 6300
30 St Mary Axe, EC3 0845 262 3030
"Dangerously delicious" cakes and "outstanding pâtisserie" – plus "a varied menu of hot dishes, soups and tartlets" – inspire ongoing raves for these (generally) "tiny" café/take-aways. / **Details:** www.konditorandcook.com; W1 11 pm, Sun 10.30 pm; Cornwall Rd & Stoney St SE1 6 pm; WC1 7 pm; WC1 & EC3 closed Sat & Sun; Cornwall Rd & Stoney St closed Sun; no booking.

Konstam WC1 £45
2 Acton St 7833 5040
Oliver Rowe's "brave", eco-conscious pub-conversion, near King's Cross, remains a "really interesting" destination – working with "a narrow range of local ingredients" (sourced from in/around the M25) inspires some notably "inventive" cooking. / **Details:** www.konstam.co.uk; 10.30 pm; closed Sat L & Sun D.

Kurumaya EC4 £31
76-77 Watling St 7236 0236
"Excellent sushi and sashimi" – some of the best-value Japanese food in the Square Mile – make this "reasonably-priced" Kaiten-Zushi outfit, near Mansion House, well worth seeking out. / **Details:** www.kurumaya.co.uk; 9.30 pm; closed Sat & Sun.

The Ladbroke Arms W11 £43
54 Ladbroke Rd 7727 6648 5–2B
"If only all pub grub was as good" as the "interesting", "seasonal" fare on offer at this hugely popular Notting Hill boozer; it's not all good news, though – "on a sunny day, don't even think about trying to bag one of the tables outside!" / **Details:** www.capitalpubcompany.com; 9.30 pm; no booking after 7.30 pm.

Lahore Kebab House E1 £22
2-4 Umberston St 7488 2551
"Ridiculous queues" advertise the "addictive" appeal of this "stupidly cheap" East End "institution", which "vies with New Tayyabs" to offer "the best kebabs this side of Karachi"; "no décor"; BYO. / **Details:** www.lahore-kebabhouse.com; midnight; need 8+ to book.

Lamberts SW12 £45
2 Station Pde 8675 2233
"Stunning value" wins acclaim for this Balham "gem", which offers an "interesting, seasonally-changing menu" and "professional, friendly service"; it's tempting to see it as "an alternative to Chez Bruce", but cognoscenti caution that its aims (and prices) are less lofty. / **Details:** www.lambertsrestaurant.com; 10.30 pm, Sun 9 pm; closed Mon, Tue-Fri L & Sun D; no Amex.

The Landau
The Langham W1   **£75**   A ✪✪
1c, Portland Pl   7965 0165   1–1B
Thanks to Andrew Turner's "exquisite" cuisine – largely served 'grazing'-style – this grand and "elegant" dining room, not far from Oxford Circus, is emerging as a real success-story (and one of the few top hotel restaurants of which Londoners can be at all proud).
/ Details: www.thelandau.com; 10 pm; closed Sat L & Sun D; no trainers.

(Winter Garden)
The Landmark NW1   **£79**   A
222 Marylebone Rd   7631 8000
A "giant glasshouse" of an atrium – "like you might find in Dubai!" – provides a "spectacular" setting at this Marylebone hotel; it has its fans, especially for afternoon tea or "champagne brunch", but "for the quite ordinary food, prices are stratospheric".
/ Details: www.landmarklondon.co.uk; 10.30 pm; no trainers; booking: max 12.

Latium W1   **£48**   ✪✪
21 Berners St   7323 9123   2–1D

Thanks to Maurizio Morelli's "magnificent" cooking, and the "classy" service too, this "hidden gem", just north of Oxford Street, is now seriously in contention as "London's finest Italian"; only the décor, perhaps, "could do with a little dressing up".
/ Details: www.latiumrestaurant.com; 10.30 pm, Fri-Sat 11pm; closed Sat L & Sun.

Latymers W6   **£28**   ✪
157 Hammersmith Rd   8741 2507   6–2C
It's "nothing to look at", but this "cheap 'n' cheerful" canteen at the rear of a huge Hammersmith gin palace serves Thai scoff that's "great, simple and reliable". / Details: 10 pm; closed Sun D; no Amex; no booking at L.

Launceston Place W8   **£72**   ✪
1a Launceston Pl   7937 6912   4–1B
"Stylish" cuisine and "charming" staff underpin a "wonderful transformation" of this "delightful" Kensington townhouse "gem", which was relaunched a year or so ago by the D&D group; it's "much more expensive" than it was, though, and its style can strike long-term fans as "pretentious". / Value tip: set weekday L £57
(FP). Details: www.danddlondon.com; 11 pm; closed Mon L.

The Ledbury W11   **£75**   A ✪✪
127 Ledbury Rd   7792 9090   5–1B
Nowadays thoroughly "top-tier" – this "consistently outstanding" Notting Hill "all-rounder" offers "rising star" Brett Graham's "flawless" and "adventurous" cuisine, in a "comfortable" and "relaxed" setting. / Value tip: set weekday L £44 (FP). Details: www.theledbury.com; 10.30 pm.

Lemonia NW1 £37 Ⓐ
89 Regent's Park Rd 7586 7454
A "huge", "vibrant" and "bustling" Primrose Hill taverna, where long-term
fans find "the owner Tony and his staff are like old friends"; nowadays,
however, the place "trades on its reputation", serving "basic" scoff that's
"mediocre and overpriced". / *Value tip:* set dinner £24
(FP). *Details:* 11.30 pm; closed Sat L & Sun D; no Amex.

Levant W1 £49 Ⓐ
Jason Ct, 76 Wigmore St 7224 1111 2–1A
"Was the money we paid for the belly dancers, not the chefs?" –
this "souk-like" Marylebone hang-out may have a "lovely, dark and
romantic" vibe (and "great cocktails" too), but its "expensive" Lebanese
fare is sometimes "awful". / *Details:* www.levant.co.uk; 11.30 pm.

The Lighthouse SW11 £32 Ⓐ★
441 Battersea Park Rd 7223 7721
"A good place in a not especially lovely area" – this Battersea gastropub
has many local fans, thanks to its "well constructed" dishes and its
"really nice" beer garden. / *Details:* 10 pm, Sun 9 pm.

LMNT E8 £30 Ⓐ
316 Queensbridge Rd 7249 6727
"With its crazy decor, and its cheap 'n' cheerful food", this "OTT" temple
of "high Egyptian kitsch", in Dalston "has all the makings of a great
party night out"; "call ahead to book one of the tree houses!"
/ *Details:* www.lmnt.co.uk; 10.45 pm; no Amex.

Lobster Pot SE11 £50 Ⓐ★
3 Kennington Ln 7582 5556
"Wacky" design (with "taped seagull noises") and "crazy" staff set
a French-surreal tone at this "strange" but "fun" stalwart, in a "dubious"-
looking bit of Kennington; its traditional Gallic fish and seafood dishes are
"first-class" too. / *Details:* www.lobsterpotrestaurant.co.uk; 10.30 pm; closed
Mon & Sun; booking: max 8.

Locanda Locatelli
Churchill InterCont'l W1 £62
8 Seymour St 7935 9088 1–2A
Giorgio Locatelli's low-lit and "sophisticated" Marylebone dining room is,
for its army of fans, "still the best Italian in London"; opinion, however,
is becoming ever more divided, and for a growing number of sceptics
"the only wow is the size of the bill!" / *Details:* www.locandalocatelli.com;
11 pm, Fri & Sat 11.30 pm; booking: max 8.

Locanda Ottomezzo W8 £69
2-4 Thackeray St 7937 2200 4–1B
According to its fans, this "low-lit" Kensington Italian is a
"neighbourhood" sort of place, offering "lovely" food – even they can find
it "a little expensive", though, and critics feel prices are plain
"outrageous". / *Details:* www.locandaottoemezzo.co.uk; 10.30 pm, Fri & Sat
10.45 pm; closed Sat L & Sun.

The Lock Dining Bar N17 £38
Heron Hs, Hale Wharf, Ferry Ln   8885 2829

This Tottenham three-year-old, at the foot of an obscurely-located office block, is not easy to find; the pay-off, however, is "great food at reasonable prices", especially the "truly unbelievable credit-crunch menus". / Value tip: set weekday L £22
(FP). Details: www.thelockrestaurant.com; 10 pm; closed Mon, Sat L & Sun D; no Amex.

Lola Rojo £29 ⭐
140 Wandsworth Bridge Rd, SW6   7371 8396
78 Northcote Rd, SW11   7350 2262
"Pushing the tapas envelope!"; these modern Spaniards put "a fantastic spin on traditional dishes" both at the "lively" Clapham original, and its "relaxed" new outpost in deepest Fulham. / Details: www.lolarojo.net; SW11 11.30 pm; SW6 11 pm; SW6 Mon-Fri D only.

Lucio SW3 £60
257 Fulham Rd   7823 3007   4–3B
"Back on form this year", this "nicely chilled" Chelsea spot is again – for its small fan club – "one of London best Italians", with "impeccable" service and food that's "always good"; look out for the "particularly good-value" lunch deal. / Value tip: set weekday L £34 (FP). Details: 11 pm.

Lucky Seven W2 £30 ⒶⒶ
127 Westbourne Park Rd   7727 6771   5–1B
You have to share booths, at Tom Conran's "really funky", "retro Americana" diner, on the fringes of Notting Hill, but it's worth it for the "awesome" burgers and "tasty" shakes.
/ Details: www.tomconranrestaurants.com; 11 pm; no Amex; no booking.

Lutyens EC4 £48
85 Fleet St   7583 8385
For the first time since the launch of Harden's almost 20 years ago, Sir Terence Conran has launched a restaurant we personally like! – a grand and comfortable (almost too pretty) Gallic brasserie, with conscientious service and Gallic favourites done to a tee; with its ultra-handy 'midtown' location it's set to become a major City/business hit. / Details: www.lutyens-restaurant.com; midnight; closed Sat & Sun.

The Luxe E1
109 Commercial St   7101 1751   1–2C
Not that far from his existing operation, Smiths of Smithfield, this long-awaited opening by John Torode (also of MasterChef fame) is expected around the publication date of this guide; as we go to press, the information available boils down to four buzzwords: 'bar, restaurant, music, art'… so now we know. / Details: www.theluxe.co.uk.

Ma Goa SW15 £34
244 Upper Richmond Rd   8780 1767
*"Extremely interesting" Goan "home cooking", with notably "friendly and professional" service, wins huge support – from Putney and beyond – for this impressive family-run restaurant. / **Details:** www.ma-goa.com; 11 pm, Sun 10 pm; closed Mon, Tue–Sat D only, Sun open L & D.*

Made in Italy SW3 £34
249 King's Rd   7352 1880   4–3C
*This popular Chelsea hang-out is usually "busy", and – thanks to the "sometimes disastrous" service – occasionally "chaotic"; it's a "fun" place, though, and its "great pizza saves the day"; "super terrace for sunny weather" too. / **Details:** www.madeinitalyrestaurant.co.uk; 11.30 pm, Sun 10.30 pm; closed weekday L; no Amex.*

Madhu's UB1 £36
39 South Rd   8574 1897
*"Well worth the schlepp to Southall"; this "consistent" high-achiever is again acclaimed for its "impeccable" service, its "deliciously different" (Kenyan-influenced) Indian food and its "bargain prices". / **Details:** www.madhusonline.com; 11.30 pm; closed Tue, Sat L & Sun L.*

Magdalen SE1 £48
152 Tooley St   7403 1342
*"Thoughtful" British cooking "bursting with flavour" underpins the lofty reputation of this foodie "haven", near the London Assembly building. / **Details:** www.magdalenrestaurant.co.uk; 10 pm; closed Sat L & Sun.*

Maggie Jones's W8 £46
6 Old Court Pl   7937 6462   4–1A
*"On a cold winter lunchtime", this "dark", rustic-style Kensington veteran is an "ideal" retreat from the world (especially for romance); for fans, its "old-fashioned comfort" food "never fails", but sceptics just find it "mediocre" nowadays. / **Details:** 11.30 pm, Sun 10.30 pm.*

Magic Wok W2 £29
100 Queensway   7792 9767   5–2C
*A "friendly", "authentic" and "no-nonsense" Bayswater Chinese, where the menu is "vast", but the food is both "surprisingly reliable" and "good value"; "great roast duck", and "good seafood" are highlights. / **Details:** 11 pm.*

Maison Bertaux W1 £11
28 Greek St   7437 6007   3–2A
*A "lovely" – if ever so slightly "mad" – Soho institution (established 1871), London's oldest pâtisserie is still worth seeking out for its "marvellous cakes and croissants". / **Details:** 11 pm, Sun 8 pm; no credit cards; no booking.*

Mandalay W2 £25
444 Edgware Rd   7258 3696
*"A warm welcome from the Ally family" happily offsets the "dive" atmosphere of this "café-style" joint, north of Edgware Road tube; its "simple and different" Burmese dishes can offer "excellent value" too. / **Value tip:** set weekday L £12 (FP). **Details:** www.mandalayway.com; 11 pm; closed Sun.*

Mandarin Kitchen W2 £34
14-16 Queensway   7727 9012   5–2C

"Lobster noodles in a class of their own" are the highpoint of the
"amazing Chinese seafood" on offer at this *"consistently fantastic"*
Bayswater spot; service is *"cursory"*, though, and the interior *"dismal"*.
/ **Details:** 11.30 pm.

Mangal Ocakbasi E8 £22
10 Arcola St   7275 8981

"Mountains of food for the money" – *"succulent"* meat, with *"fresh"*
salads – offer *"incredible"* value-for-money, at this *"basic"* and
"crammed-to-the-gills" Dalston Turk, whose front room is *"dominated"*
by a *"gigantic"* charcoal grill; BYO. / **Details:** www.mangal1.com; midnight;
no credit cards.

Mango Tree SE1 £29
5-6 Cromwell Buildings, Red Cross Way   7407 0333

"Lovely" and *"different"* Indian dishes again win praise for this
"cramped" Borough Market venture, which *"looks more like a bistro than
a curry house"*. / **Details:** www.justmangotree.co.uk; 11 pm.

Mao Tai SW6 £50
58 New King's Rd   7731 2520

"Much hipper and livelier than most Chinese places" – this evergreen
Parson's Green veteran (which is more pan-Asian really) wins continued
praise for its *"really lovely"* cuisine; it's *"not cheap"* though.
/ **Details:** www.maotai.co.uk; 11.30 pm; D only, ex Sun open L & D.

Marcus Wareing
The Berkeley SW1 £115
Wilton Pl   7235 1200   4–1D

WINNER 2010

"London's No. 1!" – *"Marcus has not just stepped out of Ramsay's
shadow but now eclipsed him"*, thanks to the *"meticulous"* and *"subtle"*
cuisine served up by *"gracious and unobtrusive"* staff at this *"absolutely
superb"* Knightsbridge dining room; the wine list is a veritable *"tome"*
too. / **Value tip:** set weekday L £98 (FP). **Details:** www.the-berkeley.co.uk;
10.30 pm; closed Sat L & Sun; no jeans or trainers; booking: max 10.

Market NW1 £40
43 Parkway 7267 9700
"The problem is that you want to eat everything on the menu!";
this year-old Camden Town "hit" is a bistro anyone would like in their
neighbourhood, offering "hearty" and "honest" British dishes
at "very competitive" prices. / **Details:** www.marketrestaurant.co.uk;
10.30 pm; closed Sun D.

Masters Super Fish SE1 £24
191 Waterloo Rd 7928 6924
"You can't get a table", such is the press of "stoutly-built cab drivers",
at this "superb chippy" near Waterloo; "nuff said!" / **Details:** 10.30 pm;
closed Mon L & Sun; no Amex; no booking Fri D.

maze W1 £65
10-13 Grosvenor Sq 7107 0000 2–2A
Jason Atherton's "pioneering", tapas-inspired approach still "wows"
visitors to this "minimalist" Ramsay-group Mayfair dining room;
"microscopic" portions twinned with "astronomical" prices, however,
contribute to the impression of a slight "loss of sparkle" of late.
/ **Details:** www.gordonramsay.com/maze; 10.30 pm.

maze Grill W1 £75
10-13 Grosvenor Sq 7107 0000 2–2A
After a good start, this "beige" and "clinical" Ramsay-group Mayfair
steakhouse has "gone down fast" in its first full year – the food seems
increasingly "underwhelming" and "overpriced", and service is too often
by the "Keystone Kops". / **Details:** www.gordonramsay.com; 10.30 pm;
no trainers.

Le Mercury N1 £25
140a Upper St 7354 4088
"For frugal romance", it's impossible to beat this "lively" bistro,
near Islington's Almeida Theatre; its basic scoff is "not high fashion",
but "astonishingly cheap" – "I feel like I'm 20 again... and so do the
prices!" / **Details:** www.lemercury.co.uk; 1 am, Sun 11.30 pm.

Mildred's W1 £32
45 Lexington St 7494 1634 2–2D
"London's best veggie" serves "imaginative" and "wholesome" dishes at a
"funky", "diner-style" Soho site, which – though "squashed" and "noisy",
and frequently "with a queue" – is usually "loads of fun".
/ **Details:** www.mildreds.co.uk; 11 pm; closed Sun; no booking.

Min Jiang
The Royal Garden Hotel W8 £55
2-24 Kensington High St 7361 1988 4–1A
"Memorable" Peking duck (the house speciality, ordered in advance),
"superb" dim sum and "extremely helpful" service are just three
highlights of this "terrific", tenth-floor Chinese yearling – all the more
remarkable for a room with "stupendous" views (over Kensington
Gardens)! / **Value tip:** set weekday L £33 (FP). **Details:** www.minjiang.co.uk;
10 pm.

Mirch Masala £27 ⭐⭐

171-173 The Broadway, UB1 8867 9222
3 Hammersmith Rd, W14 6702 4555 6–1D
1416 London Rd, SW16 8679 1828
213 Upper Tooting Rd, SW17 8767 8638
111 Commercial Rd, E1 7247 9992 1–2D
"*Don't be put off by the plastic table tops and strip-lighting!*"; you get
"*stunning*" *subcontinental scoff* – and "*at ridiculously low prices*" too –
at these "*tatty*" but "*bustling*" *Pakistani canteens; (NB. W14 actually
trades as Mirin Masala, but it's essentially identical).*
/ Details: www.mirchmasalarestaurant.co.uk; midnight.

Mitsukoshi SW1 £50 ⭐

Dorland Hs, 14-20 Lower Regent St 7930 0317 2–3D
"*The sushi bar is still the best (and most undiscovered) in town*",
say aficionados of this "*most reliable*" and "*true*" *Japanese, in an ultra-
drab department store basement, near Piccadilly Circus.* / **Value tip:** *set
weekday L £28 (FP).* **Details:** *www.mitsukoshi-restaurant.co.uk; 10 pm.*

Monkey & Me W1 £25 ⭐

114 Crawford St 7486 0400 1–1A
*Surprisingly little commented-on, this small Marylebone restaurant serves
"fresh and authentic" Thai food; the premises are set to double in size
some time during the currency of this guide, so they must be doing
something right. /*

Monmouth Coffee Company £10 🅐⭐⭐

27 Monmouth St, WC2 7379 3516 3–2B
2 Park St, SE1 7645 3585
"*The best coffee in London, undoubtedly*" – that's the draw to this
"*charming*" *Borough Market café (where "filling" Saturday breakfasts
of bread, jam and pastries are something of an institution); Covent
Garden is retail/coffee only.* / **Details:** *www.monmouthcoffee.co.uk;
6 pm-6.30 pm; closed Sun; no Amex; no booking.*

Morgan M N7 £64 ⭐⭐

489 Liverpool Rd 7609 3560

*Morgan Meunier's "clever, intricate and delicious" Gallic cuisine – among
London's very best – is "an inspiration", and well justifies a trip to his
"out-of-the-way" pub-conversion in an "unsalubrious" bit of Holloway;
the interior is rather "sober", but it is "warmed up by the personality
of the staff".* / **Value tip:** *set weekday L £39 (FP).* **Details:** *www.morganm.com;
9 pm; closed Mon, Tue L, Sat L & Sun D; no Amex; booking: max 6.*

Moro EC1 £46
34-36 Exmouth Mkt   7833 8336
"Punishing acoustics" aside, it's "really hard to fault" this "exceptional" Farringdon favourite, where "smiling" staff perennially serve up "surprising" and "mouthwatering" Spanish/Moorish dishes; "unusual" wines and "superb sherries" too. / **Details:** www.moro.co.uk; 10.30 pm; closed Sun.

Mosaica
The Chocolate Factory N22 £40
Unit C005, Clarendon Rd   8889 2400
Hidden-away in an "unpromising" location behind a factory, this Wood Green "gem" is "a real find", thanks to its "novel" setting and "very friendly" service; "interesting" and "affordable" cooking too. / **Details:** www.mosaicarestaurants.com; 9.30 pm; closed Mon, Sat L & Sun D; no Amex.

Moti Mahal WC2 £47
45 Gt Queen St   7240 9329   3–2D
"An unexpected delight!"; this "classy" contemporary Indian, in Covent Garden, can make a "great discovery" for first-timers, thanks not least to its "thoughtful" and "extremely original" cuisine. / **Details:** www.motimahal-uk.com; 11.30 pm, Sat & Sun 11.15 pm; closed Sat L & Sun L.

Mr Chow SW1 £70
151 Knightsbridge   7589 7347   4–1D
This once mega-fashionable '60s-style Chinese inspires few reports nowadays; fans still rate it highly, but "all-round disappointment" is far from unknown. / **Details:** www.mrchow.com; midnight.

Mr Wing SW5 £45
242-244 Old Brompton Rd   7370 4450   4–2A
A setting in a "supremely kitsch basement" (complete with "fish tanks, and jazz") helps make this "fun" Earl's Court veteran something of "a long-term favourite" for parties and romance; "impeccably friendly" service and "classy" Chinese cooking play honourable supporting roles. / **Details:** www.mrwing.com; midnight.

Mrs Marengos W1 £15
53 Lexington St   7287 2544   2–2D
Really good pâtisserie is hard to find in London, so we welcome this small Soho café, where the home-made gâteaux, in particular, really are exceptional. / **Details:** www.mrsmarengos.co.uk; L only, closed Sun; no Amex; no booking.

Murano W1 £77
20-22 Queen St   7592 1222   2–3B

WINNER 2010

REMY MARTIN

"Well done Angela!"; Ms Hartnett's cooking – "simple Italian dishes beautifully executed" – has proved notably "more self-assured" in this elegant new Ramsay-group Mayfair dining room than it was at The Connaught; the setting itself can seem a bit "soulless", but "fabulous" service contributes to a "charming" overall impression nonetheless. / **Details:** www.gordonramsay.com/murano; 10 pm; closed Sun.

Nahm
Halkin Hotel SW1 £82

5 Halkin St   7333 1234   1–3A

Fans of David Thompson's Belgravia Thai continue to argue that its "stunning" cuisine is "London's best" of its type; it's also "unbelievably pricey", though, and to sample it you have to endure "patronising" service in a "dead" dining room that's "very obviously part of an hotel". / **Details:** *www.nahm.como.bz; 10.30 pm; closed Sat L & Sun L.*

The Narrow E14 £42

44 Narrow St   7592 7950

"Fabulously-located" on the river, at Wapping, this "textbook" gastropub is by far the best of Gordon Ramsay's stabs at the concept … which is to say that, overall, reporters rate it "solid" (but certainly no more). / **Details:** *www.gordonramsay.com; 10 pm.*

Nautilus NW6 £32

27-29 Fortune Green Rd   7435 2532

"The rumours are true: it's the best chippy in London!" – this "cheerful" kosher West Hampstead veteran provides "massive portions of fresh fish", "perfectly cooked" in matzo meal; opinions differ, though, on whether its "old-fashioned" interior is "fun" or "dire". / **Details:** *10 pm; closed Sun; no Amex.*

New Mayflower W1 £30

68-70 Shaftesbury Ave   7734 9207   3–3A

"Don't expect a relaxing meal", at this "rudely efficient" Chinatown veteran, which is particularly of note as a late-night destination; its cooking, though, is "more authentic" than most, and comes in "huge portions". / **Details:** *4 am; D only; no Amex.*

New Tayyabs E1 £25

83 Fieldgate St   7247 9543

"The best Pakistani cooking this side of Lahore" (particularly "lamb chops to die for") comes at "ludicrously cheap" prices at this BYO East Ender – a "hectic" sort of place, with "long queues" and "slightly surly service". / **Details:** *www.tayyabs.co.uk; 11.30 pm.*

Nobu
Metropolitan Hotel W1 £88

Old Park Ln   7447 4747   2–4A

The "vibrant" Japanese-fusion dishes "still rock", at this Mayfair legend, and they are still, sadly, as "ridiculously overpriced" as ever; the place is arguably "not hip any more"… which seems to working to its advantage – service is less "snooty" than of old, and the atmosphere less "frantic and noisy". / **Details:** *www.noburestaurants.com; 10.15 pm, Fri & Sat 11 pm, Sun 9.30 pm; booking: max 12.*

Nobu Berkeley W1 £88

15-16 Berkeley St   7290 9222   2–3C

More "showy" and "fun" than its Park Lane sibling, this younger (in all respects) of the Nobus is a "vibrant" destination above a happening bar; its Japanese-fusion fare can be "divine", but it's "ludicrously expensive", and service is too often "snobbish" and "unenthusiastic". / **Details:** *www.noburestaurants.com; 11.45 pm, Thu-Sat 12.45 am, Sun 9.45 pm; closed Sat L & Sun L.*

Noor Jahan £35
2a Bina Gdns, SW5 7373 6522 4–2B
26 Sussex Pl, W2 7402 2332 5–1D
This "straightforward" but "slightly upmarket" South Kensington stalwart
has long been a key destination for a "reliable" curry, with "fast"
("brusque") service; the "cosy" Bayswater offshoot is similarly
"dependable". / **Details:** 11.30 pm.

North China W3 £30
305 Uxbridge Rd 8992 9183 6–1A
"Dingy Acton's best kept secret"; this "friendly, family-run Chinese"
is "always full of locals", thanks to its "surprisingly good" cooking that
"beats many more expensive places". / **Details:** www.northchina.co.uk;
11 pm, Fri & Sat midnight.

North Sea Fish WC1 £29
7-8 Leigh St 7387 5892
It's a bit "basic" and "faded", but this Bloomsbury institution remains
"one of the best chippies around", certainly in the centre of town.
/ **Details:** www.northseafishrestaurant.co.uk; 10.30 pm; closed Sun; no Amex.

Nozomi SW3 £72
15 Beauchamp Pl 7838 1500 4–1C
An allegedly glamorous Knightsbridge Japanese, which attracts hardly
any survey feedback... all to the effect that it's "arrogant", "tasteless" and
"disappointing"; someone must like it, though, as a new sushi bar
extension is set to open in late-2009. / **Details:** www.nozomi.co.uk;
11.30 pm; D only, closed Sun.

Number One Café W10 £20
1 Dalgarno Gdns 8968 0558 5–1A
"You'd never stumble across it by chance", but this BYO North
Kensington Thai is "always really busy", thanks to its "authentic" food
and "unbeatable value". / **Details:** www.numberonecafe.tk; 10.30 pm; closed
Sun L.

Numero Uno SW11 £41
139 Northcote Rd 7978 5837
"The very definition of a local Italian" – this "jolly", family-run Battersea
linchpin is a "fabulous" old-timer, serving "authentic" food with "bags of
charm". / **Details:** 11.30 pm; no Amex.

O'Zon TW1 £26
33-35 London Rd 8891 3611
A downtown Twickenham oriental, offering a "huge choice"
of "consistently good" food, and "smiling" service too. / **Details:** 11 pm,
Fri & Sat 11.30 pm.

The Oak W2 £42
137 Westbourne Park Rd 7221 3355 5–1B
"Terrific" atmosphere and "fantastic" wood-oven pizza make this former
boozer an "all-time favourite" for many Notting Hillbillies; "you can't
book, but wait in the comfy bar upstairs". / **Details:** www.theoaklondon.com;
10.30 pm, Sun 10 pm; closed weekday L; no booking.

Odin's W1 £54

27 Devonshire St 7935 7296 1–1A

*"Feelings of well-being" pervade visits to this "old-fashioned and elegant" Marylebone veteran (which displays the "fine art collection" of the late Peter Langan); "very friendly" staff of long standing serve up "surprisingly good" fare in "traditional" style. / **Details:** www.langansrestaurants.co.uk; 11 pm; closed Sat L & Sun; booking: max 12.*

Ye Olde Cheshire Cheese EC4 £30

145 Fleet St 7353 6170

*To follow "in the steps of centuries of men of letters" (and tourists too), visit this "venerable" inn, just off Fleet Street; the English stodge is generally "edible". / **Details:** 9.30 pm; closed Sun D; no booking, Sat & Sun.*

Oliveto SW1 £49

49 Elizabeth St 7730 0074 1–4A

*"Like being in Italy!"; "wonderful thin-crust pizzas" justify the trip to this "loud and bustling" Belgravia Sardinian; book. / **Details:** www.olivorestaurants.com; 11 pm, Sun 10.30 pm; booking: max 7 at D.*

Olivo SW1 £47

21 Eccleston St 7730 2505 1–4B

*"Fine" Sardinian cooking has long made this "buzzy" Belgravian a popular destination, and fans say a visit to its "cramped" and "basic" premises is "always a joy"; slipping ratings, however, support those who feel "value is declining" here. / **Details:** www.olivorestaurants.com; 11 pm, Sun 10.30 pm; closed Sat L & Sun L.*

Olivomare SW1 £49

10 Lower Belgrave St 7730 9022 1–4B

*"Brilliant Sardinian seafood" is served at this Belgravia two-year-old (the "fishy sibling to nearby Olivo"); its "very white" décor, though – "like a '70s-style moonscape" – can feel rather "cold". / **Details:** www.olivorestaurants.com; 11 pm; closed Sun; booking: max 12.*

1 Lombard Street EC3 £75

1 Lombard St 7929 6611

*"They've tried hard during the downturn", and the ratings at this "echoey" and "always-crowded" former City banking hall staged a recovery this year – "solid" cooking and the incredibly "convenient" location make it a "reliable" destination for a business lunch. / **Details:** www.1lombardstreet.com; 10 pm; closed Sat & Sun.*

One-O-One
Sheraton Park Tower SW1 £76

101 Knightsbridge 7290 7101 4–1D

*Pascal Proyart's "exquisite" seafood cuisine – available in "novel" tapas-style, or more conventionally – has established this Knightsbridge dining room as simply "the country's best fish restaurant"; it's a real shame about the "frigid" décor. / **Value tip:** set weekday L £41 (FP). **Details:** www.oneoonerestaurant.com; 10 pm; booking: max 6.*

L'Oranger SW1   **£85**

5 St James's St   7839 3774   2–4D
This St James's restaurant may look "elegant", but it's very much
"resting on its laurels" nowadays, with too many visitors finding
it "hushed", "clinical" and "smug"; the Gallic cuisine is still sometimes
"very refined", but prices are "alarming". / **Value tip:** set weekday L £50
(FP). **Details:** www.loranger.co.uk; 10.30 pm; closed Sat L & Sun; no jeans
or trainers; booking: max 8.

Origin Asia TW9   **£36**

100 Kew Rd   8948 0509
A "contemporary Indian" in Richmond, where the "original take
on traditional dishes" is "significantly above-average". / **Value tip:** set
weekday L £23 (FP). **Details:** www.originasia.co.uk; 11 pm.

Orrery W1   **£72**   ⭐

55 Marylebone High St   7616 8000   1–1A
"The best 'Conran'" (as D&D was formerly called) – the group's "high-
calibre" Marylebone flagship offers "gorgeous" Gallic cuisine,
"immaculate" service and "wonderful" wine; the first-floor site may
be "corridor-like", but is "airy" and "calm", and has "lovely views over
a churchyard". / **Value tip:** set always available £44
(FP). **Details:** www.orreryrestaurant.co.uk; 10.30 pm, Fri-Sat 11 pm.

Oslo Court NW8   **£52**   🅐⭐

Charlbert St, off Prince Albert Rd   7722 8795
Who cares if it's a "'70s time warp", patronised mainly by geriatric north
Londoners? – this St John's Wood "perennial" is "hard not to love", given
its "outstanding" service, décor that's "so bad it's good", and a menu
"so retro" it provides "the perfect antidote to poncy food".
/ **Details:** 11 pm; closed Sun; no jeans or trainers.

Osteria Dell'Angolo SW1   **£42**

47 Marsham St   3268 1077   1–4C
After a "shaky start", this new Westminster Italian is winning plaudits for
its "elegant" cuisine (including "extraordinary pasta") and "faultless"
service; the fantastically "dull" décor, though, is a "major
disappointment". / **Details:** www.osteriadellangolo.co.uk; 10.30 pm; closed
Sat L & Sun; booking: max 20.

Ottolenghi   **£43**

13 Motcomb St, SW1   7823 2707   4–1D
63 Ledbury Rd, W11   7727 1121   5–1B
1 Holland St, W8   7937 0003   4–1A
287 Upper St, N1   7288 1454
"Everything looks so pretty", at these "casual", communal café/delis,
and the food "tastes even better than it looks" – the "unbelievably
sublime cakes", the "incredible salads", and the "amazing brunch food"
too; the seating, though, is "not super-comfy".
/ **Details:** www.ottolenghi.co.uk; 10.15 pm; W8 & W11 8 pm, Sat 7 pm,
Sun 6 pm; N1 closed Sun D; Holland St takeaway only; W11 & SW1 no booking,
N1 booking for D only.

(Restaurant)
Oxo Tower SE1 £74 ❌

Barge House St 7803 3888
*"A dreary and expensive tourist trap"… "if only the cooking was
as good as the view"… "how do they get away with it year after year?"
– situation normal, then, at this "outrageously pricey" 8th-floor South
Bank landmark, which (as ever) is judged "a total rip-off".
/ Details: www.harveynichols.com; 11 pm, Sun 10 pm.*

The Painted Heron SW10 £46 ⭐⭐

112 Cheyne Walk 7351 5232 4–3B
*"Simply amazing", "eclectic" and "refined" Indian cuisine makes it well
worth seeking out this "hard-to-find" – and rather "unexciting"-looking –
spot, off Chelsea Embankment. / Details: www.thepaintedheron.com; 11 pm;
closed Sat L & Sun.*

The Palm SW1 £75

1 Pont St 7201 0710 4–1D
*If you "stick to the set lunch menu", you can get "very good value"
at this swanky new Belgravia outpost of a major US steakhouse chain
(once the site of Drones, RIP); otherwise, it's "extremely expensive",
and, on our early-days visit, we couldn't quite see the justification. / Value
tip: set weekday L £33 (FP). Details: www.thepalm.com; 11 pm, Sun 9 pm; closed
Mon L.*

The Palmerston SE22 £43 ⭐

91 Lordship Ln 8693 1629
*"Everything you'd want from your local, and well worth the trip if it isn't!"
– this "top gastropub", down East Dulwich way, offers "fine" and
"seasonal" British cooking "without pretence". / Value tip: set weekday L
£26 (FP). Details: www.thepalmerston.net; 10 pm, Sun 9.30 pm; no Amex.*

Pappa Ciccia £28 🅐⭐

105-107 Munster Rd, SW6 7384 1884
41 Fulham High St, SW6 7736 0900
90 Lower Richmond Rd, SW15 8789 9040
*"Delicious" pizza, a "fun" atmosphere and "good" staff win all-round
praise for this small Fulham/Putney chain; at the SW6 branches (only),
you can BYO for modest corkage. / Details: www.pappaciccia.com; 11 pm,
Sat & Sun 11.30 pm; SW6 no credit cards.*

**Paradise by Way of
Kensal Green W10** £40 🅐⭐

19 Kilburn Ln 8969 0098
*It's well off the beaten track, but this vast and "impressive" operation
(spiritually part of Notting Hill) is "hard to get into at peak times";
the food can be "excellent", but it's the "brilliant interior and real buzz"
that makes it "one of the best gastropubs in town". / Value tip: set
weekday L £25 (FP). Details: www.theparadise.co.uk; 10.30 pm, Sun 8 pm; closed
weekday L & Sat D.*

El Parador NW1 £31 🅐⭐

245 Eversholt St 7387 2789
*"Don't be deceived by the humble surroundings", or the "run down"
location – this "friendly" tapas bar, near Euston, serves "delicious food
at remarkably good prices". / Details: www.elparadorlondon.com; 11 pm,
Fri & Sat 11.30 pm, Sun 9.30 pm; closed Sat L & Sun L*

The Park

Mandarin Oriental SW1   **£68** ⭐

66 Knightsbridge   7235 2000   4–1D

*This Knightsbridge hotel's 'other' restaurant – the main one is Foliage –
is a surprisingly good all-rounder, with "top-notch" food, and views
of Hyde Park which make lunch or brunch here a "memorable"
experience; but it's to be swept away in the spring of 2010, to make way
for the arrival of Heston Blumenthal later in the year.*
/ **Details:** *www.mandarinoriental.com; 10.30 pm.*

Pasha SW7   **£49** Ⓐ Ⓧ

1 Gloucester Rd   7589 7969   4–1B

*With its "little coves", rose petals and belly dancing, this "fun" South
Kensington townhouse-Moroccan "is definitely the place to go for
romance"; shame about the food, though – it's sometimes "revolting".*
/ **Details:** *www.pasha-restaurant.co.uk; midnight, Thu-Sat 1 am.*

Patara   **£45** ⭐

15 Greek St, W1   7437 1071   3–2A
3-7 Maddox St, W1   7499 6008   2–2C
181 Fulham Rd, SW3   7351 5692   4–2C
9 Beauchamp Pl, SW3   7581 8820   4–1C

*"Lovely refined Thai cooking" and "elegantly performing" staff have won
a big following for this "pleasant" (if slightly "dull") group; however
a slight recent "drop-off in service" seems symptomatic of slipping
standards generally.* / **Details:** *www.pataralondon.com; 10.30 pm.*

Patio W12   **£30** Ⓐ

5 Goldhawk Rd   8743 5194   6–1C

*"For a fun and filling night out" (especially in a group), this "old-
fashioned" Shepherd's Bush venue – where "ebullient" staff serve
up "enormous" portions of "tasty" Polish stodge – is "a hoot".*
/ **Details:** *11.30 pm; closed Sat L & Sun L.*

Pearl WC1   **£79**

252 High Holborn   7829 7000   1–1D

*Jun Tanaka's "exquisite" cooking has made quite a name for this
"discreet" Holborn dining room, in a "vast" and "elegant" (but slightly
"soulless") former banking hall; even some fans are "dubious about the
prices", though, and ratings generally slipped a little this year.* / **Value
tip:** *set weekday L £50 (FP).* **Details:** *www.pearl-restaurant.com; 10 pm; closed
Sat L & Sun.*

Pearl Liang W2   **£37** Ⓐ ⭐

8 Sheldon Sq   7289 7000   5–1C

*"What an excellent find in bleak Paddington Basin!"; this surprisingly
atmospheric, basement all-rounder is really quite a "hidden gem", and it
serves up some "superb Chinese food" at very "decent prices" –
most notably "fantastic" dim sum "on a par with Royal China's".*
/ **Details:** *www.pearlliang.co.uk; 11 pm.*

E Pellicci E2   **£14** Ⓐ

332 Bethnal Green Rd   7739 4873   1–1C

*This East End caff is famous for its "fabulous" (listed) Art Deco interior;
while service is "adorable", the food is generally "little better than your
average greasy spoon", but fans insist that breakfast is the "best in
London by a Cockney mile!"* / **Details:** *4.15 pm; L only, closed Sun; no credit
cards.*

Petersham Nurseries TW10 £56
Church Ln, Off Petersham Rd 8605 3627

Skye Gyngell's "imaginative" cuisine is "really incredible", say fans of this "unique" venue, whose "delightful", "Boho-chic" setting – a glass house within a fully-functioning garden centre – makes a "perfect place for lunch"; the "self-conscious quirkiness" can grate, though, and critics find the operation "smug" and "overpriced".
/ **Details:** www.petershamnurseries.com; L only, closed Mon.

La Petite Maison W1 £77
54 Brooks Mews 7495 4774 2–2B

*Nice comes to London in ever-more impressive fashion, at this "casual" but "chic" Mayfair two-year-old, where the "perfect, light and delicious" take on provençal cuisine (designed for sharing) only gets better; "pricey but worth it!". / **Details:** www.lpmlondon.co.uk; 10.15 pm, Sun 9 pm.*

Pétrus SW1 £90
1 Kinnerton St 7592 1609 4–1D

*Opening in late-2009, this Belgravia newcomer from the Gordon Ramsay group revives the name until recently associated with Marcus Wareing's venture at the nearby Berkeley; an undoubted success here might do wonders for the group's somewhat battered reputation; price is our guesstimate. / **Details:** www.gordonramsay.com/petrus.*

Pham Sushi EC1 £27
159 Whitecross St 7251 6336 1–2A

*This "simple" Formica-tables Japanese café, in a "slightly dingy area" near the Barbican, again inspires raves for its "sublime" and "very original" sushi (especially the crunchy tuna roll)… and at "half the price of the big names". / **Details:** www.phamsushi.co.uk; 10 pm; closed Sat L & Sun.*

Phoenix Palace NW1 £35
3-5 Glentworth St 7486 3515 1–1A

*"Always packed with Chinese people", this "Hong Kong-style" (and "surprisingly large") spot, near Baker Street tube, is "hard to beat for dim sum", and serves a "very comprehensive" à la carte menu too; service, though, is "a lottery". / **Details:** www.phoenixpalace.uk.com; 11.15 pm, Sun 10.30 pm.*

Pied à Terre W1 £93
34 Charlotte St 7636 1178 1–1C

*David Moore's "beacon of excellence", in a Fitzrovia townhouse, continues to put in an "exemplary" performance, thanks to Shane Osborn's "truly original" cuisine, the "biblical" wine list and the "exceptionally professional" service. / **Value tip:** set weekday L £52 (FP). **Details:** www.pied-a-terre.co.uk; 10.45 pm; closed Sat L & Sun; booking: max 6.*

Pissarro's W4 £40
Corney Reach Way 8994 3111
"It's especially lovely on sunny days", in the conservatory of this "well-hidden" spot, "right on the river", near Chiswick House; perhaps unsurprisingly, the "reasonable" Gallic fare is somewhat "expensive for what it is". / **Details:** www.pissarro.co.uk; 10 pm; closed Sun D.

Planet Hollywood SW1 £41
57-60 Haymarket 7437 7639 3–4A
Following redevelopment of the original site, the new London outpost of the Tinseltown-themed chain re-opened in mid-2009 at a new West End location; we somehow didn't get there in time to review it for this guide, but early press reviews have been truly terrible. / **Details:** www.planethollywoodlondon.co.uk; 1 am, Sun 12.30 am.

Poissonnerie de l'Avenue SW3 £59
82 Sloane Ave 7589 2457 4–2C
A "timeless" Brompton Cross parlour that's still "a favourite for seafood", thanks to its "impeccable" cuisine and "discreet" service; "it's not a place for young people", though – "most of the customers are well over 60". / **Details:** www.poissonneriedelavenue.co.uk; 11.15 pm, Sun 11 pm.

Popeseye £42
108 Blythe Rd, W14 7610 4578 6–1C
277 Upper Richmond Rd, SW15 8788 7733
With their "superb quality steaks" and "sensibly-priced" clarets, these "outstanding" little steakhouses "always hit the spot"; "it hardly looks like they can have spent more than £100 on the décor", however, and Putney – in contrast to Brook Green – is often "quiet". / **Details:** www.popeseye.com; 10.30 pm; D only, closed Sun; no credit cards.

Il Portico W8 £40
277 Kensington High St 7602 6262 6–1D
"Behind a dull exterior", by the Kensington Odeon, an old-time family-run Italian that "never fails to delight"; it's the "great" ambience that makes it special, though, rather than the "staple" cuisine. / **Details:** www.ilportico.co.uk; 11.15 pm; closed Sun.

The Portrait
National Portrait Gallery WC2 £46
St Martin's Pl 7312 2490 3–4B
"Breathtaking views" ("get a window table to be at eye-level with Nelson's Column") are the star turn at this "attractive" and "bustling" top-floor venue, just off Trafalgar Square; to enjoy them, however, you risk "institutionalised" food and "awful" service. / **Details:** www.searcys.co.uk; Thu-Fri 8.30 pm; Sat-Wed closed D.

La Poule au Pot SW1 £50
231 Ebury St 7730 7763 4–2D
On a Pimlico corner, a "clichéd but perfect" slice of "rural France", which – with its "secluded and dark" nooks – is, yet again, the survey's top choice for romance; the fare is "heart-warming", and service "authentically brusque". / **Details:** 11 pm, Sun 10 pm.

Princess Garden W1 £52

8 North Audley St 7493 3223 2–2A

For a "luxurious" Chinese meal, this "little-known" stalwart offers a "very spacious" setting and "reliable" food (notably, "excellent" dim sum); the décor can seem "sterile" however, and the experience undoubtedly comes "at Mayfair prices".
/ **Details:** www.princessgardenofmayfair.co.uk; 11.15 pm.

Princi W1 £18

135 Wardour St 7478 8888 2–2D

*The new Soho outpost of Milanese baker Rocco Princi (the 'Armani del pane'), in conjunction with our own 'local hero', Alan Yau, feels like a "little bit of Milan", offering a "stunning array" of baked goods, and pizza, and "gorgeous" coffee too; "go for a calm breakfast", though – "it's too much of a scrum at other times". / **Details:** www.princi.co.uk; midnight, Sun 10 pm; no booking.*

Prism EC3 £70

147 Leadenhall St 7256 3875

Harvey Nics's "cavernous" former banking hall can "set the right tone" for a City lunch; it's easy to "feel lost" in this "soulless" space, however, and its "eye-watering" prices, and "more-show-than-substance" cuisine make it best on "someone else's expenses".
/ **Details:** www.harveynichols.com; 10 pm; closed Sat & Sun.

The Providores W1 £61

109 Marylebone High St 7935 6175 1–1A

The "intimate" ("squeezed in") restaurant above the Tapa Room offers "brilliantly creative" fusion fare plus a "terrific" Kiwi wine list; for critics, though, the premium over downstairs is "hard to justify" – "the food's the same quality, but comes at almost twice the price!"
/ **Details:** www.theprovidores.co.uk; 10.30 pm; booking: max 12.

Quadrato
Four Seasons Hotel E14 £74

Westferry Circus 7510 1857

*With its "efficient" service and "competent" cooking, this grand Canary Wharf hotel dining room has its uses, especially for business (even if it can "lack ambience"); "excellent Sunday brunch". / **Value tip:** set always available £47 (FP). **Details:** www.fourseasons.com; 10.30 pm; booking: max 14.*

The Quality Chop House EC1 £39

94 Farringdon Rd 7837 5093

"Charming, old-school décor" (with "infamously uncomfy" benches) sets an "enjoyably nostalgic" tone at this former 'working class caterer', in Farringdon – it has long been at the forefront of raising "traditional British basics" to a sometimes "brilliant" level.
/ **Details:** www.qualitychophouse.co.uk; 11 pm, Sun 10 pm; closed Sat L.

Le Querce SE23 £32

66-68 Brockley Rise 8690 3761

The exterior may look "unprepossessing", but this Sardinian "gem", in deepest Brockley, is well worth seeking out for its "terrific" fare; it "helps to know what to order", though – highlights include "excellent pasta" and "amazing ice cream in weird and wonderful flavours".
/ **Value tip:** set Sun L £22 (FP). **Details:** www.lequercerestaurant.co.uk; 10 pm, Sun 9 pm; closed Mon & Tue L.

Quilon SW1 £55
41 Buckingham Gate   7821 1899   1–4B
"You're painfully aware you're in an hotel dining room", when you visit this posh Indian, near Buckingham Palace; otherwise it really is "a star" – staff are both "efficient" and "friendly", and the cooking is "superb". / **Value tip:** *set weekday L £33 (FP).* **Details:** *www.quilon.co.uk; 11 pm, Sun 10.30 pm; closed Sat L.*

Quirinale SW1 £53
North Ct, 1 Gt Peter St   7222 7080   1–4C
"Popularity with MPs and civil servants" is a defining feature of this Westminster "gem", which is "hidden-away" in a "light and airy" basement; it offers "mouthwatering" Italian food and "brilliant" wine, and service is notably "competent" too. / **Details:** *www.quirinale.co.uk; 10.30 pm; closed Sat L & Sun.*

Racine SW3 £51
239 Brompton Rd   7584 4477   4–2C
"Forever a piece of France", Henry Harris's "high-class" Knightsbridge bistro has a big name for its "immaculate" cooking, and "attentive" service; standards remain high, but there's some feeling that the place is "not the same" since last year's departure of maître d' (and co-founder) Eric Garnier. / **Value tip:** *set Sun L £34 (FP).* **Details:** *10.30 pm.*

Ragam W1 £27
57 Cleveland St   7636 9098   1–1B
"What a dive, but what a great place"!; this "welcoming" and "overcrowded" south Indian veteran, by the Telecom Tower, was seemingly "last decorated in the '70s", but it serves up "stunning, fresh, well-flavoured and really different" food, at "incredible prices"; BYO. / **Value tip:** *set weekday L £14 (FP).* **Details:** *www.ragam.co.uk; 11 pm, Fri & Sat 11.30 pm, Sun 10.30 pm.*

Randall & Aubin W1 £45
16 Brewer St   7287 4447   2–2D
"People-watching inside, or street-watching outside" – both are attractions to rival the "simple" but "divine" fare at this "ebullient" seafood and champagne bar, "in the heart of Soho"; you may have to queue. / **Details:** *www.randallandaubin.co.uk; 11 pm, Sun 10.30 pm; closed Sun L; no booking.*

Rani N3 £26
7 Long Ln   8349 4386
This Finchley old favourite can still produce "excellent" Indian veggie dishes; it draws fans from across London for its "fantastic" buffets and "filling" thalis. / **Details:** *www.raniuk.com; 10 pm.*

Rasa N16 £27
55 Stoke Newington Church St   7249 0344
"I think about it almost every day!"; this "highly addictive" Stoke Newington Keralan – "the original and still the best" in the group – is one of the highest-rated Indians in town, thanks to its "imaginative" and "absolutely delicious" veggie cooking. / **Details:** *www.rasarestaurants.com; 10.45 pm, Fri & Sat 11.30 pm; closed weekday L.*

Rasa £30

5 Charlotte St, W1   7637 0222   1–1C
6 Dering St, W1   7629 1346   2–2B
Holiday Inn Hotel, 1 Kings Cross, WC1   7833 9787
56 Stoke Newington Church St, N16   7249 1340
"Light years ahead of typical curry houses"; these spin-offs from the N16
original also provide "wonderfully interesting" Keralan dishes and
a "cordial" welcome; though mostly veggie, Dering St and N16
(Travancore) also serve meat, while the "vividly pink" Charlotte Street
(Samudra) branch specialises in seafood.
*/ Details: www.rasarestaurants.com; 10.45 pm; variable hours especially
on weekends.*

Rasoi SW3 £87

10 Lincoln St   7225 1881   4–2D
The "kaleidoscopic" flavours offered by Vineet Bhatia's "modern fusion-
riff on subcontinental cuisine" make this Chelsea townhouse one
of London's top Indians; "slow service" and a "too-quiet ambience" can
be a let-down, though... not to mention the "second mortgage you'll
need on the way out". / **Value tip:** set weekday L £48
(FP). **Details:** www.rasoirestaurant.co.uk; 11 pm; closed Sat L & Sun; no trainers.

Rebato's SW8 £32

169 South Lambeth Rd   7735 6388
It's hard not to love this "slice of Spain in the heart of Stockwell" –
an "old-school" tapas bar, plus "cheesy" rear restaurant, where the
"pure '70s décor" only "adds to the charm"; staff are "wonderful",
and the food is "always good and hearty". / **Details:** www.rebatos.com;
10.45 pm; closed Sat L & Sun.

Red Fort W1 £58

77 Dean St   7437 2525   3–2A
This veteran Soho Indian is still "first choice" for some reporters, thanks
to its "consistently great" contemporary cuisine; with its "inattentive"
staff and lacklustre ambience, though, even supporters can find
it "outrageously expensive". / **Details:** www.redfort.co.uk; 11.15 pm,
Sun 10.30 pm; closed Sat L & Sun L.

**(Restaurant, Level 7)
Tate Modern SE1** £42

Bankside   7887 8888
"Stunning views" are the highlight of this "light and airy" 7th-floor
"canteen"; the "seasonal" British food is often "thoughtfully prepared"
too, but reports (as on service) are rather up-and-down.
/ **Details:** www.tate.org.uk; 9.30 pm; Sun-Thu closed D.

Rhodes 24 EC2 £70

25 Old Broad St   7877 7703
Fortunately, the "spectacular view" distracts from the "corporate" décor
of this 24th-floor dining room, which "couldn't be better placed for a City
lunch"; its "British classics" cuisine "doesn't embarrass", but complaints
about "sky-high" prices rocketed this year. / **Details:** www.rhodes24.co.uk;
9 pm; closed Sat & Sun; no shorts; booking essential.

Rhodes W1 Restaurant
Cumberland Hotel W1 £91
Gt Cumberland Pl 7616 5930 1–2A
Gary R's luxurious two-year-old fine dining room, near Marble Arch, inspires amazingly few reports, and they're very mixed – fans applaud it as a "fantastic all-round experience", but detractors find the food "very uninspiring". / Details: www.rhodesw1.com; 10.30 pm; closed Mon, Sat L & Sun; no trainers.

Rib Room
Jumeirah Carlton Tower Hotel SW1 £79
2 Cadogan Pl 7858 7250 4–1D
The prices at this "sterile" Knightsbridge grill room are infamously "exorbitant", but fans identify three factors to justify the expense of entertaining clients here – "melting" beef (including "the best steaks in London"), "discreetly spaced" tables, and "five-star" service. / Value tip: set weekday L £60 (FP). Details: www.jumeirah.com; 10.45 pm, Sun 10.15 pm; booking: max 24.

Riccardo's SW3 £40

126 Fulham Rd 7370 6656 4–3B
"Always fun, and full of glamorous people", this "affordable" (by Chelsea standards) Italian retains its "stalwart" charms, not least its "simple" fare (served "tapas-style" since long before it was fashionable); good terrace. / Details: www.riccardos.it; 11.30 pm, Sun 10.30 pm.

Rick's Café SW17 £34
"Rick is back, thank goodness", at "Tooting's best restaurant" (of the non-ethnic sort, anyway) – a "simple" place, with "welcoming" service and "very good" food. / Details: 11 pm, Sun 4 pm; closed Mon L; no Amex.
122 Mitcham Rd 8767 5219

El Rincón Latino SW4 £28
148 Clapham Manor St 7622 0599

An "excellent", if "noisy", family-run bar in Clapham; it serves "very good tapas", and "reasonably-priced weekend brunch menus" (featuring "full Spanish fry ups") are a highlight. / Details: www.rinconlatino.co.uk; 11.30 pm; closed Mon, Tue-Fri L & Sun D.

Ristorante Semplice W1 £56

9-10 Blenheim St 7495 1509 2–2B
"We need more West Enders like this!"; this "slick" Italian two-year-old on the northern fringe of Mayfair has "impeccable" cuisine; staff are "passionate" too, helping create "a good buzz" in the somewhat "cramped" space. / Value tip: set weekday L £25 (FP). Details: www.ristorantesemplice.com; 10.30 pm; closed Sat L & Sun; booking: max 12.

The Ritz Restaurant
The Ritz W1   **£104**   Ⓐ
150 Piccadilly   7493 8181   2–4C
*This "breathtaking" Louis XVI-style chamber, overlooking Green Park,
is often cited as "the prettiest dining room in London"; the cuisine,
though, has long been "a little average" and "horrendously expensive"
too (but, for a "special occasion", it can still be a "treat"); "top-class
breakfasts".* / **Value tip:** set dinner £66 (FP). **Details:** www.theritzlondon.com;
10 pm; jacket & tie required.

Riva SW13   **£53**   ⭐
169 Church Rd   8748 0434

*"Honest, seasonal and delicious" Italian cooking has long made Andreas
Riva's "professional" Barnes venture quite a well-known foodie
destination; the uninitiated, though, can find the atmosphere rather
"strange".* / **Details:** 10.30 pm; closed Sat L.

The River Café W6   **£69**   ⭐
Thames Wharf, Rainville Rd   7386 4200   6–2C
*Phoenix-like, this world-famous Hammersmith Italian has re-opened
(after a refurbishment forced by a fire) with "divine" food (better than
it's been for years); its "lighter" interior remains "crowded", though,
and its "eye-popping" prices are still "too high for such simple fare".*
/ **Details:** www.rivercafe.co.uk; 9 pm, Sat 9.15 pm; closed Sun D.

Roast
The Floral Hall SE1   **£55**
Stoney St   7940 1300
*"An enormous, light room overlooking Borough Market" provides the
"dynamic" location for this "showcase for British produce"; a shame,
then, that the food's "so distinctly average" – "only breakfast's really
worth eating" – and that service can be "very poor".*
/ **Details:** www.roast-restaurant.com; 10.45 pm; closed Sun D.

Roka   **£85**   Ⓐ⭐
37 Charlotte St, W1   7580 6464   1–1C
Unit 4, Park Pavilion, 40 Canada Sq, E14   7636 5228
*This "always buzzing" Zuma-sibling, in Fitzrovia, echoes to the sound
of those enjoying its "vibrant" Japanese fare – both sushi and 'robata'
(grill) dishes; it's becoming "expensive for what you get", though,
and service is increasingly "haphazard"; an offshoot opens in Canary
Wharf in October 2009.* / **Details:** www.rokarestaurant.com; 11.15 pm;
booking: max 8.

Ronnie Scott's W1   **£45**   Ⓐ⊗
47 Frith St   7439 0747   3–2A
*This famous Soho jazz club, majorly refurbished in recent years, remains
"a great place for a date"; be warned, though – "you don't go for the
food".* / **Details:** www.ronniescotts.co.uk; 3 am, Sun midnight; D only.

Roussillon SW1 £76
16 St Barnabas St   7730 5550   4–2D

Hidden-away "in deepest Pimlico" – but just five minutes' walk from Sloane Square – this "classy" but rather "sedate" outfit remains "under the radar" of many Londoners... despite the quality of Gerard Virolle's "breathtaking" Gallic cooking, and of service that just "couldn't be more friendly"; (this is also the home of London's grandest veggie menu).
/ Value tip: set weekday L £43 (FP). Details: www.roussillon.co.uk; 11 pm; closed Sat L & Sun; no trainers.

Royal China £39 ⭐
24-26 Baker St, W1   7487 4688   1–1A
805 Fulham Rd, SW6   7731 0081
13 Queensway, W2   7221 2535   5–2C
30 Westferry Circus, E14   7719 0888
Particularly as "THE place for a weekend dim sum blow-out", these weirdly "glitzy", "'70s-style" orientals are always "rammed" – beware "enormous queues", especially at Bayswater; "patchy" service, however, is a growing concern. / Details: www.rcguk.biz; 10.45 pm, Fri & Sat 11.15 pm, Sun 9.45 pm; no booking Sat & Sun L.

Royal China Club W1 £57 ⭐
40-42 Baker St   7486 3898   1–1A
"Sold as a classier option than the standard Royal Chinas", this brand's sole remaining 'premium' outlet, in Marylebone, generates a very similar feedback profile. / Details: www.royalchinagroup.co.uk; 11 pm, Fri & Sat 11.30 pm, Sun 10.30 pm.

Royal China SW15 £36 ⭐
3 Chelverton Rd   8788 0907
This Putney oriental (which long ago parted ways with the chain it spawned) may "looks like a bad '80s disco", but it offers "dependable" cuisine, which includes some "excellent dim sum".
/ Details: www.royalchinaputney.co.uk; 11 pm, Fri & Sat 11.30 pm; only Amex.

Rules WC2 £60
35 Maiden Ln   7836 5314   3–3D
"The quintessential English dining experience"; London's oldest restaurant (1798), beautifully housed in a quiet Covent Garden lane, defies its tourist trap potential with cooking (especially game) that's "much better than you might expect". / Details: www.rules.co.uk; 11.30 pm, Sun 10.30 pm; no shorts; booking: max 6.

Sagar £24
17a, Percy St, W1   7631 3319   2–2B
31 Catherine St, WC2   7836 6377   3–3D
157 King St, W6   8741 8563   6–2C
27 York St, TW1   8744 3868
"Dosas to die for" feature amongst the "delicious and very cheap" south Indian dishes on offer at this "cheerful" small chain; some of this year's visits, however, "lacked the expected wow-factor".
/ ***Details:*** *www.gosagar.com; Sun-Thu 10.45 pm, Fri & Sat 11.30 pm.*

St Alban SW1 £52
4-12 Regent St   7499 8558   2–3D
Thanks not least to a "tasteful revamp" of its "airport-lounge" styling, Messrs Corbin & King's Theatreland two-year-old now has "a real media buzz" to it, which is "much appreciated by business lunchers"; the Mediterranean cuisine is of "good quality" too, but is outshone by the "superlative" service. / ***Details:*** *www.stalban.net; 11 pm; closed Sun; booking: max 10.*

St John EC1 £52
26 St John St   7251 0848

"The flagship of British cuisine!"; Fergus Henderson's "pioneering" ex-smokehouse, in Clerkenwell is, for its many fans, "the best restaurant in the UK", thanks to its "totally unpompous" style and its "unique" and "punchy" menu (which famously features much "awesome offal").
/ ***Details:*** *www.stjohnrestaurant.com; 11 pm; closed Sat L & Sun D.*

St John Bread & Wine E1 £46
94-96 Commercial St   7251 0848   1–2C
The "younger, noisier and more laid-back" offshoot of the Clerkenwell icon – a Spitalfields canteen which offers "the best of British food" ("without any poncing about") on its "idiosyncratic and challenging" tapas-style menu. / ***Details:*** *www.stjohnbreadandwine.com; 10.30 pm, Sun 9pm.*

St Johns N19 £40
91 Junction Rd   7272 1587
A "drab" exterior gives no hint of the "cavernous" dining room – a former ballroom "charmingly" decked-out in "shabby-chic" style – at this popular Archway gastropub; its "friendly and efficient" staff serve up "straightforward" fare that's generally "well cooked". / ***Details:*** *11 pm, Sun 9.30 pm; Mon-Thu D only, Fri-Sun open L & D; booking: max 12.*

St Pancras Grand
St Pancras Int'l Station NW1 £48 Ⓐ

St Pancras International 7870 9900
"Glamorous" and *"beautiful"*, this British brasserie has been *"a very welcome addition"* to the eponymous railway station; to become a true *"destination restaurant"*, however, it would need to sharpen up its *"fine but not memorable"* cuisine, and to sort out the sometimes *"neglectful"* service. / **Details:** www.stpancrasgrand.com; 10.45 pm.

Sake No Hana SW1 £70

23 St James's St 7925 8988 2–4C
Fans insist this St James's Japanese offers *"creative"* dishes in a *"hugely glamorous"* setting; there's still a huge chorus of complaints, however, that it's *"incredibly pretentious"* and *"hugely overpriced"* – *"I went on a half-price deal, and was still shocked by the bill!"* / **Details:** 11 pm, Sat 11.30 pm; closed Sun L.

Sakura W1 £27 ★

9 Hanover St 7629 2961 2–2C
"Golly the service can be rude", at this *"dog-eared"* Japanese basement, off Regent Street; it's *"always full"*, though, and a visit can even be quite *"fun"*, thanks to its *"authentic food"* (including *"beautifully fresh"* sushi) at *"good prices"*. / **Details:** 10 pm.

Sale e Pepe SW1 £46 Ⓐ

9-15 Pavilion Rd 7235 0098 4–1D
"Brilliant staff lend a certain madness to the ambience" of this *"fun"*, *"noisy"* and *"cramped"* trattoria, hidden-away off Sloane Street; the food is *"very good"* and *"unfussy"* too. / **Details:** www.saleepepe.co.uk; 11.30 pm; closed Sun; no shorts.

Salloos SW1 £46 ★

62-64 Kinnerton St 7235 4444 4–1D
"Not flashy, but my subcontinental friends say it's the best!"; this *"old-fashioned"* establishment, hidden in a Knightsbridge mews, may be *"somewhat overpriced"*, but its *"really original"* Pakistani food is often *"divine"*. / **Details:** 11 pm; closed Sun.

Salt Yard W1 £37 ★

54 Goodge St 7637 0657 1–1B
"Tremendous" tapas (Spanish *"with an Italian twist"*), *"unusual"* wine and *"seamless"* service again inspire rave reports on this *"always-hopping"* Fitzrovia hang-out; it may be *"crowded and noisy"* (especially in the basement), but it's *"really enjoyable and relaxed"* too. / **Details:** www.saltyard.co.uk; 11 pm; closed Sat L & Sun.

San Lorenzo SW3 £68

22 Beauchamp Pl 7584 1074 4–1C
Fans of this '60s Knightsbridge trattoria still find it *"fun"*; the most eloquent commentary on this *"dated"* celeb-magnet, however, is just how few reports it attracts nowadays. / **Details:** 11.30 pm; closed Sun.

Sands End SW6 £37
135 Stephendale Rd 7731 7823
"Don't let Prince Harry's patronage put you off!"; this "nicely shabby" pub, at the back end of Fulham, may attract an easily-stereotyped clientele, but its "rustic" cuisine is part of an overall experience most reports say is "first-class". / Details: www.thesandsend.co.uk; midnight, Sun 11 pm; booking: max 24.

Santa Maria del Sur SW8 £38
129 Queenstown Rd 7622 2088
"Just like being in Buenos Aires", this Argentinean steakhouse, in Battersea, offers "huge and marvellous slabs of meat" – "a match for anywhere in London" – and a "great atmosphere" too. / Details: www.santamariadelsur.co.uk; 10.30 pm, Mon-Wed 10 pm; closed weekday L.

Santini SW1 £67
29 Ebury St 7730 4094 1–4B
A Belgravia Italian stalwart which perennially attracts a glossy crowd despite being "rather expensive for what it is"; "every year I give it one last try, and every year it disappoints!" / Details: www.santini-restaurant.com; 11 pm; closed Sat L & Sun L.

Sardo W1 £45
45 Grafton Way 7387 2521 1–1B
"Sardinian regional cuisine at its best" – served up by "a small, hard-working team" – makes it well worth discovering this "sparse" but "truly Italian-feeling" venture, "nicely hidden-away in Fitzrovia". / Details: www.sardo-restaurant.com; 11 pm; closed Sat L & Sun.

Sargasso Sea N21 £55
10 Station Rd 8360 0990
A "classy" Winchmore Hill spot, where "genuine" and "well-presented" fish and seafood dishes underpin an "excellent" all-round experience. / Details: www.sargassosea.co.uk; 10.30 pm; D only, closed Mon & Sun; booking: max 9, Sat D.

Satay House W2 £38
13 Sale Pl 7723 6763 5–1D
It's not much to look at, but this Bayswater fixture serves "very good Malaysian food" – "the menu is short, but all the favourites are here", says one (Malaysian) reporter. / Details: www.satay-house.co.uk; 11 pm.

Scott's W1 £68
20 Mount St 7495 7309 2–3A
The "great aura" of this "happening" Mayfair magnet for the "A-list" is in part due to the "super-glamorous" style of its "classic" and "elegant" interior; it's a real "all-rounder", though, also offering "exemplary" fish and seafood dishes, and "very polished" service. / Details: www.scotts-restaurant.com; 10.30 pm, Sun 10 pm; booking: max 6.

Seashell NW1 £37
49 Lisson Grove 7224 9000
"Drastically needing an updated interior", this famous, "traditional" fish 'n' chip parlour, in Marylebone, is "still among the best in town", but the setting certainly encourages you to take out. / Details: www.seashellrestaurant.co.uk; 10.30 pm; closed Sun D.

Seven Stars WC2 £31
53 Carey St 7242 8521 1–2D
Roxy Beaujolais is a "great hostess", and her "very characterful" boozer, behind the Royal Courts of Justice, provides "good home-cooking in generous portions"; just one thing — "don't try to move the cat". / **Details:** *11 pm, Sun 10.30 pm.*

1707
Fortnum & Mason W1 £44
181 Piccadilly 7734 8040 1–1B
"An incredible wine list, with a great selection of wine flights, and £10 corkage on any wine from the shop floor" is the stand-out draw to this "posh" but "relaxing" wine bar, next to the main food halls of the queen's grocer; a light menu (overseen by star chef, Shaun Hill) is served. / **Details:** *www.fortnumandmason.co.uk; 9.15 pm; closed Sun.*

Shanghai Blues WC1 £57
193-197 High Holborn 7404 1668 3–1D
"Excellent on all fronts... except the prices!" – this "upmarket" Holborn oriental offers "cracking" modern Chinese food ("yummy dim sum", in particular) and "quietly efficient" service, in a "dark" and "decadent" setting. / **Details:** *www.shanghaiblues.co.uk; 11.30 pm.*

J Sheekey WC2 £63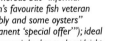
28-32 St Martin's Ct 7240 2565 3–3B

This "stellar" Theatreland "institution" was yet again the survey's most-mentioned establishment (as well as topping nominations as London's best fish restaurant); in its "maze" of "cramped" and "characterful" panelled rooms, a "stylish" menu is served (which includes some "old British favourite dishes"). / **Details:** *www.j-sheekey.co.uk; midnight, Sun 11 pm; booking: max 6.*

J Sheekey Oyster Bar WC2 £45
St Martin's Ct 7240 2565 3–3B
"Why didn't they think of it before?"; the glamorous but "informal" (indeed, slightly louche) new annex to London's favourite fish veteran really is "the perfect place for a glass of bubbly and some oysters" ("especially if you go for the seemingly-permanent 'special offer'"); ideal for "a light meal, pre/post-theatre". / **Details:** *www.j-sheekey.co.uk; midnight, Sun 11 pm; booking: max 3.*

Shilpa W6 £27
206 King St 8741 3127 6–2B
"Zingy and fresh" south Indian food at "amazing" prices makes it well worth seeking out this "subdued"-looking outfit, in Hammersmith; if you're lucky, you may get "Bollywood on the TV" too. / **Details:** *www.shilparestaurant.co.uk; 11 pm, Thu-Sat midnight; no Amex.*

Signor Sassi SW1 £45

14 Knightsbridge Grn   7584 2277   4–1D

This "friendly", traditional-style Knightsbridge trattoria is "always jumping", thanks not least to its "very good" cooking (and "superb ingredients"); "must the waiters sing?", though. / Details: 11.30 pm, Sun 10.30 pm; closed Sun.

Simpson's Tavern EC3 £29

38 1/2 Ball Ct, Cornhill   7626 9985

This "timeless" (Dickensian) back-alley chophouse makes City blokes (mainly) feel "at one with those who've been making deals round here for centuries"; its "solid" meaty fare is "never going to win any prizes", but it is "good value". / Details: www.simpsonstavern.co.uk; L only, closed Sat & Sun.

Simpsons-in-the-Strand WC2 £57

100 Strand   7836 9112   3–3D

The setting may "ooze olde-world charm", but – with its "bland" cuisine – this grand Covent Garden-fringe "institution" (famous for roast beef from the trolley) too often feels like a "tourist trap"; breakfasts, though, are "classic". / Details: www.simpsonsinthestrand.co.uk; 10.45 pm, Sun 9 pm; no trainers.

Singapore Garden NW6 £38

83a Fairfax Rd   7624 8233

An "interesting mixture of SE Asian cuisines", "attentive" (sometimes "too attentive") service and a "pleasing" ambience maintain the status of this Swiss Cottage veteran – "a 'local' with a loyal following from far and wide". / Details: www.singaporegarden.co.uk; 11 pm, Fri-Sat 11.30 pm.

Sitaaray WC2 £39

167 Drury Ln   7269 6422   3–1C

"Substantial set menus of tandoori dishes and shish kebabs" win praise for this "good-value" Covent Garden spot; a "buzzy" place – with booths and Bollywood-theming – it would equally suit a date or a party. / Details: www.sitaaray.com; 10.45 pm; closed Sun.

(Lecture Room)
Sketch W1 £95

9 Conduit St   7659 4500   2–2C

"Everything's great... until the bill arrives", at this "beautiful" ("pretentious") Mayfair dining room; true, the "elaborate" cuisine, "with an emphasis on novel flavours", can be "exciting", but... "ouch", with such "silly" prices, "who really wants to go?" / Details: www.sketch.uk.com; 10.30 pm; closed Mon, Sat L & Sun; jacket; booking: max 8.

Smithfield Bar & Grill EC1 £46

2-3 West Smithfield   7246 0900

Improved reports this year on this self-explanatory City-fringe spot, which does indeed specialise in "delicious grilled food" (especially ribs and burgers). / Details: www.blackhouse.uk.com; 11 pm, Sat 10.30 pm; closed Sat L & Sun.

Sông Quê E2 £24

134 Kingsland Rd 7613 3222 1–1B

"Probably still London's best Vietnamese" – this *"Spartan"* Shoreditch canteen serves *"wow"* dishes at *"extremely low"* prices, and remains *"very popular"*; service, though, can be *"abrupt"*. / **Details:** 11 pm; no Amex.

Soseki EC3 £50

1F, 20 Bury St 7621 9211

"Beautifully designed and thought-out", this Japanese tea house-style newcomer is surprisingly *"pretty"* for a venue right by the 'Gherkin'; *"frequent deals"* offer particularly good value. / **Details:** www.soseki.co.uk; 10 pm; closed Sat & Sun; booking: max 12.

Sotheby's Café W1 £44

34 New Bond St 7293 5077 2–2C

"Tucked-in to the auction house" – off the foyer, in fact – this small but *"very classy"* Mayfair café offers a perfect perch for a *"people-watching lunch"*; the food is *"surprisingly good value"*, too. / **Details:** www.sothebys.com; L only, closed Sat & Sun; booking: max 6.

Souk Medina WC2 £34

1A Short Gdns 7240 1796 3–2B

With its *"Arabian Nights"* atmosphere, this *"lovely"* Covent Garden 'riad' makes a great setting *"for groups and parties"*, even if the food is rather *"variable"*. / **Details:** www.soukrestaurant.co.uk; midnight.

Spacca Napoli W1 £34

101 Dean St 7437 9440 2–1D

"If you like noise and chaos", this *"authentic"* Soho trattoria (*"rammed full of Italians"*) is *"a great place"*, serving *"proper Neapolitan pizza"* (by the metre); service, however, *"needs work"*. / **Details:** www.spaccanapoli.co.uk; 11 pm.

Spianata & Co £10

41 Brushfield St, E1 7655 4411 1–2B
20 Holborn Viaduct, EC1 7236 3666
12 Moorfields, EC2 7638 6118 1–2A
29-30 Leadenhall Mkt, EC3 7929 1339
73 Watling St, EC4 7236 3666

"Proper paninis, with fresh and simple fillings", *"the best coffee"*, and *"other Italian delights"* inspire rave reviews on these *"chaotic"* but *"friendly"* pit stops. / **Details:** www.spianata.com; 3.30 pm; EC3 11 pm; closed Sat & Sun; E1 closed Sat; no credit cards; no booking.

The Square W1 £96

6-10 Bruton St 7495 7100 2–2C

Philip Howard's *"consistently superb"* cuisine and an utterly *"fabulous"* wine list have long put this *"understated and confident"* Mayfair dining room in London's first rank; the *"polished"* service has sometimes contributed to a rather *"serious"* ambience, but there are signs of late that it has 'lightened up'. / **Value tip:** set weekday L £79 (FP). **Details:** www.squarerestaurant.com; 10 pm, Sat 10.30 pm; closed Sat L & Sun L; booking: max 8.

Square Pie Company £15
Selfridges, 400 Oxford St, W1   7318 2460   2–1A
Unit 9, The Brunswick Centre, WC1   7837 6207
Westfield, Ariel Way, W12   8222 6697   6–1C
1 Canada Sq, Jubilee Line Mall, E14   7519 6071
16 Horner St, Old Spitalfields Mkt, E1   1–2C
*"Quick, simple and good-value" British pit stops, where "top pies" are indeed the star attraction. / **Details:** www.squarepie.com; E14 4 pm-8 pm; E1 4.30 pm, Sun 5.30 pm; W1 6 pm-8 pm; WC1 10.30 pm; E1 L only, closed Sat; E14 closed Sun; no booking.*

Sree Krishna SW17 £24
192-194 Tooting High St   8672 4250
*This "wonderful" Tooting veteran has forever been a "great-value" destination; it serves "some of the best south Indian cooking in London", with "especially interesting" veggie fare. / **Value tip:** set Sun L £19 (FP). **Details:** www.sreekrishna.co.uk; 10.45 pm, Fri & Sat midnight.*

Star of India SW5 £40
154 Old Brompton Rd   7373 2901   4–2B
*With its "subtle" cooking and "elegant" décor, this Earl's Court veteran curry house remains "a cut above" most subcontinentals; service, though, is "brusque". / **Details:** www.starofindia.eu; 11.45 pm, Sun 11 pm.*

Stick & Bowl W8 £22
31 Kensington High St   7937 2778   4–1A
*Ever "busy", this Kensington "hole in the wall" feels like "a little bit of Hong Kong"; perch on a "high stool" to enjoy some "tasty" and "excellent-value" chow. / **Details:** 11 pm; no credit cards; no booking.*

Story Deli
The Old Truman Brewery E1 £29
3 Dray Walk   7247 3137   1–2C
*"Brick Lane's best place to eat" isn't one of its myriad curry houses, but rather this "very cool", "rustic" haunt, which features "seriously good" pizza (with "the thinnest bases ever"); service is often off the case, but at least you get "good people-watching" while you wait. / **Details:** 10.30 pm; no booking.*

Stringray Café £25
36 Highbury Pk, N5   7354 9309
Tufnell Pk, NW5   7482 4855
109 Columbia Rd, E2   7613 1141
*"After a busy day at Columbia Road flower market", you might like to try this "chaotic" Italian for some "really tasty, crisp pizza"; it also has a pair of lesser-known north London siblings – the Highbury sibling is "great before Arsenal matches". / **Details:** www.stringraycafe.co.uk; 11 pm; NW5 11.30 pm, Sun 11 pm.*

Sufi W12 £22
70 Askew Rd   8834 4888   6–1B
*This "family-owned Persian place", in Shepherd's Bush, delivers up "wonderful" food (including "excellent" meats, "addictive" dips and "lovely fresh flat-bread"); service "couldn't be nicer". / **Details:** www.sufirestaurant.com; 11 pm.*

Suka
Sanderson W1 £70

50 Berners St 7300 1444 2–1D

*This once-trashily-trendy boutique hotel dining room, just north of Oxford Street, inspires little feedback nowadays... mainly to the effect that it's "very overpriced, and average at best". / **Details:** www.morganshotel.com; 11 pm, Sun 11.30 pm.*

Sukho Thai Cuisine SW6 £41

855 Fulham Rd 7371 7600

*"Outstanding" and "delicate" Thai cooking again wins the highest praise for this "tightly-configured" café, in the distant reaches of the Fulham Road, as does its "faultless" service; (the occasional purist, though, says the food's "too sweet"). / **Details:** www.sukhogroup.co.uk; 11 pm.*

Sumosan W1 £65

26b Albemarle St 7495 5999 2–3C

*"It's just as good as Nobu, but minus the attitude and prices", say fans of this trendy-looking but "calm" Mayfair Japanese; "they need to inject more life into the atmosphere", though, but at least the place is "much easier to get in to" than its more famous peers. / **Value tip:** set weekday L £44 (FP). **Details:** www.sumosan.com; 11.30 pm; closed Sat L & Sun L.*

Sushi-Hiro W5 £39

1 Station Pde 8896 3175

*"Still London's best place for sushi"; this "tiny" fixture, stuck out near Ealing Common tube, may look "grim", but appearances are "more than compensated for" by dishes that are "almost too good to be true" ("prepared before your eyes by a master of the art"). / **Details:** 9 pm; closed Mon; no credit cards.*

Sushi-Say NW2 £40

33b Walm Ln 8459 7512

*"You could be sitting in Ginza, Tokyo" – not Willesden Green! – at the Shimizu family's "wonderful" (recently refurbished) café, which offers "brilliantly-crafted sushi" and "unbeatable service". / **Details:** 10 pm, Sat 10.30 pm, Sun 9.30; closed Mon, Tue-Fri D only, Sat & Sun open L & D; no Amex.*

The Swan W4 £39

119 Acton Ln 8994 8262 6–1A

*"Tucked-away" in Chiswick, this "pub for all seasons" boasts a "cosy, wood-panelled" interior and "great garden"; its "good, solid food" also impresses many reporters, but a few sceptics feel the kitchen has "lost its way a bit" in recent times. / **Details:** theswanchiswick.co.uk; 10 pm, Fri & Sat 10.30 pm, Sun 10 pm; closed weekday L; no booking.*

The Table SE1 £33

83 Southwark St 7401 2760

*In a "cool" building housing a notable architectural practice, this "trendy", self-service café – serving salads, plus other "light" dishes – makes a "brisk" weekday lunch venue; it's also "perfect" for a "chilled" brunch after a trip to nearby Borough Market. / **Details:** www.thetablecafe.com; L only.*

Taiwan Village SW6 £28
85 Lillie Rd 7381 2900 4–3A

"Choose the Leave It To Us feast", to enjoy a "seemingly endless" stream of "sensational dishes", at this "off-the-beaten-track" Fulham Chinese; it's a "cosy" place too, with "lovely" staff. / **Details:** www.taiwanvillage.com; 11.30 pm; closed weekday L; booking: max 20.

Tajima Tei EC1 £31 ⭐
9-11 Leather Ln 7404 9665
"Tucked-away" off Hatton Garden, an "authentic" and "busy" Japanese, serving "excellent" sushi and other "good-quality" fare. / **Details:** www.tajima-tei.co.uk; 10 pm; closed Sat L & Sun; no booking, L.

Tamarind W1 £58 ⭐
20 Queen St 7629 3561 2–3B
Alfred Prasad's "complex and subtle" cuisine wins continued acclaim for this "high-class" Mayfair Indian, where a "slightly dark" basement setting hardly detracts from the "very superior" overall experience. / **Value tip:** set weekday L £26 (FP). **Details:** www.tamarindrestaurant.com; 11 pm, Sun 10.15 pm; closed Sat L.

Tandoori Lane SW6 £26 ⭐
131a Munster Rd 7371 0440
A "great neighbourhood Indian", at the far end of Fulham – it looks a bit "odd", but serves food that's "delicious, and cheap too". / **Details:** 11 pm; D only; no Amex.

Tandoori Nights SE22 £32
73 Lordship Ln 8299 4077
This "great non-standard curry house" offers "fresh" and "fantastic" food, say fans of this cramped East Dulwich Indian; others, though "fail to see what all the (local) fuss is about". / **Details:** www.tandoorinightsdulwich.co.uk; 11.30 pm; closed weekday L & Sat L.

Tangawizi TW1 £31 ⭐
406 Richmond Rd 8891 3737
A "better-than-average Indian restaurant with a puzzling Swahili name" – this "top-class" Twickenham local wins praise for its "incredibly friendly" service, and its "excellent" cooking. / **Details:** www.tangawizi.co.uk; 11 pm, Sun 10.30 pm; D only.

Tapas Brindisa SE1 £36
18-20 Southwark St 7357 8880
"You could be in Madrid", when you visit this Borough Market bar, run by a major firm of food importers, which serves up "exceptionally authentic tapas" in a "bustling" ("slightly manic") setting; "the only catch is that you can't book". / **Details:** www.tapasbrindisa.com; 10.45 pm; booking: max 8.

A Taste Of McClements TW9 £52 ★
8 Station Approach 8940 6617
"It's good to see John McClements returning to his roots", say fans of his ambitious Twickenham newcomer; "it's trying hard" ("maybe too hard"), and offers an "overwhelming" tasting menu, which at best is "exquisite".
/ Details: www.tasteofmcclements.com; 9.30 pm; closed Mon & Sun.

Tendido Cero SW5 £36 Ⓐ★
174 Old Brompton Rd 7370 3685 4–2B
"First-class all round", this "cool" and "very buzzy" South Kensington tapas bar – an offshoot of Cambio de Tercio, opposite – is currently on a 'high'; service is "prompt" too (but the two-seatings policy can be "a real pain"). / Details: www.cambiodetercio.co.uk; 11 pm; booking: max 16.

Tentazioni SE1 £49 ★
2 Mill St 7394 5248

Try to overlook the back street Bermondsey location and the slightly "odd" interior of this lesser-known Italian – it continues to provide "superb", "robust" cooking (with suggested wine-matches) and the "friendliest" service; ("excellent-value set menus – lunch especially").
/ Value tip: set weekday L £17 (FP). Details: www.tentazioni.co.uk; 10.45 pm; closed Mon L, Sat L & Sun.

Terroirs WC2 £36 Ⓐ★
5 William IV St 7036 0660 3–4C
"Beautifully-executed" small French plates, served with "real gusto" – plus an "epic" wine list – have made this "simple bistro", near Charing Cross, one of the year's hottest openings (to the extent that service can "struggle" to keep up). / Details: www.terroirswinebar.com; 11 pm; closed Sun.

Texture W1 £70
34 Portman St 7224 0028 1–2A
It's a shame that the "odd" location (a slightly awkward space, "sharing loos with the adjacent Quality Inn") – combined with a feeling that the menu is "grossly overpriced" – puts a cap on appreciation of this ambitious yearling, just north of Oxford Street; fans say the "very creative" cuisine is "exquisite", and there's a "strong" wine list too.
/ Value tip: set weekday L £40 (FP). Details: www.texture-restaurant.co.uk; 11 pm; closed Mon & Sun.

Theo Randall
InterContinental Hotel W1 £70 ★
1 Hamilton Pl 7318 8747 2–4A
All the "big" and "rustic" flavours of "River Café cuisine" – Theo Randall was formerly head chef there – can be had at this Mayfair two-year-old; service is "a little erratic", though, and it's a "shame about the room"… perhaps "bunker" would be a better description. / Value tip: set weekday L £44 (FP). Details: www.theorandall.com; 11.15 pm; closed Sat L & Sun.

The Thomas Cubitt SW1 £52
44 Elizabeth St   7730 6060   1–4A
This "stylish" and "very congenial" Belgravia gastropub is "always busy, with a great crowd" – there's a quieter restaurant above; it's undeniably "expensive", but – for the area – offers decent value.
/ **Details:** www.thethomascubitt.co.uk; 10 pm; booking only in restaurant.

The Three Bridges SW8 £42
153 Battersea Park Rd   7720 0204
"The owner's bonhomie" does a lot for this Italian yearling, which arguably "deserves a better location" than by Battersea Dogs Home; the cooking is "authentic", if sometimes "more competent than inspired". / **Details:** www.thethreebridges.com; 11 pm; closed Mon L & Sun D.

Tierra Brindisa W1 £40
46 Broadwick St   7534 1690   2–2D
The odd sceptic feels it's "not up to its pedigree", but this "bustling" (slightly "cramped") new Soho offshoot of the renowned Spanish importers mostly wins high praise for its "airy and modern" looks and "lovely" tapas. / **Details:** www.tierrabrindisa.com; 11 pm; closed Sun; booking: max 14.

Toff's N10 £31
38 Muswell Hill Broadway   8883 8656
It's "nothing fancy", but "vast portions" of "great fresh fish (and good chips)" have built a formidable reputation for this veteran chippy, in Muswell Hill; "very friendly" service too. / **Details:** www.toffsfish.co.uk; 10 pm; closed Sun.

Tom Aikens SW3 £96
43 Elystan St   7584 2003   4–2C
The cuisine at Tom Aikens's Chelsea flagship can be "outstanding", but – what with all its "foams and jellies" and all – it can also seem "too clever by half"; critics find prices "extortionate" too, and the ambience rather "stiff". / **Value tip:** set weekday L £50 (FP). **Details:** www.tomaikens.co.uk; 11 pm; closed Sat & Sun; jacket and/or tie; booking: max 8.

Tom Ilic SW8 £42
123 Queenstown Rd   7622 0555

Tom Illic is a "genius", say his fans, and "serious meat-eaters", in particular, will find it "well worth the trip" to his Battersea restaurant, somewhat "grim" décor notwithstanding. / **Details:** www.tomilic.com; 10.30 pm; closed Mon, Tue L, Sat L & Sun D.

Tom's Kitchen SW3 £50
27 Cale St 7349 0202 4–2C
For "food without fuss" (especially a "perfect brunch") in a "fun and
buzzy" setting, Tom Aikens's Chelsea bistro can be a "great all-rounder";
service is sometimes "the worst ever", though, and "you pay a lot" to be
so "squashed". / **Value tip:** set weekday L £32
(FP). **Details:** www.tomskitchen.co.uk; 11 pm.

Toto's SW1 £67

Lennox Gardens Mews 7589 0075 4–2C
"Slightly out-dated" but "lovely" – this Italian restaurant, tucked-away
near Harrods, is "just the place for a Eurotrashy date" (possibly of the
more mature sort); staff are "very professional", and the food – though
"pricey" and "unadventurous" – is of "really high quality"; pretty garden
too. / **Details:** 11 pm, Sun 10.30 pm.

Trinity SW4 £51

4 The Polygon 7622 1199
"A shining beacon of gastronomy in the SW4 wasteland"; Adam Byatt
has "notably raised his game" at this "laid-back" Clapham spot –
his "idiosyncratic" cuisine is often "brilliant", and service is trying
"very hard" too; "midweek prix-fixe offers exceptional value".
/ **Details:** www.trinityrestaurant.co.uk; 10.30 pm; closed Mon L & Sun D.

Trinity Stores SW12 £18
5-6 Balham Station Rd 8673 3773
"Continuing to set a standard for deli/cafés" – this "fun" Balham
"beacon" just "seems to get better and better".
/ **Details:** www.trinitystores.co.uk; 8pm, Sat 5.30 pm, Sun 4 pm; L only.

Trishna W1 £48
15-17 Blandford St 7935 5624 1–1A

"Truly wonderful Indian-style seafood" – served in a tapas format –
makes this notable newcomer a worthy namesake to the famous
Mumbai original; service can be rather "amateur", however, and the
styling of the Marylebone premises is rather "cold".
/ **Details:** www.trishnalondon.com; 10.45 pm, Sun 10 pm.

Les Trois Garçons E1 £72
1 Club Row 7613 1924 1–1C
It's "like walking into a fairy tale", when you enter this "very quirky"
East End fixture, whose "crazy" décor – "from a giraffe's head
to hanging handbags" – makes it "a great choice for a date"; the Gallic
cuisine is "adequate". / **Value tip:** set dinner £50
(FP). **Details:** www.lestroisgarcons.com; 10.15 pm; D only, closed Sun.

La Trompette W4 £57
5-7 Devonshire Rd 8747 1836 6–2A

"Perhaps the best food for the price anywhere in London" –
this "charming" and "reasonably-priced" Chiswick sibling to the fabled
Chez Bruce is similarly "outstanding" all-round; we had over 250 reports
this year, and not a single 'disappointment' – an almost unbelievable
level of consistency. / **Details:** *www.latrompette.co.uk; 10.30 pm, Sun 10 pm;*
booking: max 6.

Troubadour SW5 £33
263-267 Old Brompton Rd 7370 1434 4–3A
"A nice time warp for one's inner hippy" – this "chill-out" Earl's Court
veteran has a "wonderful café atmosphere" and "good garden" too;
the very "average" food is "not what it might be", but "good for
breakfast". / **Details:** *www.troubadour.co.uk; 11 pm.*

Two Brothers N3 £31
297-303 Regent's Park Rd 8346 0469

"Still North London's most popular chippy"; under new management,
this "busy and noisy" Finchley stalwart still wins much praise for its
"fantastic" and "efficiently-served" fish 'n' chips.
/ **Details:** *www.twobrothers.co.uk; 10.15 pm; closed Mon & Sun; no booking at D.*

Uli W11 £33
16 All Saints Rd 7727 7511 5–1B
"Michael is a wonderful host", and the "delicious and varied" pan-Asian
dishes on offer at his "unassuming" Notting Hill "favourite" make it a
real local treasure; a slight slip in ratings this year, however, supports the
long-term fan who feels "standards are down a notch recently".
/ **Details:** *www.uli-oriental.co.uk; 11 pm; D only; no Amex.*

Umu W1 £120

14-16 Bruton Pl   7499 8881   2–2C
"Transcendent sashimi and sushi" are amongst the *"exceptional"*
Japanese fare on offer at Marlon Abela's *"tranquil"* Kyoto-style venture,
in a Mayfair mews; it's *"outstandingly expensive"*, though – *"only go if an
oligarch is paying!"* / **Details:** www.umurestaurant.com; 10.30 pm; closed
Sat L & Sun; no trainers; booking: max 14.

Upstairs Bar SW2 £40

89b Acre Ln (door on Branksome Rd)   7733 8855
Entered *"speakeasy-style"*, this *"hidden"* Brixton *"jewel"* seems like
a *"great secret"*; it inspires a hymn of praise for its *"genial"* and
"romantic" style and its *"lovingly-prepared"* Gallic cuisine (albeit from
a *"limited"* menu); *"sexy"* little bar too. / **Details:** www.upstairslondon.com;
10.30 pm; D only, closed Mon & Sun.

Vama SW10 £42
438 King's Rd   7351 4118   4–3B
An *"unusual nouvelle Indian"*, in World's End, where *"some dishes are
truly mind-blowing"*; the décor, though, *"could use some smartening up"*,
and the place attracts nothing like the attention it once did.
/ **Details:** www.vama.co.uk; 11 pm, Sun 10.30 pm; D only, ex Sun open L & D.

Vanilla W1 £55
131 Great Titchfield St   3008 7763   1–1B
"Decorated like a '60s film set", this *"fun"* Fitzrovia basement
bar/restaurant scores well with a crowd – almost all of whom were born
after that decade – for its *"pure theatre"*; the cooking *"tries hard"* too,
and the results are often *"simply fantastic"*. / **Value tip:** set weekday L £26
(FP). **Details:** www.vanillalondon.com; 10 pm; closed Mon, Sat L & Sun; no trainers;
booking: max 6.

Vasco & Piero's Pavilion W1 £50
15 Poland St   7437 8774   2–1D
An age-old Italian *"hide-away"* that's *"about as un-trendy as you can get
in Soho nowadays"*, and is loved by regulars for its *"simple food, simply
done very well"*; the ambience can seem *"tepid"*, though, and the service
has been a touch *"variable"* of late. / **Details:** www.vascosfood.com;
10.30 pm; closed Sat L & Sun.

Veeraswamy W1 £54
Victory Hs, 99-101 Regent St   7734 1401   2–3D
With its *"vibrant"* contemporary décor, London's oldest Indian,
near Piccadilly Circus, has certainly moved with the times, and it serves
up some *"very subtle"* and *"gorgeous"* dishes; it has, however, become
rather *"pricey"* of late. / **Details:** www.realindianfood.com; 10.30 pm,
Sun 10.15 pm; booking: max 12.

El Vergel SE1 £19

8 Lant St   7357 0057
"Incredible South American dishes" come at *"laughably cheap prices"*,
at this *"cramped and buzzy"* refectory in a Borough side street – in fact,
"it's hard to think of anywhere in London offering better value";
"amazing" Latin breakfasts too. / **Details:** www.elvergel.co.uk; breakfast &
L only, closed Sat D & Sun; no credit cards.

Viajante E2
Patriot Sq   1–1D
With his daring experimental cuisine, chef Nuno Mendes is one of the
capital's most interesting chefs; in 2010, he will move on from the
temporary 'pop-up' restaurant ('The Loft') he has been running out of his
home, to this new venture in Bethnal Green.
/ **Details:** www.viajanterestaurant.co.uk.

Viet W1   £19 ⭐
34 Greek St   7494 9888   3–3A
"The pho soups are mouthwatering", at this "packed" and "great-value"
Soho gem (where you can BYO – £2.50 corkage); "so the tables are
bare and the service is rude – what did you expect?" / **Details:** 11 pm,
Fri 11.30 pm; closed Sun; no Amex; no booking: Fri & Sat D.

Vijay NW6   £27 ⭐
49 Willesden Ln   7328 1087
"Still my favourite!"; this "extremely cheap" and "surprisingly good"
Kilburn veteran looks little-changed since the '60s, but – thanks to its
"gorgeous" south Indian food – it "never fails to hit the spot".
/ **Details:** www.vijayrestaurant.co.uk; 10.45 pm, Fri & Sat 11.45 pm.

Vijaya Krishna SW17   £21 ⭐
114 Mitcham Rd   8767 7688
"Highly recommended" in all reports, this Tooting south Indian offers
"excellent, freshly-spiced food"; by the standards of the area, the setting
is quite "upmarket" too. / **Details:** 11 pm, Fri & Sat midnight; no Amex.

Village East SE1   £45
171-173 Bermondsey St   7357 6082
The "relaxed" vibe is the particular feature of this "fun" Bermondsey
hang-out, where the forte is a "high-end, New York-style brunch". / **Value
tip:** set Sun L £34 (FP). **Details:** www.villageeast.co.uk; 10 pm; closed Sat D &
Sun D.

Villiers Terrace N8   £34 ⭐
120 Park Rd   8245 6827

Early-days reports on this "stylish" and "quirky" new Crouch End
gastropub are all upbeat (and "they even think of vegetarians, and real
food for kids"). / **Details:** www.villierstercelondon.com; 10.30 pm; no Amex;
need 8+ to book.

Vinoteca EC1 £37
7 St John St 7253 8786
*"A truly astounding" wine list at "fair" prices, and "caring staff who know their stuff" ensure that this "very buzzy" Clerkenwell outfit is "always packed" – "expect a wait for a table"; the "hearty" food is "very decent" too. / **Details:** www.vinoteca.co.uk; 10 pm; closed Sun D; no Amex; no booking D, max 8 L.*

Vrisaki N22 £30
73 Myddleton Rd 8889 8760
*"Great mezze" in "enormous portions" draw a big following to this "busy and cheerful" – and surprisingly large-scale – Greek operation, behind a Bounds Green take-away; "not that cheap, but super value". / **Details:** midnight, Sun 9 pm.*

Wahaca £28
66 Chandos Pl, WC2 7240 1883 3–4C
Westfield, Ariel Way, W12 8749 4517 6–1C
Unit 4, Park Pavilion, 40 Canada Sq, E14
*Thanks to its "zingy" and "good-value" street-food menu, the Covent Garden original of this "designer-Mexican" duo is often full to the point of "madness" – be prepared for an "unwieldy" queue; there's also a (slightly less funky) outpost at Westfield, and a Canary Wharf branch coming soon in late 2009. / **Details:** www.wahaca.com; WC2 11 pm, Sun 10.30 pm; W12 11 pm, Sun 10 pm; no booking.*

The Wallace
The Wallace Collection W1 £46
Hertford Hs, Manchester Sq 7563 9505 2–1A
*The "beautiful" and "cleverly-designed" covered courtyard is the star turn at this Marylebone palazzo's restaurant – a "tranquil" West End rendezvous, "away from the crowds"; the Gallic cuisine is "expensive" for what it is, though, and service can be "painfully slow". / **Details:** www.thewallacerestaurant.com; Fri & Sat 9.30 pm; L only.*

Wapping Food E1 £47
Wapping Power Station, Wapping Wall 7680 2080
*This "unique" former East End pumping station makes a "most beautiful", if "very eccentric", post-industrial-chic setting – one that rather eclipses the cuisine, "well-prepared" as it is, and even the "very good" all-Ozzie wine list. / **Details:** www.thewappingproject.com; 10.30 pm; closed Sun D.*

The Warrington W9 £44
93 Warrington Cr 7592 7960
*"Gordon Ramsay, hang your head in shame!"; this "dreary" Maida Vale boozer is a "Kitchen Nightmare" of truly astonishing proportions – almost half the reporters who mention the place nominate it as their 'most disappointing meal of the year'! / **Details:** www.gordonramsay.com; 10.30 pm; Mon-Thu D only, Fri-Sun open L & D; Casual.*

Whitechapel Gallery Dining Room
Whitechapel Gallery E1
£41 ⭐⭐

77-82 Whitechapel High St 7522 7896 1–2C

The "bright and intimate" dining room of this revamped East End gallery has proved an "unexpectedly good new opening", thanks largely to the "precise modern cooking" from Maria Elia (formerly of Delfina Studios). / **Details:** www.whitechapelgallery.org; 9.30 pm; closed Mon & Sun D.

Whits W8
£44 ⭐

21 Abingdon Rd 7938 1122 4–1A

"A lady who never forgets a face" oversees this small Kensington bistro with "charm and energy"; for a place that serves "traditional" Gallic food "done very well", it's perhaps rather under-appreciated. / **Details:** www.whits.co.uk; 10.30 pm; closed Mon, Tue L, Sat L & Sun.

Wild Honey W1
£50 ⭐

12 St George St 7758 9160 2–2C

Like its sibling Arbutus, this "gourmet" favourite wins rave reviews for its "sensitively-prepared" Gallic classics, its "superb wines by the carafe" and its "decent prices" (especially the set lunch); "get a booth", though – these panelled Mayfair premises can otherwise seem a bit "dull". / **Value tip:** set pre theatre £32 (FP). **Details:** www.wildhoneyrestaurant.co.uk; 11 pm, Sun 10 pm.

Wiltons SW1
£92 Ⓐ

55 Jermyn St 7629 9955 2–3C

A "rather stuffy" clubland institution, where the "finest" British oysters, fish and game are treated "with respect", and presented in "brilliantly old-fashioned" style; critics, however, condemn the place as a "home for the elderly", and the "undemanding rich". / **Value tip:** set weekday L £74 (FP). **Details:** www.wiltons.co.uk; 10.30 pm; closed Sat & Sun; jacket required.

The Windsor Castle W8
£29 Ⓐ

114 Campden Hill Rd 7243 8797 5–2B

Just off Notting Hill Gate, an ancient coaching inn known for its quirky interior and charming walled garden; reports (relatively few this year) say its simple "traditional British" fare is usually "great". / **Details:** www.thewindsorcastlekensington.co.uk; 10 pm, Sun 9pm; no booking.

The Wine Library EC3
£24 Ⓐ

43 Trinity Sq 7481 0415

A selection of "over 200 wines" (all at shop price plus corkage) make this City cellar "hide-away" a "super venue for serious wine browsers"; don't expect much of the food, however – it's just a simple buffet of pâté and cheese. / **Details:** www.winelibrary.co.uk; 8 pm, Mon 6 pm; L & early evening only, closed Sat & Sun.

The Wolseley W1 £55
160 Piccadilly 7499 6996 2–3C
"A buzzing hub of London life!"; Corbin & King's "electric" grand café, by the Ritz, suits most occasions, not least a "peerless breakfast", "impressing a client" or "discreet celeb-spotting" (or all three at once!); the "steadfast" food is rather beside the point.
/ **Details:** www.thewolseley.com; midnight, Sun 11 pm.

Wright Brothers SE1 £42
11 Stoney St 7403 9554
*"Three cheers for the best oysters in London!" – they're "incomparable", at this "cramped" but "fun" seafood bar in Borough Market; "be warned, it gets VERY busy". / **Details:** www.wrightbros.eu.com; 10.30 pm; closed Sun; booking: max 8.*

Yalla Yalla W1 £22
1 Greens Ct 7287 7663 2–2D
*This "sweet" new heart-of-Soho café has been an instant hit with its "authentic Beirut-style cooking and baking"; it is already invariably full. / **Details:** www.yalla-yalla.co.uk; 11 pm, Sun 10 pm; no Amex.*

Yauatcha W1 £55
Broadwick Hs, 15-17 Broadwick St 7494 8888 2–2D
*"The most ravishing dim sum in London" inspire rave reports on Alan Yau's "über-trendy" Soho oriental – it doesn't seem to matter than the experience is "rushed", or that service sometimes "sucks"; NB above the "dark and funky" basement, there's a "lovely" room additionally offering "exquisite" teas and "jewel-like" pâtisserie. / **Details:** www.yauatcha.com; 11.30 pm.*

The Yellow House SE16 £33
126 Lower Rd 7231 8777
*Recently moved to larger premises, this "excellent local restaurant" is all the more worth knowing about in the Surrey Quays "sea of mediocrity" – Jamie is a "passionate" chef/patron, and it shows. / **Details:** www.theyellowhouse.eu; 10.30 pm, Sun 9.30 pm; closed Mon, Tue-Fri D only, Sat & Sun open L & D.*

Yi-Ban £31
Imperial Wharf, Imperial Rd, SW6 7731 6606 4–4B
Regatta Centre, Dockside Rd, E16 7473 6699
*With its "lovely views of City airport", this "lively" dockside oriental is certainly "in the middle of nowhere", and its Fulham sibling, lost in a soulless riverside development, is even more obscure; both establishments, however, are worth seeking out for their "fresh and tasty" Chinese fare (including top dim sum). / **Details:** www.yi-ban.co.uk; 10.45 pm; SW6 closed Sun.*

Yming W1 £33
35-36 Greek St 7734 2721 3–2A
*"How they remember so many customers is amazing" – Christine Lau's "charming" Soho restaurant is an unusually "personal" venture, and always has some "interesting" dishes on its "North Chinese-focussed" menu; let's hope a few recent 'off' reports are just a wobble. / **Value tip:** set pre theatre £20 (FP). **Details:** www.yminglondon.com; 11.45 pm; closed Sun.*

Yoshino W1 £38 ⭐

3 Piccadilly Pl   7287 6622   2–3D

"Hidden-away" off Piccadilly, a "super, secret Japanese" that's "always packed with an oriental crowd"; there was the odd misfire this year, but most feedback is still a hymn of praise to its "smiling" staff and "mouth-wateringly good" sushi and sashimi; the interior, though, is slightly "cold". / *Details: www.yoshino.net; 9 pm; closed Sun.*

Zaika W8 £52 ⭐⭐

1 Kensington High St   7795 6533   4–1A

Sanjay Dwivedi's "subtle but confident" cooking at this "innovative" Kensington spot is nigh on "the very definition of gourmet Indian cuisine"; the former banking-hall premises, however, can seem "cavernous". / *Details: www.zaika-restaurant.co.uk; 10.45 pm, Sun 9.45 pm.*

Zuma SW7 £69 Ⓐ⭐⭐

5 Raphael St   7584 1010   4–1C

"Move over Nobu!"; this "happening" Knightsbridge hang-out – with its "stunning" Japanese fusion fare and a "super-chic" vibe – is "so much better"; if you want to eat, though, be prepared to "fight your way through the flash younger crowd at the bar".

/ *Details: www.zumarestaurant.com; 10.45 pm, Sun 9.45 pm; booking: max 8.*

LONDON AREA
OVERVIEWS

CENTRAL

Soho, Covent Garden & Bloomsbury
(Parts of W1, all WC2 and WC1)

£80+	L'Atelier de Joel Robuchon	*French*	Ⓐ✪
	Asia de Cuba	*Fusion*	
£70+	Pearl	*French*	
£60+	The Ivy	*British, Modern*	Ⓐ
	Homage	*"*	
	Rules	*British, Traditional*	Ⓐ
	J Sheekey	*Fish & seafood*	Ⓐ✪✪
£50+	Alastair Little	*British, Modern*	
	Simpsons-in-the-Strand	*British, Traditional*	
	Vasco & Piero's Pavilion	*Italian*	✪
	Yauatcha	*Chinese*	Ⓐ✪✪
	Shanghai Blues	*"*	✪
	Red Fort	*Indian*	✪
£40+	Joe Allen	*American*	Ⓐ
	Arbutus	*British, Modern*	✪
	Konstam	*"*	✪
	The Portrait	*"*	Ⓐ
	J Sheekey Oyster Bar	*Fish & seafood*	Ⓐ✪✪
	Clos Maggiore	*French*	Ⓐ✪
	Randall & Aubin	*"*	Ⓐ✪
	Ronnie Scott's	*International*	Ⓐ✪
	Dehesa	*Italian*	Ⓐ✪
	Barrafina	*Spanish*	Ⓐ✪✪
	Tierra Brindisa	*"*	✪
	Moti Mahal	*Indian*	✪
	Edokko	*Japanese*	✪
	Benja	*Thai*	✪
	Patara	*"*	✪
£35+	Andrew Edmunds	*British, Modern*	Ⓐ
	Great Queen Street	*British, Traditional*	✪
	Terroirs	*French*	Ⓐ✪
	The Giaconda	*"*	✪
	Bocca Di Lupo	*Italian*	Ⓐ✪
	Barshu	*Chinese*	✪
	Fung Shing	*"*	✪
	Sitaaray	*Indian*	Ⓐ✪
	Haozhan	*Pan-Asian*	✪✪
£30+	Seven Stars	*International*	Ⓐ
	Spacca Napoli	*Italian*	✪
	Ciao Bella	*"*	Ⓐ
	Mildred's	*Vegetarian*	Ⓐ✪
	Souk Medina	*Moroccan*	Ⓐ
	New Mayflower	*Chinese*	✪
	Yming	*"*	✪
	Rasa Maricham	*Indian, Southern*	✪
	Inamo	*Japanese*	Ⓐ
	Bincho Yakitori	*"*	
£25+	North Sea Fish	*Fish & chips*	✪
	Fernandez & Wells	*Sandwiches, cakes, etc*	Ⓐ✪✪
	Wahaca	*Mexican/TexMex*	✪
	Harbour City	*Chinese*	✪

	Joy King Lau	"	✪
	Busaba Eathai	Thai	Ⓐ✪
	C&R Cafe	"	✪
£20+	Gordon's Wine Bar	International	Ⓐ✪
	Konditor & Cook	Sandwiches, cakes, etc	✪
	Yalla Yalla	Lebanese	✪
	Sagar	Indian	✪
£15+	Square Pie Company	British, Traditional	✪
	Princi	Italian	Ⓐ
	Food for Thought	Vegetarian	✪
	Mrs Marengos	Sandwiches, cakes, etc	✪
	Bar Italia	"	Ⓐ
	Abokado	Japanese	✪
	Viet	Vietnamese	✪
£10+	Fryer's Delight	Fish & chips	Ⓐ
	Monmouth Coffee Co	Sandwiches, cakes, etc	Ⓐ✪✪
	Kastner & Ovens	"	✪✪
	Maison Bertaux	"	Ⓐ✪
£5+	Flat White	"	Ⓐ✪✪

Mayfair & St James's (Parts of W1 and SW1)

£120+	Umu	Japanese	✪
£110+	Le Gavroche	French	Ⓐ✪
£100+	Hélène Darroze	"	✪
	The Ritz Restaurant	"	Ⓐ
£90+	Wiltons	British, Traditional	Ⓐ
	Sketch (Lecture Rm)	French	✪
	The Square	"	✪
	The Greenhouse	"	Ⓐ
	Alain Ducasse	"	
	G Ramsay at Claridges	"	
£80+	Dorchester Grill	British, Modern	
	Hibiscus	French	
	L'Oranger	"	
	Kai Mayfair	Chinese	
	Nobu	Japanese	✪
	Nobu Berkeley	"	
£70+	Bellamy's	British, Modern	
	The Albemarle	British, Traditional	Ⓐ
	La Petite Maison	French	Ⓐ✪
	Galvin at Windows	"	Ⓐ
	maze Grill	"	
	Cipriani	Italian	✪
	Murano	"	✪
	Theo Randall	"	✪
	The Palm	Steaks & grills	
	China Tang	Chinese	
	Benares	Indian	✪
	Ikeda	Japanese	Ⓐ✪
	Sake No Hana	"	
£60+	Corrigan's Mayfair	British, Traditional	

Price	Restaurant	Cuisine	Awards
	Scott's	*Fish & seafood*	Ⓐ✪
	Bentley's	*"*	✪
	maze	*French*	✪
	L'Incontro	*Italian*	
	Kiku	*Japanese*	✪
	Sumosan	*"*	✪
£50+	Le Caprice	*British, Modern*	Ⓐ✪
	Wild Honey	*"*	✪
	The Wolseley	*"*	Ⓐ
	Fortnum's, The Fountain	*British, Traditional*	
	Boudin Blanc	*French*	Ⓐ✪
	Ristorante Semplice	*Italian*	✪
	Cecconi's	*"*	Ⓐ
	St Alban	*Mediterranean*	Ⓐ
	Goodman	*Steaks & grills*	✪
	The Guinea Grill	*"*	✪
	Fakhreldine	*Lebanese*	
	Princess Garden	*Chinese*	✪
	Veeraswamy	*Indian*	Ⓐ✪
	Tamarind	*"*	✪
	Quilon	*Indian, Southern*	✪
	Mitsukoshi	*Japanese*	✪
£40+	Automat	*American*	
	The Duke of Wellington	*British, Modern*	Ⓐ✪
	Sotheby's Café	*"*	Ⓐ✪
	1707	*"*	Ⓐ
	Osteria Dell'Angolo	*Italian*	
	Planet Hollywood	*Burgers, etc*	
	Levant	*Lebanese*	Ⓐ
	Chor Bizarre	*Indian*	Ⓐ✪
	Patara	*Thai*	✪
£35+	Chisou	*Japanese*	✪
	Yoshino	*"*	✪
£30+	Rasa	*Indian, Southern*	✪
£25+	Sakura	*Japanese*	✪
	Busaba Eathai	*Thai*	Ⓐ✪
£10+	Fuzzy's Grub	*Sandwiches, cakes, etc*	✪

Fitzrovia & Marylebone (Part of W1)

Price	Restaurant	Cuisine	Awards
£90+	Rhodes W1 Restaurant	*British, Modern*	
	Pied à Terre	*French*	✪
£80+	Roka	*Japanese*	Ⓐ✪
£70+	The Landau	*British, Modern*	Ⓐ✪
	Orrery	*French*	✪
	Texture	*Scandinavian*	
	Hakkasan	*Chinese*	Ⓐ✪
	Suka	*Malaysian*	
£60+	The Providores	*Fusion*	
	5 Cavendish Square	*Italian*	✪
	Locanda Locatelli	*"*	
£50+	Vanilla	*British, Modern*	Ⓐ✪

	Odin's	*British, Traditional*	Ⓐ
	Archipelago	*Fusion*	Ⓐ
	Fino	*Spanish*	Ⓐ✪
	Royal China Club	*Chinese*	✪
	Crazy Bear	*Thai*	Ⓐ
£40+	Back to Basics	*Fish & seafood*	✪✪
	Trishna	"	✪✪
	Galvin Bistrot de Luxe	*French*	Ⓐ✪✪
	L'Autre Pied	"	✪
	The Wallace	"	Ⓐ
	Latium	*Italian*	✪✪
	Sardo	"	✪
	Ibérica	*Spanish*	✪
	Bam-Bou	*Vietnamese*	Ⓐ✪
£35+	Hellenik	*Greek*	✪
	Salt Yard	*Spanish*	✪
	Royal China	*Chinese*	✪
	Defune	*Japanese*	✪✪
£30+	Rasa Samudra	*Indian, Southern*	✪
	Dinings	*Japanese*	✪✪
£25+	La Fromagerie Café	*Sandwiches, cakes, etc*	Ⓐ✪
	Ragam	*Indian*	✪✪
	Monkey & Me	*Thai*	✪
£20+	Golden Hind	*Fish & chips*	✪✪
	Sagar	*Indian*	✪
£15+	Square Pie Company	*British, Traditional*	✪
	Atari-Ya	*Japanese*	✪✪

Belgravia, Pimlico, Victoria & Westminster (SW1, except St James's)

£110+	Marcus Wareing	*French*	Ⓐ✪✪
£90+	Pétrus	"	
£80+	Foliage	"	
	Apsleys	*Italian*	
	Nahm	*Thai*	
£70+	Rib Room	*British, Traditional*	
	One-O-One	*Fish & seafood*	✪✪
	Roussillon	*French*	✪✪
	Mr Chow	*Chinese*	
£60+	The Goring Hotel	*British, Modern*	Ⓐ
	The Park	*International*	✪
	Toto's	*Italian*	Ⓐ
	Santini	"	
	The Cinnamon Club	*Indian*	Ⓐ✪
£50+	The Thomas Cubitt	*British, Modern*	Ⓐ
	La Poule au Pot	*French*	Ⓐ
	Il Convivio	*Italian*	✪
	Quirinale	"	✪
	Ken Lo's Memories	*Chinese*	✪
	Amaya	*Indian*	Ⓐ✪✪

£40+	Grenadier	British, Traditional	Ⓐ Ⓧ
	Olivomare	Fish & seafood	Ⓧ
	Le Cercle	French	Ⓐ Ⓧ Ⓧ
	Ottolenghi	Italian	Ⓧ Ⓧ
	Signor Sassi	"	Ⓐ Ⓧ
	Olivo	"	Ⓧ
	Sale e Pepe	"	Ⓐ
	Caraffini	"	
	About Thyme	Mediterranean	Ⓧ
	Oliveto	Pizza	Ⓧ Ⓧ
	Ishbilia	Lebanese	Ⓧ
	Hunan	Chinese	Ⓧ Ⓧ
	Salloos	Pakistani	Ⓧ
£35+	Kazan	Turkish	Ⓧ
£30+	Blue Jade	Thai	
£25+	Cyprus Mangal	Turkish	Ⓧ
	Jenny Lo's	Chinese	Ⓧ

WEST

**Chelsea, South Kensington,
Kensington, Earl's Court &
Fulham (SW3, SW5, SW6, SW7, SW10 & W8)**

£110+	Gordon Ramsay	*French*	
£100+	Blakes	*International*	🅐❌
£90+	Tom Aikens	*British, Modern*	
	Aubergine	*French*	
£80+	The Capital Restaurant	*"*	❌❌
	Rasoi	*Indian*	❌
£70+	Launceston Place	*British, Modern*	❌
	Brunello	*Italian*	
	Bombay Brasserie	*Indian*	
	Nozomi	*Japanese*	
£60+	Bibendum	*French*	🅐
	Lucio	*Italian*	
	San Lorenzo	*"*	
	Locanda Ottomezzo	*Mediterranean*	
	Zuma	*Japanese*	🅐❌❌
	The Collection	*Pan-Asian*	❌
£50+	Clarke's	*British, Modern*	❌
	Tom's Kitchen	*"*	
	Poissonnerie de l'Av.	*Fish & seafood*	❌
	Racine	*French*	❌
	Belvedere	*"*	🅐
	Min Jiang	*Chinese*	🅐❌
	Zaika	*Indian*	❌❌
	Chutney Mary	*"*	🅐❌
	Mao Tai	*Pan-Asian*	🅐❌
	Blue Elephant	*Thai*	🅐
£40+	Whits	*British, Modern*	❌
	Ffiona's	*British, Traditional*	🅐
	Maggie Jones's	*"*	🅐
	Chez Patrick	*Fish & seafood*	❌
	Le Colombier	*French*	🅐
	Ottolenghi	*Italian*	❌❌
	Riccardo's	*"*	🅐❌
	Frantoio	*"*	🅐
	Il Portico	*"*	🅐
	Cambio de Tercio	*Spanish*	🅐❌
	Pasha	*Moroccan*	🅐❌
	Mr Wing	*Chinese*	🅐
	The Painted Heron	*Indian*	❌❌
	Star of India	*"*	❌
	Vama	*"*	❌
	Eight Over Eight	*Pan-Asian*	🅐❌
	Sukho Thai Cuisine	*Thai*	❌❌
	Patara	*"*	❌
£35+	Harwood Arms	*British, Modern*	🅐❌
	The Cabin	*International*	🅐❌
	The Atlas	*Mediterranean*	🅐❌
	Tendido Cero	*Spanish*	🅐❌
	Beirut Express	*Lebanese*	❌

Price	Name	Cuisine	
	Royal China	*Chinese*	★
	Haandi	*Indian*	★
	Noor Jahan	*"*	★
£30+	Aglio e Olio	*Italian*	A★
	Made in Italy	*"*	A★
	Troubadour	*Sandwiches, cakes, etc*	A★
	Yi-Ban	*Chinese*	A★
£25+	The Windsor Castle	*International*	A
	Pappa Ciccia	*Italian*	A★
	Lola Rojo	*Spanish*	★
	Haché	*Steaks & grills*	A★
	Taiwan Village	*Chinese*	★★
	Tandoori Lane	*Indian*	★
	Addie's Thai Café	*Thai*	★
£20+	Stick & Bowl	*Chinese*	★
	Churchill Arms	*Thai*	A★
	Café 209	*"*	A

Notting Hill, Holland Park, Bayswater, North Kensington & Maida Vale (W2, W9, W10, W11)

Price	Name	Cuisine	
£70+	The Ledbury	*British, Modern*	A★★
£60+	Angelus	*French*	★
£50+	Julie's	*British, Modern*	A
	Le Café Anglais	*French*	
	Assaggi	*Italian*	A★★
	Essenza	*"*	A★
£40+	The Cow	*British, Modern*	A★
	The Ladbroke Arms	*"*	A★
	Paradise, Kensal Green	*"*	A★
	The Warrington	*"*	★
	First Floor	*"*	A
	Hereford Road	*British, Traditional*	★
	Ottolenghi	*Italian*	★★
	The Oak	*"*	A★
	Bombay Palace	*Indian*	★★
	E&O	*Pan-Asian*	A★★
£35+	The Academy	*International*	A★
	Electric Brasserie	*"*	A
	Crazy Homies	*Mexican/TexMex*	A★
	Beirut Express	*Lebanese*	★
	Pearl Liang	*Chinese*	A★
	Royal China	*"*	★
	Noor Jahan	*Indian*	★
	Satay House	*Malaysian*	★
£30+	Lucky Seven	*American*	A★
	Al-Waha	*Lebanese*	★
	Mandarin Kitchen	*Chinese*	★★
	Inaho	*Japanese*	★★
	Uli	*Pan-Asian*	★
£25+	Mandalay	*Burmese*	★
	The Four Seasons	*Chinese*	★
	Magic Wok	*"*	★

	C&R Cafe	*Thai*	✪
£20+	Khan's	*Indian*	✪
	Number One Café	*Thai*	✪✪
£15+	Fresco	*Lebanese*	✪

Hammersmith, Shepherd's Bush, Olympia, Chiswick, Acton & Ealing (W4, W3, W5, W6, W12, W14)

£60+	The River Café	*Italian*	✪
£50+	La Trompette	*French*	Ⓐ✪✪
£40+	The Anglesea Arms	*British, Modern*	Ⓐ✪
	Pissarro's	"	Ⓐ
	High Road Brasserie	"	
	Fish Hook	*Fish & seafood*	✪
	Annie's	*International*	Ⓐ
	Bianco Nero	*Italian*	✪
	Popeseye	*Steaks & grills*	✪
£35+	The Swan	*Mediterranean*	Ⓐ
	The Gate	*Vegetarian*	✪
	Indian Zing	*Indian*	✪✪
	Madhu's	"	✪✪
	Brilliant	"	✪
	Sushi-Hiro	*Japanese*	✪✪
£30+	Patio	*Polish*	Ⓐ
	North China	*Chinese*	✪
£25+	Ground	*Burgers, etc*	✪
	Wahaca	*Mexican/TexMex*	Ⓐ
	Adams Café	*Moroccan*	
	Chez Marcelle	*Lebanese*	✪✪
	Mirch Masala	*Indian*	✪✪
	Anarkali	"	✪
	Shilpa	*Indian, Southern*	✪✪
	Esarn Kheaw	*Thai*	✪✪
	Latymers	"	✪
£20+	Sufi	*Persian*	✪
	Abu Zaad	*Syrian*	✪
	Sagar	*Indian*	✪
£15+	Square Pie Company	*British, Traditional*	✪

NORTH

Hampstead, West Hampstead, St John's Wood, Regent's Park, Kilburn & Camden Town (NW postcodes)

£70+	Landmark (Winter Gdn)	British, Modern	Ⓐ
£50+	L'Aventure	French	Ⓐ✪
	Oslo Court	"	Ⓐ✪
£40+	Market	British, Modern	✪
	The Engineer	"	✪
	St Pancras Grand	"	Ⓐ
	Bull & Last	British, Traditional	Ⓐ✪✪
	Atma	Indian	✪
	Sushi-Say	Japanese	✪✪
£35+	Holly Bush	British, Traditional	Ⓐ
	Lemonia	Greek	Ⓐ
	Seashell	Fish & chips	✪
	Goldfish	Chinese	✪
	Phoenix Palace	"	✪
	Eriki	Indian	✪✪
	Jin Kichi	Japanese	✪✪
	Singapore Garden	Malaysian	✪
£30+	Daphne	Greek	Ⓐ
	El Parador	Spanish	Ⓐ✪
	Nautilus	Fish & chips	✪✪
	Alisan	Chinese	✪
	Gung-Ho	"	Ⓐ
	Café Japan	Japanese	✪✪
	Bento Cafe	"	✪
£25+	Stringray Café	Mediterranean	✪
	Haché	Steaks & grills	Ⓐ✪
	Vijay	Indian	✪
	Asakusa	Japanese	✪
£20+	Five Hot Chillies	Indian	✪
£15+	Geeta	"	✪
	Atari-Ya	Japanese	✪✪

Hoxton, Islington, Highgate, Crouch End, Stoke Newington, Finsbury Park, Muswell Hill & Finchley (N postcodes)

£80+	Fifteen Restaurant	Italian	
£60+	Morgan M	French	✪✪
£50+	Sargasso Sea	Fish & seafood	Ⓐ✪
£40+	Mosaica	British, Modern	Ⓐ✪
	St Johns	British, Traditional	Ⓐ
	Fig	French	Ⓐ✪
	Ottolenghi	Italian	✪✪
£35+	The Lock Dining Bar	British, Modern	Ⓐ✪
	Chez Liline	Fish & seafood	✪✪

	Les Associés	French	✪
	Isarn	Thai	✪
£30+	Villiers Terrace	British, Modern	✪
	The Flask	British, Traditional	✪
	Vrisaki	Greek	
	500	Italian	✪
	Toff's	Fish & chips	✪
	Two Brothers	"	✪
	Rasa Travancore	Indian, Southern	✪
£25+	Le Mercury	French	✪
	Stringray Café	Mediterranean	✪
	Rani	Indian	✪
	Rasa	Indian, Southern	✪✪
£20+	Anglo Asian Tandoori	Indian	✪
	Huong-Viet	Vietnamese	✪

SOUTH

South Bank (SE1)

£70+	Oxo Tower (Rest')	*British, Modern*	✪
£50+	Roast	*British, Traditional*	
£40+	Magdalen	*British, Modern*	✪
	Garrison	*"*	Ⓐ
	Wright Brothers	*Fish & seafood*	Ⓐ✪✪
	Champor-Champor	*Fusion*	Ⓐ✪
	Village East	*"*	
	Tate Modern (Level 7)	*International*	Ⓐ
	Tentazioni	*Italian*	✪
£35+	The Anchor & Hope	*British, Traditional*	✪✪
	Applebee's Cafe	*International*	✪
	Tapas Brindisa	*Spanish*	✪
£30+	The Table	*British, Modern*	Ⓐ✪
£25+	Mango Tree	*Indian*	✪
£20+	Masters Super Fish	*Fish & chips*	✪
£15+	El Vergel	*South American*	Ⓐ✪✪
£10+	Monmouth Coffee Co	*Sandwiches, cakes, etc*	Ⓐ✪✪
	Fuzzy's Grub	*"*	✪

Greenwich, Lewisham & Blackheath
(All SE postcodes, except SE1)

£50+	Lobster Pot	*Fish & seafood*	Ⓐ✪
£40+	Inside	*British, Modern*	✪
	The Palmerston	*"*	✪
£35+	Babur	*Indian*	Ⓐ✪✪
£30+	The Yellow House	*International*	✪
	Le Querce	*Italian*	✪
	Dragon Castle	*Chinese*	Ⓐ✪✪
	Tandoori Nights	*Indian*	Ⓐ✪
£25+	The Gowlett	*Pizza*	Ⓐ✪
	Ganapati	*Indian*	Ⓐ✪

Battersea, Brixton, Clapham, Wandsworth
Barnes, Putney & Wimbledon
(All SW postcodes south of the river)

£50+	Chez Bruce	*British, Modern*	Ⓐ✪✪
	Trinity	*"*	✪
	Enoteca Turi	*Italian*	✪
	Riva	*"*	✪
£40+	Lamberts	*British, Modern*	Ⓐ✪✪
	Tom Ilic	*"*	✪✪
	Four O Nine	*"*	Ⓐ✪

	Upstairs Bar	French	Ⓐ✪
	Annie's	International	Ⓐ
	Numero Uno	Italian	Ⓐ✪
	The Three Bridges	"	
	Popeseye	Steaks & grills	✪
£35+	Sands End	British, Modern	Ⓐ✪
	Emile's	"	✪
	Donna Margherita	Italian	✪
	Isola del Sole	"	Ⓐ
	The Fox & Hounds	Mediterranean	Ⓐ✪
	Santa Maria del Sur	Argentinian	Ⓐ✪
	Royal China	Chinese	✪
	Cho-San	Japanese	✪
£30+	The Lighthouse	British, Modern	Ⓐ✪
	Rick's Café	"	Ⓐ✪
	The Duke's Head	"	Ⓐ
	Fish Club	Fish & seafood	✪
	Rebato's	Spanish	Ⓐ
	Fish Club	Fish & chips	✪
	Ma Goa	Indian	Ⓐ✪
£25+	Pappa Ciccia	Italian	Ⓐ✪
	Lola Rojo	Spanish	✪
	El Rincón Latino	"	Ⓐ
	Kastoori	Indian	✪✪
	Mirch Masala SW16	"	✪✪
	Chutney	"	✪
	Indian Ocean	"	✪
£20+	Hot Stuff	"	Ⓐ✪✪
	Sree Krishna	"	✪
	Vijaya Krishna	Indian, Southern	✪
£15+	Trinity Stores	British, Modern	Ⓐ✪
£10+	Franco Manca	Pizza	✪✪

Outer western suburbs
Kew, Richmond, Twickenham, Teddington

£50+	The Glasshouse	British, Modern	✪✪
	Petersham Nurseries	"	Ⓐ✪
	A Taste Of McClements	French	✪
£40+	Brula	"	Ⓐ✪
	A Cena	Italian	Ⓐ✪
£35+	Origin Asia	Indian	✪
£30+	Tangawizi	"	✪
£25+	O'Zon	Chinese	
£20+	Sagar	Indian	✪

129

EAST

Smithfield & Farringdon (EC1)

£60+	Club Gascon	French	✪
£50+	St John	British, Traditional	✪✪
£40+	Smithfield Bar & Grill	British, Modern	Ⓐ✪
	Bleeding Heart	French	Ⓐ✪
	Café du Marché	"	Ⓐ✪
	Comptoir Gascon	"	Ⓐ✪
	Moro	Spanish	Ⓐ✪✪
£35+	Vinoteca	British, Modern	Ⓐ
	The Quality Chop House	British, Traditional	✪
	The Fox and Anchor	"	Ⓐ
	Cellar Gascon	French	
	Fabrizio	Italian	✪
	54 Farringdon Road	Malaysian	✪
£30+	Tajima Tei	Japanese	✪
£25+	The Eagle	Mediterranean	Ⓐ
	Pham Sushi	Japanese	✪✪
£10+	Spianata & Co	Sandwiches, cakes, etc	✪

The City (EC2, EC3, EC4)

£70+	Prism	British, Modern	✪
	Rhodes 24	"	Ⓐ
	1 Lombard Street	"	
	Bel Canto	French	Ⓐ
£60+	Catch	Fish & seafood	
£50+	Coq d'Argent	French	
	L'Anima	Italian	Ⓐ✪
	Cinnamon Kitchen	Indian	✪✪
	Soseki	Japanese	Ⓐ
£40+	The Hoxton Grille	American	Ⓐ✪
	The Don	British, Modern	✪
	The Chancery	"	
	Lutyens	French	
	The East Room	International	Ⓐ
£35+	Kazan	Turkish	✪
£30+	Ye Olde Cheshire Cheese	British, Traditional	Ⓐ
	Kurumaya	Japanese	Ⓐ✪✪
£25+	Hilliard	British, Modern	✪✪
	Simpson's Tavern	British, Traditional	Ⓐ
£20+	The Wine Library	"	Ⓐ
	Konditor & Cook	Sandwiches, cakes, etc	✪
	Chi Noodle & Wine Bar	Pan-Asian	✪
£10+	Fuzzy's Grub	Sandwiches, cakes, etc	✪
	Spianata & Co	"	✪

East End & Docklands (All E postcodes)

£80+	Roka	*Japanese*	❷✪
£70+	Les Trois Garçons	*French*	❷
	Quadrato	*Italian*	
£40+	Whitechapel Gallery	*British, Modern*	❷✪
	The Gun	*"*	❷
	Wapping Food	*"*	❷
	The Narrow	*"*	
	St John Bread & Wine	*British, Traditional*	❷✪
	Forman's	*Fish & seafood*	
	El Faro	*Spanish*	❷✪
	Buen Ayre	*Argentinian*	✪
	Café Spice Namaste	*Indian*	✪
£35+	Applebee's	*International*	✪
	Il Bordello	*Italian*	❷✪
	La Figa	*"*	✪
	Jamie's Italian	*"*	
	Ark Fish	*Fish & chips*	✪
	Royal China	*Chinese*	✪
£30+	LMNT	*International*	❷
	Faulkner's	*Fish & chips*	✪
	Yi-Ban	*Chinese*	❷✪
£25+	Stringray Globe Café	*Mediterranean*	✪
	Story Deli	*Organic*	❷✪
	Wahaca	*Mexican/TexMex*	❷
	The Drunken Monkey	*Chinese*	❷✪
	Mirch Masala	*Indian*	❷✪
	New Tayyabs	*Pakistani*	❷✪✪
£20+	Mangal Ocakbasi	*Turkish*	❷✪
	Clifton	*Indian*	✪
	Lahore Kebab House	*Pakistani*	❷✪
	Sông Quê	*Vietnamese*	✪
£15+	Square Pie Company	*British, Traditional*	✪
	Gourmet San	*Chinese*	❷✪
£10+	E Pellicci	*Italian*	❷
	Spianata & Co	*Sandwiches, cakes, etc*	✪
£5+	Brick Lane Beigel Bake	*"*	❷✪

LONDON INDEXES

BREAKFAST
(with opening times)

Central
Abokado *(7.30)*
The Albemarle *(7.30)*
Apsleys *(7)*
Asia de Cuba *(6, Sun 7.30)*
Automat *(7, Sat 10)*
Bar Italia *(7)*
Cecconi's *(7)*
The Cinnamon Club *(Mon-Fri 7.30)*
Dorchester Grill *(7, Sat & Sun 8)*
Fernandez & Wells: *Lexington St W1 (7 am)*
5 Cavendish Square *(8)*
Flat White *(8, Sat & Sun 9)*
Fortnum's, The Fountain *(7.30)*
La Fromagerie Café *(8, Sat 9, Sun 10)*
Fuzzy's Grub: *SW1 (7)*
Galvin at Windows *(7)*
The Goring Hotel *(7, Sun 7.30)*
Homage *(7)*
Joe Allen *(8)*
Kastner & Ovens *(8)*
Konditor & Cook: *WC1 (9.30); W1 (9.30, Sun 10.30)*
The Landau *(7)*
Maison Bertaux *(8.30, Sun 9)*
Monmouth Coffee Company: *WC2 (8)*
Mrs Marengos *(8, Sat noon)*
Ottolenghi: *SW1 (8, Sun 9)*
The Park *(6.30)*
Pearl *(6.30, Sat & Sun 7)*
The Portrait *(10)*
The Providores *(9, Sat & Sun 10)*
Rib Room *(7, Sun 8)*
The Ritz Restaurant *(7, Sun 8)*
Simpsons-in-the-Strand *(Mon-Fri 7.30)*
Sotheby's Café *(9.30)*
Square Pie Company: *W1 (10, Sat 9.30, Sun midday)*
Suka *(6.30, Sat & Sun 7)*
The Wallace *(10)*
The Wolseley *(7, Sat & Sun 8)*
Yalla Yalla *(8, Sat & Sun 10)*

West
Adams Café *(7.30, Sat 8.30)*
Annie's: *W4 (Tue - Thu 10, Fri & Sat 10.30, Sun 10)*
Beirut Express: *W2 (7)*
Blakes *(7.30)*
Brunello *(7)*
Le Café Anglais *(Sat 9.30)*
Electric Brasserie *(8)*
Fresco *(8)*
High Road Brasserie *(7, Sat & Sun 8)*
Julie's *(9)*
Lucky Seven *(Mon noon, Tue-Thu 10, Fri-Sun 9)*
Ottolenghi: *W11 (8, Sun 8.30)*
Pappa Ciccia: *Fulham High St SW6 (7.30)*

Paradise by Way of Kensal Green *(Sat noon)*
Pissarro's *(Sat & Sun 9)*
Square Pie Company: *W12 (7, Sat 9, Sun midday)*
Tom's Kitchen *(7, Sat 10, Sun 11)*
Troubadour *(9)*

North
The Engineer *(9)*
Landmark (Winter Gdn) *(7)*
Ottolenghi: *N1 (8, Sun 9)*
Stringray Café: *N5 (11); NW5 (Fri-Sun 11)*

South
Annie's: *SW13 (Tue-Sun 10)*
The Duke's Head *(11, Sun noon)*
Garrison *(8, Sat & Sun 9)*
Lola Rojo: *SW11 (Sat & Sun 11)*
Monmouth Coffee Company: *SE1 (7.30)*
El Rincón Latino *(Sat & Sun 11)*
Roast *(7, Sat 8)*
The Table *(7.30, Sat & Sun 9)*
Tapas Brindisa *(Fri & Sat 9, Sun 10)*
Tate Modern (Level 7) *(10)*
Trinity Stores *(9)*
El Vergel *(8.30, Sat 10.30)*

East
L'Anima *(9)*
Bleeding Heart *(7.30)*
Brick Lane Beigel Bake *(24 hrs)*
Comptoir Gascon *(9, Sat 10.30)*
Coq d'Argent *(Mon-Fri 7.30)*
Forman's *(Sat 7 am, Sun 9 am)*
The Fox and Anchor *(7, Sat 8)*
Fuzzy's Grub: *Cornhill EC3 (7); EC2, Fleet St EC4, Well Ct EC4 (7.30); Houndsditch EC3 (7.30 am); Carter Ln EC4 (7 am)*
The Gun *(Sat & Sun 11.30)*
Hilliard *(8)*
The Hoxton Grille *(7, Sat & Sun 8)*
Lutyens *(7.30)*
1 Lombard Street *(7.30)*
E Pellicci *(7)*
Quadrato *(6.30, Sun 8)*
St John Bread & Wine *(9, Sat & Sun 10)*
Spianata & Co: *E1, EC2, EC3, EC4 (7.30)*
Square Pie Company: *E1 (10.30); E14 (7)*
Wapping Food *(Sat & Sun 10)*

BRUNCH MENUS

Central
Automat
Le Caprice
Cecconi's
La Fromagerie Café
Galvin at Windows
The Ivy
Joe Allen

Ottolenghi: *all branches*
The Providores
The Wolseley

West
Annie's: *all branches*
The Cabin
Electric Brasserie
First Floor
High Road Brasserie
Lucky Seven
The Oak
Ottolenghi: *all branches*
Tom's Kitchen
Troubadour
Zuma

North
The Engineer
Landmark (Winter Gdn)
Ottolenghi: *all branches*

South
Annie's: *all branches*
Garrison
Inside
Lamberts
Roast
The Table
El Vergel
Village East

East
The Hoxton Grille
Quadrato
Wapping Food

BUSINESS

Central
Alain Ducasse
Amaya
Apsleys
Bellamy's
Benares
Bentley's
Boudin Blanc
Le Caprice
Cecconi's
China Tang
The Cinnamon Club
Corrigan's Mayfair
Dorchester Grill
Fino
Foliage
Galvin at Windows
Galvin Bistrot de Luxe
Le Gavroche
Goodman
Gordon Ramsay at Claridge's
The Goring Hotel
The Greenhouse
The Guinea Grill
Hakkasan
Hélène Darroze
Hibiscus

Homage
The Ivy
Kai Mayfair
Ken Lo's Memories
The Landau
Locanda Locatelli
Marcus Wareing
maze Grill
Murano
Nobu
Odin's
One-O-One
L'Oranger
Orrery
The Palm
Pearl
Pétrus
Pied à Terre
Quilon
Quirinale
Rhodes W1 Restaurant
Rib Room
Roka: *W1*
Roussillon
Rules
St Alban
Santini
Scott's
J Sheekey
Simpsons-in-the-Strand
The Square
Tamarind
Theo Randall
Veeraswamy
The Wallace
Wild Honey
Wiltons
The Wolseley

West
Aubergine
Bibendum
The Capital Restaurant
Gordon Ramsay
The Ledbury
Poissonnerie de l'Avenue
Racine
Tom Aikens
La Trompette
Zuma

North
Landmark (Winter Gdn)
St Pancras Grand

South
Oxo Tower (Rest')
Roast
A Taste Of McClements

East
L'Anima
Bleeding Heart
Café du Marché
The Chancery
Club Gascon

INDEXES

Coq d'Argent
The Don
Forman's
The Fox and Anchor
Galvin La Chapelle
The Hoxton Grille
Lutyens
Moro
1 Lombard Street
Prism
Quadrato
Rhodes 24
St John

BYO

(Bring your own wine at no or low – less than £3 – corkage. Note for £5-£15 per bottle, you can normally negotiate to take your own wine to many, if not most, places.)

Central
Food for Thought
Golden Hind
Ragam
Viet

West
Adams Café
Café 209
Five Hot Chillies
Mirch Masala: *all branches*
Number One Café
Pappa Ciccia: *Munster Rd SW6*

North
Geeta
Huong-Viet

South
Hot Stuff
Mirch Masala: *all branches*

East
Lahore Kebab House
Mangal Ocakbasi
Mirch Masala: *all branches*
New Tayyabs

CHILDREN

*(h – high or special chairs
m – children's menu
p – children's portions
e – weekend entertainments
o – other facilities)*

Central
About Thyme *(hm)*
Alastair Little *(hm)*
The Albemarle *(hmp)*
Apsleys *(ehmp)*
Arbutus *(h)*
Asia de Cuba *(hp)*
L'Autre Pied *(hp)*

Back to Basics *(hp)*
Bar Italia *(hp)*
Barshu *(h)*
Bellamy's *(h)*
Benares *(h)*
Benja *(h)*
Bentley's *(h)*
Bincho Yakitori *(hp)*
Bocca Di Lupo *(hp)*
Boudin Blanc *(hp)*
Le Caprice *(hp)*
Caraffini *(h)*
Cecconi's *(hp)*
Le Cercle *(p)*
Chisou *(h)*
Chor Bizarre *(h)*
Ciao Bella *(h)*
The Cinnamon Club *(h)*
Cipriani *(hp)*
Clos Maggiore *(p)*
Cyprus Mangal *(hm)*
Dorchester Grill *(hm)*
The Duke of Wellington *(hp)*
Fakhreldine *(h)*
Fino *(hp)*
Foliage *(hm)*
Fortnum's, The Fountain *(hp)*
La Fromagerie Café *(p)*
Fung Shing *(h)*
Galvin at Windows *(hm)*
Galvin Bistrot de Luxe *(hm)*
Golden Hind *(h)*
Gordon Ramsay at Claridge's *(hp)*
The Goring Hotel *(hm)*
The Guinea Grill *(p)*
Haozhan *(h)*
Harbour City *(hp)*
Hélène Darroze *(hp)*
Hellenik *(hp)*
Hibiscus *(hp)*
Homage *(hpm)*
Ibérica *(p)*
L'Incontro *(hp)*
The Ivy *(hp)*
Joe Allen *(h)*
Joy King Lau *(h)*
Kai Mayfair *(h)*
Kazan: *all branches (hp)*
Ken Lo's Memories *(p)*
Konstam *(h)*
The Landau *(hm)*
Latium *(hp)*
Locanda Locatelli *(hop)*
Marcus Wareing *(hp)*
maze *(h)*
maze Grill *(hm)*
Mildred's *(h)*
Mitsukoshi *(h)*
Moti Mahal *(hp)*
Mrs Marengos *(hp)*
Murano *(hp)*
Nahm *(hm)*
New Mayflower *(h)*
Nobu *(h)*
Nobu Berkeley *(hm)*

INDEXES

Gourmet San *(h)*
The Gun *(hp)*
Hilliard *(p)*
The Hoxton Grille *(hm)*
Kazan: *all branches (hp)*
Lahore Kebab House *(h)*
Lutyens *(hp)*
Mangal Ocakbasi *(m)*
Moro *(h)*
The Narrow *(hp)*
New Tayyabs *(h)*
E Pellicci *(p)*
Prism *(hp)*
Quadrato *(hm)*
The Quality Chop House *(hp)*
Royal China: *all branches (h)*
St John *(h)*
St John Bread & Wine *(hp)*
Smithfield Bar & Grill *(hm)*
Sông Quê *(h)*
Square Pie Company: *all east branches (m)*
Story Deli *(o)*
Stringray Globe Café: *all branches (hm)*
Vinoteca *(p)*
Wapping Food *(h)*
Whitechapel Gallery *(hp)*
Yi-Ban: *E16 (h)*

ENTERTAINMENT
(Check times before you go)

Central
Apsleys
    (jazz brunch, Sun)
Bentley's
    (live piano, Wed-Sat)
Bincho Yakitori
    (DJ, Mon, occasional live music, Wed)
Le Caprice
    (pianist, nightly)
Ciao Bella
    (pianist, nightly)
Fakhreldine
    (bellydancer, Thu-Sat)
Hakkasan
    (DJ, nightly)
Joe Allen
    (pianist, Mon-Sat)
Kai Mayfair
    (harpist & cellist, Tue & Thu)
Levant
    (belly dancer, nightly)
L'Oranger
    (pianist, Fri & Sat)
Pearl
    (pianist, Wed-Sat)
Planet Hollywood
    (DJ, nightly)
Red Fort
    (DJ, Fri & Sat)
The Ritz Restaurant
    (live music, Fri & Sat)
Roka: *W1*
    (DJ, Thu-Sat)

Ronnie Scott's
    (jazz, nightly)
Shanghai Blues
    (live jazz, Fri & Sat)
Simpsons-in-the-Strand
    (pianist, nightly)
Souk Medina
    (belly dancer, Thu-Sat)

West
Belvedere
    (pianist, nightly Sat & Sun all day)
Le Café Anglais
    (magician Sun lunch)
Chutney Mary
    (jazz, Sun L)
The Collection
    (DJ, nightly)
Harwood Arms
    (quiz night, Tue)
Mr Wing
    (jazz, Thu-Sat)
Nozomi
    (DJ, Tue-Sat)
Paradise by Way of Kensal Green
    (live music and burlesque, Tue & Thu; comedy nights, Wed; DJ, Fri-Sun; jazz, Sun)
Pasha
    (belly dancer, nightly; tarot card reader, Wed)
Troubadour
    (live music, most nights)

North
Bull & Last
    (pub quiz, Sun; live band, occasional)
Isarn
    (live music)
Landmark (Winter Gdn)
    (pianist & musicians, daily)
St Pancras Grand
    (live jazz, Sun)
Villiers Terrace
    (DJ, Fri & Sat)

South
The Gowlett
    (DJ, Sun; Lucky 7s, Thu)
Roast
    (jazz, Sun)
Santa Maria del Sur
    (live music, Mon)
Tentazioni
    (various, monthly)

East
Bel Canto
    (opera singers & pianists)
Café du Marché
    (pianist & bass, Mon-Thu, pianist, Fri & Sat)
Cinnamon Kitchen
    (DJ, occasionally)
Coq d'Argent
    (jazz Sun L)
The Drunken Monkey
    (DJ, Wed-Sun)

INDEXES

The Hoxton Grille
  (DJ, Thu-Sat)
Kazan: *EC3*
  (Turkish night, occasional)
LMNT
  (opera, Sun)
Prism
  (circus acts and DJ, Fri)
Smithfield Bar & Grill
  (live music, Thu & Fri)
Yi-Ban: *E16*
  (live music, Fri & Sat)

LATE
(open till midnight or later as shown; may be earlier Sunday)

Central
Asia de Cuba *(midnight, Thu-Sat 12.30 am)*
Automat
Bar Italia *(open 24 hours, Sun 3 am)*
Bentley's
Le Caprice
Cecconi's *(1am, Sun midnight)*
Cyprus Mangal *(Sun-Thu midnight, Fri & Sat 1 am)*
Fakhreldine
Hakkasan *(Thu-Sat 12.30 am)*
Haozhan *(Fri & Sat midnight)*
Harbour City *(Fri & Sat midnight)*
Ibérica
Inamo
The Ivy
Joe Allen *(12.45 am, not Sun)*
Moti Mahal
Mr Chow
New Mayflower *(4 am)*
Nobu Berkeley *(Thu-Sat 12.45 am)*
Planet Hollywood *(1 am, Sun 12.30 am)*
Princi
Ronnie Scott's *(3 am, Sun midnight)*
J Sheekey
J Sheekey Oyster Bar
Souk Medina
The Wolseley

West
Anarkali
Beirut Express: *SW7; W2 (2 am)*
Brilliant *(Fri & Sat midnight)*
The Collection
High Road Brasserie *(Fri & Sat midnight)*
Mirch Masala: *UB1*
Mr Wing
North China *(Fri & Sat midnight)*
Pasha *(midnight, Thu-Sat 1 am)*
Shilpa *(Thu-Sat midnight)*

North
Landmark (Winter Gdn) *(1 am)*
Le Mercury *(1 am, not Sun)*
Vrisaki

South
The Duke's Head *(Fri & Sat midnight)*
Mirch Masala: *all south branches*
Sands End
Sree Krishna *(Fri & Sat midnight)*
Vijaya Krishna *(Fri & Sat midnight)*

East
Brick Lane Beigel Bake *(24 hours)*
Cellar Gascon
Clifton *(midnight, Sat & Sun 1am)*
The Drunken Monkey
Lahore Kebab House
Lutyens
Mangal Ocakbasi

OUTSIDE TABLES
(* particularly recommended)

Central
Andrew Edmunds
aqua kyoto
Archipelago
Atari-Ya: *W1*
L'Autre Pied
Back to Basics
Bam-Bou
Bar Italia
Barrafina
Bentley's
Bincho Yakitori
Boudin Blanc
Busaba Eathai: *WC1*
Caraffini
Cecconi's
Chisou
Ciao Bella
Dehesa
The Duke of Wellington
Golden Hind
Goodman
Gordon's Wine Bar*
Great Queen Street
Hellenik
Ishbilia
Jenny Lo's Tea House
Kazan: *SW1*
Levant
Maison Bertaux
Olivomare
L'Oranger
Orrery
Osteria Dell'Angolo
The Park
La Petite Maison
La Poule au Pot
The Ritz Restaurant
Roka: *W1*
Salt Yard
Santini
Sardo
Scott's
Suka
The Thomas Cubitt
Toto's
Yalla Yalla

PRIVATE ROOMS

**(for the most comprehensive
listing of venues for functions –
from palaces to pubs – visit
www.hardens.com/party, or buy
*Harden's London Party, Event &
Conference Guide*, available in all
good bookshops)
* particularly recommended**

INDEXES

ROMANTIC

Archipelago
Bam-Bou
Boudin Blanc
Le Caprice
Cecconi's
Le Cercle
Chor Bizarre
Clos Maggiore
Corrigan's Mayfair
Crazy Bear
Galvin at Windows
Le Gavroche
Gordon Ramsay at Claridge's
Gordon's Wine Bar
Hakkasan
The Ivy
Levant
Locanda Locatelli
Marcus Wareing
Odin's
L'Oranger
Orrery
Pied à Terre
La Poule au Pot
The Ritz Restaurant
Roussillon
Rules
J Sheekey
Souk Medina
Toto's
Vanilla
The Wolseley

West
Assaggi
Belvedere
Bibendum
Blakes
Blue Elephant
Le Colombier
E&O
Eight Over Eight
Ffiona's
Julie's
The Ledbury
Maggie Jones's
Mr Wing
Paradise by Way of Kensal
   Green
Pasha
Patio
Pissarro's
Racine
The River Café
Star of India
La Trompette
Zuma

North
Anglo Asian Tandoori
L'Aventure
The Engineer
Fig
The Flask
Le Mercury
Oslo Court

South
A Cena
Brula
Champor-Champor
Chez Bruce
Enoteca Turi
Four O Nine
The Glasshouse
Lobster Pot
Petersham Nurseries
Upstairs Bar

East
Bleeding Heart
Café du Marché
Club Gascon
LMNT
Moro
Soseki
Les Trois Garçons
Wapping Food

ROOMS WITH A VIEW

Central
Fakhreldine
Foliage
Galvin at Windows
The Park
The Portrait

West
Belvedere
Min Jiang
Pissarro's

South
The Duke's Head
Oxo Tower (Rest')
Tate Modern (Level 7)
Upstairs Bar

East
Coq d'Argent
The Gun
The Narrow
Rhodes 24
Yi-Ban: *E16*

NOTABLE WINE LISTS

Central
Andrew Edmunds
Arbutus
Le Cercle
Clos Maggiore
Dehesa
Fino
Foliage
Fortnum's, The Fountain
La Fromagerie Café
Galvin Bistrot de Luxe
Le Gavroche
Gordon Ramsay at Claridge's

LONDON MAPS

MAP 1 - WEST END OVERVIEW

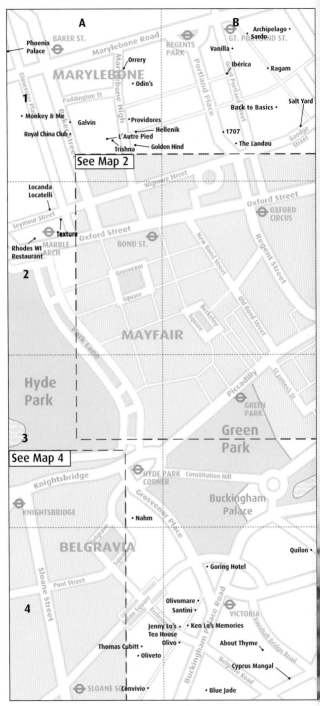

MAP 1 - WEST END OVERVIEW

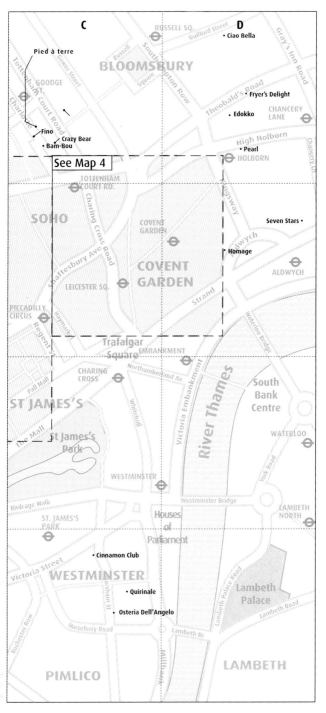

MAP 2 - MAYFAIR, ST JAMES'S & WEST SOHO

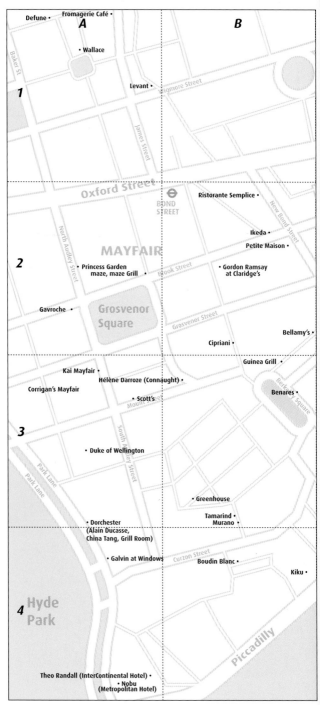

MAP 2 - MAYFAIR, ST JAMES'S & WEST SOHO

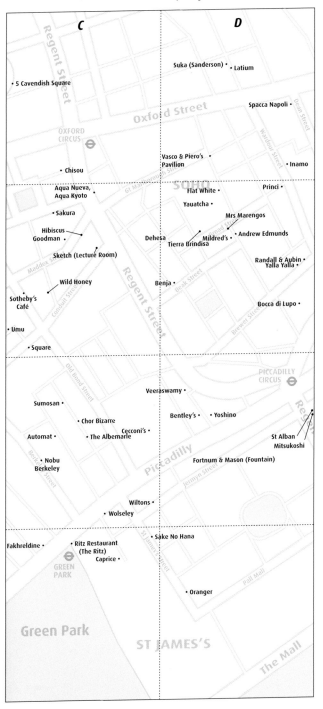

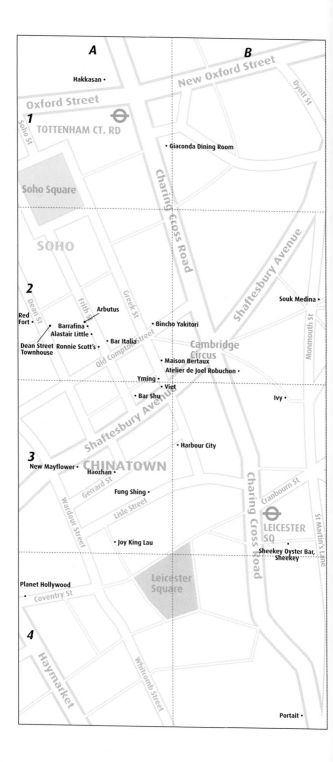

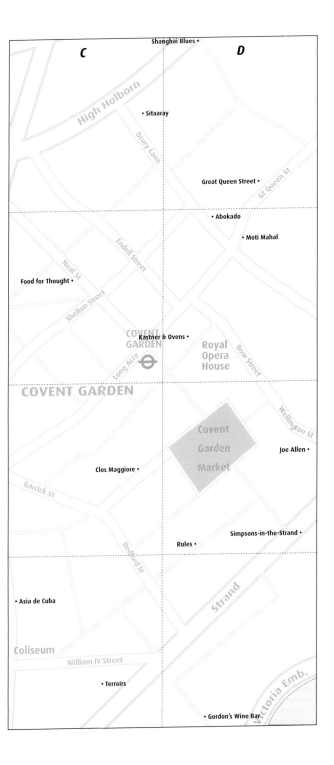

C

D

Shanghai Blues •

High Holborn

• Sitaaray

Drury Lane

Great Queen Street •

Gt Queen St

• Abokado

• Moti Mahal

Endell Street

Neal St

Food for Thought •

Shelton Street

COVENT
GARDEN   Kastner & Ovens •

Royal
Opera
House

Long Acre

Bow Street

COVENT GARDEN

Wellington St

Covent

Garden

Market

Joe Allen •

Clos Maggiore •

Garrick St

Bedford St

Simpsons-in-the-Strand •

Rules •

• Asia de Cuba

Strand

Coliseum

William IV Street

• Terroirs

Victoria Emb.

• Gordon's Wine Bar

MAP 4 - KNIGHTSBRIDGE, CHELSEA & SOUTH KENSINGTON

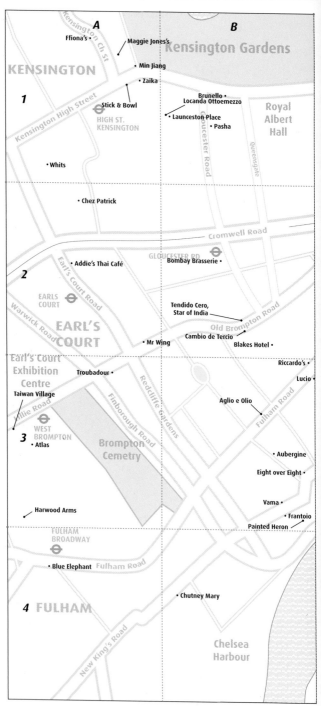

A

B

Ffiona's •

Maggie Jones's •

Kensington Ch St

Kensington Gardens

• Min Jiang

KENSINGTON

• Zaika

1

Brunello •
Locanda Ottoemezzo

Royal
Albert
Hall

Stick & Bowl •

**HIGH ST.
KENSINGTON**

• Launceston Place

• Pasha

Kensington High Street

Gloucester Road

Queensgate

• Whits

• Chez Patrick

Cromwell Road

GLOUCESTER RD

2

• Addie's Thai Café

Bombay Brasserie •

Earl's Court Road

**EARLS
COURT**

Warwick Road

**EARL'S
COURT**

Tendido Cero,
Star of India

Old Brompton Road

• Mr Wing

Cambio de Tercio •

Blakes Hotel •

**Earl's Court
Exhibition
Centre**

Troubadour •

Riccardo's •

Lucio •

Fulham Road

Taiwan Village

Lillie Road

Finborough Road

Redcliffe Gardens

Aglio e Olio •

**WEST
BROMPTON**

3

• Atlas

**Brompton
Cemetery**

• Aubergine

Eight over Eight •

Vama •

• Frantoio

Harwood Arms

Painted Heron •

**FULHAM
BROADWAY**

• Blue Elephant   Fulham Road

4 FULHAM

• Chutney Mary

New King's Road

**Chelsea
Harbour**

MAP 4 - KNIGHTSBRIDGE, CHELSEA & SOUTH KENSINGTON

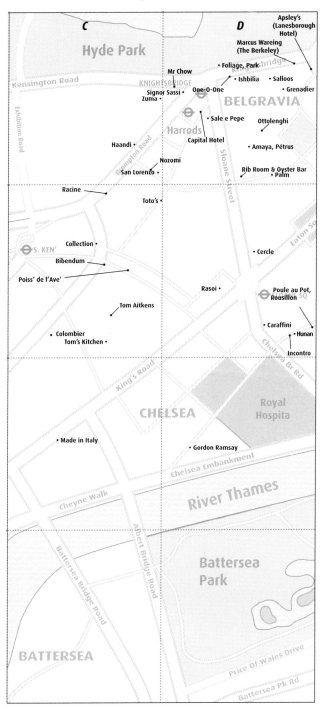

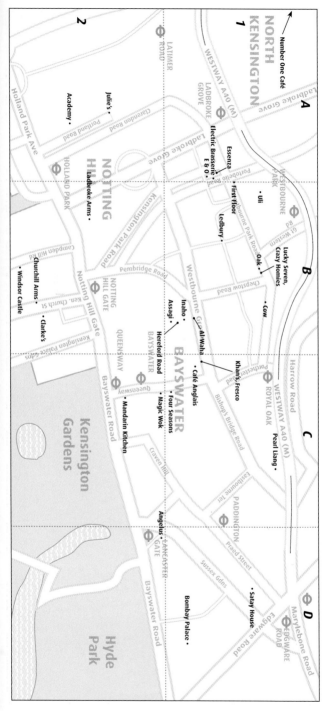

MAP 5 – NOTTING HILL & BAYSWATER

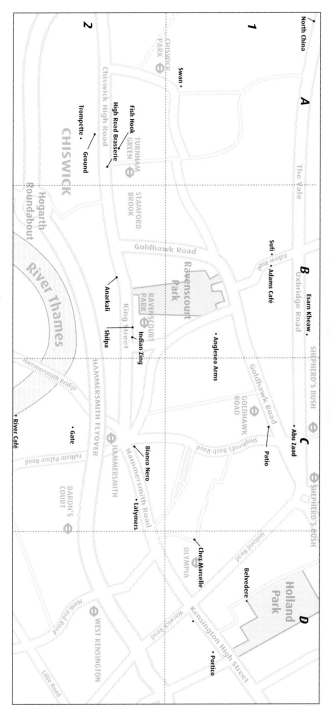

MAP 6 - HAMMERSMITH & CHISWICK

North China

CHISWICK PARK

Swan

The Vale

Esarn Kheaw

Uxbridge Road

SHEPHERD'S BUSH

Chiswick High Road

TURNHAM GREEN

Fish Hook

High Road Brasserie

Trompette

Ground

CHISWICK

STAMFORD BROOK

Hogarth Roundabout

River Thames

Goldhawk Road

Sufi

Adams Café

Askew Road

Ravenscourt Park

RAVENSCOURT PARK

Anarkali

Shilpa

King Street

Indian Zing

Anglesea Arms

Goldhawk Road

GOLDHAWK ROAD

Abu Zaad

Patio

Shepherd's Bush Road

Hammersmith Bridge

HAMMERSMITH FLYOVER

Gate

Bianco Nero

HAMMERSMITH

Hammersmith Road

Fulham Palace Road

River Café

Latymers

BARON'S COURT

Chez Marcelle

OLYMPIA

Belvedere

Holland Park

North End Road

WEST KENSINGTON

Lillie Road

Kensington High Street

Holland Road

SHEPHERD'S BUSH

Kharia Road

Portico

A

B

C

D

1

2

UK SURVEY RESULTS
& TOP SCORERS

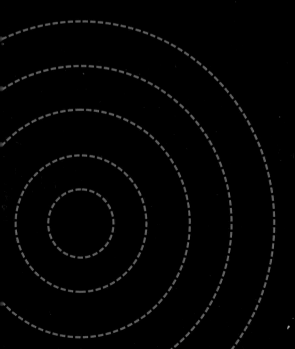

PLACES PEOPLE TALK ABOUT

These are the restaurants outside London that were mentioned most frequently by reporters (last year's position is shown in brackets). For the list of London's most mentioned restaurants, see page 34.

1	Fat Duck (1)	
	Bray, Berks	
2	Manoir aux Quat' Saisons (2)	
	Great Milton, Oxon	
3	Waterside Inn (3)	
	Bray, Berks	
4	Hind's Head (4)	
	Bray, Berks	
5	Seafood Restaurant (6=)	
	Padstow, Cornwall	

Waterside Inn

6	Yang Sing (6)	
	Manchester	
7	Star Inn (13=)	
	Harome, N Yorks	
8	Magpie (10)	
	Whitby, N Yorks	
9	Chapter One (6)	
	Locksbottom, Kent	
10	Northcote (19=)	
	Langho, Lancs	

Star Inn

11	Terre à Terre (13=)	
	Brighton	
12	Vineyard/Stockcross (9)	
	Stockcross, Berkshire	
13	Gidleigh Park (–)	
	Chagford, Devon	
14	Champignon Sauvage (13=)	
	Cheltenham, Gloucs	
15	Rick Stein's Café (18)	
	Padstow, Cornwall	

Terre à Terre

16=	Anthony's (8)	
	Leeds	
16=	Olive Branch (17)	
	Clipsham, Rutland	
18	Three Fishes	
	Whalley, Lancs	
19=	Hambleton Hall (-)	
	Hambleton, Rutland	
19=	Hand & Flowers (11)	
	Marlow, Bucks	
19=	The Company Shed (–)	
	West Mersea, Essex	

Three Fishes

TOP SCORERS

All restaurants whose food rating is ○○; plus restaurants whose price is £50+ with a food rating of ○.

£120+	Le Manoir aux Quat' Saisons *(Great Milton)*	○○Ⓐ
	Waterside Inn *(Bray)*	○○Ⓐ
£110+	The Fat Duck *(Bray)*	○○
£100+	Gidleigh Park *(Chagford)*	○○Ⓐ
	Andrew Fairlie *(Auchterarder)*	○
£90+	Dining Room *(Easton Gray)*	○
	Restaurant Sat Bains *(Nottingham)*	○
£80+	Hambleton Hall *(Hambleton)*	○○Ⓐ
	Lucknam Park *(Colerne)*	○○Ⓐ
	Bybrook Restaurant *(Castle Combe)*	○○
	The Dower House *(Bath)*	○○Ⓐ
	The Oak Room *(Marlow)*	○○Ⓐ
	The White Room *(Seaham)*	○○Ⓐ
	Colette's *(Chandler's Cross)*	○
	Midsummer House *(Cambridge)*	○
	Restaurant Martin Wishart *(Edinburgh)*	○
£70+	Restaurant Nathan Outlaw *(Fowey)*	○○Ⓐ
	Terrace *(Taplow)*	○○Ⓐ
	Yorke Arms *(Ramsgill-in-Nidderdale)*	○○Ⓐ
	Bohemia *(Jersey)*	○○
	La Bécasse *(Ludlow)*	○○
	Number One *(Edinburgh)*	○○
	The Kitchin *(Edinburgh)*	○○
	Ardeonaig Hotel & Restaurant *(Killin)*	○○Ⓐ
	Kinloch Lodge *(Sleat)*	○○Ⓐ
	Sharrow Bay *(Ullswater)*	○○Ⓐ
	The French Horn *(Sonning-on-Thames)*	○○Ⓐ
	Harry's Place *(Great Gonerby)*	○
	L'Enclume *(Cartmel)*	○
	Seafood Restaurant *(Padstow)*	○
	Summer Lodge *(Evershot)*	○
	The Devonshire Arms *(Bolton Abbey)*	○
	The Old Vicarage *(Ridgeway)*	○
£60+	Airds Hotel *(Port Appin)*	○○Ⓐ
	Hipping Hall *(Kirkby Lonsdale)*	○○Ⓐ
	Knockinaam Lodge *(Portpatrick)*	○○Ⓐ
	Monachyle Mhor *(Balquhidder)*	○○Ⓐ
	Mr Underhill's *(Ludlow)*	○○Ⓐ
	Northcote *(Langho)*	○○Ⓐ
	The Albannach *(Lochinver)*	○○Ⓐ
	The Three Chimneys *(Dunvegan)*	○○Ⓐ
	Tyddyn Llan *(Llandrillo)*	○○Ⓐ
	Abstract *(Inverness)*	○○

TOP SCORERS

Drakes *(Ripley)*	✪✪
Holbeck Ghyll *(Windermere)*	✪✪
Le Champignon Sauvage *(Cheltenham)*	✪✪
Purnells *(Birmingham)*	✪✪
Turners *(Birmingham)*	✪✪
Bailiffscourt Hotel *(Climping)*	✪Ⓐ
Darroch Learg *(Ballater)*	✪Ⓐ
Gilpin Lodge *(Windermere)*	✪Ⓐ
Linthwaite House *(Windermere)*	✪Ⓐ
Llangoed Hall *(Llyswen)*	✪Ⓐ
Newick Park *(Newick)*	✪Ⓐ
Read's *(Faversham)*	✪Ⓐ
Rhubarb *(Edinburgh)*	✪Ⓐ
Samuel's *(Masham)*	✪Ⓐ
Seafood Restaurant *(St Andrews)*	✪Ⓐ
Simpsons *(Birmingham)*	✪Ⓐ
Summer Isles Hotel *(Achiltibuie)*	✪Ⓐ
The Cross *(Kingussie)*	✪Ⓐ
Thornbury Castle *(Thornbury)*	✪Ⓐ
36 on the Quay *(Emsworth)*	✪
Abstract *(Edinburgh)*	✪
Anthony's *(Leeds)*	✪
Deanes *(Belfast)*	✪
Horn of Plenty *(Gulworthy)*	✪
Mallory Court *(Bishops Tachbrook)*	✪
Michael Caines *(Exeter)*	✪
Ramsons *(Ramsbottom)*	✪
Simon Radley *(Chester)*	✪
The Crown at Whitebrook *(Whitebrook)*	✪
The Hambrough *(Ventnor)*	✪
The Harrow at Little Bedwyn *(Marlborough)*	✪
Underscar Manor *(Applethwaite)*	✪
West Stoke House *(Chichester)*	✪

£50+	Plas Bodegroes *(Pwllheli)*	✪✪Ⓐ
	The Cellar *(Anstruther)*	✪✪Ⓐ
	The Fish House *(Chilgrove)*	✪✪Ⓐ
	The Peat Inn *(Cupar)*	✪✪Ⓐ
	The Star Inn *(Harome)*	✪✪Ⓐ
	Braidwoods *(Dalry)*	✪✪
	Fraiche *(Oxton)*	✪✪
	Gamba *(Glasgow)*	✪✪
	Gourmet Spot *(Durham)*	✪✪
	Le Poussin at Whitley Ridge *(Brockenhurst)*	✪✪
	Ostlers Close *(Cupar)*	✪✪
	Black Bull *(Moulton)*	✪Ⓐ
	Brummells *(Norwich)*	✪Ⓐ
	By Appointment *(Norwich)*	✪Ⓐ
	Crab & Lobster *(Asenby)*	✪Ⓐ
	Driftwood *(Rosevine)*	✪Ⓐ
	Estbek House *(Sandsend)*	✪Ⓐ
	Gaucho *(Manchester)*	✪Ⓐ

TOP SCORERS

	Gravetye Manor *(East Grinstead)*	✪Ⓐ
	Hartwell House *(Aylesbury)*	✪Ⓐ
	Hassop Hall *(Bakewell)*	✪Ⓐ
	Hix Oyster and Fish House *(Lyme Regis)*	✪Ⓐ
	Hotel Tresanton *(St Mawes)*	✪Ⓐ
	Lavender House *(Brundall)*	✪Ⓐ
	Little Barwick House *(Barwick)*	✪Ⓐ
	Riverside Brasserie *(Bray)*	✪Ⓐ
	Rookery Hall Hotel & Spa *(Nantwich)*	✪Ⓐ
	Smiths Brasserie *(Ongar)*	✪Ⓐ
	St Helena *(Elstow)*	✪Ⓐ
	The Castle Hotel *(Taunton)*	✪Ⓐ
	The Loft Restaurant *(Beaumaris)*	✪Ⓐ
	Vintners Rooms *(Edinburgh)*	✪Ⓐ
	22 Mill Street *(Chagford)*	✪
	5 North Street *(Winchcombe)*	✪
	Allium *(Fairford)*	✪
	Bosquet *(Kenilworth)*	✪
	Brockencote Hall *(Chaddesley Corbett)*	✪
	Chino Latino *(Nottingham)*	✪
	Edmunds *(Birmingham)*	✪
	Fairyhill *(Reynoldston)*	✪
	La Potinière *(Gullane)*	✪
	Lanterna *(Scarborough)*	✪
	Moss Nook *(Manchester)*	✪
	Ode *(Shaldon)*	✪
	Percy's *(Virginstow)*	✪
	Restaurant Gilmore *(Uttoxeter)*	✪
	Royal Oak *(White Waltham)*	✪
	Sienna *(Dorchester)*	✪
	The Dining Room *(Ashbourne)*	✪
	The Neptune *(Old Hunstanton)*	✪
	The Old Passage Inn *(Arlingham)*	✪
	The Olive Tree *(Bath)*	✪
	The Plough Wavendon *(Wavendon)*	✪
	The Seafood Restaurant *(St Monans)*	✪
	The Vanilla Pod *(Marlow)*	✪
	The Weavers Shed *(Golcar)*	✪
	The Well House *(St Keyne)*	✪
	Three Lions *(Stuckton)*	✪
	Tony Tobin @ The Dining Room *(Reigate)*	✪
	Vatika *(Southampton)*	✪
£40+	Ee-Usk (Seafood Restaurant) *(Oban)*	✪✪Ⓐ
	Great House *(Lavenham)*	✪✪Ⓐ
	Llys Meddyg *(Newport)*	✪✪Ⓐ
	Porthminster Café *(St Ives)*	✪✪Ⓐ
	Stagg Inn *(Titley)*	✪✪Ⓐ
	The Wheatsheaf *(Bath)*	✪✪Ⓐ
	Trawlers *(East Looe)*	✪✪Ⓐ
	Apicius *(Cranbrook)*	✪✪
	Chapter One *(Locksbottom)*	✪✪

TOP SCORERS

	Choice *(Manchester)*	✪✪
	Crab & Winkle *(Whitstable)*	✪✪
	Culinaria *(Bristol)*	✪✪
	Ginger *(Belfast)*	✪✪
	Gingerman *(Brighton)*	✪✪
	Goodfellows *(Wells)*	✪✪
	J Baker's Bistro Moderne *(York)*	✪✪
	Maliks *(Cookham)*	✪✪
	Plumed Horse *(Edinburgh)*	✪✪
	Sportsman *(Whitstable)*	✪✪
	Terre à Terre *(Brighton)*	✪✪
	The Dining Room *(Rawtenstall)*	✪✪
	The Hind's Head *(Bray)*	✪✪
	The Marquis *(Alkham)*	✪✪
	The Walnut Tree *(Abergavenny)*	✪✪
	Vine Leaf *(St Andrews)*	✪✪
	Wedgwood *(Edinburgh)*	✪✪
	West House *(Biddenden)*	✪✪
	Wing's *(Manchester)*	✪✪
£30+	Barley Bree *(Muthill)*	✪✪Ⓐ
	Cafe Tabou *(Perth)*	✪✪Ⓐ
	Langmans *(Callington)*	✪✪Ⓐ
	Michael's *(Southport)*	✪✪Ⓐ
	Quince & Medlar *(Cockermouth)*	✪✪Ⓐ
	The Malt Shovel *(Brearton)*	✪✪Ⓐ
	Baipo *(Ipswich)*	✪✪
	Cafe Maitreya *(Bristol)*	✪✪
	Dusit *(Edinburgh)*	✪✪
	Food by Breda Murphy *(Whalley)*	✪✪
	Lian *(Witham)*	✪✪
	Mother India *(Glasgow)*	✪✪
	Roti *(Edinburgh)*	✪✪
	The Old Deanery *(Ripon)*	✪✪
	The Ship Inn *(Ipswich)*	✪✪
	The Three Mariners *(Oare)*	✪✪
	Wheeler's Oyster Bar *(Whitstable)*	✪✪
£25+	Aagrah *(Bradford)*	✪✪Ⓐ
	Aagrah *(Leeds)*	✪✪Ⓐ
	Aagrah *(Shipley)*	✪✪
	Hansa's *(Leeds)*	✪✪
	Magpie Café *(Whitby)*	✪✪
	Punjab Tandoori *(Manchester)*	✪✪
£20+	Anstruther Fish Bar *(Anstruther)*	✪✪
	Mumtaz Paan House *(Bradford)*	✪✪
£15+	Kashmir Curry Centre *(Sheffield)*	✪✪
	The Company Shed *(West Mersea)*	✪✪
£10+	This & That *(Manchester)*	✪✪

ABBOTS LANGLEY, HERTFORDSHIRE 3–2A

Pin Wei £ 20
35 High St WD5 0AA (01923) 268028
In a town with seemingly little to offer the traveller, this bright and spacious pan-Asian establishment is our top tip; not all reporters, though, are convinced that standards are being maintained.
/ **Details:** www.pinwei.co.uk.

ABERAERON, CEREDIGION 4–3C

Harbourmaster £ 40
Quay Pde SA46 0BA (01545) 570755
"Superb locally-sourced seafood and a fabulous location" have made a very big name for the dining options at this harbourside hotel; expansion doesn't seem to have done much for the atmosphere though, and there are also somewhat unsettled reports on the cuisine.
/ **Details:** www.harbour-master.com; 9 pm; no Amex. **Accommodation:** 13 rooms, from £100.

ABERDEEN, ABERDEENSHIRE 9–2D

Cafe 52 £ 34
52 The Green AB11 6PE (01224) 590094
A "cheap and cheerful" spot, tipped for "locally-sourced seasonal food prepared with imagination"; in the transition year to a new chef, however, reports were a little variable. / **Details:** www.cafe52.net; 9.30 pm; closed Sun D; no Amex.

Cafe Boheme £ 38
23 Windmill Brae AB11 6HU (01224) 210677
A small, candle-lit dining room, tipped for "good and reliable French cooking, well presented and well served".
/ **Details:** www.cafebohemerestaurant.co.uk; 9 pm; closed Mon & Sun; no Amex.

Carmelite
Carmelite Hotel £ 34
Stirling St AB11 6JU (01224) 589101
A city-centre hotel dining room, consistently tipped by reporters as an all-round-impressive destination. / **Details:** 10 pm. **Accommodation:** 50 rooms, from £75.

Cinnamon £ 46
476 Union St AB10 1TS (01224) 633328
It's sometimes tipped for its "tireless innovation", but there's also a feeling among reporters that this locally prominent Indian is somewhat "over-hyped". / **Details:** www.cinnamon-aberdeen.com; midnight.

Howies £ 34
50 Chapel St AB10 1SN (01224) 639500
A "cosy" bistro which extends a "very warm welcome on a cold Aberdeen night"; for the quality of the food, it's "priced very reasonably" too. / **Details:** www.howies.uk.com; 10 pm.

Silver Darling £ 62

Pocra Quay, North Pier AB11 5DQ   (01224) 576229

You get "surprisingly good food in an unlikely dockland setting" at this former lighthouse – the city's grandest restaurant; it's fish-based cuisine can be "a little inconsistent", but at best it's "impeccable".
/ **Details:** www.silverdarlingrestaurant.co.uk; beside harbour master's tower; 9 pm; closed Sat L & Sun; children: +16 after 8 pm.

ABERFORD, WEST YORKSHIRE 5–1C

Swan Hotel £ 27

Great North Rd LS25 3AA   (0113) 281 3205

It's no foodie haunt, but this 16th-century coaching inn is tipped as a "safe haven" in these parts – a "smashing" carvery is the lead attraction (but beware "long waits"). / **Details:** www.theswanaberford.co.uk; 10 pm, Sun 9.30 pm; D only, ex Sun open L & D; no Amex; book only for restaurant.

ABERGAVENNY, MONMOUTHSHIRE 2–1A

Angel Hotel £ 42

15 Cross St NP7 5EN   (01873) 857121

Of note for being under the same ownership as the famous Walnut Tree, this town-centre hotel attracts rather less consistent reports; the food, though, is generally "good" (with afternoon tea coming highly recommended). / **Details:** www.angelhotelabergavenny.com; 10 pm.
Accommodation: 32 rooms, from £85.

The Bayleaf £ 23

7 Market St NP7 5SD   (01873) 851212

Not many good Indians in these parts, so those with curry cravings may wish to seek out this "friendly" rural eatery tipped – including by a South London reporter, who ought to know! – for good standards of the "usual staples", and "some more unusual dishes too". / **Details:** www.the-bayleaf.co.uk; 11pm, Fri & Sat midnight; D only.

Clytha Arms £ 41

NP7 9BW   (01873) 840206

A "wide choice" of "adventurous dishes" makes this "relaxed" inn quite a local destination; the décor, however, "may be in need of a re-think". / **Details:** www.clytha-arms.com; on Old Abergavenny to Raglan Rd; 9.30 pm; closed Mon L & Sun D. **Accommodation:** 4 rooms, from £80.

The Hardwick £ 44

Old Raglan Rd NP7 9AA   (01873) 854220

"Beautifully crafted food" – "far above gastro-standards" – comes "with a home-style touch" at Stephen Terry's "informal" inn; it is not only with reporters that it is hugely popular, and an extension was completed shortly before this guide went to press.
/ **Details:** www.thehardwick.co.uk; 10 pm; closed Mon & Sun D; no Amex.

The Walnut Tree   £ 48
Llandewi Skirrid NP7 8AW   (01873) 852797

*Shaun Hill has achieved a special mix of "astonishing value" and
"outstanding cooking" at this brilliantly revitalised Welsh institution;
his "unusual" and "imaginative" use of "modest" ingredients is a big
hit with reporters, and service is "friendly" and "informed" too.
/ **Details:** www.thewalnuttreeinn.com; 3m NE of Abergavenny on B4521; 10 pm;
closed Mon & Sun.* **Accommodation:** *2 rooms, from £160.*

ABERYSTWYTH, POWYS   4–3C

Gwesty Cymru   £ 39
19 Marine Ter SY23 2AZ   (01970) 612252
*"Astonishingly good food for Aberystwyth!" – the restaurant at this
five-star guesthouse impresses all reporters with its "fresh" and
"inventive" locally-sourced cuisine (and "very reasonable prices too").
/ **Details:** www.gwestycymru.com; 9 pm; closed Tue L; no Amex.*
Accommodation: *8 rooms, from £85.*

Ultracomida   £ 31
31 Pier St SY23 2LN   (01970) 630686
*"Lunches only, but excellent"; this two-year-old town-centre bar
is tipped for its "good-size" tapas, and its "reasonable prices".
/ **Details:** www.ultracomida.com; 9 pm; closed Mon D, Tue D, Wed D, Thu D,
Sat D & Sun.*

ABINGDON, OXFORDSHIRE   2–2D

Limoncello   £ 25
13 Ock St OX14 5AL   (01235) 530900
*Tipped for its "above-average" Southern Italian fare, a much-muralled
restaurant, where the staff "really make you feel at home".
/ **Details:** www.limoncello-restaurant.co.uk.*

ABINGER HAMMER, SURREY   3–3A

Drakes On The Pond   £ 62
Dorking Rd RH5 6SA   (01306) 731174
*It's not just the "Travelodge-style" décor that makes this village
restaurant rather an odd recipient of a Michelin star – yes, the food
can sometimes be "beautiful", but it can sometimes be "below
expectations" too. / **Details:** www.drakesonthepond.com; 9 pm; closed Mon,
Sat L & Sun; no Amex; no trainers; booking: max 6; children: 8+.*

Summer Isles Hotel £ 67
IV26 2YQ (01854) 622282

*It's not thanks only to the "unique" and "lovely" (and very remote)
location that this waterside hotel has long had a big reputation –
its "simply prepared" food can be "fabulous"; initial reports, however,
suggests some dishes have lacked inventiveness since a recent change
of ownership. / **Details:** www.summerisleshotel.com; 25m N of Ullapool
on A835; 8 pm; no Amex; children: 8+. **Accommodation:** 13 rooms, from £140.*

ACTON TRUSSELL, STAFFORDSHIRE 5–3B

Moat House £ 45
Lower Penkridge Rd ST17 0RJ (01785) 712217
*Tipped as an "atmospheric" destination ("despite its proximity to the
M6"), this an hotel which enjoys "a big local reputation as the
best place to eat". / **Details:** www.thelewispartnership.co.uk; Junction 13 off
the M6, follow signs for A449; 9.30 pm; no jeans. **Accommodation:** 41 rooms,
from £150.*

ADDINGHAM, WEST YORKSHIRE 5–1C

Fleece £ 35
152-4 Main St LS29 0LY (01943) 830491
*Tipped as "exactly what a pub should be" – "a place which does
good food, not a restaurant trying to pretend it's terribly down
to earth"; there's no booking, so "get there early".
/ **Details:** www.thefleeceaddingham.co.uk; 9.15 pm, Sun 8pm.*

ADDINGTON, SURREY 3–3B

Planet Spice £ 30
88 Selsdon Park Rd CR2 8JT (020) 8651 3300
*This colourful dining room is quite a "local favourite", and it attracts
praise from further afield too for its "delicate" and "mouthwatering"
Indian cuisine, from a menu that's "interesting" and "inventive".
/ **Details:** www.planet-spice.com; 11.30 pm.*

ALBOURNE, WEST SUSSEX 3–4B

The Ginger Fox £ 32
Henfield Rd BN6 9EA (01273) 857 888
*A new rural offshoot of Brighton's Gingerman group, offering "above-
average" pub food, and already attracting quite a few reports; it's a
"noisy" place, though, and – in the early days – service has sometimes
tended to "chaotic". / **Details:** www.gingermanrestaurants.com; 10 pm,
Sun 9 pm.*

Aldeburgh Fish And Chips   £ 13   ⭐
225 High St IP16 4BZ   (01728) 454685
A seaside chippy which, insist fans, serves "the best fish 'n' chips in England" – ideally these should be enjoyed "eaten out of the paper sitting on the shingle beach, beside the upturned fishing boats"; beware "long queues". / Details: 8 pm; no credit cards.

The Lighthouse   £ 36
77 High St IP15 5AU   (01728) 453377
A local favourite, this seaside bistro specialising in seafood gains praise for "good fresh fish" which is not "spoilt by heavy sauces"; the atmosphere is "lively" bordering on "very loud", and fans find the experience best when the owner, Peter Hill, is in attendance. / Details: www.thelighthouserestaurant.co.uk; 10 pm; closed one week in Jan and one week in Oct.

152   £ 38
152 High St IP15 5AX   (01728) 454594
In the style of a "simple café", an establishment that's long had quite a name as a dinner-destination too (not least for "fresh fish"); most reporters find the reputation justified, but this year's reports were rather up-and-down, and included some outright disappointments. / Details: www.152aldeburgh.co.uk; 10 pm; closed Tue.

Regatta   £ 33
171-173 High St IP15 5AN   (01728) 452011
An "old-favourite" bistro, which serves "a fine selection of fresh fish"; its "no-pretensions" setting can sometimes get rather "noisy". / Details: www.regattaaldeburgh.com; 10 pm; closed Sun D Nov-Feb.

The Wentworth Hotel   £ 32
Wentworth Rd IP15 5BD   (01728) 452312
*A "classic seaside hotel" tipped for "a good bar menu including good fish 'n' chips washed down with Adnams beer", and "surprisingly good" food in the dining room too. / Details: www.wentworth-aldeburgh.com; 9 pm. **Accommodation:** 35 rooms, from £140.*

The Grosvenor Arms   £ 32   Ⓣ
Chester Rd CH3 6HJ   (01244) 620228
A huge, very handsome inn, tipped as a good all-rounder with a "lovely setting" and beautiful garden; the food is "steady and predictable, though, rather than innovative". / Details: www.grosvenorarms-aldford.co.uk; 6m S of Chester on B5130; 10 pm, Sun 9 pm.

The Marquis   £ 46   ⭐⭐
Alkham Valley Rd CT15 7DF   (01304) 873410
*"A new modern minimalist venue, offering very good food"; the dining room of this recently revamped restaurant-with-rooms may be a bit "stark", but the cooking – from a chef who once cooked at the Star at Harome – is "superb". / Details: www.themarquisatalkham.co.uk; 9.30 pm; closed Mon L & Sun D. **Accommodation:** 5 rooms, from £95.*

Blackmore's £ 35

Bondgate Without NE66 1PN (01665) 602395

Tipped as "a rising local 'in' place", this town-centre spot comprises hotel, brasserie and restaurant; it "caters well for its different markets", but, when downstairs gets "busy", service can suffer.
/ **Details:** www.blackmoresofalnwick.com; 9.30 pm. **Accommodation:** 14 rooms, from £105.

The Tree House
The Alnwick Garden £ 37

Denwick Ln NE66 1YU (01665) 511852

It's the "fantastic" setting – it really is "built around a huge tree!" – that makes this an "outstanding" destination, most obviously for a "well-heeled family day out"; that's not to say that the food isn't "good" – just that it can seem (unsurprisingly) "pricey" for what it is.
/ **Details:** www.alnwickgarden.com; 9.15 pm; closed Mon D, Tue D, Wed D & Sun D; no Amex.

Dilli £ 33

60 Stamford New Rd WA14 1EE (0161) 929 7484

It's still "a cut above the ordinary" (well, Rusholme anyway), but reporters are beginning to feel that this much-hailed suburban subcontinental (based on Ayurvedic principles) is, at least to some extent, "trading on past glories" nowadays. / **Details:** www.dilli.co.uk; on A538; 11 pm, Sun 10 pm.

Amberley Castle £ 85

BN18 9LT (01798) 831992

Tipped for its "exquisite" surroundings, this ancient castle is a "wonderful" destination for a romantic dinner (and the rooms are "lovely" too) – the food at this Von Essen hotel, however, can sometimes seem rather incidental.
/ **Details:** www.amberleycastle.co.uk; N of Arundel on B2139; 9 pm; jacket or tie required; booking: max 8; children: 12+. **Accommodation:** 19 rooms, from £190.

Britannia Inn £ 32

Elterwater LA22 9HP (01539) 437210

"An excellent watering hole for walkers", which is "always busy", thanks to a "hearty" cuisine, which matches up to the "stunning location"; service is "helpful and friendly" too.
/ **Details:** www.britinn.co.uk; 9.30 pm; no Amex; booking: max 6; children: 18+ after 9 pm. **Accommodation:** 9 rooms, from £100.

Drunken Duck £ 49

Barngates LA22 0NG (01539) 436347

Still lots of feedback on this famous Lakeland inn-cum-microbrewery – fans insist that it offers "perfect food, wine and accommodation", but there are also rather too many reports of an "unfriendly" place that's now rather "past its sell-by date".
/ **Details:** www.drunkenduckinn.co.uk; 3m from Ambleside, towards Hawkshead; 9.30 pm; no Amex; no trainers; booking: max 6. **Accommodation:** 17 rooms, from £95.

The Glass House £ 36

Rydal Rd LA22 9AN (01539) 432137

Rather up-and-down commentary on this former mill (which achieved some fame as the subject of one of Gordon Ramsay's TV visits); if you're looking for a "relaxing" sort of place, it's still tipped as offering "the best food in Ambleside".
/ **Details:** www.theglasshouserestaurant.co.uk; behind Little Bridge House; 9.30 pm, Sat 10 pm; no Amex; children: 5+ at D.

Lucy's on a Plate £ 39

Church St LA22 0BU (01539) 431191

Fans still find this "fantastic small bistro" to be a "very friendly" place with "excellent local food", but there's no getting away from the feeling that standards have "deteriorated" as the Lucy's empire has grown over the years – the puddings, however remain notably "excellent". / **Details:** www.lucysofambleside.co.uk; centre of Ambleside; 9 pm.

Rothay Manor £ 51

Rothay Bridge LA22 0EH (01539) 433605

All-round satisfaction is the watchword in reports on this Regency country house hotel (where the proprietor/chef duo collectively have nearly 70 years experience) – a "welcoming" and "comfortable" place, where the cuisine is "beautifully prepared and presented".
/ **Details:** www.rothaymanor.co.uk; 9 pm; no jeans or trainers; no booking, Sat D; children: 7+ at D. **Accommodation:** 19 rooms, from £155.

Zeffirelli's £ 32

Compston Rd LA22 9AD (01539) 433845

An "always-busy" and "buzzy" restaurant attached to a cinema, which serves Italian food that's all-vegetarian (but "doesn't make a song and dance about it"); there's "live jazz" upstairs, or – for a complete evening's entertainment – seek out one of the "cinema meal deals".
/ **Details:** www.zeffirellis.com; 10 pm; no Amex.

AMERSHAM, BUCKINGHAMSHIRE 3–2A

Gilbey's £ 45

1 Market Sq HP7 0DF (01494) 727242

"Efficient and friendly staff" generally figure prominently in reports on this "intimate" local restaurant in Old Amersham, which also attracts praise for its "simple but pleasant" cuisine, and its wine list – the place is, after all, owned by the eponymous gin family.
/ **Details:** www.gilbeygroup.com; in Old Amersham; 9.30 pm, Sat 9.45 pm.

ANDOVER, HAMPSHIRE 2–3D

Jade Cottage £ 22

49 Bridge St SP10 1BG (01264) 324888

The décor may be "a bit dull", but this Thai/Chinese operation is tipped for its "first-rate" cuisine and service.
/ **Details:** www.jadecottage.co.uk; 11 pm.

Anstruther Fish Bar   £ 21   ⭐⭐

42-44 Shore St   KY10 3AQ   (01333) 310518

"The best fish 'n' chips in Scotland" – or arguably even *"the whole of the UK"!* – are to be had in this *"old-fashioned"* harbourside chippy; it even claims to source sustainably.
/ **Details:** www.anstrutherfishbar.co.uk; 10 pm; no Amex; no booking.

The Cellar   £ 57   Ⓐ⭐⭐

24 East Grn   KY10 3AA   (01333) 310378

"Nowhere else comes close", say fans of Peter & Susan Jukes's long-running, cave-like venture near the harbour, which offers *"superlative cooking of fish straight out of the sea"*; if there is a reservation, it is that the establishment (est. 1982) is now arguably a little settled in its ways. / **Details:** www.cellaranstruther.co.uk; in the harbour area; 9 pm; closed Mon & Sun.

Applecross Inn   £ 31   ⭐

Shore St   IV54 8LT   (01520) 744262

A remote and *"spectacularly-located"* inn, where *"fabulous fresh seafood"* is served *"with minimal fuss"*, and at *"great prices"* too.
/ **Details:** www.applecross.uk.com; off A896, S of Shieldaig; 9 pm; no Amex; need 4+ to book. **Accommodation:** 7 rooms, from £100.

Underscar Manor   £ 67   ⭐

CA12 4PH   (01768) 775000

"It's better than Sharrow Bay!", say fans; this *"wonderfully staid"* but *"reliable"* country house hotel offers food – and service too – that's most definitely *"out of the top drawer"*; lake views here, though, are only distant. / **Details:** www.underscarmanor.co.uk; on A66, 17m W of M6, J40; 8.30 pm; no Amex; no jeans or trainers; children: 12+. **Accommodation:** 11 rooms, from £190.

ARLINGHAM, GLOUCESTERSHIRE 2–2B

The Old Passage Inn £ 52

Passage Rd GL2 7JR (01452) 740547

"Terrific seafood in a beautiful setting by the River Severn" – the new régime is making a real hit of this *"hidden gem"* of a restaurant, where the terrace makes a *"perfect place to eat on a sunny day"*.
/ **Details:** www.theoldpassage.com; 9.30 pm; closed Mon & Sun D.
Accommodation: 3 rooms, from £95.

ARUNDEL, WEST SUSSEX 3–4A

Arundel House £ 40

11 High St BN18 9AD (01903) 882136

A restaurant-with-rooms, in the shadow of the castle, which is praised with impressive consistency for its "warm welcome" and its "good cooking at reasonable prices"; there's a "great wine list" too, offering "something for everyone". / **Details:** www.arundelhouseonline.com; 9.30 pm; closed Sun; children: 12+ D. **Accommodation:** 5 rooms, from £80.

The Town House £ 34

65 High St BN18 9AJ (01903) 883847

A splendid Regency building overlooking Arundel Castle; this "gem" of a restaurant offers "fantastic value for money", with excellent "locally sourced food" and a "wonderful atmosphere" – the "beautiful" dining room even has a (genuine) Venetian ceiling!
/ **Details:** www.thetownhouse.co.uk; 9.30 pm; closed Mon & Sun.
Accommodation: 3 rooms, from £120.

ASCOT, BERKSHIRE 3–3A

Ascot Oriental £ 41

London Rd SL5 0PU (01344) 621877

This is no run-of-the-mill Home Counties oriental – with its "innovative" and "freshly-prepared" Chinese fare, Konrad Liu's establishment is a real cut-above. / **Details:** www.ascotoriental.com; 2m E of Ascot on A329; 10.30 pm.

The Thatched Tavern £ 35

Cheapside Rd SL5 7QG (01344) 620874

"Consistently of a good standard", "interesting" and "good-value" – the dining experience at this "attractive" and "friendly" old pub is praised by all who comment on it.
/ **Details:** www.thethatchedtavern.co.uk; 2m from Ascot, signed to Cheapside village; 9.30 pm.

ASENBY, NORTH YORKSHIRE 8–4C

Crab & Lobster £ 51

Dishforth Rd YO7 3QL (01845) 577286

"Great seafood in quirky, kitsch surroundings with a surreal French vibe to them" – that's the formula that's long made this *"romantic"*, thatched gastropub a top Yorkshire destination for nearly two decades. / **Details:** www.crabandlobster.co.uk; at junction of Asenby Rd & Topcliffe Rd; 9 pm, 9.30 pm Sat. **Accommodation:** 14 rooms, from £150.

ASHBOURNE, DERBYSHIRE 5–3C

The Dining Room £ 53 ⭐
33 St. John's St DE6 1GP (01335) 300666
*A small restaurant whose ambition certainly comes as "a surprise
in rural Derbyshire", and where even critics concede that there's
"considerable ability" in the kitchen; (the fear is also expressed,
though, that the chef can succumb to bouts of "self-indulgence").*
/ **Details:** www.thediningroomashbourne.co.uk; D only, closed Mon & Sun;
no Amex; children: 12+.

ASHBURTON, DEVON 1–3D

Agaric £ 47
30 North St TQ13 7QD (01364) 654478
*"A small, small-town restaurant that's worth a small detour" –
a "lovely" place with "friendly" service, "low" lighting and a "log fire";
the "innovative" food is generally "well cooked" too; also "great
cookery classes".* / **Details:** www.agaricrestaurant.co.uk; 9.30 pm; closed
Mon & Tue, Sat L & Sun D; no Amex. **Accommodation:** 5 rooms, from £110.

ASTON TIRROLD, OXFORDSHIRE 2–2D

Sweet Olive £ 43 ⭐
Baker St OX11 9DD (01235) 851272
*A "welcoming" gastropub that impresses all reporters as a
"good dining experience", thanks not least to its "interesting" Gallic
menu, and its "very fine" wine list too; it can get rather "noisy".*
/ **Details:** www.sweet-olive.com; Half a mile off the A417 between Streatley &
Wantage; 9 pm; closed Feb.

AUCHTERARDER, PERTH & KINROSS 9–3C

Andrew Fairlie 🅷⭐
Gleneagles Hotel £102
PH3 1NF (01764) 694267

*"A dramatic room and all-round experience with inspirational flavours
and cooking", and "perfect" service; it thrills most reporters, but there
are also a few critics who feel that its performance "isn't quite
as memorable as the very high prices demand"; (note, though
"gorgeous", the space has "no windows").*
/ **Details:** www.andrewfairlie.com; 10 pm; L only, closed Sun; children: 12+.
Accommodation: 273 rooms, from £320.

AXMINSTER, DEVON   2–4A

River Cottage Canteen   £ 44
Trinity Sq EX13 5AN   (01297) 631862
*Hugh Fearnley-Whittingstall's "top-drawer" canteen-style operation,
adjacent to his food store, is an "enthusiastic" venture which serves
a "short" menu of "simple", "straightforward" dishes food,
complemented by an "extensive" list of English wines.*
/ **Details:** *www.rivercottage.net; 9.30 pm; closed Mon D & Sun D.*

AYLESBURY, BUCKINGHAMSHIRE   3–2A

Hartwell House   £ 59
Oxford Rd HP17 8NR   (01296) 747444*This "grand country
house" – well, it was good enough for Louis XVI in exile – makes
an "exceptionally pretty" dining, or residential, location (with spa);
all aspects of the operation achieve impressively consistent high
ratings.* / **Details:** *www.hartwell-house.com; 2m W of Aylesbury on A418;
9.45 pm; no jeans or trainers; children: 6+.* **Accommodation:** *49 rooms,
from £280.*

BABINGTON, SOMERSET   2–3B

Babington House   £ 64
BA11 3RW   (01373) 812266

*The fashionable rural outpost of the Soho House group offers "simple
good food at sensible prices", in a "vibrant" country setting, and with
"attentive" service too; to eat, though, you have to stay (which
is generally reckoned a fine overall experience – the 'Cowshed' has
impressive leisure facilities).* / **Details:** *www.babingtonhouse.co.uk; 11 pm;
open to residents & members only; children: 16+ in the Orangery.*
Accommodation: *32 rooms, from £260.*

BAGSHOT, SURREY   3–3A

The Latymer
Pennyhill Park Hotel   £ 86
London Rd GU19 5EU   (01276) 471774
*"Full of frills and fripperies", the style of this "fancy" hotel dining
dining room seems judged to please Michelin (from whom it has now
received its due); the occasional reporter does indeed find the cooking
"excellent", but it can also seem disappointing and overpriced.*
/ **Details:** *www.exclusivehotels.co.uk; 10 pm; closed Mon, Sat L & Sun; booking:
max 8; children: 11.* **Accommodation:** *123 rooms, from £195.*

BAKEWELL, DERBYSHIRE 5–2C

Hassop Hall £ 50
DE45 1NS (01629) 640488
*The Chapman family's "fine and gracious" country house hotel of over
four decades' standing "continues its excellent tradition of quality
cooking", and of "personal" service too.* / **Details:** *www.hassophall.co.uk;
on the B6001 Bakewell - Hathersage Road, Junction 29 of M1; 9 pm; closed
Mon L, Sat L & Sun D.* **Accommodation:** *13 rooms, from £95.*

The Monsal Head Hotel £ 31
DE45 1NL (01629) 640250
*With its "peerless" views, its own pub ('The Stables'), and a restaurant
serving up an "eclectic menu of traditional British staples", this small
Peak District hotel is "highly recommended" by all who comment
on it.* / **Details:** *www.monsalhead.com; Just up from Ashford in the Water on the
B6465; 9.30 pm, Sat & Sun 9 pm; no Amex.* **Accommodation:** *7 rooms,
from £90.*

BALLANTRAE, SOUTH AYRSHIRE 7–2A

Glenapp Castle £ 74
KA26 0NZ (01465) 831212
*Less commentary than we'd like on this "beautiful castle,
and grounds", which is tipped as having an "exciting" young chef
whose cooking is "stylish" and "precise".*
/ **Details:** *www.glenappcastle.com; 9.30 pm; D only; no shorts.*
Accommodation: *17 rooms, from £415.*

BALLATER, ABERDEENSHIRE 9–3C

Darroch Learg £ 60
Braemar Rd AB35 5UX (01339) 755443
*This "superb" and "cosseting" country house hotel, now heading for
half a century in the ownership of the Franks family, is hailed by all
reporters as a "wonderful place to eat, especially for a special
occasion"; the kitchen shows "talent in all areas", and its efforts are
complemented by a "very extensive" wine list.*
/ **Details:** *www.darrochlearg.co.uk; on A93 W of Ballater; 9 pm; D only, ex Sun
open L & D; no Amex.* **Accommodation:** *17 rooms, from £130.*

BALQUHIDDER, PERTHSHIRE 9–3C

Monachyle Mhor £ 60
FK19 8PQ (01877) 384622

*"A faultless dining experience, offering truly exceptional food
in awesome surroundings" – many reports attest to the "stunning"
standards of Tom Lewis's "relaxing" restaurant-with-rooms, which
enjoys a wonderful, remote location with loch views.*
/ **Details:** *www.mhor.net; Take the Kings House turning off the A84; 8.45 pm;
children: 12+ at D.* **Accommodation:** *14 rooms, from £105.*

BANBURY, OXFORDSHIRE 2–1D

Thai Orchid £ 33
56 Northbar St OX16 0TL (01295) 270833
*A handy tip if you're looking for an "ornate" oriental in an area
"without much competition" in such things; reports on the food,
though, range from "fantastic" to "ordinary".*
/ **Details:** www.thaiorchidbanbury.co.uk; 10.30 pm.

BARFRESTON, KENT 3–3D

The Yew Tree £ 30
CT15 7JH (01304) 831000
*"Reliable and intelligent" cooking and "excellent" wine make this
"isolated" inn an all-round crowd-pleaser.* / **Details:** www.yewtree.info;
9 pm; closed Sun D; no Amex.

BARNET, HERTFORDSHIRE 3–2B

Emchai £ 25
78 High St EN5 5SN (020) 8364 9993
*"Interesting, appetising and tasty" oriental fusion fare makes this
"consistently good" spot quite a "gem", and a consistently "buzzy" one
too – don't be put off by the "lousy" location.* / **Details:** 11 pm.

BARNSLEY, GLOUCESTERSHIRE 2–2C

Barnsley House £ 62
GL7 5EE (01285) 740000
*Tipped mainly for its "lovely grounds" (with "romantic corners
in which to dine"), this pricey country house hotel otherwise inspires
little excitement from reporters.* / **Details:** www.barnsleyhouse.com;
9.30 pm, Sat & Sun 10 pm; no Amex. **Accommodation:** 18 rooms, from £295.

BARRASFORD, NORTHUMBERLAND 8–2A

Barrasford Arms £ 34
NE48 4AA (01434) 681237
*An "off-the-beaten-track" country inn where the food "is worth a bit
of a journey" (with the steaks attracting particular praise), and the
service is "relaxed" and "professional" too; the "cosy" bar, though,
is sometimes preferred to the dining room.*
/ **Details:** www.barrasfordarms.co.uk; 9 pm; closed Mon L & Sun D; no Amex.
Accommodation: 7 rooms, from £85.

BARROW, LANCASHIRE 5–1B

Eagle at Barrow £ 26
Clitheroe Rd BB7 9AQ (01254) 825285
*Ex-butcher turned chef Kevin Berkins is making a big name for meat
dishes of "exceptional quality", at his grandly-subdued new gastropub;
all reports are very clear that this is a most "impressive" destination
all-round.*

BARTON-ON-SEA, HAMPSHIRE

2–4C

Pebble Beach £ 44

Marine Drive BH25 7DZ   (01425) 627777

"Superb" is a term applied to both food and service at this clifftop
restaurant, where the "fabulous" terrace (with "views over the water
to the Isle of Wight") is one highlight, and "truly local seafood"
is another; otherwise, however, the experience can seem curiously
"impersonal". / **Details:** www.pebblebeach-uk.com; 9 pm, Fri & Sat 9.30 pm;
booking essential. **Accommodation:** 3 rooms, from £89.95.

BARWICK, SOMERSET

2–3B

Little Barwick House £ 50

BA22 9TD   (01935) 423902

This "superb" country restaurant-with-rooms offers cooking
to challenge "anything in London"; indeed the "consistently good" food
and service have drawn unanimous praise from reporters.
/ **Details:** www.littlebarwick.co.uk; Take the A37 Yeovil to Dorchester road,
turn left at the brown sign for Little Barwick House; 9 Tue-Fri, 9.30 Sat; closed
Mon, Tue L & Sun D; no Amex; children: 5+ D. **Accommodation:** 6 rooms,
from £100.

BASHALL EAVES, LANCASHIRE

5–1B

The Red Pump Inn £ 31

Clitheroe Rd BB7 3DA   (01254) 826227

Tipped for its "particularly good" game dishes, and "well-kept" ales
too – an inn upon which reports are otherwise a little up-and-down.
/ **Details:** www.theredpumpinn.co.uk; 9 pm, Sun 7.30 pm; closed Mon; no Amex.
Accommodation: 3 rooms, from £70.

BASLOW, DERBYSHIRE

5–2C

Cavendish £ 51

Church Ln DE45 1SP   (01246) 582311

It's still tipped as a "very pleasant" destination (especially in the no-
bookings conservatory), but this grand hotel, on the Chatsworth
Estate, has inspired only a rather modest level of feedback of late,
and a little bit mixed too. / **Details:** www.cavendish-hotel.net; J29 of the M1,
follow tourist signs to Chatsworth; 10 pm; no jeans or trainers.
Accommodation: 24 rooms, from £160.

Fischers at Baslow Hall £ 58

Calver Rd DE45 1RR   (01246) 583259

Though still often acclaimed for "interesting" cuisine that's arguably
the "best food in Derbyshire", this well-known country house hotel
risks slipping into a "condescending" and "pretentious" rut, with gripes
about "finicky", "overpriced" cooking and a "snooty" attitude.
/ **Details:** www.fischers-baslowhall.co.uk; on the A623 ; 9 pm; closed Mon L &
Sun D; no jeans or trainers; children: 9+ at D. **Accommodation:** 11 rooms,
from £140.

Rowley's £ 44

Church Ln DE45 1RY   (01246) 583880

"An upmarket brasserie where the food is dusted with a little magic
from its big brother Baslow Hall"; it remains "popular with the locals,
and those travelling through the Derbyshire Dales", but reports in the
year that's seen the transition to a new chef have been somewhat
mixed. / **Details:** www.rowleysrestaurant.co.uk; 9 pm, Fri & Sat 10 pm; closed
Sun D; no Amex.

Pheasant Hotel £ 49

CA13 9YE (01768) 776234

An "elegant" and "old-fashioned" coaching inn nestled in a "beautiful" setting; it's tipped for "the best breakfast in England", and also as "excellent for lunch or morning coffee".
/ **Details:** www.the-pheasant.co.uk; 8.30 pm; no Amex; no jeans or trainers; children: 12+ at D. **Accommodation:** 15 rooms, from £156.

BATH, SOMERSET 2–2B

Is Bath finally looking up? There are some signs that this most beautiful of English cities is finally beginning to offer dining options above the level of a superior tourist trap. At the top end of the market *Dower House* is setting an impressive standard, and there are a couple of noteworthy gastropubs too – the *King William* and also the (less accessible) *Wheatsheaf* and *White Hart Inn*. There's even a good-quality bistro in the heart of the city nowadays, *Circus*. Let's hope it's the beginning of a trend!

Bath Priory Hotel £ 93

Weston Rd BA1 2XT (01225) 331922

Chris Horridge left this "immaculate" country house hotel all-rounder just as our survey for the year was concluding; we do hope that Michael Caines – based at Gidleigh Park, but now nominally also in charge here – can maintain anything like the same standards; in the circumstances, however, a rating seems inappropriate.
/ **Details:** www.thebathpriory.co.uk; 1m W of city centre, past Victoria Park; 9.30 pm; no jeans or trainers; children: 8+ D. **Accommodation:** 27 rooms, from £260.

Casanis £ 36

4 Saville Row BA1 2QP (01225) 780055

An "intimate" Gallic bistro, near the Assembly Rooms, praised for its "unassuming" but "pleasing" style. / **Details:** www.casanis.co.uk; 10.30 pm; closed Mon & Sun; no Amex.

The Circus £ 35

34 Brock St BA1 2LN (01225) 466020

This newcomer between the Royal Crescent and The Circus is hailed as a "rare find" – an "authentic" bistro with an "ever-changing" menu, "delightful" staff, and a "buzzing" atmosphere, and "fairly-priced" too; in this of all cities, can it possibly last?
/ **Details:** www.thecircuscafeandrestaurant.co.uk; 10 pm; closed Sun; no Amex; children: 7+ at D.

Demuths £ 40

2 North Parade Pas BA1 1NX (01225) 446059

Rachel Demuth's vegetarian restaurant, in the heart of the city, has won a big following, thanks to its "inspired" and "tasty" fare that's "always interesting"; open all day. / **Details:** www.demuths.co.uk; 10 pm; no Amex; booking: max 4 at D, Fri & Sat; children: 6+ at D.

The Dower House
Royal Crescent Hotel   **£ 86**
16 Royal Cr BA1 2LS   (01225) 823333
As you'd sort of hope, given the prices, the restaurant to the rear
of this famous hotel (Von Essen) has "the best location in Bath",
and the set-up – "top-notch food in a lovely room overlooking
secluded gardens" – certainly pleases most reporters; it's certainly
no bargain overall, but the "huge" wine list does include some
*relatively inexpensive choices. / **Details:** www.royalcrescent.co.uk; 9.30 pm;*
*no jeans or trainers; booking: max 8. **Accommodation:** 45 rooms, from £235.*

The Eastern Eye   **£ 32**
8a Quiet St BA1 2JS   (01225) 422323
A "consistently buzzy" Indian restaurant, grandly housed in a Georgian
room, tipped for its "superb" curries (and its notably "cosmopolitan"
*following too). / **Details:** www.easterneye.co.uk; 11.30 pm.*

The Garrick's Head   **£ 39**
7-8 St. John's Pl BA1 1ET   (01225) 318368
A town-centre gastropub, tipped for its "great" ("bewildering") wine
selection; the food generally pleases too.
*/ **Details:** www.garricksheadpub.com; 10 pm.*

Hole in the Wall   **£ 36**
16 George St BA1 2EH   (01225) 425242
Perhaps this famous site (home to one of England's seminal post-War
restaurants) is finally getting its act together? – it's not attracted many
reports of late, but all tip the food as "lovely", and service is "happy"
*too. / **Details:** www.theholeinthewall.co.uk; 10 pm, Sun 9.30 pm; closed Sun L.*

Jamie's Italian   **£ 34**
10 Milsom Pl BA1 1BZ   (01225) 510051
"The boy done good" – even cynics have tended to find this
outpost of Jamie O's new mock-rustic Italian chain "better than
expected"; "the hour-long queue", though, "can be a bit frustrating".
*/ **Details:** www.jamiesitalian.com; 11 pm, Sun 10.30 pm.*

Jamuna   **£ 20**
10 Cheap St BA1 1NE   (01225) 464631
Up a flight of stairs, with impressive views of the Abbey, a long
established Indian tipped for curries cooked with "panache".
*/ **Details:** www.jamunabath.co.uk; midnight.*

King William   **£ 38**
36 London Rd BA1 5NN   (01225) 428096
"A quaint gastropub in a rough part of town"; there is the occasional
misfire, but its "old-fashioned favourite dishes with a twist" continue
to make this place, for most reporters, quite a "find".
*/ **Details:** www.kingwilliampub.com; 11 pm, midnight weekends.*

Loch Fyne   **£ 39**
24 Milsom St BA1 1DG   (01225) 750120
"Like the rest of this chain, a reliable if not outstanding, first port
of call for a fish meal", tipped as a good choice for "diners with young
*families in tow". / **Details:** www.lochfyne.com; 9.45 pm, Fri & Sat 10.45.*
Accommodation: 9 rooms, from £85.

Mai Thai £ 30
6 Pierrepont St BA2 4AA (01225) 445557
Tipped for its "consistently good" food and its "pleasant" service,
a "traditional" Thai operation that's usually "dependable".
/ Details: www.maithai.co.uk; 10.30 pm, Fri & Sat 10.45 pm.

The Olive Tree
Queensberry Hotel £ 51
Russell St BA1 2QF (01225) 447928
Reports of "excellent" and "imaginative" cuisine feature in most (if not
quite all) reports on this popular cellar, beneath a family-owned
boutique hotel; tables are, however, rather "shoehorned-in".
/ Details: www.thequeensberry.co.uk; 9.45 pm; closed Mon L.
Accommodation: *29 rooms, from £115.*

Pump Rooms £ 39
The Pump Room, Stall St BA1 1LZ (01225) 444477
"Great for a tourist tea" – this gracious Georgian chamber has been
at the heart of Bath life for over 200 years, and it certainly has
a "fantastic ambience"; the food is incidental.
/ Details: www.searcys.co.uk; by the Abbey; L only; no booking, Sat & Sun.

Raphael £ 35
Gascoyne Hs, Upper Borough Walls BA1 1RN (01225) 480042
"A wonderful and intimate small restaurant", in the heart of the town,
hailed by one reporter as "perfect in every way" – even if that's
overdoing it, this is certainly a "slick" operation, and "ideal pre-
theatre". / Details: www.raphaelrestaurant.co.uk; 10.15 pm.

The Walrus & Carpenter £ 31
28 Barton St BA1 1HH (01225) 314864
A "quirky" corner bistro, tipped for its "good portions" (albeit from
a "limited" menu), and its "friendly" service.
/ Details: www.walrusandcarpenter.com; 11 pm; no Amex.

The Wheatsheaf £ 48
Combe Hay BA2 7EG (01225) 833504
It's worth the ten minute drive from the city-centre to seek out this
"hidden-away" but "convivial" rustic-chic establishment, which was
a farmhouse before it became a boozer in the 18th century –
the food is "stunning", and the wine list is "amazing" too.
/ Details: www.wheatsheafcombehay.com; 9.30 pm; closed Mon & Sun D;
no Amex. **Accommodation:** *3 rooms, from £105.*

The White Hart Inn £ 34
Widcombe Hill BA2 6AA (01225) 338053
A "modest" pub, "slightly on the edge of the city", that's worth seeking
out for the quality of its cuisine – the style may be "basic", but quality
is impressively consistent. / Details: www.whitehartbath.co.uk; 10 pm; closed
Sun D; no Amex. **Accommodation:** *4 private, 24 dormitory beds rooms,*
from £25.

Yen Sushi £ 18
11 Bartlett St BA1 2QZ (01225) 333313
In an area rather devoid of Japanese restaurants, this place is tipped
for its "friendly staff" and vast array of "delicious sushi"; expect
to wait for the conveyor belt seats though. / Details: www.yensushi.co.uk.

BAUGHURST, HAMPSHIRE 2–3D

The Wellington Arms **£ 42**
Baughurst Rd RG26 5LP (0118) 982 0110
*A "great little pub" where "tremendous" food is as locally-sourced
as you can get – the chickens and honey bees, for example, live on
a nearby farm; as there are only eight tables, though,
it's safest to book ahead. / **Details:** www.thewellingtonarms.com; 9.30 pm;
closed Mon, Tue L & Sun D; no Amex.*

BAWTRY, SOUTH YORKSHIRE 5–2D

China Rose **£ 35**
16 South Pde DN10 6JH (01302) 710461
*A long-established Chinese that "still delivers" (in the metaphorical
sense), and it's all the more worth knowing about as "the best in an
area where all the restaurants are very mediocre".
/ **Details:** www.chinarose-bawtry.co.uk; 10 pm, Fri & Sat 10.30 pm; D only.*

BEACONSFIELD, BUCKINGHAMSHIRE 3–3A

Crazy Bear **£ 33**
HP9 1LX (01494) 673086
*If you're looking for an "OTT sexy extravaganza", this "bordello-style"
restaurant-with-rooms – which features both Thai and British dining
rooms – may well be the place; commentary on the food, however,
is remarkably wide-ranging, and critics say it is grossly overpriced.
/ **Details:** www.crazybeargroup.co.uk/beaconsfield; 10 pm; no Amex.
Accommodation: 10 rooms, from £345.*

Spice Merchant **£ 45**
33 London End HP9 2HW (01494) 675474
*"Well above-average Indian food" makes this "smart"
(but "characterless") Old Beaconsfield spot popular with all who
report on it. / **Details:** www.spicemerchantgroup.com; opposite the Beaconsfield
wine cellar; 11 pm, Sun 9.30 pm.*

BEARSTED, KENT 3–3C

Soufflé **£ 42**
31 The Green ME14 4DN (01622) 737065
*A tip "convenient for Leeds Castle", this is a well-established
restaurant on the village green; the style is smartly-traditional – "white
tablecloths and crystal glasses" – but sceptical reporters feel its
approach "could do with freshening up".
/ **Details:** www.soufflerestaurant.net; off M20; 9.30 pm; closed Mon, Sat L &
Sun D.*

BEAUMARIS, ISLE OF ANGLESEY 4–1C

**The Loft Restaurant
Ye Olde Bull's Head** **£ 50**
Castle St LL58 8AP (01248) 810329
*A surprise find in an ancient coaching inn – a "lovely" modern
restaurant that continues to inspire all-round satisfaction from all who
comment on it; there's also an excellent cheaper brasserie.
/ **Details:** www.bullsheadinn.co.uk; On the High Street, opposite the Spar shop;
9.30 pm; D only, closed Sun; no jeans; children: 7+ at D. **Accommodation:** 26
rooms, from £110.*

BECKENHAM, KENT 3–3B

Mello £ 40 🌕

2 Southend Rd BR3 ISD   (020) 8663 0994

*"Just about the only place round here for well-cooked food
at reasonable prices"; the style can sometimes seem a little "dated",
but the food is invariably tipped as "good value".*

/ **Details:** www.mello.uk.com; Opposite Beckenham Junction Station; 10 pm; closed
Sun D.

BEELEY, DERBYSHIRE 5–2C

Devonshire Arms £ 41

Devonshire Sq DE4 2NR   (01629) 733259

*"I believe the Duchess had something to do with turning this very
rustic pub into a bright blue and purple gastro-experience!";
Her Grace's decorative scheme is, however, higher rated than either
the food or service at this "gorgeous gastropub".*

/ **Details:** www.devonshirebeeley.co.uk; 9.30 pm. **Accommodation:** 8 rooms,
from £120.

BEER, DEVON 2–4A

Steamers £ 38 🌕

New Cut EX12 3DU   (01297) 22922

*Near the 'Jurassic Coast', a "modern" family-run restaurant in an old
fishing village, which is tipped for "good-quality" cuisine (including
seafood that's "fresh" and "very well presented").*

/ **Details:** www.steamersrestaurant.co.uk; 9 pm; closed Mon & Sun; no Amex.

BELFAST, COUNTY ANTRIM 10–1D

Although the Belfast restaurant scene is not particularly
extensive (especially when it comes to good-quality ethnic
choices), it does include a range of very creditable ventures,
most of quite long standing. Although the volume
of comments on *Ginger* is not that great, these do suggest that
it is currently the most interesting of the options.

Aldens £ 38 ⭐

229 Upper Newtownards Rd BT4 3JF   (028) 9065 0079

*Still sometimes hailed as "Belfast's finest", this "unsalubriously-
located" restaurant seems to have been a little "hit-and-miss" over the
period of a (much-needed) major refurbishment; a new-era report,
however, says that "very high standards" have now been restored.*

/ **Details:** www.aldensrestaurant.com; 2m from Stormont Buildings; 10 pm, Fri &
Sat 10.30 pm; closed Sun D.

Bo Tree £ 37 🅐⭐

31 University Rd BT7 INA   (02890) 247722

*"Excellent authentic Thai food" is served in this "lively" former bank
building, near the University – a setting where the proprietors,
formerly of the famous Chiang Mai in Oxford, must feel right
at home!* / **Details:** www.botreethai.com; 10.30 pm; closed Sun; no Amex.

Cayenne £ 45

7 Ascot Hs, Shaftesbury Sq BT2 7DB   (028) 9033 1532

Proprietor and TV chef Paul Rankin has had his "financial concerns" of late, but this "chic" and "stylish" city-centre spot is "on top form" regardless, with all reports confirming that the food is "imaginative" and "well-prepared". / Details: www.cayenne-restaurant.co.uk; near Botanic Railway Station; 10 pm, Fri & Sat 11 pm; D only except Thu & Fri.

Deanes £ 61

36-40 Howard St BT1 6PF   (028) 9056 0000

For some reporters this city-centre spot is Belfast city's "only really serious foodie hang-out", offering "exceptional" food and notably "courteous" service too, in an "informal" atmosphere; for a small minority of critics, though, standards are "strangely inconsistent". / Details: www.michaeldeane.co.uk; near Grand Opera House; 9.30 pm; closed Mon D & Sun.

Ginger £ 40

7-8 Hope St BT12 5EE   (0871) 426 7885

The style may be "basic" (and perhaps a bit self-consciously Bohemian too) but the cuisine at Simon McCance's bistro is judged "outstanding" by all who report on it, and the prices demanded are "decent" too. / Details: www.gingerbistro.com; 9.30 pm, Mon 9 pm, Fri-Sat 10 pm; closed Mon L & Sun; no Amex.

James Street South £ 48

21 James Street South BT2 7GA   (028) 9043 4310

"Arguably the best restaurant in Belfast" – Niall McKenna's city-centre establishment wins praise for its "courteous" service, and cooking showing great "attention to detail"; the décor, though, strikes critics as "featureless". / Details: www.jamesstreetsouth.co.uk; behind the City Hall, off Bedford Street ; 10.30 pm; closed Sun L.

Nick's Warehouse £ 36

35 Hill St BT1 2LB   (028) 9043 9690

Tipped as "the best place in town for lunch", this long-established wine bar otherwise attracts little interest from reporters, perhaps because it can seem "pricey, for what you get". / Details: www.nickswarehouse.co.uk; behind St Anne's Cathedral; 9.30 pm; closed Mon & Sun; children: 18+ after 9 pm.

Soul Food Co £ 15

395 Ormeau Rd BT7 3GP   (028) 9064 6464

The destination for "a top Irish breakfast with a twist"; fans hail "the best bacon sandwiches in Ireland… no small achievement!"

Zen £ 38

55-59 Adelaide St BT2 8FE   (028) 9023 2244

"You'd be hard pushed to find a better restaurant in the whole of Belfast", says one of the fans of this large and "swish" Japanese – you certainly "need to book". / Details: www.zenbelfast.co.uk; 11.30 pm, Sun 10.30 pm; closed Sat L.

BENDERLOCH, ARGYLL & BUTE 9–3B

Isle of Eriska £ 51
PA37 1SD (01631) 720371
A grand and remote hotel, on its own island, where the dining room (recently refurbished) is tipped for its "sumptuous" cuisine… indeed, it can be "too rich for some tastes". / Details: www.eriska-hotel.co.uk; 9 pm; D only; no jeans or trainers; children: 6pm; high tea for resident's chldren. **Accommodation:** *25 rooms, from £310.*

BERKHAMSTED, HERTFORDSHIRE 3–2A

Eat Fish £ 38
163-165 High St HP4 3HB (01442) 879988
"Very fresh fish" and "good value" have won quite a following for this well-regarded local eatery; of late, however, reports on the cooking have been a little up-and-down. / Details: www.eatfish.co.uk; 10 pm, Sun 9 pm.

BEVERLEY, EAST YORKSHIRE 6–2A

The Pipe & Glass Inn £ 43
West End HU17 7PN (01430) 810246
The odd reporter claims this "laid-back" gastropub is "better than the Star at Harome"; it certainly has a style "more like a quality restaurant than a pub", and the consistency of praise for its "interesting" and "original" cuisine is impressive in both volume and consistency. / Details: www.pipeandglass.co.uk; 9.30 pm; closed Mon & Sun D; no Amex.

BIBURY, GLOUCESTERSHIRE 2–2C

Bibury Court
Bibury Court Hotel £ 43
GL7 5NT (01285) 740337
"Surprisingly adventurous" cooking helps win unanimous reporter approval for this Jacobean country house hotel, tipped for its "bargain set lunches". / Details: www.biburycourt.co.uk; 9 pm. **Accommodation:** *18 rooms, from £170.*

BIDDENDEN, KENT 3–4C

West House £ 48
28 High St TN27 8AH (01580) 291341
"Graham Garrett's cooking gets better every year", and his "refined" and "cultured" dishes are praised for their "outstanding" value; despite occupying an ancient cottage in a "lovely" village, however, atmosphere can sometimes prove elusive. / Details: www.thewesthouserestaurant.com; 9.30 pm; closed Mon, Sat L & Sun D; no Amex.

BIGBURY-ON-SEA, DEVON 1–4C

Burgh Island Hotel £ 73
TQ7 4BG (01548) 810514
You "need to like 30's style", but if you do it's hard to beat a trip – by sea tractor! – to this Agatha Christie-esque hotel (where "black tie and posh frocks are essential"); the food is a bit incidental, but it rarely actually disappoints. / Details: www.burghisland.com; 8.30 pm; D only, ex Sun open L & D; no Amex; jacket & tie at D; children: 12+ at D. **Accommodation:** *25 rooms, from £360.*

Oyster Shack £ 46 🅐⭐

Millburn Orchard Farm, Stakes Hills TQ7 4BE (01548) 810876

"One of best places to spend a Devon afternoon", this "quirky" restaurant serves up "fantastic, fresh fish" in a "laid back" but "professional" style; the views are "wonderful" too.
/ **Details:** www.oystershack.co.uk; 9 pm; L only, closed Mon.

BILDESTON, SUFFOLK 3–1C

⭐

The Bildeston Crown
The Crown Hotel £ 45

High St IP7 7EB (01449) 740510

"A very good restaurant in a beautifully renovated country pub/hotel" – some reporters are "astonished" by the quality on offer at this "out-of-the-way" location; service can be "haphazard", but seemed "improved" this year. / **Details:** www.thebildestoncrown.com; from the A14, take the B115 to Bildeston; 10 pm, Sun 9.30 pm . **Accommodation:** 12 rooms, from £150.

BILLERICAY, ESSEX 3–2C

🅣

The Magic Mushroom £ 42

Barleyland Rd CM11 2UD (01268) 289963

A "great local restaurant", tipped for "wonderful food, reasonably priced" – even a reporter who finds the food "a bit hit-and-miss sometimes" proclaims the overall formula "very reliable"!
/ **Details:** www.magicmushroomrestaurant.co.uk; next to "Barleylands Farm"; midnight; closed Mon L & Sun D.

BIRCHANGER, ESSEX 3–2B

🅣

The Three Willows £ 23

Birchanger Ln CM23 5QR (01279) 815913

Near Stansted Airport, a village boozer that's "always packed" (but not with children, who are banned); it's tipped for its "reliable" cuisine (in which "excellent fresh fish" stands out).

BIRCHOVER, DERBYSHIRE 5–2C

❌

Druid Inn £ 38

Main St DE4 2BL (01629) 650302

This "beautifully located" pub seems to have been ruined by the receipt of one of Michelin's 'bibs'; the place inspires many reports – including some of "excellent food" – but far too many visits are spoilt by service and ambience somewhere round the level of "Fawlty Towers"! / **Details:** www.thedruidinn.co.uk; SW of Bakewell off B5056; 9 pm, Fri & Sat 9.30 pm ; closed Sun D; no Amex.

In a culinary revolution without precedent in modern times, Birmingham has emerged over the past few years as a dining destination of indubitable note. With its five – yes, five – ambitious Anglo/French restaurants, all of some interest, the city is in that respect exceeded only by London and Edinburgh. This is all the more bizarre when you consider that these five restaurants have no visible means of support. They are not at the apex of any sort of pyramid of quality restaurants, as – with the exception of a some Indian curry houses – the dining-out scene is otherwise almost entirely without interest!

Bank   £ 40   Ⓣ
4 Brindleyplace B1 2JB   (0121) 633 4466
A large, rather '90s-style brasserie, with a "good location overlooking the canal". / Details: www.bankrestaurants.com; 10.30 pm, Fri & Sat 11 pm.

Buonissimo   £ 32
1 Albany Rd B17 9JX   (0121) 426 2444
"A pleasant Italian surprise"; this Harborne spot is a "popular local restaurant", where "outstanding" staff serve up "fresh seasonal food" in "hearty portions". / Details: www.buonissimouk.com; 10.15 pm; closed Mon L & Sun; no Amex.

Café Ikon
Ikon Gallery   £ 28
Oozells Sq, Brindley Place B1 2HS   (0121) 248 3226
A "stimulating" tapas bar which has long been regarded as central Brum's best informal rendezvous; it moved into new ownership (possibly no bad thing) after our survey had closed, so an assessment of the new régime will have to wait until next year's guide. / Details: www.ikon-gallery.co.uk; 11 pm; closed Sun D; no Amex; children: 18+ after 9 pm.

Chez Jules   £ 29   Ⓣ
5a Ethel St, off New St B2 4BG   (0121) 633 4664
A "fun French-ish restaurant", tipped for "excellent lunchtime value" – even fans, though, may proclaim food quality to be only "just about OK"! / Details: www.chezjules.co.uk; 11 pm; closed Sun D; no Amex.

Chung Ying   £ 32
16-18 Wrottesley St B5 4RT   (0121) 622 5669
This long-established city-centre behemoth is "always full of Chinese people", and offers a "wide" and "varied" menu, on which dim sum is a highlight; on balance, reporters marginally prefer it to the broadly similar Chung Ying Gardens (16-18 Wrottesley St, tel 622 5669) nearby. / Details: 11.30 pm.

Cielo   £ 51
6 Oozells Sq B1 2JB   (0121) 632 6882
Not all reporters would necessarily agree that the food at this Brindleyplace Italian is "marvellous", but even more sceptical reporters concede it has its attractions – "at least there's a bit of glamour about the place, and it's still going strong after 10pm". / Details: www.cielobirmingham.com; 11 pm, 10 pm Sun; Max booking: 20, Sat & Sun D.

Edmunds £ 50
6 Central Sq B1 2JB (0121) 633 4944
*"Fast becoming Brum's number one destination", say fans, this "very professional" Brindleyplace outfit offers "wonderful, innovative and tasty" food, and at "very reasonable" prices too. / **Details:** www.edmundsbirmingham.com; 10 pm; closed Sat L & Sun.*

Hotel du Vin et Bistro £ 45

25 Church St B3 2NR (0121) 200 0600
*"Very buzzing and popular", this city-centre outpost of the boutique-hotel chain (complete with spa) is "always a safe bet" for a night out, and is a top recommendation as a place to stay too; in the bistro, though, the "phenomenal" wine completely outpaces the food, and service is sometimes poor. / **Details:** www.hotelduvin.co.uk; 10 pm, Fri & Sat 10.30 pm; booking: max 10. **Accommodation:** 66 rooms, from £160.*

Kinnaree Thai Restaurant
The Mailbox, Holiday Wharf Building £ 32
22 Water Front Walk B1 1SN (0121) 665 6568
*Not far from the Mailbox, a "busy" oriental tipped for both its "tasty" food and for its "great location by the canal". / **Details:** www.kinnaree.co.uk; 11 pm, 10.30 pm Sun.*

Lasan £ 44
3-4 Dakota Buildings, James St B3 1SD (0121) 212 3664
*"Different and adventurous" Indian cooking and "marvellous" service have come together to make this "smooth" Indian restaurant one of the city-centre's most notable restaurants; there's now a Hall Green "satellite" too ('Lasan Eatery'), which "shows the suburban competition how it should be done". / **Details:** www.lasan.co.uk; 11 pm, 10 pm Sun; closed Sat L.*

Maharaja £ 24
23-25 Hurst St B5 4SA (0121) 622 2641
*"A shining beacon"; this "classical" city-centre curry house of very long standing – much smartened up in recent times – still attracts praise for its "superb" and "authentic" North Indian cuisine. / **Details:** www.maharajarestaurant.co.uk; 11 pm; closed Sun.*

Opus Restaurant £ 44
54 Cornwall St B3 2DE (0121) 200 2323
*A "blingy" city-centre destination, with "good space between the tables", and where the food is often "lovely"; of late, however, reports have become rather inconsistent. / **Details:** www.opusrestaurant.co.uk; 9.30 pm; closed Sat L & Sun.*

Pascal's £ 47

1 Montague Rd B16 9HN (0121) 455 0999
*Still relatively little feedback on the Edgbaston townhouse which originally found fame as Jessica's – the Gallic cuisine has a "distinctly Mediterranean influence" nowadays, but all reports confirm that this remains "a really enjoyable place to eat". / **Details:** www.pascalsrestaurant.co.uk; 10 pm; closed Mon, Tue, Sat L & Sun D; no Amex.*

Purnells £ 60
55 Cornwall St B3 2BH (0121) 212 9799
*For "stylish, inventive and witty food in businesslike surroundings",
Glynn Purnell's centrally-located restaurant really is hard to beat –
this is a venue where, for once, "you can impress the clients and enjoy
yourself, all at the same time!" /* **Details:** *www.purnellsrestaurant.com;
9.30 pm; closed Mon, Sat L & Sun; children: 6+.*

San Carlo £ 40
4 Temple St B2 5BN (0121) 633 0251
*The city-centre's longest-established quality restaurant – a rather
glitzy Italian – is usually "mega-busy"; reports on it remain rather
mixed, however, not helped by service that can be "unhelpful".
/* **Details:** *www.sancarlo.co.uk; near St Philips Cathedral; 11 pm.*

Simpsons £ 65
20 Highfield Rd B15 3DU (0121) 454 3434
*"Really delightful" food and "unstuffy" service combine to make
Andreas Antona's Edgbaston townhouse-restaurant one of the handful
of establishments which closely contend for the title of "Brum's best";
you can also stay the night. /* **Details:** *www.simpsonsrestaurant.co.uk; 9 pm;
closed Sun D.* **Accommodation:** *4 rooms, from £160.*

Turners £ 66
69 High St B17 9NS (0121) 426 4440
*"Top-class ingredients" are handled "with real skill" at this "top-notch"
but "unpretentious" restaurant, in the lucky village of Harborne;
supporting attractions include a "really well-chosen wine list",
and service that's notably "friendly" and "professional".
/* **Details:** *www.turnersofharborne.com; 9.30 pm; closed Mon, Sat L & Sun;
no Amex.*

Warehouse Café £ 23
54-57 Allison St B5 5TH (0121) 633 0261
*A "friendly" vegetarian café nestled amongst a number of other
ethical businesses, behind Moor Street Station; the daily specials board
presents the "freshest produce" and "most creative ideas"; do not
miss the puddings! /* **Details:** *www.thewarehousecafe.com.*

BISHOPS STORTFORD, HERTFORDSHIRE 3–2B

Anton's Restaurant
Great Hallingbury Manor £ 48
Great Hallingbury Manor CM22 7TJ (01279) 506475
*"Anton Edelmann's new restaurant by Stansted Airport" attracts
reports of every shade of opinion – from "consistently good"
to "extremely expensive and pleased with itself"; you can't help
feeling that the famous ex-Savoy chef ought to be able to achieve
rather more consistent customer satisfaction!
/* **Details:** *www.antonsrestaurant.co.uk; 9.30 pm; closed Sat L & Sun D.*
Accommodation: *55 rooms, from £130.*

Baan Thitiya £ 35
102 London Rd CM23 3DS (01279) 658575
*In a multi-level former pub, a Thai restaurant with many "cosy" nooks,
and "very friendly" staff too; thanks to cuisine that's "fresh" and
"full of oriental flavour", it has quickly established quite a following.
/* **Details:** *www.baan-thitiya.com; 11 pm.*

The Lemon Tree £ 42
14-16 Water Ln CM23 2LB   (01279) 757788
Tipped for its "high-quality" fare, this long-established restaurant often pleases all-round, even if it can sometimes seem a little "tired".
/ **Details:** www.lemontree.co.uk; past 'Coopers', then 1st left; 9.30 pm; closed Sun D.

BISHOPS TACHBROOK, WARWICKSHIRE   5–4C

Mallory Court £ 68
Harbury Ln CV33 9QB   (01926) 330214
On most reports, this "very comfortable" Lutyens-designed country house hotel is "a real gem", where the food is often "excellent"; both the main restaurant and the "attractive" conservatory-brasserie, however, are sometimes noted for their "ups and downs".
/ **Details:** www.mallory.co.uk; 2m S of Leamington Spa, off B4087; 8.30 pm.
Accommodation: 30 rooms, from £149.

BISPHAM GREEN, LANCASHIRE   5–1A

Eagle & Child £ 35
Maltkiln Ln L40 3SG   (01257) 462297
"Top pub grub" – standards at this ancient inn are "consistently high", and presentation is "beautiful" too. / **Details:** www.ainscoughs.co.uk; M6, J27; 8.30 pm; no Amex.

BLACKPOOL, LANCASHIRE   5–1A

Kwizeen £ 35
47-49 King St FY1 3EJ   (01253) 290045
"A great find in an area short of good eateries"; this "back street" beacon is tipped for its "very good" cooking, and its particularly good value lunchtime and early-evening menus.
/ **Details:** www.kwizeenrestaurant.co.uk; 100 yards inland from the Winter Gardens; 9 pm; closed Sat L & Sun; no Amex; no shorts.

BLAIRGOWRIE, PERTH & KINROSS   9–3C

Kinloch House £ 58
PH10 6SG   (01250) 884237
A "proper Scottish country house", with a rather "genteel" vibe, tipped for its "excellent" food and "wonderful" location.
/ **Details:** www.kinlochhouse.com; past the Cottage Hospital, turn L, procede 3m along A923, (signposted Dunkeld Road); 8.30 pm; jacket required; children: 7+ at D. **Accommodation:** 18 rooms, from £210.

BOLNHURST, BEDFORDSHIRE   3–1A

The Plough at Bolnhurst £ 38
MK44 2EX   (01234) 376274
"The best in the area by a long way"; "thoughtful, flavoursome and well sourced dishes" – mainly Gallic – help make this "sympathetically restored" village inn an "impressive" destination for all of the many reporters who comment on it. / **Details:** www.bolnhurst.com; 9.30 pm; closed Mon & Sun D; no Amex.

BOLTON ABBEY, NORTH YORKSHIRE 8–4B

The Devonshire Arms £ 70 ⭐

BD23 6AJ (01756) 710441

*"An expensive Dales hotel which does everything right... at a price";
but since the arrival of new chef Steve Smith, this grand but "friendly"
ducally-owned inn has a much more solid claim to being "one of the
country's best dining rooms" (and with an "unbelievably extensive"
wine list too); there's also a brasserie.*

/ Details: www.devonshirehotels.co.uk; on A59, 5m NE of Skipton; 9.30 pm; closed
Mon, Tue-Sat D only, Sun open L & D; no jeans or trainers. **Accommodation:** 40
rooms, from £235.

BOLTON, LANCASHIRE 5–2B

Spice Valley £ 18 ⭐

17 Eagley Brook Way BL1 8TS (01204) 388609

*Indian cooking "par excellence" makes this tastefully decorated spot
well worth seeking out; "the special menus of Thai-with-a-
twist or Indo-Chinese dishes are always worth a try".*

BONCHURCH, ISLE OF WIGHT 2–4D

The Pond Café £ 42 ⓣ

Pond Church Village Rd PO38 1RG (01983) 855666

*An airy bistro, in an "idyllic location", that was generally tipped
as "worth a detour" in this year's reports – the chef changed as our
survey was concluding, however, so this assessment is a provisional
one.* **/ Details:** www.thepondcafe.com; 9.30 pm; closed Tue & Wed; no Amex.

BOREHAM, ESSEX 3–2C

The Lion Inn £ 33 Ⓐ

Main Rd CM3 3JA (01245) 394900

*A "buzzy" new "top-end" gastropub outpost of the Blue Strawberry
(Hatfield Peverel) that's quickly become "very popular locally";
any establishment which claims (uniquely) to have prosecco on tap
can't be all bad!* **/ Details:** www.lioninnhotel.co.uk; 9 pm, Sun 8 pm; no Amex.
Accommodation: 15 rooms, from £79.

BOSHAM, WEST SUSSEX 3–4A

Millstream Hotel £ 46 ⓣ

PO18 8HL (01243) 573234

*If you're looking for a "pleasant" destination in a "tourist-trap" part
of the world, this traditional hotel is tipped for the "wide choice
of good food" it offers; "my 90-year-old aunt loved it".*

/ Details: www.millstream-hotel.co.uk; A259 from Chichester; 9.15 pm; no jeans
or trainers. **Accommodation:** 35 rooms, from £142.

BOURNEMOUTH, DORSET 2–4C

Chez Fred £ 18 ⭐

10 Seamoor Rd BH4 9AN (01202) 761023

*"The best fish 'n' chip restaurant in the area"; it's "consistently good",
but you can "expect to queue" for entry to the "busy" and "crowded"
dining room; the lunchtime deal is outstanding value.*

/ Details: www.chezfred.co.uk; 1m W of town centre; 9.45 pm, 9 Sun; closed
Sun L; no Amex; no booking.

Ocean Palace £ 32

8 Priory Rd BH2 5DG   (01202) 559127
*A Chinese veteran tipped for fare that's sometimes "very tasty";
"very good-value midweek lunch menu" too.*
/ **Details:** www.oceanpalace.co.uk; 11 pm.

Print Room £ 39

Richmond Hill BH2 6HH   (01202) 789669
*This "stylish" brasserie has a "beautiful" setting (in a former
newspaper HQ), and offers "an excellent choice of food, from snacks
to main meals"; the fare has generally been reported as "imaginative"
too (though the chef changed just as our survey for the year was
drawing to a close). / **Details:** www.theprintroom-bournemouth.co.uk; 10 pm,
Fri & Sat 11 pm.*

West Beach £ 43

Pier Approach BH2 5AA   (01202) 587785
*An "excellent" location ("virtually on the beach") is not the only
attraction which makes this bar-restaurant-terrace a massive hit with
reporters, as its seafood dishes are often "first-rate" too; service,
though, often tends to "average". / **Details:** www.west-beach.co.uk; 10 pm.*

BOWNESS-ON-WINDERMERE, CUMBRIA   7–3D

Miller Howe £ 55

Rayrigg Rd LA23 1EY   (01539) 442536
*A once-famous country house hotel, sometimes tipped as "nearly back
to the standards of John Tovey's day" after its "sensitive" recent
refurbishment; reports remain few, however, and are still not quite
consistent. / **Details:** www.millerhowe.com; on A592 between Windermere &
Bowness; 8.45 pm. **Accommodation:** 15 rooms, from £105.*

BRADFORD, WEST YORKSHIRE   5–1C

Aagrah £ 28

483 Bradford Rd LS28 8ED   (01274) 668818
*In the curry capital of the UK, an outstanding member of the
subcontinental chain that "sets the standards" (around Yorkshire,
and beyond); it's a "plush" place too, with notably "friendly" staff.
/ **Details:** www.aagrah.com; on A647; 11.30 pm; D only, ex Sun open L & D.*

Akbar's Balti £ 25

1276 Leeds Rd BD3 3LF   (01274) 773311
*"Simply the best", say fans, this famous curry house "always offers
great food, and at reasonable prices"; survey ratings tend to confirm
that it's "not as good as the Aagrah", but it still gets "busy as hell"
at weekends. / **Details:** www.akbars.co.uk; midnight; D only; no Amex.*

Karachi £ 11
15-17 Neal St BD5 0BX (01274) 732015

The city's oldest subcontinental "still does the best curries" (says an attendee since the early days, in the '70s); the dining room may be "really basic", but the food is "always reliable". / **Details:** *I am, 2 am Fri & Sat; no credit cards.*

Kashmir £ 15
27 Morley St BD7 1AG (01274) 726513

"You don't go for the décor", but the food at this long-established subcontinental can be "amazing" ("especially the chapatis"), and it's "cheap" too. / **Details:** *3 am.*

Mumtaz Paan House £ 24
Great Horton Rd BD7 3HS (01274) 571861

The curry house of curry houses, nearly 30 years old, with a huge reputation for its "authentic and tasty" dishes, and "helpful and warm" service too; no booze, though. / **Details:** *www.mumtaz.com; midnight.*

BRAMFIELD, SUFFOLK 3–1D

The Queen's Head £ 32
The St IP19 9HT (01986) 784214

"A dining pub in a small village off the A12"; it's universally hailed as a "charming" place, where the food is "imaginative" and "wholesome". / **Details:** *www.queensheadbramfield.co.uk; 9.15 pm, Sat 10 pm, Sun 9 pm; no Amex.*

BRAMLEY, SURREY 3–3A

Jolly Farmer £ 22
High St GU5 0HB (01483) 890484

A traditional boozer, tipped for its "reliable" pub staples that can "stump even the most hearty appetite"; there's an impressive selection of beers too. / **Details:** *www.jollyfarmer.co.uk.*

BRAMPTON, CUMBRIA 7–2D

Farlam Hall £ 52
CA8 2NG (01697) 746234

Not least because reports often mention the "very good" breakfast, it's "worth staying overnight" at this country house hotel; it pleases across the board, but service – perhaps because of hands-on involvement of the proprietors – stands out as truly exceptional. / **Details:** *www.farlamhall.co.uk; 2.5m S.E of Brampton on A689, not in Farlam Village; 8.30 pm; D only; no shorts; children: 5+.* **Accommodation:** *12 rooms, from £280.*

BRANCASTER STAITHE, NORFOLK 6–3B

The White Horse £ 35
Main Rd PE31 8BY (01485) 210262
"You get no fireworks – just reliable cooking served by very friendly, efficient staff in a lovely conservatory, with sea views" – at this contemporary seaside inn whose local fish and shellfish dishes are "always worth the trip". / **Details:** *www.whitehorsebrancaster.co.uk; 9 pm; no Amex.* **Accommodation:** *15 rooms, from £120.*

BRANSCOMBE, DEVON 2–4A

Masons Arms £ 32
Main St EX12 3DJ (01297) 680300
In the heart of a hugely picturesque village, an ancient inn tipped as a "delightful" dining destination; "go when it's quiet", though, as "standards slip when they're busy". / **Details:** *www.masonsarms.co.uk; 9 pm; no Amex; children: 14+ in restaurant.* **Accommodation:** *21 rooms, from £80.*

BRAY, BERKSHIRE 3–3A

Caldesi In Campagna £ 48
Old Mill Ln SL6 2BG (01628) 788500
"Adding lustre to Bray's already faultless gastronomic credentials", this "buzzy" and "elegant" newcomer – which offers a notionally rustic Italian cucina – has pleased almost all reporters who've commented on it. / **Details:** *www.campagna.caldesi.com; 10.30 pm; closed Mon & Sun D.*

The Fat Duck £115
High St SL6 2AQ (01628) 580333
"Genius verging on insanity"; Heston Blumenthal's "brilliantly imaginative" and "witty" food – in the 'molecular gastronomy' school of El Bulli – found greater favour with reporters this year; refuseniks, though (about one reporter in seven) still find the whole experience "nonsensical" and "overpriced". / **Details:** *www.thefatduck.co.uk; 9 pm; closed Mon & Sun D.*

The Hind's Head £ 46
High St SL6 2AB (01628) 626151

"The best chips in the known universe" are far from being the only attraction of Heston Blumenthal's "wonderful" inn, just over the road from the Fat Duck; it offers a "superb modern take on pub classics", and at "pub prices too... well, almost".
/ **Details:** *www.hindsheadhotel.co.uk; From the M4 take exit to Maidenhead Central, then go to Bray village; 9.30 pm; closed Sun D.*

Riverside Brasserie £ 56

Monkey Island Ln, Bray Marina SL6 2EB   (01628) 780553

It may be "little more than a shed on the riverbank, but on a sunny summer's day this relaxed hang out in hard-to-find Bray Marina really is idyllic", and the "well-executed" food and "friendly" service do nothing to spoil the experience. / **Details:** *www.riversidebrasserie.co.uk; follow signs for Bray Marina off A308; 9.30 pm.*

Waterside Inn £129

Ferry Rd SL6 2AT   (01628) 620691

A "beautiful" and "romantic" spot that's hard to beat... as long as you can stand the "eye-watering" prices; if you're looking for a rather ancien régime approach, you won't find it done better that at Michel Roux's famous establishment in a Thames-side cottage, which is "still one of the best restaurants in England". / **Details:** *www.waterside-inn.co.uk; off A308 between Windsor & Maidenhead; 10 pm; closed Mon & Tue; no jeans or trainers; booking: max 10; children: 14+ D.* **Accommodation:** *11 rooms, from £200.*

BREARTON, NORTH YORKSHIRE 8–4B

The Malt Shovel £ 39

HG3 3BX   (01423) 862929

For "the most fantastic food", served in a "lovely, friendly setting", it's "really worth seeking out" the Bleiker family's 16th-century country pub, where all aspects of the operation show "great attention to detail"; its occasional opera nights seem to go down well too. / **Details:** *www.themaltshovelbrearton.co.uk; off A61, 6m N of Harrogate; 10 pm; closed Mon, Tue & Sun D; no Amex; need 8+ to book.*

BRECON, POWYS 2–1A

Felin Fach Griffin £ 43

Felin Fach LD3 0UB   (01874) 620111

You get "everything one would want in a 'country' dining room – warm greeting, good service and the highest-quality food" – at this "outstanding" gastropub in the Brecon Beacons, which wins unanimous praise from reporters. / **Details:** *www.eatdrinksleep.ltd.uk; 20 mins NW of Abergavenny on A470; 9.30 pm; closed Mon L; no Amex.* **Accommodation:** *7 rooms, from £115.*

BRENTFORD, GREATER LONDON

3–3B

Pappadums £ 33
Ferry Quays, Ferry Ln TW8 0BT   (020) 8847 1123
*This may be just a "canteen", but this is the place where "all the local Indians eat"; the food is "tasty" and "light", and complemented – rather intriguingly – by Portuguese wines chosen by guru Charles Metcalfe. / **Details:** www.pappadums.co.uk; 9 pm, Sat 11 pm, Sun 10.30 pm.*

BRIDGE OF ALLAN, STIRLING

9–4C

Clive Ramsay £ 32
26 Henderson St FK9 4HR   (01786) 831616
*The overall experience may not always 'gel', but even critics tip this impressive café/deli for its "good and reasonably-priced food".
/ **Details:** www.cliveramsay.com; 10 pm; no Amex.*

BRIDPORT, DORSET

2–4B

Hive Beach Cafe £ 34
Beach Rd DT6 4RF   (01308) 897070
*"Fantastic fish served in a genuine beach café ambience" – that's the "fun" formula which makes this place "very busy, as soon as the sun shines"; the no-booking policy can, however, be rather "frustrating".
/ **Details:** www.hivebeachcafe.co.uk; L only, varies seasonally.*

Riverside £ 45
West Bay DT6 4EZ   (01308) 422011
*"Arthur Watson is a local legend, who knows his fish and knows his France" – both of which enthusiasms are on full display at this "wonderfully located" riverside café, which is usually "fully booked", thanks to the "consistent" quality of the cooking; it's sometimes suggested, though, that "the simplest dishes are best".
/ **Details:** www.thefishrestaurant-westbay.co.uk; 9 pm; closed Mon & Sun D; no Amex.*

BRIGHOUSE, WEST YORKSHIRE

5–1C

Brook's £ 38
6 Bradford Rd HD6 1RW   (01484) 715284
*Over twenty years in business, this "excellent Pennines stand-by" is still tipped for its "dependable" cuisine (and for extending a "warm Yorkshire welcome" too). / **Details:** www.brooks-restaurant.co.uk; 11 pm; D only, closed Sun; no Amex.*

BRIGHTON, EAST SUSSEX

3–4B

It is perhaps disappointing that there is not a more pronounced trend for standards of restaurants in 'London By the Sea' to improve in the same way as they have in the capital itself in recent years. However, the city remains a brunching heaven, and also one for veggies – *Terre à Terre* is probably the UK's best establishment of that type. *Gingerman* – now the HQ of a small local empire – is also a very creditable performer.

Bill's at the Depot £ 30

100 North Rd, The Depot BN1 1YE (01273) 692894

"Great food in the middle of a grocery shop!" – that's the formula that makes this "buzzing slice of foodie heaven" an "essential" lunch or brunch destination; it can feel "cramped", though, and a queue is "inevitable". / Details: www.billsproducestore.co.uk; 10 pm; closed Sun D; no Amex.

Casa Don Carlos £ 26

5 Union St BN1 1HA (01273) 327177

Your classic "friendly", "buzzy" and "authentic" tapas bar; after more than two decades under the same ownership, this "lovely" Lanes destination is just as popular as ever. / Details: 11 pm.

China Garden £ 34

88-91 Preston St BN1 2HG (01273) 325124

"Rocking" dim sum is the top proposition at this Chinese on the Hove/Brighton borders, but its "extensive" menu attracts general praise for offering "fresh" dishes at other times too. / Details: www.chinagarden.name; opp West Pier; 11.30 pm.

Donatello £ 28

1-3 Brighton Pl BN1 1HJ (01273) 775477

A popular "value-for-money" tip in the Lanes, offering "good but not great pizza", and the like. / Details: www.donatello.co.uk; 11.30 pm.

Due South £ 43

139 King's Road Arches BN1 2FN (01273) 821218

"Bag a table upstairs with a view over the beach and sea and you'll have the perfect setting for a date", at this very popular (and sometimes rather "chaotic") restaurant, "just yards from the beach"; the cooking is "fresh", "interesting" and "good value" too. / Details: www.duesouth.co.uk; Brighton Beach, below the Odeon cinema; 9.30 pm; no trainers.

L'Eglise £ 33

196 Church Rd BN3 2DJ (01273) 220868

"A proper French bistro", in Hove, offering "reassuringly old-fashioned" food in "generous portions"; top marks too for such indications of authenticity as "rather close-set tables" and "wines from Madame's own family vineyard"! / Details: www.legliserestaurant.co.uk; 11 pm, Sun 10 pm; closed Mon.

English's £ 45

29-31 East St BN1 1HL (01273) 327980

A new chef has improved the food at this "fadedly splendid" Victorian institution (which has some great outside tables) in the Lanes, and the seafood can be "amazing"; "average" results, however, are still not unknown. / Details: www.englishs.co.uk; 10 pm, Sun 9.30 pm.

Food for Friends £ 37

17-18 Prince Albert St BN1 1HF (01273) 202310

This "buzzing" veggie, in the Lanes, is consistently praised for its "good food" and "friendly" service; the no-booking policy, however, leads to "long waits" at busy times. / Details: www.foodforfriends.com; 10 pm, Fri & Sat 10.30 pm.

La Fourchette £ 38
105 Western Rd BN1 2AA (01273) 722556
Part of a four-strong local group, which includes both this restaurant and three café/bar establishments; they're all pretty French in style, and "generally reliable". / **Details:** www.lafourchette.co.uk; 10.30 pm.

The Ginger Pig £ 33
3 Hove St BN3 2TR (01273) 736123
In Hove, a "nice airy restaurant/pub with an interesting menu and lots of good specials" (including, as you might hope, "good pork dishes"), and which seems "even better now you can book"; it inspires almost as much feedback as Gingerman (same owner).
/ **Details:** www.gingermanrestaurant.com; 10 pm; no trainers.

Gingerman £ 40
21a Norfolk Sq BN1 2PD (01273) 326688
Ben McKellar's "small but classy local restaurant", on the Hove/Brighton border, serves up "tasteful" British dishes that are "probably the best in town"; service is "very helpful" too.
/ **Details:** www.gingermanrestaurants.com; off Norfolk Square; 9.15 pm; closed Mon.

Graze £ 42
42 Western Rd BN3 1JD (01273) 823707
The eclectic 'grazing' (small plates) fare on offer at this wacky Hove outfit offers fans "a real eating experience" that's sometimes proclaimed "the best in town"; it can seem "a bit pricey" for what it is, though, and not all reporters are convinced.
/ **Details:** www.graze-restaurant.co.uk; 9.30 pm; closed Mon & Sun D.

Havana £ 48
32 Duke St BN1 1AG (01273) 773388
This airy Lanes establishment – where the décor takes inspiration from the Caribbean, but the food does not – has long been tipped for its "charming" ambience; of late, however, standards have sometimes seemed a mite "jaded". / **Details:** www.havana.uk.com; 10.30 pm, Fri & Sat 11 pm, Sun 10 pm; no shorts; children: 5+ at D.

Hotel du Vin et Bistro £ 45
Ship St BN1 1AD (01273) 718588
"Buzzy and welcoming" or "busy and mediocre"?; this "relaxed" outpost of the wine-led brasserie chain, just off the seafront, still attracts many reports, but critics say "the food needs more care and attention" – "the template seemed fresh and exciting ten years ago, but it's not really up to best current standards".
/ **Details:** www.hotelduvin.com; 9.45 pm, Fri & Sat 10.15 pm; booking: max 10.
Accommodation: 49 rooms, from £170.

Indian Summer £ 32
69 East St BN1 1HQ (01273) 711001
"By far the best in Brighton" – the "unusual twist" on Indian cuisine ("bordering on fusion") inspires many, and unanimously favourable, reports on this "very central" spot; "excellent-value set lunch".
/ **Details:** www.indian-summer.org.uk; 10.30 pm, Sun & Mon 10 pm; closed Mon L.

Jamie's Italian £ 34

11 Black Lion St BN1 1ND (01273) 915480

The "funky" décor may be a bit "self-conscious" for some tastes, but even reporters who "rarely go to anything resembling a chain" are swept away by the all-round value on offer at Jamie O's "unfussy" and "unmissable" Italian outfit – "a sort of better Carluccio's"; "pity about the long queues". / **Details:** www.jamiesitalian.com; 11 pm, Sun 10.30 pm.

Moshi Moshi £ 27

Opticon, Bartholomew Sq BN1 1JS (01273) 719195

Counterpart to the small London chain, a place tipped for "the best sushi in Brighton", and using "locally sourced fish" too. / **Details:** www.moshimoshi.co.uk; 10.30 pm; no Amex.

Murasaki £ 34

115 Dyke Rd BN1 3JE (01273) 326231

A "buzzy" Seven Dials spot, tipped for its "consistently excellent and very fresh sushi"; it's a "friendly" place too, where children are "made welcome". / **Details:** 11 pm; closed Mon; no Amex.

Regency £ 26

131 Kings Rd BN1 2HH (01273) 325014

A "cheap and cheerful" sea-front institution, serving "good fish 'n' chips with a view"; the seafood platter is "good value" too, but more ambitious dishes are "better avoided".
/ **Details:** www.theregencyrestaurant.co.uk; opp West Pier; 11 pm.
Accommodation: 30 rooms, from £65.

The Restaurant at Drakes
Drakes Hotel £ 53

44 Marine Pde BN2 1PE (01273) 696934

The departure of the Gingerman team has not been to the advantage of this hotel dining room – yes, there are still reports of "very high-quality cuisine", but there are some very critical ones too.
/ **Details:** www.therestaurantatdrakes.co.uk; 9.30 pm. **Accommodation:** 20 rooms, from £100.

Riddle & Finns £ 46

12b, Meeting House Ln BN1 1HB (01273) 323008

"Excellent seafood, as fresh as can be" and "charming staff" help make this marble-countered oyster bar, in the Lanes, "one of Brighton's most pleasureable dining experiences", and hugely popular; beware the wine selection, though – "champagnes offer the best choice!" / **Details:** www.riddleandfinns.co.uk.

Sam's Of Brighton £ 36

1 Paston Pl BN2 1HA (01273) 676222

Sam Metcalfe rather seems to have transferred his affections from Hove's declining Seven Dials (which we no longer list) to this informal new restaurant in Kemp Town – its "great English fare" attracts impressively consistent reports. / **Details:** www.samsofbrighton.co.uk; 10 pm, Sun 9 pm; closed Mon.

Terre à Terre £ 43
71 East St BN1 1HQ (01273) 729051

"The best vegetarian in the UK, bar none"; this Lanes institution retains a huge fan club (including many carnivores) for its "staggeringly inventive food... which happens to have been created without the use of meat". / **Details:** www.terreaterre.co.uk; 10.30 pm; closed Mon; booking: max 8 at weekends.

BRINKWORTH, WILTSHIRE 2–2C

The Three Crowns £ 39
The Street SN15 5AF (01666) 510366
A dining pub that's "renowned locally for its food" (though, arguably this may be as much a reflection of the "lack of good restaurants in the area", as it is of standards of the establishment concerned). / **Details:** www.threecrowns.co.uk; 9.30 pm, Sun 9 pm.

BRISTOL, CITY OF BRISTOL 2–2B

Although it has only one undoubted culinary 'star' – Culinaria – Bristol has in recent years acquired an impressive range of restaurants offering both good food and a good ambience (remarkably better than, say, not-so-distant Oxford). The range includes not only what's threatening to become England's best veggie restaurant (Cafe Maitreya), but also good exponents of most of the major 'ethnic' cuisines (particularly Indian). Many neighbourhoods also have good non-ethnic champions.

The Albion £ 43
Boyces Ave BS8 4AA (0117) 973 3522
"Decent" and "adventurous" food has made this pretty Clifton gastroboozer very popular... even if it does sometimes seem "not inexpensive" for what it is. / **Details:** www.thealbionclifton.co.uk; 9.30; closed Mon & Sun D.

La Barrique £ 31
225 Gloucester Rd BS7 8NR (0117) 944 5500
"A genuine French place in the northern suburbs", where Michel Lemoine dishes up "imaginative" and seasonal petits-plats (small-plate dishes), with something of a Mediterranean twist; the setting, though, can seem "rather cold and echoey". / **Details:** www.bistrolabarrique.co.uk; 10 pm; no Amex.

Bell's Diner £ 43
1 York Rd BS6 5QB (0117) 924 0357
"An unexpected jewel in a rough area"; Chris Wicks's "cramped" Montpelier bistro is a longstanding "gastronomic oasis" with a serious local following for its "innovative" and "interesting" cuisine; "unusual" wines too. / **Details:** www.bellsdiner.co.uk; 10 pm; closed Mon L, Sat L & Sun.

Bordeaux Quay £ 44
Canons Rd BS1 5UH (0117) 943 1200
*This "buzzing" two-level brasserie, down on the docks, has made quite
a name as an eco-destination, and it attracts a large number
of reports – supporters insist that it demonstrates that "ethics and
quality aren't mutually exclusive", but the middle view is that this is a
destination which is "nice, but not special".*
/ **Details:** www.bordeaux-quay.co.uk; 10 pm; closed Mon & Sun D.

Boston Tea Party £ 18
75 Park St BS1 5PF (0117) 929 8601
*Part of a small westerly chain of "informal eateries" (with three
representatives in Bristol), an "eccentric" and "popular" rendezvous,
offering "great coffee", "a huge range of breakfasting options" and
lunches which are "more than adequate for the style of the place".*
/ **Details:** www.bostonteaparty.co.uk; 8 pm; no Amex; no booking.

Brasserie Blanc £ 37
Bakers And Cutlers Halls, The Friary Building BS1 3DF
(01179) 102410
*A new addition to the improving Blanc empire – in an "attractively
converted old building" in the Cabot Circus shopping centre – that's
already attracting a lot of commentary; its "enthusiastic" service helps
create "a good imitation of the French brasserie experience" (even if
some niggles have yet to be fully ironed out).*
/ **Details:** www.brasserieblanc.com.

Budokan £ 31
31 Colston St BS1 5AP (0117) 914 1488
*This small pan-Asian chain attracts praise for its "consistently good
food at reasonable prices"; the rapid refuel menu, in particular, offers
"excellent value".* / **Details:** www.budokan.co.uk; 11 pm; closed Sun.

Cafe Maitreya £ 32
89 St Marks Rd, Easton BS5 6HY (0117) 951 0100
*"Vegetarian heaven!" – Terre à Terre (Brighton) better watch out,
as this "dodgily-located" and "basic" spot is making a serious play for
the title of "just the best veggie ever".* / **Details:** www.cafemaitreya.co.uk;
9.45; closed Mon, Tue L, Wed L & Sun; no Amex.

Casamia £ 45
38 High St B9 3DZ (0117) 959 2884
*"An intimate, family-run Italian fine-dining venue serving sublime
food"; the cuisine may be "stunning" but – in Michelin-pleasing style –
the atmosphere can sometimes seem a touch "pretentious".*

Culinaria £ 40
1 Chandos Rd BS6 6PG (0117) 973 7999
*"Lovingly prepared from the freshest ingredients", Stephen Markwick's
cooking makes this "simply-converted shop unit", in Redland, a place
of gastronomic pilgrimage (and, accordingly, booked-up far
in advance); bizarrely, it's "also good for take-away".*
/ **Details:** www.culinariabristol.co.uk; 9.30 pm; closed Sun-Wed; no Amex.

Dynasty £ 38
16a St. Thomas St BS1 6JJ (0117) 925 0888
*"The best Chinese in Bristol", this barn-like spot is particularly worth
knowing about for its "lovely dim sum" – other fare, though, can tend
to "undistinguished".* / **Details:** www.dynasty-bristol.co.uk; 11.30 pm; jacket.*

Fishers
£ 34

35 Princess Victoria St BS8 4BX (0117) 974 7044

With some of the national fish chains having quit the city, this "reliable", "enthusiastic" and "buzzy" Clifton seafood restaurant is finding even more favour than ever; "the 'light-lunch' menu offers incredible value". / *Details:* www.fishers-restaurant.com; 10.30 pm, Sun 10 pm.

The Glass Boat
£ 40

Welsh Back BS1 4SB (0117) 929 0704

A moored barge, tipped for its "romantic setting overlooking the river, with swans floating by"; "if only the food was up to the location…" / *Details:* www.glassboat.co.uk; below Bristol Bridge; 10 pm; closed Sat L & Sun; no Amex.

Goldbrick House
£ 38

69 Park St BS1 5PB (0117) 945 1950

This "happening and trendy" two-year-old bar/restaurant pleases most reporters with its "diverse range of dining options"; critics, however, aren't quite sure the quality of the cooking lives up to the prices. / *Details:* www.goldbrickhouse.co.uk; 11 pm; closed Sun.

Green's Dining Room
£ 40

25 Zetland Rd BS6 7AH (0117) 924 6437

"An excellent local restaurant", whose backers have some starry London names on their cvs; it's a "consistently good" all-rounder, with "pleasant" service, but the tables can seem "a bit close for comfort". / *Details:* www.greensdiningroom.com; 10.30 pm; closed Mon & Sun; no Amex.

Hotel du Vin et Bistro
£ 45

Sugar Hs, Narrow Lewins Mead BS1 2NU (0117) 925 5577

An "atmospheric" outpost of the boutique-hotel chain, in a former warehouse, which always makes a "safe" choice for lunch or dinner; as always with this brand, though, it's the "superb wine list" which is the real star. / *Details:* www.hotelduvin.com; 9.45 pm, Fri-Sun 10.15 pm; booking: max 10. **Accommodation:** 40 rooms, from £145.

Kathmandu
£ 34

Colston Tower, Colston St BS1 5AQ (0117) 929 4455

Some "outstanding" Nepalese specialities add interest to a visit to this "reliable" subcontinental, near the Colston Hall. / *Details:* www.kathmandu-curry.com; 11 pm, Sat 11.30 pm; D only.

The Kensington Arms
£ 32

35-37 Stanley Rd BS6 6NP (0117) 944 6444

A Redland gastropub, three years old in its current incarnation, tipped as having "one of Bristol's best kitchens"; the menu is "fairly carnivorous". / *Details:* www.thekensingtonarms.co.uk; 10 pm; closed Sun D; no Amex.

Krishna's Inn
£ 27

4 Byron Pl, Triangle South BS8 1JT (0117) 927 6864

"What a gem!" – if you're looking for "excellent South Indian food at silly prices", this café-style operation is just the ticket. / *Details:* www.keralagroup.co.uk; 11 pm Fri & Sat midnight.

Lido £ 36

Oakfield Pl BS8 2BJ (0117) 933 9533

An interesting new restaurant overlooking a recently restored Victorian swimming pool, in Clifton; the Italianate food is sometimes said to be "wonderful" too, but reports aren't quite consistent.
/ **Details:** www.lidobristol.com; 10 pm; no Amex.

Mud Dock Café
CycleWorks £ 36

40 The Grove BS1 4RB (0117) 934 9734

An "unusual" all-day venue, tipped for its "great waterside views from the rooftop terrace" (above a cycle-shop); it's "slightly overpriced", though, and staff can be "more interested in gossiping than service".
/ **Details:** www.mud-dock.com; close to the Industrial Museum & Arnolfini Gallery; 10 pm; closed Mon D & Sun D.

Obento £ 20

69 Baldwin St BS1 1QZ (01179) 297392

Tipped for "delicious sushi, fresh and beautifully presented", this well priced city-centre spot impresses reporters across the board; for karaoke, head on upstairs. / **Details:** www.obento-bristol.co.uk; no Amex.

Primrose Café £ 33

1 Boyces Ave BS8 4AA (0117) 946 6577

A "busy" café, whose "quirky" Clifton premises make a "consistently atmospheric" destination at any time of day – from "top-quality" breakfasts, via tea and "special" cakes, all the way through to "really sweet" suppers (when the romantic vibe is perhaps the main attraction). / **Details:** 10 pm; Sun D; no booking at L.

Prosecco £ 36

25 The Mall BS8 4JG (0117) 973 4499

A rather smart and metropolitan-looking Clifton Italian, tipped for "consistently superb" cuisine, "very friendly" service and "excellent choice of wines". / **Details:** www.proseccoclifton.com; 11.30 pm; closed Mon L, Tue L, Wed L & Sun; no Amex.

Rajpoot £ 38

52 Upper Belgrave Rd BS8 2XP (0117) 973 3515

An "unusually attractive" Clifton Indian of long standing, consistently acclaimed for its "tasty" food and "helpful" service.
/ **Details:** www.rajpootrestaurant.co.uk; 11 pm; D only, closed Sun.

riverstation £ 40

The Grove BS1 4RB (0117) 914 4434

"Location, location, location" – this former river-police station, with an attractive upstairs dining room (and busier ground-floor bar), certainly has a fab position on the dockside; the food has traditionally played second fiddle, but seemed "improved" this year.
/ **Details:** www.riverstation.co.uk; 10.30 pm, Fri & Sat 11 pm; closed Sat L & Sun D; no Amex.

Sands £ 33

95 Queens Rd BS8 1LW (0117) 973 9734

It's not just the "authentic" Lebanese cuisine (including "excellent mezze") which makes it worth seeking out this Clifton spot – its "intimate" atmosphere makes it "ideal for a date".
/ **Details:** www.sandsrestaurant.co.uk; 11 pm.

Severnshed £ 35

The Grove, Harbourside BS1 4RB (0117) 925 1212

It's the "beautiful waterside setting" in a "lovely old building" that makes this trendy bar/brasserie of particular note, but the food is generally hailed as being pretty "reliable" too.
/ **Details:** www.shed-restaurants.com; 10.30 pm.

The Thali Café £ 22

12 York Rd BS6 5QE (0117) 942 6687

"I come back again and again", says a (young, London-based) reporter, who is among those "wowed" by the "charming, exotic and crazy" formula of these "fun" subcontinentals; also in Easton and Totterdown. / **Details:** www.thethalicafe.co.uk; 10 pm; D only, closed Mon; no Amex.

BRITWELL SALOME, OXFORDSHIRE 2–2D

The Goose £ 49

OX49 5LG (01491) 612304

Tipped as "a good find", this "remote" but "friendly" gastropub still seems to be settling after a change of chef; no one seems to doubt, however, that "they are still trying hard".
/ **Details:** www.thegooserestaurant.co.uk; M40, J6 near Watlington; 9.30 pm; closed Mon & Sun D.

BROADWAY, WORCESTERSHIRE 2–1C

Buckland Manor £ 72

WR12 7LY (01386) 852626

A Central Castings-perfect Cotswold manor house hotel, tipped for "first-class food and service"; one regular, however, suggests the cooking has "lost its edge" since ownership became "remote" (Von Essen). / **Details:** www.bucklandmanor.co.uk; 2m SW of Broadway on B4632; 9 pm; jacket & tie at D; booking: max 8; children: 10+.
Accommodation: 13 rooms, from £275.

The Lygon Arms £ 64

High St WR12 7DU (01386) 852255

For once, new owners (Barcelo) appear to be making a "great improvement" to an historic hotel... but then this famously grand coaching inn has been so "terrible" in recent times that the only way was up! / **Details:** www.barcelo-hotels.co.uk; just off A44; 9 pm; closed Sat L; no jeans; booking: max 8.* **Accommodation:** 77 rooms, from £133.

Russell's £ 48

20 High St WR12 7DT (01386) 853555

This stylish restaurant-with-rooms can seem a "breath of fresh air", in the centre of this picturebook-perfect Cotswold village; it's "not cheap", but its "simple and modern" approach generally pleases most reporters. / **Details:** www.russellsofbroadway.co.uk; 9.30 pm; closed Sun D. **Accommodation:** 7 rooms, from £120.

BROCKENHURST, HAMPSHIRE 2–4D

Le Poussin at Whitley Ridge £ 56 ●○
Beaulieu Rd SO42 7QL (0238) 028 2944
"Great consistency" is the theme of most of the commentary on Alex
Aitken's *"wonderful"* restaurant-with-rooms in the heart of the New
Forest; its style, however, can sometimes seem a little *"stuffy"*.
/ **Details:** www.lepoussin.co.uk; 9.30 pm; children: . **Accommodation:** 18
rooms, from £190.

Simply Poussin £ 37
The Courtyard, Brookley Rd SO42 7RB (01590) 623063
A village bistro tipped as a place where you can eat *"inexpensively but
well"* – indeed, there's some concern that *"the bargain prices are
beginning to undercut the quality"*. / **Details:** www.simplypoussin.co.uk;
behind Bestsellers Bookshop; 9 pm; closed Mon & Sun; no Amex.

BROMLEY, KENT 3–3B

Tamasha £ 41
131 Widmore Rd BR1 3AX (020) 8460 3240
*"An expensive but superb curry house, with a lively atmosphere and
attentive service"*; its all-round charms make it *"a great place for
a lively evening out with friends"*. / **Details:** www.tamasha.co.uk; 10.30 pm;
no shorts. **Accommodation:** 7 rooms, from £65.

BRUNDALL, NORFOLK 6–4D

Lavender House £ 50 ●○
39 The St NR13 5AA (01603) 712215
Chef/patron Richard Hughes is *"very much in evidence"* at this
thatched-roof restaurant, in a *"lovely"* village, which *"tries very hard
to please"*, and is *"becoming very popular"*; there's no denying,
however, that the occasional reporter finds food *"not up
to expectations"*. / **Details:** www.thelavenderhouse.co.uk; 9.30 pm; D only,
closed Sun & Mon; no Amex.

BUCKFASTLEIGH, DEVON 1–3D

Riverford Field Kitchen £ 32 ●○
Wash Barn, Buckfast Leigh TQ11 0LD (01803) 762074
"A million miles from sackcloth-and-ashes style", this elegant
communal-dining shed – in a large organic farm – really does offer
"the freshest vegetables in the world", as well as *"mountains"* of other
"great and freshly-prepared food"; two sittings daily – leave time for
a farm tour. / **Details:** www.riverford.co.uk; closed Mon D, Tue D, Wed D,
Thu D & Sun D; no Amex.

BUCKHORN WESTON, DORSET 2–3B

The Stapleton Arms £ 34
Church Hill SP8 5HS (01963) 370396
"A welcoming gastropub in a picture perfect country village", tipped
as a *"deservedly popular"* destination, if arguably on the *"expensive"*
side for what it is. / **Details:** www.thestapletonarms.com; 10 pm, 9.30 pm Sun.
Accommodation: 4 rooms, from £90.

BULWICK, NORTHAMPTONSHIRE

6–4A

Queen's Head Inn
£ 34

Main St NN17 3DY (01780) 450272

"A quintessential country pub in a stone-built village", which comes complete with a "cosy" dining room; it's a "no-frills" affair, but its "delicious and local" food is all part of the package that makes it "a real delight". / **Details:** 9.30 pm; closed Mon.

BUNBURY, CHESHIRE

5–3B

The Dysart Arms
£ 34

Bowes Gate Rd CW6 9PH (01829) 260183

A classic church-side boozer, tipped as a "popular and friendly dining pub", and offering a good choice of real ales too.
/ **Details:** www.dysartarms-bunbury.co.uk; 9.30 pm, Sun 9 pm.

BURFORD, OXFORDSHIRE

2–2C

The Lamb
£ 47

Sheep St OX18 4LR (01993) 823155

This well-known, grand and "charming" Cotswold inn, is tipped for its "consistent" culinary standards.
/ **Details:** www.cotswold-inns-hotels.co.uk/lamb; A40 from Oxford toward Cheltenham; 9.30 pm, Sun 9 pm; no jeans or trainers. **Accommodation:** 17 rooms, from £142.

BURGHCLERE, BERKSHIRE

2–2D

Carnarvon Arms
£ 40

Winchester Rd RG20 9LE (01635) 278222

A "modern day country inn" (so they say), handy for Newbury Racecourse, and tipped for its "really reliable" and "good-value" pub food. / **Details:** www.carnarvonarms.com; 9 pm, Sun 8.15 pm.
Accommodation: 23 rooms, from £89.95.

BURNHAM MARKET, NORFOLK

6–3B

Hoste Arms
£ 43

The Green PE31 8HD (01328) 738777

This fashionable former coaching inn continues to draw flak for being "a victim of its own success" – many reporters do still find it a "lovely" place with food that's "a cut above your average gastropub", but, for critics, it's just "dreadfully overrated". / **Details:** www.hostearms.co.uk; 6m W of Wells; 9 pm; no Amex. **Accommodation:** 36 rooms, from £128.

BURPHAM, WEST SUSSEX

3–4A

The George & Dragon
£ 39

BN18 9RR (01903) 883131

A "fantastic village location" – "with views across the Arun valley to Arundel Castle" – makes this "tucked-away" boozer particularly worth seeking out; its "home-made food" almost invariably satisfies too. / **Details:** www.burphamgeorgeanddragoninn.com; 3m from Arundel station, off A27; 9 pm; D only, except Sun when L only; no Amex.

Northcote Manor   £ 43
EX37 9LZ   (01769) 560501
A beautiful wisteria-covered country house hotel in the Devon Hills (popular with wedding parties, and also for shooting parties); most reports are of "faultless" cooking and "well trained and helpful" staff, but there's also a feeling in some quarters that "food and wine mark-ups are getting out of hand". / Details: www.northcotemanor.co.uk; 9 pm; no jeans. Accommodation: 11 rooms, from £155.

Maison Bleue   £ 38
30-31 Churchgate St IP33 1RG   (01284) 760623
The Crépy family's "very French" restaurant shines even more brightly as a "beacon of excellence" since its recent refurbishment; "beautifully cooked and presented fish" is the highlight culinary attraction, but the cheeseboard also contends for "best ever" status. / Details: www.maisonbleue.co.uk; near the Cathedral; 9.30 pm; closed Mon & Sun; no Amex.

St James   £ 41
30 High St WD23 3HL   (020) 8950 2480
A "sophisticated" spot, by local standards, sometimes tipped as a "perfect neighbourhood restaurant" (and with particularly "cheery" service); reports, though, are too variable to make this an entirely safe endorsement. / Details: www.stjamesrestaurant.co.uk; opp St James Church; 9 pm; closed Sun; booking essential.

Columbine   £ 35
7 Hall Bank SK17 6EW   (01298) 78752
If you're visiting this lovely bit of the world, this family-owned establishment is tipped as "the best in town"… which is to say that meals can be "a little predictable", and service can be "cool". / Details: www.buxtononline.net/columbine; nr top of Hall Bank; 10 pm; D only, closed Sun; no Amex.

Langmans   £ 38
3 Church St PL17 7RE   (01579) 384933
"Easily the most impressive gastronomic experience in East Cornwall"; the (self-taught) Anton Buttery offers a "true gourmet experience" (tasting menu only), at this "surprising" small restaurant, and a "well balanced" wine list to go with it too. / Details: www.langmansrestauran.co.uk; D only, closed Mon–Wed & Sun; booking essential.

The Place £ 40
New Lydd Rd TN31 7RB (01797) 225057
"A former motel, now a cool hotel with brasserie close to Camber Sands"; it's of much more culinary note than its external appearances might suggest, but the year that's seen a change of ownership has seen very mixed reports (hence we've left it un-rated for the time being). / Details: www.theplacecambersands.co.uk; 9 pm, Fri & Sat 9.30 pm. Accommodation: 18 rooms, from £80.

CAMBRIDGE, CAMBRIDGESHIRE 3–1B

At the top end of the market, some clear blue water remains on the dining out front between Cambridge and its ancient rival, but the lead does look to be shrinking. The city's eminent restaurant *Midsummer House*, having secured high approval from Michelin, seems to be getting rather complacent, and *22 Chesterton Road* – long the top mid-range option – has slipped a bit on a change of ownership. *Alimentum* offers hope, but a change of chef unfortunately happened at just the wrong point in the year for our survey to give any authoritative judgement on the new régime. Otherwise, the choices the city offers remain very dull.

Alimentum £ 44
152-154 Hills Rd CB2 8PB (01223) 413000
Despite a location "on a junction plagued by roadworks" (and "strange décor" too), this ambitious two-year-old has quite a name for "amazing" cooking; the chef changed just as our survey for the year was concluding, however, so a proper assessment of the new régime will have to wait till next year. / Details: www.restaurantalimentum.co.uk; 9.30 pm, Fri & Sat 10 pm; closed Sun D; booking essential.

Backstreet Bistro £ 37
2 Sturton St CB1 2QA (01223) 306306
Tipped as a "real gem", a "friendly" and generally "reliable" spot that precisely lives up to its name. / Details: www.back-street.co.uk; 9.30 pm, Fri & Sat 10 pm; closed Mon.

The Cambridge Chop House £ 36
1 Kings Pde CB2 1SJ (01223) 359506
Only a couple of years in business, this "good city-centre stand-by" has exercised its "reliable" and "relaxed" charms to gather quite a following among reporters; there's no denying, however, that critics just find it "very ordinary". / Details: www.cambscuisine.com/chophouse; 10.30 pm, Sat 11 pm, Sun 9.30 pm.

Charlie Chan £ 25
14 Regent St CB2 1DB (01223) 359336
An ages-old standby, still tipped for "Chinese food of the usual English variety, but really well done!" / Details: 11 pm.

Hotel Du Vin £ 45
15-19 Trumpington St CB2 1QA (01223) 227330
One of the newer branches of the celebrated wine-led hotel-and-bistro chain; it got off to a very "shaky" start, striking many reporters as "expensive" and "very average" – let's hope that supporters who speak of "recent improvements" have got it right. / Details: www.hotelduvin.com; 10 pm, Fri & Sat 10.30 pm.

Loch Fyne £ 37
37 Trumpington St CB2 1QY (01223) 362433
A central chain-outlet surprisingly often tipped as "an old favourite for quality seafood" (too many instances of "dire" service notwithstanding). / Details: www.lochfyne.com; opp Fitzwilliam Museum; 10 pm.

Midsummer House £ 87
Midsummer Common CB4 1HA (01223) 369299
It has a "wonderful" location (by the Cam) and Daniel Clifford's food is often "sublime", but the two Michelin stars awarded to his "polished" establishment seem to be weaving their evil spell – service can be "obsequious-cum-patronising", and the cuisine has too often seemed "less-special-than-expected" of late.
/ Details: www.midsummerhouse.co.uk; On the river Cam, near Mitchams Corner and the boat sheds; 9.30 pm; closed Mon, Tue L & Sun.

Rainbow Café £ 28
9a King's Pde CB2 1SJ (01223) 321551
A "homely" and "eclectic" cellar-vegetarian, tipped for its "large portions" and its wonderfully central location (opposite King's); no booking, though, is a "pain". / Details: www.rainbowcafe.co.uk; 9 pm; closed Mon D & Sun D; no Amex.

22 Chesterton Road £ 43
22 Chesterton Rd CB4 3AX (01223) 351880
For most reporters, "consistently good" (and sometimes "exquisite") cooking remains the watchword at this "tiny" and "intimate" restaurant in a terrace house; there's some feeling, however, that standards are "not quite what they were under the former régime". / Details: www.restaurant22.co.uk; 9.45 pm; D only, closed Mon & Sun; children: 12+.

CANTERBURY, KENT 3–3D

Apeksha £ 24
24 St Peters St CT1 2BQ (01227) 780079
"A really pleasant surprise", this "modern" establishment, a few minutes walk from the city-centre, is unanimously hailed for "superb Indian food", and notably "polite" service too.
/ Details: www.apeksha.co.uk; 11.30 pm.

Café des Amis £ 31
95 St Dunstan's St CT2 8AD (01227) 464390
In a city remarkably devoid of quality eating places, this long-established Mexican, by Westgate Towers, is tipped as a "very reliable" destination, and it's usually "heaving".
/ Details: www.cafedez.com; by Westgate Towers; 10 pm, Fri & Sat 10.30 pm, Sun 9.30 pm; booking: max 6 at D, Fri & Sat.

Cafe Mauresque £ 33
8 Butchery Ln CT1 2JR (01227) 464300
It's perhaps the (downstairs) setting – "all-in-all a sensory delight" – which makes this Moorish/North African city-centre spot of particular note, but the cuisine is usually reported as "delicious and spicy", and it's "inexpensive" too. / Details: www.cafemauresque.com; 10 pm, Fri & Sat 10.30 pm.

Goods Shed **£ 39**
Station Road West CT2 8AN   (01227) 459153
Traditionally "a welcome find in a city without much in the way
of good eating", this "former railway building" (which also houses
a Farmers' Market) has quite a name for its "earthy" cuisine; for what
it is, though, there is a growing feeling among reporters that it's
*"just too expensive". / **Details:** www.thegoodsshed.net; 9.30 pm; closed*
Mon & Sun D.

Michael Caines
ABode Canterbury **£ 53**
High St CT1 2RX   (01227) 766266
Of all the restaurants associated with the celebrity (Gidleigh Park)
chef, this town-centre hotel dining room is by far the weakest –
the "amazing" lunch offer has its fans, but otherwise reports tend
*to be very negative. / **Details:** www.ABodehotels.co.uk; 10 pm; closed Sun D.*
***Accommodation:** 72 rooms, from £.*

CARDIFF, CARDIFF   2–2A

Cardiff remains a city without a great deal of dining-out
interest. If one's looking for good news, however, the once-
celebrated *Le Gallois Y Cymro*, in the smart suburb of Canton,
is currently staging something of a renaissance. Whatever the
food may be like, the waterside restaurants at the Bay are
pleasant on a sunny day.

The Armless Dragon **£ 39**
97 Wyeverne Rd CF2 4BG   (029) 2038 2357
Tipped for a "truly Welsh experience", a stalwart bistro in Cathays,
where the "locally sourced" dishes are sometimes "very good".
*/ **Details:** www.thearmlessdragon.co.uk; 10 min outside city-centre; 9 pm, Fri &*
Sat 9.30 pm; closed Mon, Sat L & Sun.

La Brasserie **£ 25**
60 St Mary St CF10 1FE   (029) 2023 4134
"Central, popular and long-established", this large-scale operation
specialises in "a decent range of quickly cooked meats and fish"
(which you choose at the counter yourself).
*/ **Details:** www.labrasserierestaurant.co.uk; midnight; closed Sun D; need 8+*
to book.

Le Gallois Y Cymro **£ 48**
6-10 Romilly Cr CF11 9NR   (029) 2034 1264
"Transformed under its new chef", this Canton brasserie – until recent
years, undisputedly Cardiff's pre-eminent place – is "working hard
to regain lost ground", and is strongly re-emerging as a "consistent
*performer that's worth the money". / **Details:** www.legallois-ycymro.com;*
1.5m W of Cardiff Castle; 9.30 pm, Fri & Sat 10 pm; closed Mon & Sun D;
no Amex.

Happy Gathering **£ 28**
233 Cowbridge Road East CF11 9AL   (029) 2039 7531
An "authentic" oriental, in the city-centre, that's consistently praised for
*its "excellent Chinese food". / **Details:** www.happygathering.co.uk; 10.30 pm,*
Sun 9 pm.

Le Monde £ 37 ★

62 St Mary St CF10 1FE   (029) 2038 7376

"You get to pick from the display" at the grander upstairs adjunct to La Brasserie, where the same "cooked to order" procedure applies; there's "a great choice of seafood" and "good fresh fish".
/ **Details:** *www.le-monde.co.uk; 11 pm; closed Sun; need 10+ to book.*

Patagonia £ 42

11 Kings Rd CF11 9BZ   (029) 2019 0265

"Cardiff may be a culinary desert, but this is an oasis" – it still attracts disappointingly few reports, but this plain Spanish-run restaurant (cum-'coffee house') is vociferously tipped for its "inventive" and "delicate" contemporary cuisine; more reports please.
/ **Details:** *www.patagonia-restaurant.co.uk; 10.30 pm, Sat 11 pm; D only, closed Mon & Sun; no Amex.*

Thai House £ 38

3-5 Guiford Cr CF10 2HJ   (029) 2038 7404

Near the Cardiff International Arena, a Thai restaurant tipped as "better than most in Cardiff", and where some dishes come "very powerfully spiced". / **Details:** *www.thaihouse.biz; 10.30 pm; closed Sun.*

Tides Bar And Grill ✖
St David's Hotel & Spa £ 48

Havannah St CF10 5SD   (029) 2045 4045

Cardiff's grandest hotel may be a landmark of the Bay, but we mention it as usual only for completeness – commentary on its restaurant is modest in volume, but it all continues to suggest that it's "very ordinary", and "extortionately overpriced".
/ **Details:** *www.thestdavidshotel.com; in Cardiff Bay; 10 pm; no shorts.*
Accommodation: *132 rooms, from £99.*

Woods Brasserie £ 40 ⓣ

Pilotage Building, Stuart St CF10 5BW   (029) 2049 2400

A "modern" brasserie with a "fantastic harbourside setting" at Cardiff Bay, tipped for general "attention to detail", and for "attentive" (but not "overbearing") service. / **Details:** *www.woods-brasserie.com; next to the Mermaid Quay Complex; 10 pm.*

CARTHORPE, NORTH YORKSHIRE 8–4B

The Fox and Hounds Inn £ 35 ★

DL8 2LG   (01845) 567433

This "typical country inn" is "very handy for a break from the A1", but its "all-round" charms make it worth seeking out whether or not you're travelling. / **Details:** *www.foxandhoundscarthorpe.co.uk; 9.30 pm; closed Mon.*

CARTMEL, CUMBRIA 7–4D

Aynsome Manor £ 38 ⓣ

LA11 6HH   (01539) 536653

"Not adventurous, but reliable", this "very comfortable" and "efficient" country house hotel is tipped for its "value-for-money" cuisine.
/ **Details:** *www.aynsomemanorhotel.co.uk; off A590, 0.5m N of village; 8.30 pm; D only, ex Sun open L only; no shorts; children: 5+ in restaurant at D.*
Accommodation: *12 rooms, from £95.*

L'Enclume **£ 75** ★

Cavendish St LA11 6PZ   (01539) 536362

"Startlingly creative" food (*"from the Fat Duck school"*) makes a visit to Simon Rogan's restaurant-with-rooms an undoubted *"experience"*; even fans, though, may proclaim this is *"food as entertainment, not sustenance"*, and critics say the menu here is *"ego on a plate"*, at prices which are *"taking the p***"*. / **Details:** www.lenclume.co.uk; Junction 36 from M6, down A590 towards Cartmel; 9 pm; closed Mon L & Tue L; children: no children at D. **Accommodation:** 12 rooms, from £98.

Rogan & Co **£ 40**

Devonshire Sq LA11 6QD   (01539) 535917

It inhabits a *"fabulous"* building, but there are some question marks over the level of consistency at Simon Rogan's bistro yearling; most reporters enjoyed the *"well-prepared"* food, but teething problems have also been in evidence.

/ **Details:** www.roganandcompany.co.uk; 9 pm; no Amex.

CASTLE COMBE, WILTSHIRE 2–2B

★★

Bybrook Restaurant
Manor House Hotel **£ 80**

SN14 7HR   (01249) 782206

The dining room of this *"beautiful manor house"*, in a *"scenic village"*, almost invariably impresses reporters with its *"top-notch"* food and its *"very impressive"* service; the ambience though can sometimes be *"stiff"* (in Michelin-pleasing style), and critics find the lighting *"unsympathetic"*. / **Details:** www.exclusivehotels.co.uk; 9.30 pm, Fri & Sat 10 pm; closed Sat L; no trainers. **Accommodation:** 48 rooms, from £235.

CAUNTON, NOTTINGHAMSHIRE 5–3D

Caunton Beck **£ 38**

Main St NG23 6AB   (01636) 636793

"The perfect local" – this all-day boozer is unanimously hailed by reporters for its *"pleasant"* food and its *"very reasonable"* prices. / **Details:** www.wigandmitre.com; 6m NW of Newark past British Sugar factory on A616; 10 pm, Sun 9.30 pm .

CHADDESLEY CORBETT, WORCESTERSHIRE 5–4B

Ⓗ★

Brockencote Hall **£ 53**

DY10 4PY   (01562) 777876

Fans hail this recently-expanded traditional country house hotel – which looks very English, but where the staff tend to be very French – as an example of *"sheer perfection"*; reports, however, are not entirely consistent. / **Details:** www.brockencotehall.com; on A448, just outside village; 9.30 pm; no trainers. **Accommodation:** 17 rooms, from £120.

Gidleigh Park   £ 105
TQ13 8HH   (01647) 432367

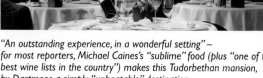

"An outstanding experience, in a wonderful setting" –
for most reporters, Michael Caines's *"sublime"* food (plus *"one of the best wine lists in the country"*) makes this Tudorbethan mansion, by Dartmoor, a simply *"unbeatable"* destination.
/ **Details:** www.gidleigh.com; from village, right at Lloyds TSB, take right fork to end of lane; 9 pm; no jeans or shorts; children: 8+ at D. **Accommodation:** 24 rooms, from £310.

22 Mill Street   £ 54
22 Mill St TQ13 8AW   (01647) 432244
Continuing good feedback on the new régime at this popular town-centre restaurant; it doesn't raise reporters to great heights of eloquence, but ratings confirm that realisation of the menu, which is quite ambitious, can be *"excellent"*. / **Details:** www.22millst.com; 9.30 pm; closed Mon & Sun; no trainers; children: 12+. **Accommodation:** 2 rooms, from £75.

The Clarendon   £ 46
Redhall Ln WD3 4LU   (01923) 270009
Difficult to appraise this *"all singing/all dancing"* pub-conversion, which offers everything from bar-dining to a hugely pricey chef's table – there's some agreement that it's *"expensive"*, but thereafter reporters differ as to whether it's *"a real discovery"*, or just *"way OTT"*.
/ **Details:** www.theclarendon.co.uk; 10 pm.

Colette's
The Grove   £ 86
WD3 4TG   (01923) 296015
"Pricey, but a good experience overall" – almost all of the reports on this *"posh"* modern country house hotel dining room are in a remarkably similar vein, and *"it's hard to beat for many miles around for a romantic evening"*. / **Details:** www.thegrove.co.uk; J19 or 20 on M25; 9.30 pm; D only, closed Mon & Sun; jacket; children: 16+. **Accommodation:** 227 rooms, from £295.

The Glasshouse
The Grove   £ 55
WD3 4TG   (01923) 296015
Views divide on the buffet-restaurant at this groovy–grand country house hotel; fans insist it's a *"wonderful"* experience offering *"a new taste sensation every second"*, but critics just find the whole experience *"horrendous"* – *"like feeding time at the zoo"*.
/ **Details:** www.thegrove.co.uk; 9.30 pm, Sat 10.30 pm, Sun 9.30 pm.
Accommodation: 227 rooms, from £280.

Seven Spices £ 25

2 Mellor Rd SK8 5AU (0161) 485 4700

A very orange restaurant which doesn't inspire reporters to great heights of poetry – the ratings they award, however, make it clear that this is a top tip for Indian cuisine in the area.

/ **Details:** www.7spices.co.uk/.

Brasserie Blanc

The Queen's Hotel £ 37

The Promenade GL50 1NN (01242) 266800

"Very good-value lunches" are the highlight attraction of this handily-located outpost of a national chain; otherwise, however, the many reports tend to suggest that improvements apparent elsewhere in the group are yet to show through here. / **Details:** www.brasserieblanc.com; 10.30 pm, Sat 11 pm, Sun 10 pm.

Le Champignon Sauvage £ 66

24-28 Suffolk Rd GL50 2AQ (01242) 573449

"Husband and wife in perfect harmony" – David Everitt-Mathias delivers the "versatile" and "amazing" cuisine, while Helen runs front-of-house – help make this city-centre veteran (est. 1987) perhaps the UK's "best-value gourmet restaurant"; this year's feedback, however, did include the occasional 'wobble'.

/ **Details:** www.lechampignonsauvage.co.uk; near Cheltenham Boys College; 9 pm; closed Mon & Sun.

The Daffodil £ 41

18-20 Suffolk Pde GL50 2AE (01242) 700055

It's the setting – a "gorgeous former Art Deco cinema" featuring "private and intimate" booths – which makes this an establishment of some note, especially for romance; the food may be a bit incidental, but it rarely disappoints, and the set menus offer "good value".

/ **Details:** www.thedaffodil.com; just off Suffolk Square; 10 pm, Sat 10.30 pm; closed Sun.

Lumière £ 51

Clarence Pde GL50 3PA (01242) 222200

Still not many reports, but this smart city-centre restaurant is recommended for "improved" cooking, since it moved into new ownership in 2009 – a proper appraisal of the new régime, however, will have to wait until next year. / **Details:** www.lumiere.cc; off the promenade on the inner ring; 9 pm; D only, closed Mon & Sun; booking: max 10; children: 8+ D.

The Royal Well Tavern £ 38

5 Royal Well Pl GL50 3DN (01242) 221212

"Spot-on food" and "fine service" make this smartly-furnished gastropub yearling ("more gastro than pub") popular with all who comment on it; for those who wish to eat pre-7pm, the prix-fixe menu offers a "satisfying" option. / **Details:** www.theroyalwelltavern.com; by the main bus station; 10 pm, Sat 10.30 pm; closed Sun D.

Ruby £ 31 ⭐

52 Suffolk Rd GL50 2AQ   (01242) 250909

Twenty years on, this town-centre Cantonese still offers "Chinese food at its best", and meals here can be "memorable".
/ **Details:** *www.rubycantonese.co.uk; near Cheltenham Boys College; 11.15 pm.*

Storyteller £ 34 Ⓐ⭐

11 North Pl GL50 4DW   (01242) 250343

Although it's tempting to single out the "excellent wines" – chosen in the walk-in wine room – for praise at this "novel" establishment, all aspects please reporters; for the best ambience, "book in the conservatory". / **Details:** *www.storyteller.co.uk; near the cinema; 10 pm; no Amex.*

Thai Emerald £ 37

60 St. Georges Pl GL50 3PN   (01242) 522004

A large and "beautifully-furnished" Thai restaurant, part of a small chain, which is tipped for its "great-value buffet lunch".
/ **Details:** *www.thai-emerald.co.uk; 10.30 pm.*

CHESTER, CHESHIRE 5–2A

Aqua-Vitus £ 33

58 Watergate St CH1 2LA   (01244) 313721

"Not a great gastronomic experience, but good-value" – in this bizarrely under-served city, tips such as this Swedish/French establishment are not to be sneezed at, with the set lunch menu particularly worth seeking out. / **Details:** *www.aquavitus.co.uk; 10.30 pm; closed Sun; no Amex.*

La Brasserie Ⓐ

Chester Grosvenor £ 49

Eastgate CH1 1LT   (01244) 324024

The "expensive but delightful" brasserie of the city's grandest hotel has a good number of fans in its own right – "it's often seen as the poor relation to Simon Radley, but I prefer the fun atmosphere, and the decoration is beautiful too". / **Details:** *www.chestergrosvenor.com; 10 pm.* **Accommodation:** *80 rooms, from £169.50.*

Moules A Go Go £ 35

39 Watergate Row CH1 2LE   (01244) 348818

Especially worth knowing about in a city with so very many dreary options, a "bustling" bistro, on the famous first-floor 'rows', where "good" mussels are tipped as the highlight of a "varied" menu.
/ **Details:** *www.moulesagogo.co.uk; 10 pm, Sun 9 pm.*

Simon Radley
The Chester Grosvenor   **£ 61**
Eastgate CH1 1LT   (01244) 324024

Putting the name of the long-standing chef over the door of the former 'Arkle' restaurant has contributed to an extraordinary transformation of this grand – and now "memorable" and "sophisticated" – city-centre hotel (and spa) dining room; the tempting wine list ("to suit most budgets") includes some "good-value vintage champagnes". / **Details:** www.chestergrosvenor.com; 11 pm; D only, closed Mon & Sun; no Amex; no trainers; children: 12+. **Accommodation:** 82 rooms, from £180.

Upstairs at The Grill   **£ 37**
70 Watergate St CH1 2LA   (01244) 344883
Consistent praise from reporters for this small and recently-established steakhouse "gem", which is of particular note for its "funky" and extensive wine list. / **Details:** www.upstairsatthegrill.co.uk; D only.

CHETTLE, DORSET   2–3C

Castleman Hotel   **£ 35**
DT11 8DB   (01258) 830096
A "rather old-fashioned manor house", where the food – if "slightly unadventurous" – is tipped as being of "good quality" and "very fairly priced". / **Details:** www.castlemanhotel.co.uk; 1m off the A354, signposted; 9 pm; D only, ex Wed & Sun open L & D; no Amex. **Accommodation:** 8 rooms, from £80.

CHICHESTER, WEST SUSSEX   3–4A

Comme Ça   **£ 50**
67 Broyle Rd PO19 6BD   (01243) 788724
"A charming, old-fashioned, French restaurant, convenient for the Festival Theatre"; almost all reports confirm that it's a "consistently satisfying" destination, and it has a "beautiful outside eating area" too. / **Details:** www.commeca.co.uk; 0.5m N of city-centre; 9.30 pm, Sat & Sun 10.30 pm; closed Mon & Tue L.

Field & Fork
Pallant House Gallery   **£ 43**
9 North Pallant PO19 1TJ   (01243) 770 827
"A café by day and a small, cosy restaurant space in the evening"; "tacked on" to an "attractive" art gallery, this is tipped as the sort of of place that's good for a "shopping lunch", or "sophisticated brunch". / **Details:** www.fieldandfork.co.uk; 10.30 pm; closed Mon, Tue D & Sun D.

West Stoke House £ 62
PO18 9BN (01243) 575226
*A recent internal reorganisation seems to have unsettled reports
on this "slightly eccentric" restaurant-with-rooms; most reporters still
say it "deserves its high local reputation", but it's often seemed rather
"impersonal" of late, with too many meals rated as "underwhelming".*
/ **Details:** www.weststokehouse.co.uk; 9 pm; closed Mon & Tue; children: 12+
D. **Accommodation:** 8 rooms, from £140.

CHIGWELL, ESSEX 3–2B

The Bluebell £ 48
117 High Rd IG7 6QQ (020) 8500 6282
*"A cosy little restaurant in an old cottage"; both quantities and prices
strike some reporters as a little generous, but there's not much
dispute that the quality is "very good".*
/ **Details:** www.thebluebellrestaurant.co.uk; 10 pm, Sat 12.30 am; closed Mon,
Sat L & Sun D.

CHILGROVE, WEST SUSSEX 3–4A

The Fish House £ 59
High St PO18 9HX (01243) 519444

*From David Barnard (former proprietor of the celebrated Crab
at Chieveley), a small but supremely "professional" new hotel –
"nestled in the glorious South Downs" – that's had a rapturous
reception from early-days reporters; highlights include "superb" fish
dishes and extensive al fresco seating.* / **Details:** www.thefishhouse.co.uk;
9.30 pm, Fri & Sat 10 pm; no Amex. **Accommodation:** 15 rooms, from £100.

CHILLESFORD, WOODBRIDGE, SUFFOLK 3–1D

The Froize Free House Restaurant £ 40
The St IP12 3PU (01394) 450282
*"Don't let the carvery-style put you off, the food here is great!" –
thus speaks one of the fans of the spread put on by the "hospitable"
chef/patron of this attractive inn; puddings, in particular,
are "fantastic".* / **Details:** www.froize.co.uk; 8.30 pm but varies seasonally;
closed Mon, Tue D, Wed D & Sun D.

CHINNOR, OXFORDSHIRE 2–2D

The Sir Charles Napier £ 47
Spriggs Alley OX39 4BX (01494) 483011

Thirty-five years in its current ownership, this "perfect little retreat" has long had a reputation such that it's "besieged by 4x4s" (and it's certainly "not cheap") – to a remarkable extent, though, it maintains its "hidden gem"-style charm, and the menu is (almost) "always good". / Details: www.sircharlesnapier.co.uk; M40, J6 into Chinnor, turn right at roundabout, carry on straight up hill for 2 miles; 9.30 pm; closed Mon & Sun D.

CHIPPING CAMPDEN, GLOUCESTERSHIRE 2–1C

Eight Bells £ 38
Church St GL55 6JG (01386) 840371
A "real 'winter' pub", tipped for "just the sort of food you really want to eat – not messed with or pretentious".
/ Details: www.eightbellsinn.co.uk; 10m S of Stratford upon Avon; 9 pm, Fri & Sat 9.30 pm, Sun 8.45 pm; no Amex; children: 11+ after 6 pm. Accommodation: 7 rooms, from £85.

**Juliana's
Cotswold House Hotel** £ 73
High Street GL55 6AN (01386) 840330
In a "painfully picturesque" village, an elegant hotel tipped for its "superb food and presentation"; the chef changed, however, shortly before this guide went to press. / Details: www.cotswoldhouse.com; 9.45 pm; D only, closed Mon & Sun. Accommodation: 28 rooms, from £150.

CHIPPING, LANCASHIRE 5–1B

Gibbon Bridge £ 42
Green Ln PR3 2TQ (01995) 61456
A "superb setting", in the Forest of Bowland, is not the only thing that makes this prettified hotel dining room "well worth a detour" – the food is (almost) invariably "of the same good standard".
/ Details: www.gibbon-bridge.co.uk; 8.30 pm; no shorts. Accommodation: 30 rooms, from £130.

CHRISTCHURCH, DORSET 2–4C

**Rhodes South
Christchurch Harbour Hotel** £ 47
95 Mudeford BH23 3NJ (01202) 483434
It may be "very much to the Gary R brand formula", but this modern sea-front spot impresses most reporters as an "extremely nice" venue all-round; "wonderful views", however, are the highlight; (NB Do not confuse this establishment with King's Rhodes, nearby, which is "a real let-down"). / Details: www.rhodes-south.co.uk; 10 pm; closed Mon & Sun.

CHURCH STRETTON, SHROPSHIRE 5–4A

Berry's £ 27
17 High St SY6 6BU (01694) 724452
A village-centre café, tipped for "good home-made soups, tasty and imaginative pies and very good coffee".
/ Details: www.berryscoffeehouse.co.uk; 10 pm; closed for D Mon-Thu & Sun D; no credit cards.

CLACHAN, CAIRNDOW 9–3B

Loch Fyne Oyster Bar £ 48
PA26 8BL (01499) 600236
With its "stunning" lochside location, the original LFOB (run separately from the chain) is still a hit with reporters who say its "deliciously fresh fish" can be "out of this world"; service, though, can be "poor" at busy times. / Details: www.loch-fyne.com; 10m E of Inveraray on A83; 8.30 pm.

CLAVERING, ESSEX 3–2B

The Cricketers £ 39
Wicken Rd CB11 4QT (01799) 550442
On the village green, a "friendly", old-fashioned boozer, run by Jamie Oliver's parents; arguably, it's "not as good as its reputation might suggest", but still "as good as it gets around this area for pub grub".
/ Details: www.thecricketers.co.uk; on B1038 between Newport & Buntingford; 9.30 pm. Accommodation: 14 rooms, from £110.

CLIFTON, CUMBRIA 8–3A

George & Dragon Clifton £ 33
CA10 2ER (01768) 865381
"A superb addition to the Cumbria dining scene", this recently relaunched inn is a relaxed sort of place, where the menu puts much emphasis on local sourcing. / Details: www.georgeanddragonclifton.co.uk; 9.30 pm. Accommodation: 10 rooms, from £85.

CLIMPING, WEST SUSSEX 3–4A

Bailiffscourt Hotel £ 68
BN17 5RW (01903) 723511
The medieval dining room of this "fabulous" country house hotel (with beautiful spa and leisure facilities) offers a "magical" setting for dinner, and the food – though attracting rather less in the way of commentary – is usually pretty "sumptuous" too.
/ Details: www.hshotels.co.uk; 9.30 pm; booking: max 8; children: 7+. Accommodation: 39 rooms, from £135.

CLIPSHAM, RUTLAND 6–4A

The Olive Branch £ 44
Main St LE15 7SH (01780) 410355
Well, it's had a great run, but this famous gastropub, near the A1, is now "losing its sparkle" – "it has terrific days and bad days... sometimes even at the same meal"; though "wonderful" reports still predominate, some reporters now find the place simply "dreary".
/ Details: www.theolivebranchpub.com; 2m E from A1 on B664; 9.30 pm; no Amex. Accommodation: 6 rooms, from £100.

Inn at Whitewell £ 40
Forest of Bowland BD7 3AT (01200) 448222

"A wonderfully romantic inn, buried away in the Forest of Bowland";
it's not just the "amazingly beautiful" setting which makes it of note
either – the "beautiful home-cooked" food has many admirers,
as does the "more-exciting-than-usual wine list".
/ **Details:** www.innatwhitewell.com; 9.30 pm; D only; no Amex.
Accommodation: 23 rooms, from £93.

COBHAM, SURREY 3–3A

The Old Bear £ 41
Riverhill KT11 3DX (01932) 862116
"Transformed, this formerly ordinary pub is now a decent eatery with
an interesting menu" – its "good, straightforward food" is always well
prepared, and service is often "excellent" too.
/ **Details:** www.theoldbearcobham.co.uk; 10 pm; closed Sun D.

COCKERMOUTH, CUMBRIA 7–3C

Kirkstile Inn £ 33
Loweswater CA13 0RU (01900) 85219
Tipped as a safe choice "for basic traditional meals", this "out-of-the-
way" pub but "busy" pub but also of note for its "fine setting" and,
in winter, its "roaring fires". / **Details:** www.kirkstile.com; 9 pm; no Amex.
Accommodation: 8 rooms, from £44.50.

Quince & Medlar £ 35
13 Castlegate CA13 9EU (01900) 823579

In an elegant townhouse, a "friendly" establishment that's been
of note for more than twenty years on account of its "innovative",
"delicate" and "delicious" vegetarian fare.
/ **Details:** www.quinceandmedlar.co.uk; next to Cockermouth Castle; 9.30 pm;
D only, closed Mon & Sun; no Amex; children: 5+.

COLERNE, WILTSHIRE   2–2B

Lucknam Park   **£ 88**   H A ✪ ✪
SN14 8AZ   (01225) 742777

Superlative experiences are again reported at this "gorgeous" country
house (complete with spa), where the food is "consistently brilliant"
and service "unexpectedly friendly"; Chef Hywel Jones and the
rest of the staff "simply cannot do enough for you".
/ **Details:** www.lucknampark.co.uk; 6m NE of Bath; 9.30 pm; no jeans or trainers;
children: 5+ at D. **Accommodation:** 41 rooms, from £280.

COLNE, LANCASHIRE   5–1B

Banny's Restaurant   **£ 12**   ✪
1 Vivary Way BB8 9NW   (01282) 856220
A bright brasserie-style operation, on quite a scale (280 seats); this is,
say fans, "the best cheap 'n' cheerful restaurant in Lancashire",
with "traditional fish 'n' chips" the menu star.
/ **Details:** www.bannys.co.uk.

COMPTON, SURREY   3–3A

The Withies Inn   **£ 42**   T
Withies Ln GU3 1JA   (01483) 421158
It's perhaps the "beautiful seating outside" which is the
surest strength of this "quaint" and "very popular" – but "pricey" –
destination pub in the Surrey Hills; a menu like "a '70s throw-back",
however, disenchants some reporters. / **Details:** www.thewithiesinn.com;
off A3 near Guildford, signposted on B3000; 9.30 pm, Sun 4 pm; closed Sun D.

CONGLETON, CHESHIRE   5–2B

Pecks   **£ 48**   ✪
Newcastle Rd CW12 4SB   (01260) 275161
Though revamped under new ownership, this is a rare North Western
restaurant with a true "theatrical" style all of its own – book ahead
for one of their seven-course (Thu-Sat) single-sitting dining
experiences; make sure you leave space for the "great selection
of desserts". / **Details:** www.pecksrest.co.uk; off A34; 8 pm; closed Mon &
Sun D; booking essential.

COOKHAM, BERKSHIRE   3–3A

Bel & The Dragon   **£ 39**   T
High St SL6 9SQ   (01628) 521263
Handy for the Stanley Spencer museum (opposite), this "high-quality
pub/restaurant" attracts only a modest level of feedback, but all
positive. / **Details:** www.belandthedragon-cookham.co.uk; opp Stanley Spencer
Gallery; 10 pm; no Amex.

Ferry £ 35

Sutton Rd SL6 9SN (01628) 525123
*This former 'Harvester' inn is particularly tipped for its "attractive surroundings" (and "great views of Cookham Bridge"), but the food is generally pretty "tasty" too. / **Details:** www.theferry.co.uk; 10 pm.*

Maliks £ 46

High St SL6 9SF (01628) 520085

*An Indian restaurant whose "very fresh and innovative" food is "among the best of its type in the UK"; it's thanks to the quality of the cooking, though – not the service or ambience – that the place is usually "packed". / **Details:** www.maliks.co.uk; from the M4, Junction 7 for A4 for Maidenhead; 11.30 pm, Sun 10.30 pm.*

COPSTER GREEN, LANCASHIRE 5–1B

Yu And You £ 30

500 Longsight Rd BB1 9EU (01254) 247111
*"High quality" food and "great" service win all-round plaudits for this rather unlikely "upper crust" Chinese; some reporters, though, complain of prices which are just "too high".
/ **Details:** www.yuandyou.com; 11 pm, Sat & Sun midnight; D only; no Amex.*

CORBRIDGE, NORTHUMBERLAND 8–2B

The Angel of Corbridge £ 36

Main St NE45 5LA (01434) 632119
*A large Georgian coaching inn sometimes tipped for its "great value"; to be quite frank, though, it's really the paucity of other suggestions in this part of the world which is our prime justification for tipping it. / **Details:** www.theangelofcorbridge.co.uk; 8.45 pm, Fri & Sat 9.25 pm; closed Sun D; no Amex. **Accommodation:** 15 rooms, from £105.*

CORSCOMBE, DORSET 2–4B

The Fox Inn £ 34

DT2 0NS (01935) 891330
*It's not just the "remarkable wine list" which makes this village boozer a consistent hit – even a reporter who thought it an "expensive" destination found it "well worth it". / **Details:** www.thefoxinn.co.uk; 5m off A37; 9 pm; no Amex; children: 5+ D. **Accommodation:** 4 rooms, from £80.*

CORSE LAWN, GLOUCESTERSHIRE 2–1B

Corse Lawn Hotel £ 44
GL19 4LZ (01452) 780771
"Consistently good food and service" makes the Hine family's village
house hotel (in Queen Anne style) a destination that's popular with all
who comment on it; a *"good-value set lunch"* attracts particular
praise. / **Details:** www.corselawn.com; 5m SW of Tewkesbury on B4211;
9.30 pm. **Accommodation:** 19 rooms, from £150.

CORTON DENHAM, SOMERSET 2–3B

The Queen's Arms £ 34
DT9 4LR (01963) 220317
"Friendly, rural and consistent", this *"dog and wellie-friendly"* boozer
is a destination often tipped for those in search of *"great pub food
served in a relaxed and informal atmosphere"*.
/ **Details:** www.thequeenarms.com; 10 pm, Sun 9.30 pm. **Accommodation:** 5
rooms, from £100.

CRANBROOK, KENT 3–4C

Apicius £ 45
23 Stone St TN17 3HF (01580) 714666
"A wonderful reminder of why you should eat out" - Tim Johnson's
restaurant serves up *"consistently outstanding"* food in a *"small but
pleasant"* dining room; its keen prices are *"remarkable for
an establishment of this standard"*, which helps make it worth the
"long wait for a reservation". / **Details:** www.restaurant-apicius.co.uk;
take the A21, turn left through Goudhurst, take the 3rd exit left on the roundabout;
9 pm; closed Mon, Tue L, Sat L & Sun D; no Amex; children: 8+.

CRASTER, NORTHUMBERLAND 8–1B

Jolly Fisherman £ 21
NE66 3TR (01665) 576461
A coastal boozer whose continuing popularity may account for its
sometimes iffy service; even critics, though, tip it for its *"excellent"* crab
sandwiches, and its *"lovely sea views"* too.
/ **Details:** www.thejollyfisherman.org.uk; near Dunstanburgh Castle; 11 pm; L only;
no credit cards; no booking.

CRAYKE, NORTH YORKSHIRE 5–1D

Durham Ox £ 42
Westway YO61 4TE (01347) 821506

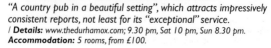

"A country pub in a beautiful setting", which attracts impressively
consistent reports, not least for its *"exceptional"* service.
/ **Details:** www.thedurhamox.com; 9.30 pm, Sat 10 pm, Sun 8.30 pm.
Accommodation: 5 rooms, from £100.

CREIGIAU, CARDIFF 2–2A

Caesars Arms £ 39

Cardiff Rd CF15 9NN (029) 2089 0486

"A fantastic range of fresh produce" (including good fish) – individually chosen by the customer at the counter – is "cooked to order" at this rural institution, which is "always busy". / Details: beyond Creigiau, past golf club; 10 pm; closed Sun D.

CRICK, NORTHAMPTONSHIRE 5–4D

Edwards £ 32

West Haddon Rd NN6 7SQ (01788) 822517

"Great for lunch when travelling up the M1", this "handy" canalside restaurant is a "very pleasant" and airy spot, which offers "fine food" at "fair prices". / Details: www.edwardsrestaurant.co.uk; 9.30 pm; closed Mon & Sun D; no Amex.

CRICKHOWELL, POWYS 2–1A

The Bear £ 36

High St NP8 1BW (01873) 810408

A well-known, "atmospheric" old coaching inn, complete with "open fires" in the heart of the Brecon Beacons, which serves "hearty portions" of "straightforward" local produce ("albeit not in huge variety"). / Details: www.bearhotel.co.uk; 9.30 pm; D only, ex Sun open L only, closed Mon; children: 7+. Accommodation: 34 rooms, from £86.

Nantyffin Cider Mill £ 41

Brecon Rd NP8 1SG (01873) 810775

"Back, and better than ever"; new owners have breathed new life into this sometimes "crowded" ancient coaching inn, where the service is "lovely" and the food of "top quality". / Details: www.cidermill.co.uk; on A40 between Brecon & Crickhowell; 9.30 pm; closed Mon; no Amex.

CRINAN BY LOCHGILPHEAD, ARGYLL & BUTE 9–4B

Crinan Hotel £ 58

PA31 8SR (01546) 830261

Admittedly it's tipped for its "great sea views" rather than its cuisine, but this elegant hotel is still worth knowing about in an area without a huge number of alternatives. / Details: www.crinanhotel.com; 8.30 pm; no Amex. Accommodation: 20 rooms, from £95/person.

CROSTHWAITE, CUMBRIA 7–4D

The Punch Bowl £ 45

LA8 8HR (01539) 568237

An inn that's "well off the beaten track" but tipped for the "sustained high quality" of its food; service, however, can be "dreadfully slow". / Details: www.the-punchbowl.co.uk; off A5074 towards Bowness, turn right after Lyth Hotel; 9.30 pm. Accommodation: 9 rooms, from £110.

The Mark Cross Inn   £ 30
Mark Cross TN6 3NP   (01892) 852423
"Local produce is cooked to a very high standard" at this "friendly" inn (which is one of a trio under common ownership); it offers "outstanding" views too, especially from the outside tables.
/ **Details:** *www.themarkcross.co.uk; 9.30 pm, Sun 9 pm; no Amex.*

Albert's Table   £ 35
49 South End CR0 1BF   (020) 8680 2010
Most reports on this ambitious newcomer speak of "superb cooking in a welcoming ambience, where nothing is too much trouble", or say it's "not cheap, but good value" – there are also some doubters, though, and the 'star' we've awarded gives the benefit of a certain amount of doubt. / **Details:** *www.albertstable.co.uk; 10.30 pm; closed Mon L & Sun D; no Amex.*

Banana Leaf   £ 28
7 Lower Addiscombe Rd CR0 6PQ   (020) 8688 0297
"Excellent South Indian food at incredibly cheap prices, but in far from beautiful surroundings" – that's the concept that's made this East Croydon spot very popular for over two decades.
/ **Details:** *www.a222.co.uk/bananaleaf; near East Croydon station; 11 pm.*

McDermotts Fish & Chips   £ 22
5-7 The Forestdale Shopping Centre Featherbed Ln CR0 9AS
(020) 8651 1440
A modern chippy, unanimously tipped by reporters for the "very high standard" of its cuisine. / **Details:** *ww.mcdermottsfishandchips.co.uk; 9.30 pm, Sat 9 pm; closed Sun.*

The Potting Shed   £ 34
The St SN16 9EW   (01666) 577833
Consistently positive reports all-round on this elegantly furnished village boozer, which offers "beautifully prepared, no-nonsense fare", including "the best ploughman's ever".
/ **Details:** *www.thepottingshedpub.com; 9.30 pm; closed Sun D; no Amex.*

Ockenden Manor   £ 70
Ockenden Ln RH17 5LD   (01444) 416111
Bizarrely mixed reviews on this "attractive" and "comfortable" country house hotel – on most accounts, the food is "splendid" and the overall experience "never disappoints", but the occasional critic is vocal in criticism of both prices and standards. / **Details:** *www.hshotels.co.uk; 9 pm; no jeans or trainers.* **Accommodation:** *22 rooms, from £183.*

CUPAR, FIFE
9–3D

Ostlers Close £ 52 ⚝⚝
25 Bonnygate KY15 4BU (01334) 655574
"Intimate… friendly… great food" – such is the gist of all reports on the Grahams' "friendly" town-centre stalwart (est. 1981), which continues to offer "imaginative" cuisine in "cosy" surroundings.
/ **Details:** www.ostlersclose.co.uk; centrally situated in the Howe of Fife; 9.30 pm; closed Sun & Mon, Tue-Fri D only, Sat L & D; children: 5+.

The Peat Inn £ 50 ⓗⒶ⚝⚝
KY15 5LH (01334) 840206

"Well worth beating a path to!"; this famous country inn has, under the Smeddle family (who bought it three years ago), maintained its "superb" cuisine, showcasing "very high quality" local ingredients; "cosy" dining rooms and "attentive service" do nothing to diminish an exceptional all-round experience. / **Details:** www.thepeatinn.co.uk; at junction of B940 & B941, SW of St Andrews; 9 pm; closed Mon & Sun.
Accommodation: 8 rooms, from £190.

DALRY, NORTH AYRSHIRE
9–4B

Braidwoods £ 57 ⚝⚝
Drumastle Mill Cottage KA24 4LN (01294) 833544

Thanks to the "utterly superb" cooking, reporters are pretty much unanimous that this remote cottage-restaurant is "worth a long drive" – the Braidwoods simply go "the extra mile", and the "interesting wine list" and "impeccable service" all add to the experience.
/ **Details:** www.braidwoods.co.uk; 9 pm; closed Mon, Tue L & Sun D; children: 12+ at D.

DANEHILL, EAST SUSSEX
3–4B

Coach And Horses £ 34 ⓣ
School Ln RH17 7JF (01825) 740369
"A very comfortable old pub with excellent beer", tipped for its "consistently good food from local produce".
/ **Details:** www.coachandhorses.danehill.biz; off A275; 9 pm, Fri & Sat 9.30 pm.

DARLINGTON, COUNTY DURHAM 8–3B

Oven £ 31
30 Duke St DL3 7AQ (01325) 466668
This local restaurant is a "gem" of a place (if one which arguably "lacks a little finesse"), offering "very good food" in "huge portions"; service can slow towards the end of the evening.
/ **Details:** www.ovenrestaurant.com; 9.30 pm, Sat 10 pm; closed Mon L & Sun D.

DARTMOUTH, DEVON 1–4D

New Angel £ 58
2 South Embankment TQ6 9BH (01803) 839425
Perhaps celebrity-besotted Michelin's most absurd star of all – John Burton-Race's "woeful" destination inspired a barrage of abuse, including from one (admittedly younger) reporter who recorded "the most disappointing restaurant experience of my entire life".
/ **Details:** www.thenewangel.co.uk; opp passenger ferry pontoon; 9.30 pm; closed Mon, Tue L & Sun D; no Amex. **Accommodation:** 6 rooms, from £125.

The Seahorse £ 48
5 South Embankment TQ6 9BH (01803) 835147
Mitch Tonks, founder of the FishWorks chain, offers "fine food" – including fish from the establishment's own boat – at this "unpretentious" yearling, overlooking the River Dart.
/ **Details:** www.seahorserestaurant.co.uk; 10 pm, Fri & Sat 10.30 pm; closed Mon, Tue L, Sat L & Sun.

DATCHWORTH, HERTFORDSHIRE 3–2B

The Tilbury £ 39
Watton Rd SG3 6TB (01438) 815 550
A village pub and (slightly "noisy") dining room, where the chef is "amazing", and where the cuisine offers "very good value".
/ **Details:** www.thetilbury.co.uk; 9 pm, Fri & Sat 9.30 pm; closed Mon & Sun D.

DAVENTRY, NORTHAMPTONSHIRE 2–1D

Fawsley Hall £ 50
NN11 3BA (01327) 892000
It has a "stunning" setting, and the "original" style of this "wonderfully atmospheric" country house hotel wins it some very positive reviews; feedback on the food, however, is a little up-and-down.
/ **Details:** www.fawsleyhall.com; on A361 between Daventry & Banbury; 9.30 pm, Sun 9 pm. **Accommodation:** 59 rooms, from £175.

DEAL, KENT 3–3D

Dunkerley's £ 37
19 Beach St CT14 7AH (01304) 375016
There's no denying that this 30+ year-old seafront restaurant is "time-warped"; fans still find the food "generally good", but for critics it's just too "'70s" for comfort. / **Details:** www.dunkerleys.co.uk; 9.30 pm; closed Mon L. **Accommodation:** 16 rooms, from £100.

Milsoms £ 36
Stratford Rd CO7 6HW (01206) 322795
In Constable Country, an informal (and no-booking) offshoot of the celebrated Tolbooth restaurant; it's tipped for "useful all-day dining", even if the cuisine does tend to be "unexciting".
/ **Details:** www.milsomhotels.com; Just off the A12, the Stratford St Mary turning; 9.30 pm; no booking. **Accommodation:** 15 rooms, from £108.

The Sun Inn £ 36
High St CO7 6DF (01206) 323351
This Constable Country inn pleases most reporters with its "very superior bar food" – even those who find it "solid but unspectacular" say it's "good value for money".
/ **Details:** www.thesuninndedham.com; opposite the church on the high street; 11 pm, Sun 9.30 pm. **Accommodation:** 5 rooms, from £90.

Le Talbooth £ 58
Gun Hill CO7 6HP (01206) 323150
Nearly 60 years old, this riverside Constable Country spot has "the best restaurant location in Essex"; its "special occasion" charms can still work their magic, but too often nowadays the formula seems "overpriced" or "disappointing". / **Details:** www.milsomhotels.com; 5m N of Colchester on A12, take B1029; 9.30 pm; closed Sun D; no jeans or trainers.

Swan Inn £ 36
Village Rd UB9 5BH (01895) 832085

Just off the M4 (J1), a "lively" and "popular" gastropub ("with a small car park!") – it's certainly a "pleasant" destination, and the food is usually "tasty", but service is sometimes "not very professional".
/ **Details:** www.swaninndenham.co.uk; 9.30 pm, Fri & Sat 10 pm .

Anoki £ 44
First Floor, 129 London Rd DE1 2QN (01332) 292888
"A former cinema now converted into a wondrous Indian palace of a dining room"; who cares if the style can seem "slightly cheesy"? – both food and service are "first-rate". / **Details:** www.anoki.co.uk; 2m from town centre, opposite hospital; 11.30 pm; D only, closed Sun.

Le Bistrot Pierre £ 30
18 Friar Gate DE1 1BX (01332) 370470
"An excellent slice of Gallic style", in the heart of the city; "it's always full, so book". / **Details:** www.lebistrotpierre.co.uk; 10.30 pm, Sun & Mon 10 pm, Fri & Sat 11 pm; no Amex.

Darleys £ 46

Darley Abbey Mill DE22 IDZ (01332) 364987

A pretty former mill tipped for its riverside location (and charming terrace); the food "rarely disappoints", but – perhaps unsurprisingly – it can seem rather "overpriced" for what it is. / Details: www.darleys.com; 2m N of city centre by River Derwent; 9 pm; closed Sun D; no Amex.

Ebi Sushi £ 25

Abbey St DE22 3SJ (01332) 265656

Here's a real tip! – this unsigned (in English) spot is "where the executives from the town's Toyota plant go to sit at the sushi bar and enjoy rawfish, drink Japanese beer and talk with their colleagues"; "I took my discerning Japanese mother-in-law, and she says it's better than most sushi bars in Japan!"

Masala Art £ 35

6-7 Midland Rd DE1 2SN (01332) 292629

A useful tip for Indian cuisine, in a city hardly renowned for its restaurants, and "offering even better choice now they have a daily-changing menu". / Details: www.masala-art.co.uk; 11 pm; D only, closed Sun; children: 10+ after 7.30 pm.

Restaurant Zest £ 39

16d, George St, Friar Gate DE1 1EH (01332) 381101

"A smart and cosy edge-of-town restaurant that's clearly aiming high" – the "charming" service perhaps slightly eclipses the cuisine, but most reporters leave very satisfied overall. / Details: www.restaurantzest.co.uk; 10 pm; closed Sun.

DINTON, BUCKINGHAMSHIRE 2–3C

La Chouette £ 49

Westlington Grn HP17 8UW (01296) 747422

Chef Frederic is as opinionated as they come, so brace yourself for the "idiosyncratic floor show" if you visit this Belgian outfit, now two decades old; it's worth it, though, for food which is often "fantastic"; "beers abound" too, and there's also a good range of wines. / Details: off A418 between Aylesbury & Thame; 9 pm; closed Sat L & Sun; no Amex.

DODDISCOMBSLEIGH, DEVON 1–3D

Nobody Inn £ 35

EX6 7PS (01647) 252394

A countryside inn known for its notably "good wine list" and still tipped as a "lovely" spot; it's occasionally hailed as "the best pub in Devon", but reports are too varied to make it a safe recommendation. / Details: www.nobodyinn.co.uk; off A38 at Haldon Hill (signed Dunchidrock); 9 pm, Fri & Sat 9.30 pm; D only; no Amex.
Accommodation: *5 rooms, from £60.*

DONCASTER, SOUTH YORKSHIRE 5–2D

Aagrah £ 30

Great North Rd DN6 7RA (01302) 728888

A "good and reliable" outpost of the celebrated North Eastern Indian chain; the 'raves' the group normally inspires, however, are notable by their absence. / Details: www.aagrah.com; 2m S of A1 on A638; 11.30 pm, Fri & Sat midnight; D only.

DONHEAD ST ANDREW, WILTSHIRE 2–3C

The Forester Inn £ 36
Lower St SP7 9EE (01747) 828038
Tipped as more a "top restaurant" than a gastropub (and certainly "worth the drive"), this "charming", "cosy" and "hospitable" thatched inn, in a pretty village, attracts particular praise for "excellent fish". / **Details:** *Off A30; 9 pm; closed Sun D.*

DONNINGTON, BERKSHIRE 2–2D

Wine Press
Donnington Valley Hotel £ 45
Old Oxford Rd RG14 3AG (01635) 551199
A privately-owned modern country hotel and spa ("lovely"), tipped – bizarrely – as a perfect destination for chocoholics; the chef has won awards, apparently, and his covered strawberries are not-to-be-missed; also, a "biggest ever" wine list. / **Details:** *www.donningtonvalley.co.uk; 9 pm.*
Accommodation: *111 rooms, from £99.*

DORCHESTER, DORSET 2–4B

Sienna £ 55
36 High West St DT1 1UP (01305) 250022
The premises may be "tiny", but the "classy" fare at this family-run town-centre restaurant pleases almost all who comment on it. / **Details:** *www.siennarestaurant.co.uk; 9 pm; closed Mon & Sun; no Amex; children: 12+.*

Yalbury Cottage £ 45
DT2 8PZ (01305) 262382

"Brilliant use of local ingredients" characterises the cooking at this recently-established hotel (in a part-thatched building), whose "relaxed" and "pleasant" style has found much favour with reporters. / **Details:** *www.yalburycottage.com; 9 pm; D only, closed Mon & Sun.*
Accommodation: *8 rooms, from £110.*

DORE, SOUTH YORKSHIRE 5–2C

Moran's £ 43
289 Abbeydale Road South S17 3LB (01142) 350101
"Very promising", or "greatly hyped"? – both views are expressed in reports on this "small local restaurant"; overall the optimists have the upper hand, and if there is a middle-course assessment, it's that "food and service are great, but the location leaves something to be desired". / **Details:** *www.moranssheffield.co.uk; 9.30 pm; closed Mon, Tue L & Sun D; no Amex.*

DORKING, SURREY

3–3A

The Stephan Langton £ 40 Ⓣ
Friday St, Abinger Common RH5 6JR (01306) 730775
*A well-known pub with a marvellously "picturesque location in the
Surrey Hills"; it changed hands (again) as this guide was going
to press. / Details: www.stephan-langton.co.uk; off A25 at Wotton; 9 pm, Fri &
Sat 9.30 pm; closed Mon & Sun D.*

DUNBAR, EAST LOTHIAN

9–4D

The Rocks £ 36 Ⓣ
Marine Rd EH42 1AR (01368) 862287
*"Jimmy Findlay and his team just can't do anything wrong", say fans,
and this clifftop hotel is strongly tipped for the quality of its
"interesting" menus, using "locally-sourced fish and seafood".
/ Details: www.experiencetherocks.co.uk; 9 pm.* **Accommodation:** *11 rooms,
from £65.*

DUNTON GREEN, KENT

3–3B

Taj Tandoori £ 25 Ⓣ
110 London Rd TN13 2UT (01732) 462277
*"A family business that is the equal of any tandoori restaurant I have
ever eaten in!" – this quarter-centenarian establishment is a top tip
in a part of the world without a great deal of subcontinental
competition, and is often very busy.*

DUNVEGAN, HIGHLAND

9–2A

The Three Chimneys £ 65 Ⓗ Ⓐ ✪ ✪
Colbost IV55 8ZT (01470) 511258

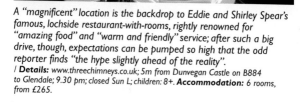

*A "magnificent" location is the backdrop to Eddie and Shirley Spear's
famous, lochside restaurant-with-rooms, rightly renowned for
"amazing food" and "warm and friendly" service; after such a big
drive, though, expectations can be pumped so high that the odd
reporter finds "the hype slightly ahead of the reality".
/ Details: www.threechimneys.co.uk; 5m from Dunvegan Castle on B884
to Glendale; 9.30 pm; closed Sun L; children: 8+.* **Accommodation:** *6 rooms,
from £265.*

DURHAM, COUNTY DURHAM

8–3B

Bistro 21 £ 42
Aykley Heads Hs DH1 5TS (0191) 384 4354
*"Still the best local place for a nice meal, but resting on its laurels
a bit" – this "beautifully-located" bistro has quite a name, and in
particular is an "excellent venue for lunch"; the early-evening menu
(Mon-Thu) also "offers great value". / Details: www.bistrotwentyone.co.uk;
near Durham Trinity School; 10 pm; closed Sun D.*

Gourmet Spot ★★

Farnley Tower Hotel £ 53

The Ave DH1 4DX (0191) 384 6655

Under new chef Ashley Paynton, this "über-modern" dining room –
oddly "tucked away in the basement of a guest house" – continues
on the path to establish itself as "the Fat Duck of the North";
all reports (but one!) speak of "absolutely superb" dishes, which are
"incredibly creative" and "beautifully presented".

/ **Details:** www.gourmet-spot.co.uk; 9.30 pm; D only, closed Mon & Sun.
Accommodation: 13 rooms, from £80.

Oldfields £ 31

18 Claypath DH1 1RH (0191) 370 9595

"One of the few places round here for straightforward non-ethnic
food", this all-day brasserie pleases most reporters with its "good-
quality" cuisine; "good-value early bird and pre-theatre menus" find
particular favour. / **Details:** www.oldfieldsrestaurants.com; 10 pm, Sun 9 pm.

Pump House £ 46 ⓣ

Farm Rd DH1 3PJ (0191) 386 9189

Attracting more consistent reports of late (but still modest in volume),
this "interestingly-housed" restaurant is tipped as a "genuinely good"
all-rounder. / **Details:** www.thepumphouserestaurant.co.uk; 9.30 pm, Sun 9 pm .

EAST CHILTINGTON, EAST SUSSEX 3–4B

Jolly Sportsman £ 42

Chapel Ln BN7 3BA (01273) 890400

"A lovely pub with a beautiful garden, good beers and locally-sourced
food"; despite its "off-the-beaten-track" location, its "enthusiastic"
proprietor has built up quite a following (and, at busy times, service
can suffer quite badly). / **Details:** www.thejollysportsman.com; NW of Lewes;
midnight; closed Mon & Sun D; no Amex.

EAST DEAN, WEST SUSSEX 2–3D

Star & Garter £ 38 Ⓐ★

PO18 0JG (01243) 811318

"A fabulous gastropub specialising in seafood", in a "beautiful village";
"lots of photos of Goodwood, both horses and motors" set the tone.
/ **Details:** www.thestarandgarter.co.uk; 10 pm, Sun 9.30 pm; no Amex.
Accommodation: 6 rooms, from £90.

EAST GRINSTEAD, WEST SUSSEX 3–4B

Gravetye Manor £ 58
Vowels Ln RH19 4LJ (01342) 810567

"A timeless island of England as it once was"; this Elizabethan country house hotel has a particularly *"lovely setting"*, and is hailed by most reporters as a *"good all-rounder"*, with *"top-notch"* food, *"interesting"* wines and *"very good"* service; it is, needless to say, a little *"pricey"*. / **Details:** www.gravetyemanor.co.uk; 2m outside Turner's Hill; 9.30 pm; jacket & tie; children: 7+. **Accommodation:** 18 rooms, from £170.

EAST HADDON, NORTHAMPTONSHIRE 5–4D

The Red Lion £ 32 (T)
Main St NN6 8BU (01604) 770223
"A good country pub with rooms" that's *"flourished under the landlords who took it over a few years ago"* – tipped as *"pleasant"* all-round, it is *"very popular with the locals"*.
/ **Details:** www.redlioneasthaddon.co.uk; 9.30 pm, 10 pm; no Amex.
Accommodation: 5 rooms, from £75.

EAST HENDRED, OXFORDSHIRE 2–2D

The Eyston Arms £ 43
High St OX12 8JY (01235) 833320
A "real winner" of a pub, in a *"beautiful village setting"*; it's unanimously acclaimed by reporters for its *"terrific"* (and quite ambitious) food, its *"engaging"* staff and its *"first-rate"* wine list.
/ **Details:** www.eystons.co.uk; 9 pm; closed Sun D.

EAST LAVANT, WEST SUSSEX 2–4D

The Royal Oak £ 36
Pook Ln PO18 0AX (01243) 527 434
"Cosy" and *"atmospheric"*, this *"dining pub"* offers some *"great bedrooms and cottages to stay in"*; the food – a *"good blend of high-class pub staples with more 'refined' gastrofood"* – generally pleases too. / **Details:** www.royaloaklavant.co.uk.

EAST LOOE, CORNWALL 1–4C

Trawlers £ 42
On The Quay PL13 1AH (01503) 263593
"A great place to eat seafood, right on the dock" – this *"excellent small restaurant"* attracts a hymn of praise from almost all who comment on it; steaks and puddings are particular highlights.
/ **Details:** www.trawlersrestaurant.co.uk; 9.30 pm; D only, closed Mon & Sun.

EAST WITTON, NORTH YORKSHIRE 8–4B

The Blue Lion £ 42
DL8 4SN (01969) 624273
*It's "the best pub in the land!", claim fans, and it's not just the "lovely
candlelit room" at this "cosy" and "atmospheric" Dales inn which
so impresses reporters – the "bold" cuisine (especially the liquorice
dishes!) almost invariably satisfies too. / **Details:** www.thebluelion.co.uk;
between Masham & Leyburn on A6108; 9.15 pm; D only, ex Sun open L &
D; no Amex. **Accommodation:** 15 rooms, from £89.*

EASTBOURNE, EAST SUSSEX 3–4B

The Mirabelle
The Grand Hotel £ 55
King Edwards Pde BN21 4EQ (01323) 412345
*"Much improved service" is boosting feedback generally about this
unusually grand seaside hotel dining room; the food is often "highly
competent" too, but both the cuisine and its style of presentation can
seem "fussy". / **Details:** www.grandeastbourne.com; 9.45 pm; closed Mon &
Sun; jacket or tie required at D. **Accommodation:** 152 rooms, from £190.*

EASTON GRAY, WILTSHIRE 2–2C

Dining Room
Whatley Manor £ 94
SN16 0RB (01666) 822888
*The food at this contemporary-style country house hotel often comes
with "a real wow-factor" – "exemplary, from the amuses-bouches
to the petits-fours"; the ambience, though, is almost invariably thought
"staid" or "sterile"… but, as we all know, that's how the men from the
tyre company like it! / **Details:** www.whatleymanor.com; 9.30 pm, Sat & Sun
9.45 pm; D only, closed Mon-Tue; children: 12+. **Accommodation:** 23 rooms,
from £295.*

EDGWARE, MIDDLESEX 3–2A

Amaretto £ 25
12 The Promenade HA8 7JZ (020) 8958 9044
*Out in the 'burbs, a "good family Italian restaurant", tipped for
"huge bowls of steaming hot pasta", and the like.
/ **Details:** www.amarettoristorante.co.uk.*

EDINBURGH, CITY OF EDINBURGH 9–4C

On the basis of our survey, we allot – curiously – almost exactly
the same number of our stars to Auld Reekie as we do to
Manchester. The pattern of restaurants in the two cities,
however, could not be more different. In this, the ultimate
bourgeois city, many of the establishments worthy of stars are
pitched at a high level, to catch the affluent local professionals,
and the visitors too. Places receiving high acclaim for serving that
particular market well include *Number One*, *Restaurant Martin
Wishart* and *The Kitchin*. Perhaps, before too long, Paul Kitching's
21212 will be mentioned in that sort of company too.

There are also some particularly charming all-round destinations,
one of which should be on any (affluent) visitor's list, including
the *Witchery by the Castle* and the *Vintners' Rooms*. There is also
an impressive supporting cast of mid-range restaurants,
both ethnic and otherwise, whose ranks have been boosted in
recent times with the opening of *Wedgwood*.

For casual dining, Leith, and its waterside, remains the best place
to go for a range of fun and relatively inexpensive options. **235**

Abstract £ 62
33-35 Castle Ter EH1 2EL (0131) 229 1222

Near the Castle, this is a "stylish" and "very professional" – and very Gallic – operation; the cooking is in an "innovative and surprising" mould, although the "skilful" dishes can also seem "over-elaborate".
/ Details: www.abstractedinburgh.com; 10 pm; closed Mon & Sun; no Amex.

Atrium £ 50
10 Cambridge St EH1 2ED (0131) 228 8882
Reports on the city's original trendy restaurant continue to improve; the setting inspires mixed reviews, but the food rarely fails to satisfy nowadays, and it's complemented by "an excellent range of wines, all available by the glass". / Details: www.atriumrestaurant.co.uk; by the Usher Hall; 10 pm; closed Sat L & Sun (ex during Festival).

Bell's Diner £ 30
7 St Stephen St EH3 5EN (0131) 225 8116
"Still good after all these years", this long-established Stockbridge diner is tipped for its "consistently good" cuisine (including some "great burgers"), and also its "friendly" service. / Details: 10 pm; closed weekday L & Sun L; no Amex.

blue bar café £ 43
10 Cambridge St EH1 2ED (0131) 221 1222
Especially handy given the location (by the Usher Hall), this "informal" West End brasserie is tipped for its "terrific-value early-evening meal" (and "good for a bite during the Festival" too).
/ Details: www.bluescotland.co.uk; by the Usher Hall; 10.30 pm, Fri & Sat 11 pm; closed Sun (except during Festival).

Cafe Andaluz £ 33
77B, George St EH2 3EE (0131) 220 9980
"Don't expect haute cuisine", but this "already popular" New Town tapas bar is a newcomer that's been universally welcomed by reporters; it's "always busy". / Details: www.cafeandaluz.com; 10.30 pm, Sun 10 pm; no Amex.

Cafe Marlayne £ 33
7 Old Fishmarket Close EH1 1RW (0131) 225 3838
A "cramped" and "busy" Gallic bistro in the New Town which is tipped for its "interesting" and "varied" cuisine (and "not overpriced" either); there is a branch in the Old Town. / Details: www.cafemarlayne.com; 10 pm; no Amex.

Le Café St-Honoré £ 43 Ⓐ
34 NW Thistle Street Ln EH2 IEA (0131) 226 2211
"Still good" under its new management, this *"cosy"*, *"romantic"* and
extremely authentic-looking New Town bistro remains very popular;
it's still *"not quite as good as it once was"*, though, and not all
reporters are convinced that the prices are fully justified.
/ **Details:** www.cafesthonore.com; 10 pm.

Calistoga £ 35 ⭐
93 St Leonards St EH8 9QY (0131) 668 4207
"A great surprise"; this *"good-value local eatery"* benefits from
an *"unusual"* and well-priced (fixed mark-up) Californian wine list;
it now has a more central offshoot, on the former Martin's/Roti site,
at 70 Rose Street Lane North (tel 225 1233).
/ **Details:** www.calistoga.co.uk; 10 pm; closed Mon, Tue-Thu L & Sun.

Centotre £ 42
103 George St EH2 3ES (0131) 225 1550
From the same family who own Valvona & Crolla, this all-day New
Town spot is a *"favourite"* for some reporters, who applaud its *"great
pizzas and décor"*; critics, though, find the food *"underwhelming"*,
or *"overpriced"*. / **Details:** www.centotre.com; 10 pm, Fri & Sat 11 pm,
Sun 8 pm.

Creelers £ 46 Ⓣ
3 Hunter Sq EH1 1QW (0131) 220 4447
A small fish restaurant, just off the Royal Mile, tipped for *"superb
seafood"*, and its *"fish of the day"*. / **Details:** www.creelers.co.uk; 10.30 pm.

Daniel's £ 34 Ⓐ⭐
88 Commercial St EH6 6LX (0131) 553 5933
"Excellent value, in fashionable Leith"; this *"buzzy"* and *"affordable"*
bistro is an all-round crowd-pleaser, thanks not least to its *"unusual"*
Scottish/Alsatian cuisine – surprisingly, *"it works!"*
/ **Details:** www.daniels-bistro.co.uk; 10 pm.

David Bann £ 34 ⭐
56-58 St Marys St EH1 1SX (0131) 556 5888
"Delicate and flavoursome" veggie fare – and *"with a bit of style"*
thrown in too – has won a huge following (including many carnivores)
for David Bann's *"relaxed"* Old Town venture; a few former fans have
found it *"not as good as it was"* of late, however.
/ **Details:** www.davidbann.com; 10 pm, Fri & Sat 10.30 pm.

The Dogs £ 31 ⭐
110 Hanover St EH2 1DR (0131) 220 1208
"A very welcome addition to Edinburgh", this *"eccentric"* and *"buzzy"*
canine-themed spot in the New Town is *"fast becoming
an institution"*, thanks not least to a menu which offers *"big portions"*
of *"rustic food"* (*"using interesting ingredients"*), at *"reasonable
prices"*. / **Details:** www.thedogsonline.co.uk; 10 pm.

Dusit £ 37 ⭐⭐
49a Thistle St EH2 1DY (0131) 220 6846
*"Wonderful Thai cooking, beautifully presented and with fabulous
flavours"* continues to make this New Town spot extremely popular
(and service is *"spot on"* too); the only real downside is that it can
be a touch *"noisy"*. / **Details:** www.dusit.co.uk; 11 pm.

Favorita £ 34

325 Leith Walk EH6 8JA (0131) 554 2430

"Buzzy, busy and always fun", this bright, modern and colourful dining room is a top destination for those in search of a "delicious" wood-fired pizza. / **Details:** *www.la-favorita.com; 11 pm; no Amex.*

First Coast £ 30

97-101 Dalry Rd EH11 2AB (0131) 313 4404

A bit of a "secret" destination, hidden-away near Haymarket Station, this "reasonably-priced" bistro (where fish is a speciality) retains quite a fan club; there's just a slight feeling, though, that "value isn't quite as good as it used to be". / **Details:** *www.first-coast.co.uk; 10.30 pm; closed Sun.*

Fishers Bistro £ 37

1 The Shore EH6 6QW (0131) 554 5666

"Excellent" fish dishes have made quite a name for this "bare" Leith waterfront cradle of a local group of seafood restaurants; most reporters find it a "fun" destination too, but feedback of late has been a little variable. / **Details:** *www.fishersbistros.co.uk; 10.30 pm.*

Fishers in the City £ 37

58 Thistle St EH2 1EN (0131) 225 5109

In the New Town, this warehouse-conversion fish restaurant is still a "dependable" attraction for some reporters, and it still attracts a good number of reports; service is often "indifferent", though, contributing to the feeling that the place is "not as good as it used to be". / **Details:** *www.fishersbistros.co.uk; 10.30 pm.*

Forth Floor
Harvey Nichols £ 59

30-34 St Andrew Sq EH2 2AD (0131) 524 8350

The setting may be "fabulous" and the views "superb", but they "do not compensate" for the "ordinary" food and "uninterested" service too often observed at this elevated department-store dining room. / **Details:** *www.harveynichols.com; 10 pm; closed Mon D & Sun D; booking: max 8.*

La Garrigue £ 42

31 Jeffrey St EH1 1DH (0131) 557 3032

Thanks to its "very genuine" SW French cuisine, this "first-class" Old Town spot is often praised for offering "intense flavours" at "amazing" prices; critics say it has "lost its edge", though, and reports are certainly much more mixed than once they were. / **Details:** *www.lagarrigue.co.uk; 9.30 pm; closed Sun.*

Glass & Thompson £ 26

2 Dundas St EH3 6HZ (0131) 557 0909

A smart and elegant café/deli handy for New Town ladies who lunch, by at least one of whom it is tipped as an "all-time favourite". / **Details:** *L only.*

Grain Store £ 48

30 Victoria St EH1 2JW (0131) 225 7635

A "well-executed", "slightly Scottish" menu ("like you might hope for at a good dinner party"), with "pleasant" service too, has helped win wide popularity for this "relaxed" and "atmospheric" spot, in the Old Town. / **Details:** *www.grainstore-restaurant.co.uk; 10 pm.*

Henderson's £ 29
94 Hanover St EH2 IDR (0131) 225 2131
"A veggie legend"; two years off its half-century, this no-frills New Town basement "continues to serve up basic food at good-value prices, right in the heart of the city".
/ **Details:** www.hendersonsofedinburgh.co.uk; 10 pm; closed Sun; no Amex.

Indian Cavalry Club £ 44
22 Coates Cr EH3 7AF (0131) 220 0138
It's still sometimes tipped for serving "well-prepared standard Indian dishes in pleasing modern surroundings" but this New Town spot seems to have lost much of its special charm since its recent change of premises. / **Details:** www.indiancavalryclub.co.uk; between Caledonian Hotel & Haymarket Station; 10.45 pm.

Kalpna £ 29
2-3 St Patrick Sq EH8 9EZ (0131) 667 9890
"If you can overlook the ambience, the food is amazing", says one of the fans of the "exceptional veggie fare" on offer at this Gujarati canteen of long standing, near the University; lunch, in particular, is "great value". / **Details:** www.kalpnarestaurant.com; 10.30 pm; closed Sun; no Amex; no booking at L.

The Kitchin £ 76
78 Commercial Quay EH6 6LX (0131) 555 1755

"A true experience"; for "excellent food in a relaxed atmosphere", it's hard to beat Tom Kitchin's much-acclaimed Leith warehouse-conversion, with its "imaginative" cuisine (featuring "particularly effective use of herbs") that's "beautifully served"; "superb" service too. / **Details:** www.thekitchin.com; 10 pm; closed Mon & Sun.

Kweilin £ 33
19-21 Dundas St EH3 6QG (0131) 557 1875
Little feedback on this New Town Cantonese, but it's consistently well reported on, and tipped in particular for the quality of its fish-specials.
/ **Details:** www.kweilin.co.uk.

Loch Fyne £ 37
25 Pier Pl EH6 4LP (0131) 559 3900
"Right by the sea", this is an establishment with a "great location" for a fish restaurant, even a chain one; some (but not all) reporters say the cooking is "better than average" too. / **Details:** www.lochfyne.com; 10 pm, Sat 10.30 pm.

Loon Fung £ 25
2 Warriston Pl EH3 5LE (0131) 556 1781
A Canonmills establishment tipped as "a staple choice for good oriental food"; there are also suggestions, however, that it is "in need of an overhaul". / **Details:** near Botanical Gardens; 11.30 pm.

Maison Bleue £ 40
36-38 Victoria St EH1 2GW (0131) 226 1900
*"Popular with tourists", it may be, but this rustic Old Town spot
is tipped for its "good French cooking" nonetheless.*
/ ***Details:*** *www.maisonbleuerestaurant.com; 11 pm.*

Malmaison £ 39

1 Tower Pl EH6 7DB (0131) 468 5000

*"More like a laid-back brasserie than an hotel dining room",
this "buzzy" Leith spot – the 'original' Malmaison – pleases all
reporters, not least with its "decent" food and its "efficient" service;
it's also commended as a place to stay.* / ***Details:*** *www.malmaison.com;
10.15 pm.* ***Accommodation:*** *100 rooms, from £170.*

Mother India's Cafe £ 21
3-5 Infirmary St EH1 1LT (0131) 524 9801
*"Superb Indian tapas" have made this new offshoot of Mother India
(Glasgow!) instantly popular; its Old Town premises are "very buzzy"
too.* / ***Details:*** *www.motherindiaglasgow.co.uk; 10 pm, Fri & Sat 10.30 pm;
no Amex.*

Mussel Inn £ 35
61-65 Rose St EH2 2NH (0131) 225 5979
*A "speedy" and "reliable" seafood bistro not far from Princes Street;
the menu "doesn't change" – "no problem... if you like mussels".*
/ ***Details:*** *www.mussel-inn.com; 10 pm.*

Number One
Balmoral Hotel £ 75
1 Princes St EH2 2EQ (0131) 557 6727
*Jeff Bland's food "just gets better and better", and service
is consummately "professional" too in the basement dining room
of the city's grandest hotel – an operation where "there is simply
nothing to fault"... except perhaps for a style that's a bit "stately" for
some tastes.* / ***Details:*** *www.roccofortehotels.com; 10.30 pm; D only; no jeans
or trainers.* ***Accommodation:*** *188 rooms, from £290.*

Oloroso £ 57
33 Castle St EH2 3DN (0131) 226 7614
*A fashionable, elevated dining room, whose terrace seats are at a real
premium on "warm and non-windy days" (which are "few in
Edinburgh"); the cooking, though, is "not up to the prices", and service
is sometimes "off-hand"; "the bar menu is better value".*
/ ***Details:*** *www.oloroso.co.uk; 10.15 pm; no Amex.*

Outsider £ 37

15-16 George IV Bridge EH1 1EE (0131) 226 3131

*"A stylish bistro serving up great food in a laid-back and spacious setting", and offering "spectacular castle-views"; a "loud" and "busy" place, it is especially recommended "for groups". / **Details:** 11 pm; no Amex; booking: max 10.*

Le Petit Paris £ 36

38-40 Grassmarket EH1 2JU (0131) 226 2442

*"A genuine Parisian feel" distinguishes this "cramped" and "ever-packed" Grassmarket bistro, where "classic" dishes are prepared to "consistently high standards", and served at "fabulous" prices. / **Details:** www.petitparis-restaurant.co.uk; near the Castle; 11 pm.*

Plumed Horse £ 48

50-54 Henderson St EH6 6DE (0131) 554 5556

*"Fantastic food" (albeit from a "short menu") makes this small Leith restaurant well worth making a bee-line for; service can be "over-attentive", though, and the décor of the small room does not excite. / **Details:** www.plumedhorse.co.uk; 9 pm; closed Mon & Sun.*

Restaurant Martin Wishart £ 87

54 The Shore EH6 6RA (0131) 553 3557

*A "complex" menu that's "beautifully executed" with "elegance" and "finesse" has made a very big name for Mr Wishart's Leith operation; the cynics, though – who say "the food is great, but the bills are greater" – have grown in number of late. / **Details:** www.martin-wishart.co.uk; near Royal Yacht Britannia; 9 pm, Fri & Sat 9.30 pm; closed Mon & Sun; no trainers; booking: max 10.*

Rhubarb
Prestonfield Hotel £ 67

Priestfield Rd EH16 5UT (0131) 225 1333

*"Completely OTT in every sense, but the experience lives on in your memory for a long time"; this "lovely" country house is popular with almost all who comment on it thanks to its "first-class" food, and "very good" service too; "for the full romantic experience, you need to stay". / **Details:** www.rhubarb-restaurant.com; 10 pm, Fri & Sat 11 pm; children: 12+ at D, none after 7pm. **Accommodation:** 23 rooms, from £225.*

Roti £ 38

73 Morrison St EH3 8BU (0131) 221 9998

*The setting may be a touch "cavernous", but "amazing" food, in "Indian-fusion" style, makes this New Town operation well worth seeking out. / **Details:** www.roti.uk.com; midnight; no Amex.*

The Shore £ 38

3-4 The Shore EH6 6QW (0131) 553 5080

*An "unassuming" Leith bistro of longstanding, tipped for "fabulous food at reasonable prices"; feedback, however, is not entirely consistent. / **Details:** www.theshore.biz; 10.30 pm.*

Skippers £ 39

1a Dock Pl EH6 6LU (0131) 554 1018

*"A good option, among the many in Leith" – this longrunning bistro in a former dock building, is a "cosy" sort of place, whose "short" fish-centric menu almost invariably satisfies. / **Details:** 10 pm.*

The Stockbridge £ 44
54 St Stephen's St EH3 5AL   (0131) 226 6766
In a small but strikingly-furnished basement, a "cosy" and "tucked-away" New Town spot, tipped as a "very good neighbourhood restaurant". / Details: www.thestockbridgerestaurant.co.uk; 9.30 pm; closed Mon, Tue-Fri D only, Sat & Sun open L & D; children: 18+ after 8 pm.

Sweet Melindas £ 34
11 Roseneath St EH9 1JH   (0131) 229 7953
A Marchmont bistro offering a "short menu with focus on fresh ingredients and a heavy bias towards fish" ("presumably from the excellent shop next door"); "inventive" puddings find favour too. / Details: www.sweetmelindas.co.uk; 10 pm; closed Mon L & Sun.

Tigerlily £ 42
125 George St EH2 4JN   (0131) 225 5005
*Well, it's "certainly modern", and the blingy design of this hotel dining room (and bar) certainly helps it stand out; the cooking is "good", on most accounts, too, if "slightly marred by the over-bright, over-noisy setting", which is "always bursting at the seams". / Details: www.tigerlilyedinburgh.co.uk; 10 pm; no Amex. **Accommodation:** 33 rooms, from £110.*

The Tower
Museum of Scotland £ 50
Chambers St EH1 1JF   (0131) 225 3003
"Beautiful and striking" views help make this elevated dining room a true "Edinburgh highlight"; it continues, however, to attract too many critical reports of food that's "pedestrian" and "overpriced". / Details: www.tower-restaurant.com; 11 pm.

21212 £ 77
3 Royal Ter EH7 5AB   (0845) 222 1212
Opening too late for proper survey feedback, this plush Calton town house has been one of the UK's top openings of the year; chef/patron Paul Kitching delivers his trademark wackily creative cuisine (last seen at Juniper near Manchester, RIP) — one early fan says it's "the most exciting dining in town". / Details: www.21212restaurant.co.uk; 9.30 pm; closed Mon & Sun.

Urban Angel £ 34
121 Hanover St EH2 1DJ   (0131) 225 6215
In the New Town, an "all-day café-cum-restaurant", sometimes tipped as "the best budget option for a casual meal with friends" (and with "lots of veggie options"); opinions differ on whether the new Forth Street offshoot is an improvement on the original or not. / Details: www.urban-angel.co.uk; 10 pm; closed Sun D.

Valvona & Crolla £ 36
19 Elm Row EH7 4AA   (0131) 556 6066
This famous deli/café of long standing, on the way to Leith, has a huge name as a "reliable lunch stop" (and you may well have to queue); some reporters still find the fare "ordinary" and prices "outrageous", but — after a prolonged dip — standards seem to be somewhat on the mend. / Details: www.valvonacrolla.com; at top of Leith Walk, near Playhouse Theatre; L only.

Vintners Rooms £ 52
87a Giles St EH6 6BZ (0131) 554 6767
"A wonderful intimate restaurant, with great food" – this Leith "hidden gem", in an ancient, partly candle-lit wine warehouse, continues to be on "top form"; service is particularly outstanding.
/ **Details:** www.thevintnersrooms.com; 10 pm; closed Mon & Sun.

Wedgwood £ 43
267 Canongate EH8 8BQ (0131) 558 8737

WINNER 2010
RÉMY MARTIN

For one reporter "reminiscent of Raymond Blanc's first venture, in Oxford, thirty years ago", Paul Wedgwood's "small but perfectly-formed" Old Town establishment, just two years old, is already universally hailed by reporters as a truly "fantastic" destination – "everything they serve is excellent".
/ **Details:** www.wedgwoodtherestaurant.co.uk; 10 pm.

The Witchery by the Castle £ 58
Castlehill, The Royal Mile EH1 2NF (0131) 225 5613
By the Castle, this destination restaurant of 30 years' standing boasts a "beautiful" and "intimate" Gothic atmosphere, and a famously "encyclopaedic" wine list too; traditionally, the food has been "nothing special" in comparison, but those who judge it "excellent" have become more vocal of late. / **Details:** www.thewitchery.com; 11.30 pm.
Accommodation: 7 rooms, from £295.

EGHAM, SURREY 3–3A

The Oak Room
Great Fosters Hotel £ 56
Stroude Rd TW20 9UR (01784) 433822

"Back on form with a new chef and a new approach", this "beautiful" country house dining room is – certainly on the appearances front – a "perfect place for an anniversary or birthday party"; most reporters, however, tend to note that, for what it is, it's "a little pricey".
/ **Details:** www.greatfosters.co.uk; 9.15 pm; closed Sat L; no jeans or trainers; booking: max 12. **Accommodation:** 44 rooms, from £155.

La Cachette   £ 30
31 Huddersfield Rd HX5 9AW   (01422) 378833
*Not many reports this year on this long-running brasserie success,
but it's still tipped for its "consistently high standards".*
/ **Details:** www.lacachette-elland.com; 9.30 pm, Fri & Sat 10 pm; closed Sun;
no Amex.

St Helena   £ 50
High St MK42 9XP   (01234) 344848
*A "well-run country restaurant" with a rare degree of "character";
the cuisine − from a menu which includes "numerous specials" −
is praised by all reporters, and there is an "amazing selection of wines
for every budget".* / **Details:** www.sthelenarestaurant.co.uk; off A6, S of
Bedford; 9 pm; closed Mon, Sat L & Sun; no trainers; children: 12+ at D, +8 at L.

The Boathouse   £ 30
5-5A, Annesdale CB7 4BN   (01353) 664388
*A riverside location that's "lovely on a sunny day" is the particular
attraction of this former boathouse, but the "basic" fare can
be "very good" too.* / **Details:** www.cambscuisine.com/theboathouse.

Old Fire Engine House   £ 40
25 St Mary's St CB7 4ER   (01353) 662582
*"An Ely institution" (of over 40 years' standing), which offers
"generous portions" of "plain" English cooking, plus a surprisingly
"great" (and "not overpriced") wine list; critics may feel the place
"lacks spark", but its (fairly mature) following seems to like things
just the way they are!* / **Details:** www.theoldfireenginehouse.co.uk; 9 pm;
closed Sun D; no Amex.

Fat Olives   £ 41
30 South St PO10 7EH   (01243) 377914
*"A cosy bistro that's gorgeous for an intimate meal", this "small"
former cottage a short walk up the hill from the waterfront is hailed
in all reports as simply an "excellent all-rounder"; "advanced booking
essential!"* / **Details:** www.fatolives.co.uk; 10 pm; closed Mon & Sun; no Amex;
children: 8+.

36 on the Quay   £ 66

47 South St PO10 7EG   (01243) 375592
*Too often "remote", "brittle" and "very slow", the service at this
"quaint" and "crammed" harboursider sometimes seems a sort
of parody of the style that so appeals to Michelin… which is a
shame, as the food itself is often "excellent".*
/ **Details:** www.36onthequay.co.uk; off A27 between Portsmouth & Chichester;
9.45 pm; closed Mon & Sun; no Amex. **Accommodation:** 4 (plus cottage) rooms,
from £95.

EPSOM, SURREY
3–3B

Le Raj £ 29 ⭐
211 Fir Tree Rd KT17 3LB (01737) 371371
An "innovative" approach to subcontinental cuisine puts this colourful restaurant "in a class of its own" locally; service, though, can be "patchy". / **Details:** www.lerajrestaurant.co.uk; next to Derby race course; 11 pm; no jeans or trainers.

ESCRICK, NORTH YORKSHIRE
5–1D

Sangthai £ 33 ⭐
Church Cottage YO19 6EX (01904) 728462
"Fabulous and very authentic food" – "the curries are better than you get in Thailand!", according to fans – makes this "friendly" restaurant popular with all who comment on it (even if "the ambience is more coffee shop than restaurant"). / **Details:** www.sangthai.co.uk; flexible; closed Mon, Tue-Thu & Sat D only.

ESHER, SURREY
3–3A

Good Earth £ 43 ⭐
14-18 High St KT10 9RT (01372) 462489
"A stand-out among the usual run-of-the-mill Chineses"; this "palatial" restaurant of thirty years standing still generally hits the spot, and – though "a bit expensive" – is "worth it for special occasions".
/ **Details:** www.goodearthgroup.co.uk; 11.15 pm, Sun 10.45 pm; booking: max 12, Fri & Sat.

Sherpa £ 31 ⓣ
132 High St KT10 9QJ (01372) 470777
An "attractive" spot, tipped for its "well-flavoured" Nepalese food, and its "friendly" service too. / **Details:** www.sherpakitchen.co.uk; 11 pm; no Amex.

Siam Food Gallery £ 40 ⓣ
95-97 High St KT10 9QE (01372) 477139
An "authentic", "reliable" and "hospitable" establishment, tipped as "the best Thai in this part of Surrey".
/ **Details:** www.siamfoodgallery.co.uk; 11 pm; closed Mon L.

ESKMILLS, EAST LOTHIAN
9–4C

The Glasshouse at Eskmills £ 37
Stuart Hs, Station Rd EH21 7PQ (0131) 273 5240
It's not just the "very interesting" modern building, in the courtyard of a former ropeworks, that makes this a restaurant of some note – it's the "short" but "interesting" menu of "local and fresh" fare, "simply cooked". / **Details:** www.theglasshouseateskmills.com; 10 pm; closed Mon & Sun; children: 16+ after 8 pm.

ETON, BERKSHIRE 3–3A

Gilbey's £ 40

T

82-83 High St SL4 6AF (01753) 854921

This "cosy" high street wine bar, near the College, has been in the same ownership for over 30 years, and is tipped for its consistently "enjoyable" food; tables at the front are "great for people-watching", while the "huge" rear conservatory is best in summer.
/ **Details:** www.gilbeygroup.com; 5 min walk from Windsor Castle; 9.30 pm, Fri & Sat 10 pm.

EVERSHOT, DORSET 2–4B

★

Summer Lodge
Country House Hotel & Restaurant £ 78

Summer Lodge DT2 0JR (01935) 482000

One of our longest-established reporters says this "beautifully-located" country house hotel has "now taken over from Chewton Glen as top all-rounder" ("even if the amenities are more limited"); overall, however, reports are not entirely consistent.
/ **Details:** www.summerlodgehotel.co.uk; 12m NW of Dorchester on A37; 9.30 pm; no shorts. **Accommodation:** 24 rooms, from £300.

EVESHAM, WORCESTERSHIRE 2–1C

T

Evesham Hotel £ 42

Coopers Ln WR11 1DA (01386) 765566

John Jenkinson brings much "humour and eccentricity" to running the hotel he has owned for over thirty years; it's most famous for its wine list, but also tipped for some "excellent" cooking from the new chef too. / **Details:** www.eveshamhotel.com; 9.30 pm; booking: max 12.
Accommodation: 40 rooms, from £120.

EXETER, DEVON 1–3D

★

Michael Caines
Royal Clarence Hotel £ 63

Cathedral Yd EX1 1HD (01392) 223 638

Beginning (at last!) to live up to the name of the celebrated Gidleigh Park chef, this "gloriously-located" dining room by the Cathedral pleases most (but still not quite all) reporters with its "beautiful" cuisine; as elsewhere in the chain, though, "good lunch deals" are still the undoubted highlight. / **Details:** www.abodehotels.co.uk; 9.30 pm; closed Sun; booking essential. **Accommodation:** 53 rooms, from £125.

EXTON, RUTLAND 5–3D

The Fox And Hounds £ 20

19 The Grn LE15 8AP (01572) 812403

This ivy-clad coaching inn is a "friendly" place, where local food comes "freshly cooked"; pizzas (evenings only) are something of a menu speciality, but most feedback focuses on "succulent roasts" and the like. / **Details:** www.foxandhoundsrutland.co.uk; 9 pm; closed Mon & Sun D.
Accommodation: 4 rooms, from £45.

FAIRFORD, GLOUCESTERSHIRE 2–2C

Allium **£ 55** ⭐
1 London St GL7 4AH (01285) 712200
'Contemporary Cotswold dining' is the motto of Erica and James
Graham's "small country restaurant" – an "intimate" and "relaxing"
spot, where the food is "imaginative" and "well presented".
/ **Details:** www.allium.uk.net; 9 pm; closed Mon, Tue L, Sun D; no Amex; booking:
max 10.

FALMOUTH, CORNWALL 1–4B

Bistro de la Mer **£ 41** Ⓣ
28 Arwenack St TR11 3JB (01326) 316509
This is a case where you should "ignore appearances" ("more café
than bistro") – stick to the local seafood, and the cuisine here
is tipped as "excellent". / **Details:** www.bistrodelamer.com; 9.30 pm, Fri & Sat
10 pm; no Amex.

Harbourside Restaurant
Greenbank Hotel **£ 43** Ⓣ
Harbourside TR11 2SR (01326) 312440
A "great romantic setting" (with a 180° harbour-view) is not the only
attraction of this waterside restaurant – it is also tipped for
"particularly good" fish dishes. / **Details:** www.greenbank-hotel.co.uk; 1m E
of Falmouth marina; 9 pm. **Accommodation:** 60 rooms, from £139.

FARNHAM, DORSET 2–3C

Museum Inn **£ 47** ⭐
DT11 8DE (01725) 516261
A "posh" pub in a pretty village, offering "wonderfully cooked local
produce" which, if "not cheap", is "worth the premium"; given the
setting, though, the styling can sometimes seem a touch "clinical".
/ **Details:** www.museuminn.co.uk; Off the A354, signposted to Farnham; 9.30 pm,
9 pm Sun; no Amex. **Accommodation:** 8 rooms, from £110.

FAVERSHAM, KENT 3–3C

Read's **£ 69** ⒶⒶ⭐
Macknade Manor, Canterbury Rd ME13 8XE (01795) 535344
"Definitely one of Kent's finest restaurants" – this "elegant",
"comfortable" and "traditional" Georgian manor house restaurant-
with-rooms is notable for the general all-round consistency of the
many reports which it inspires. / **Details:** www.reads.com; 9.30 pm; closed
Mon & Sun. **Accommodation:** 6 rooms, from £250.

FENCE, LANCASHIRE 5–1B

Fence Gate Inn & Banqueting Centre **£ 33** Ⓣ
Wheatley Lane Rd BB12 9EE (01282) 618101
A bright contemporary brasserie in a banqueting complex in a period
building, sometimes tipped as "the best place to eat
in East Lancashire". / **Details:** www.fencegate.co.uk; 9 pm, Fri 9.30 pm,
Sat 10 pm, Sun 8 pm; no Amex.

FERRENSBY, NORTH YORKSHIRE

8–4B

⭐

General Tarleton £ 38
Boroughbridge Rd HG5 0PZ (01423) 340284
More consistent feedback of late on this "friendly" and popular
gastropub, where "all the food is great, especially the fish", and where
the wine list "covers the globe". / **Details:** www.generaltarleton.co.uk;
2m from A1, J48 towards Knaresborough; 9.15 pm. **Accommodation:** 14 rooms,
from £129.

FLAUNDEN, HERTFORDSHIRE

3–2A

The Bricklayers Arms £ 44
Hogpits Bottom HP3 0PH (01442) 833322
"One of those special little surprises you want to keep to yourself",
or "crassly overpriced and mediocre"? – in the large volume
of feedback on this "great country pub", positive reports
do predominate, but there's also a lingering feeling that it's become
rather "over-hyped". / **Details:** www.bricklayersarms.com; J18 off the M25,
past Chorleywood; 9.30 pm, Sun 8.30 pm.

FLETCHING, EAST SUSSEX

3–4B

🅐⭐

The Griffin Inn £ 45
TN22 3SS (01825) 722890
"The perfect country pub" ("beautifully lit and decorated, and homely
and smart all at the same time"), and with "fabulous outdoor dining"
too; it has a very big reputation for "terrific" food – this is largely
upheld by reporters, but "prices are rising" and the occasional critic
fears complacency may be setting in. / **Details:** www.thegriffininn.co.uk;
off A272; 9.30 pm. **Accommodation:** 13 rooms, from £85.

FOREST GREEN, SURREY

3–3A

The Parrot Inn £ 36
RH5 5RZ (01306) 621339
A village-pub-cum-farm-shop which sources meat from its own farm;
dishes are of a "consistently high standard" (and often "delicious"),
but prices can seem to be on the "steep side".
/ **Details:** www.theparrot.co.uk; 10 pm; closed Sun D; no Amex.

FOREST ROW, WEST SUSSEX

3–4B

🆃

Anderida Restaurant
Ashdown Park Hotel £ 49
Wych Cross RH18 5JR (01342) 824988
This "vast" (and rather ecclesiastical) dining room of a country-house
resort-hotel is tipped for its "fabulous" food; even fans, though,
can complain of exorbitant pricing of wine and incidentals.
/ **Details:** www.ashdownpark.com; 9.30 pm, Fri & Sat 10 pm; jacket and/or tie.
Accommodation: 106 rooms, from £170.

FORT WILLIAM, HIGHLAND

9–3B

🆃

Crannog £ 43
Town Pier PH33 6DB (01397) 705589
A seafood restaurant, on the pier, which continues to attract particular
praise for its high-quality cooking.
/ **Details:** www.crannog.net/restaurant.asp; 9.30 pm; no Amex.

Inverlochy Castle £ 90
Torlundy PH33 6SN (01397) 702177
This famously grand Baronial lochside hotel inspires little reporter feedback; such as there is tips the food as "excellent" (as you'd hope at the prices), and the wines are "good" too.
/ **Details:** www.inverlochycastlehotel.com; off A82, 4 m N of Ft. William; 10 pm; jacket & tie required at D; children: 8+ at D. **Accommodation:** 17 & gate lodge rooms, from £300.

FOWEY, CORNWALL 1–4B

The Q Restaurant
The Old Quay House £ 50
28 Fore St PL23 1AQ (01726) 833302
Tipped for its "fabulous" setting, with "wonderful views over the estuary", this "straightforward" institution otherwise put in something of a "curate's egg" performance in this year's reports.
/ **Details:** www.theoldquayhouse.com; 9 pm; closed Tue L; children: 8+ at D. **Accommodation:** 11 rooms, from £140.

Restaurant Nathan Outlaw
Marina Villa Hotel £ 70
17 Esplanade PL23 1HY (01726) 833315
*"A superb seven-course tasting menu, all beautifully cooked and presented by a friendly and enthusiastic staff" – that's the sort of experience which makes a visit to this "beautiful" riverside restaurant "wonderful in every way"; indeed, it is undoubtedly now one of England's very best. / **Details:*** www.themarinahotel.co.uk; 9 pm; closed Mon L, Tue L, Wed L, Thu L & Sun; no jeans or trainers; children: 12+ at D. **Accommodation:** 37 rooms, from £160.

Sam's £ 35
20 Fore St PL23 1AQ (01726) 832273
*"The fish is good but the best asset is the wonderfully buzzy atmosphere" at this "brilliant" bistro; apart from the fact that it can be "impossible" to get a table in season, it's an almost invariable crowd-pleaser. / **Details:*** www.samsfowey.co.uk; 10 pm; no Amex.

FOWLMERE, CAMBRIDGESHIRE 3–1B

The Chequers at Fowlmere £ 44
SG8 7SR (01763) 208369
*An inn not far from Cambridge, which has had something of a name as a gastropub since before that term came into general use; nowadays, it's mainly tipped for its "lovely and timeless setting, especially in the garden". / **Details:*** www.thechequersfowlmere.co.uk; on B1368 between Royston & Cambridge; 9.30 pm; children: 14+ in bar.

FRESSINGFIELD, SUFFOLK 3–1D

The Fox & Goose £ 39
IP21 5PB (01379) 586247
*"The food just keeps getting better", at this "gorgeous" and rather "grand" country inn, where "military efficiency" is applied to the delivery of "well-prepared" locally-sourced food; "they manage a good balance between fine dining and keeping the local clientele happy" too. / **Details:*** www.foxandgoose.net; off A143; 8.45 pm, Fri & Sat 9 pm, Sun 8.15 pm; closed Mon; no Amex; children: 9+ for D.

⭐

The Alford Arms   £ 37
HP1 3DD   (01442) 864480
*"A very popular pub restaurant that's very difficult to book but well worth it when you do get in"; almost all of the many reports confirm that it is a "very satisfactory all-rounder", with "great puddings" a culinary highlight. / **Details:** www.alfordarmsfrithsden.co.uk; near Ashridge College and vineyard; 9.30 pm, Fri & Sat 10 pm; booking: max 12.*

GILLINGHAM, DORSET   2–3B

Ⓣ

Stock Hill House   £ 53
SP8 5NR   (01747) 823626
This "formal" country house hotel of long standing ("trying unsuccessfully to maintain its jacket-and-tie code!") still seems a "relaxed" destination to those who like that sort of thing; it's tipped as a good all-rounder, but most particularly for the cooking – the chef, Austrian, can dish up some "delightful surprises".
*/ **Details:** www.stockhillhouse.co.uk; 8.30 pm; no Amex; no jeans; children: 8+ at D in dining room. **Accommodation:** 10 rooms, from £250.*

GLASGOW, CITY OF GLASGOW   9–4C

Glasgow is rare among British cities in having a long-established restaurant which is truly famous, but it is a pity that *Rogano* – the Art Deco seafood establishment – currently appears to be trading almost exclusively on the basis of that fame. Other institutions, more recent, and somewhat less complacent, are the *Ubiquitous Chip* and – from the same local restaurant 'dynasty' – *Stravaigin*.

The city offers much better seafood restaurants than *Rogano* nowadays, most obviously *Gamba*, probably the best restaurant in town, as well as the popular *Two Fat Ladies at the Buttery*. Otherwise, it is for Indian restaurants – particularly *Mother India* – that the city in any way stands out.

Ⓣ

The Butterfly & The Pig   £ 29
153 Bath St G2 4SQ   (0141) 221 7711
*Tipped for "brilliant food at very reasonable prices", this informal city-centre spot is especially worth seeking out at weekends, when "live music" adds charm. / **Details:** www.thebutterflyandthepig.com; 9 pm, Sun 8 pm; no Amex.*

Ⓣ

Café Gandolfi   £ 37
64 Albion St G1 1NY   (0141) 552 6813
*"Bright, airy and well-designed", an "efficient" café – with a bar upstairs – tipped for its "tasty" fare generally, and for breakfast in particular. / **Details:** www.cafegandolfi.com; near Tron Theatre; 11.30 pm; no booking, Sat.*

The Dhabba   £ 34
44 Candleriggs G1 1LE   (0141) 553 1249
*A "trendy" Merchant City Indian that's generally – but this year, not quite invariably – hailed for its "authentic" dishes and its "good all-round standards". / **Details:** www.thedhabba.com; 11 pm.*

Gamba   **£ 55**   ⭐⭐
225a West George St G2 2ND   (0141) 572 0899
*"Still the place for top-notch fish cuisine", this city-centre basement
is "highly-recommended" for its sometimes "unusual" cuisine – "it can
be expensive, but the pre-theatre menu and other deals are a steal".*
/ **Details:** *www.gamba.co.uk; 10.30 pm; closed Sun L.*

Michael Caines   ⓣ
ABode Hotel   **£ 45**
The Arthouse, Bath St G2 2SZ   (0141) 572 6011
*Tipped for the "excellent value of the set lunch deal", this city-centre
outpost of the chef based at far-off Gidleigh Park (Chagford)
otherwise inspires only a modest volume of commentary from
reporters.* / **Details:** *www.michaelcaines.com; 10 pm; closed Mon & Sun;
no jeans or trainers.* **Accommodation:** *59 rooms, from £130.*

Mother India   **£ 30**   ⭐⭐
28 Westminster Ter G3 7RU   (0141) 221 1663
*"The best Indian food in Scotland!"; if you're looking for
"huge portions of delicious curry", and "elegantly presented" too,
this "busy" veteran, near Kelvingrove Park, is undoubtedly well worth
seeking out – it inspired more reports even than the famous 'Chip'!*
/ **Details:** *www.motherindia.co.uk; beside Kelvingrove Hotel; 10.30 pm; closed
Mon L & Tue L.*

Nanakusa   **£ 23**   ⓣ
441 Sauchiehall St G2 3LG   (0141) 332 6303
*"Quick, cheap and always a pleasure", a city-centre Japanese
especially tipped for its "great sushi".* / **Details:** *www.nanakusa.co.uk;
11 pm, Fri & Sat midnight; closed Sun L; no Amex.*

Rogano Seafood Bar & Restaurant   **£ 52**   ❌
11 Exchange Pl G1 3AN   (0141) 248 4055
*The Art Deco interior may be "stunning", but this famous city-centre
fish restaurant otherwise disappoints almost all who report on it –
"talk about laurel-resting, the local chippy could do better!"*
/ **Details:** *www.roganoglasgow.com; 10.30 pm; no Amex.*

Sarti's   **£ 30**   Ⓐ
121 Bath St G2 2SZ   (0141) 204 0440
*"Plenty of marble and Murano chandeliers" add character to this
"lively" Italian institution; its "authentic" atmosphere is perhaps
a greater strength than the "honest" cuisine, but both aspects please
most reporters.* / **Details:** *www.sarti.co.uk; 10.30 pm; no booking at L.*

Stravaigin   **£ 40**   ⭐
28 Gibson St G12 8NX   (0141) 334 2665
*Colin Clydesdale's well-known bar/restaurant wins consistent praise
as an "excellent-value" destination, where the cooking "becomes more
accomplished by the year" (and where the wine is "great and
unusual" too); on balance the less formal part of the operation
is marginally preferred.* / **Details:** *www.stravaigin.com; 11 pm;
Mon-Thu D only, Fri-Sun open L & D.*

(Two Fat Ladies at) The Buttery   **£ 41** Ⓐ ⭐
652 Argyle St G3 8UF   (0141) 221 8188
It may be "marooned" in "one of Glasgow's worst urban deserts",
but this "landmark" Victorian establishment near the SECC turns out
to be a surprisingly "romantic" destination, where seafood,
in particular, is "first-class"; the pre-theatre menu is especially worth
seeking out for its "fabulous" value.
/ Details: www.twofatladiesrestaurant.com; 10 pm.

Ubiquitous Chip   **£ 58** Ⓐ
12 Ashton Ln G12 8SJ   (0141) 334 5007
Some of its 'modern Scottish' dishes may seem "odd", and realisation
nowadays tends to "hit-and-miss", but – for long-term fans –
the 'Chip' is a "lovely institution" which "retains its appeal", both for
business and romance; the wine list is "excellent" too (if "rather
pricey"). / Details: www.ubiquitouschip.co.uk; behind Hillhead station; 11 pm.

Wee Curry Shop   **£ 27** ⭐
Buccleuch St G3 6SJ   (0141) 353 0777
Superlatives abound in reports on this Byres Road offshoot of Mother
India, whose "subtly flavoured" curries are "fantastic" and "great
value". / **Details:** www.motherindia.co.uk; 10.30 pm; closed Sun L; no credit
cards.

GODALMING, SURREY   3–3A

Bel & The Dragon   **£ 42** Ⓣ
Bridge St GU7 3DU   (01483) 527333
Tipped for its "gorgeous" setting in an old church, a "welcoming"
gastropub (part of a small chain) where the food "can be good, but it
can be average". / **Details:** www.belandthedragon-godalming.co.uk; at the
bottom of Godalming High St, directly opposite Waitrose; 10 pm, Sat 10.30,
Sun 9 pm; no Amex.

La Luna   **£ 44**
10-14 Wharf St GU7 1NN   (01483) 414155
"An inventive modern Italian with an interesting wine list";
most reporters concede that dishes are "interesting" (and sometimes
"brilliant"), but "inconsistency" remains something of a problem.
/ **Details:** www.lalunarestaurant.co.uk; Between the High Street and Flambard
Way; 10 pm; closed Mon & Sun.

GODSTONE, SURREY   3–3B

The Bell   **£ 38** Ⓣ
128 High St RH9 8DX   (01883) 743216
This "prettily located" 'contemporary pub' (their term) is tipped for
offering the sort of traditional grub that's "perfect for Sunday lunch";
it's quite a "comfortable" sort of place too.
/ **Details:** www.thebellgodstone.co.uk; 9 pm, Sat & Sun 10 pm.

GOLCAR, WEST YORKSHIRE   5–1C

The Weavers Shed   **£ 55**
Knowl Rd HD7 4AN   (01484) 654284

Not all reporters find this long-established (1973) restaurant-with-rooms – in a former weaver's shed – especially atmospheric; all is forgiven, though, as the food from long-term chef Stephen Jackson, is "excellent", and the wines are "reasonably priced" too.
/ **Details:** www.weaversshed.co.uk; 9 pm; closed Mon, Sat L & Sun.
Accommodation: 5 rooms, from £100.

GOLDSBOROUGH, NORTH YORKSHIRE   8–3D

The Fox And Hounds Inn   **£ 43**
YO21 3RX   (01947) 893372
"River Café-style food" and "very friendly" service win rave reviews for this "quirky" and "delightful" small inn, in a "lovely part of the country"; it's like its Hammersmith inspiration in other ways too – "if only it was a bit cheaper…"!
/ **Details:** www.foxandhoundsgoldsborough.co.uk; 8.30 pm; D only, closed Sun-Tue; no Amex.

GORING-ON-THAMES, BERKSHIRE   2–2D

Leatherne Bottel   **£ 70**
Bridleway RG8 0HS   (01491) 872667
On most reports "a real out-of-town treat", this long-established Thames-side spot undoubtedly has "a wonderful setting", and many fans find the food "excellent" too; harsher critics, however, complain that "flashes of high culinary skill do appear, but not really with enough consistency". / **Details:** www.leathernebottel.co.uk; 0.5m outside Goring on B4009; 9 pm; closed Sun D; children: 10+ for D.

GRANGE MOOR, WEST YORKSHIRE   5–1C

The Kaye Arms   **£ 37**
29 Wakefield Rd WF4 4BG   (01924) 848385
"Still as popular as ever"; most (but not quite all) reporters are still very up on this "comfortable" gastropub, since its recent change of ownership. / **Details:** www.thekayearms.com; 9.30 pm; no Amex.

GRANGE-OVER-SANDS, CUMBRIA   7–4D

Hazelmere   **£ 31**
1-2 Yewbarrow Ter LA11 6ED   (01539) 532972
A "delightful" café, offering a "large choice of teas" (with leaves!), and a "massive choice of coffees" too; perhaps most remarkably in this sedate town, it's a "child-friendly" place too.
/ **Details:** www.hazelmerecafe.co.uk; L only; no Amex.

The Jumble Room   £ 43
Langdale Rd   LA22 9SU   (01539) 435188
A well-established restaurant, in a pretty village; reporters unanimously praise its "excellent and generous home cooking", which is served in an atmosphere that's "very friendly and welcoming".
/ **Details:** www.thejumbleroom.co.uk; Halfway along the Langdale road, between two hotels; midnight; closed Mon L & Tue; no Amex. **Accommodation:** 2 rooms, from £180.

Lancrigg Country House Hotel   £ 38
Easedale Rd   LA22 9QN   (01539) 435317
A quarter of a century in business, this rare vegetarian country house hotel attracts little, but consistently positive, feedback; it's especially tipped for "afternoon tea with a view". / **Details:** www.lancrigg.co.uk; 1/2 mile up the Easedale road from the centre of Grasmere; 8 pm; no Amex. **Accommodation:** 12 rooms, from £120.

The Grassington House Hotel   £ 45
5 The Sq   BD23 5AQ   (01756) 752406
A large Georgian house, recently launched as a guesthouse, tipped for "mouthwatering" cooking – whether for a "light snack in the bar terrace, or good food in the restaurant".
/ **Details:** www.grassingtonhousehotel.co.uk; 9.30pm (Mo-Sa) 7.30pm (Su). **Accommodation:** 7 rooms, from £85.

Starr   £ 50
Market Pl   CM6 1AX   (01371) 874321
Irreconcilably mixed reports on this long-established town-centre restaurant-with-rooms – fans praise "imaginative dishes" and "superb service", but critics decry a place that's "trying too hard to be a fine dining experience" (and charging prices to match).
/ **Details:** www.the-starr.co.uk; 8m E of M11, J8 on A120; 9.30 pm; closed Mon & Sun D; no jeans or trainers. **Accommodation:** 8 rooms, from £130.

Harry's Place   £ 75
17 High St   NG31 8JS   (01476) 561780
"Small but perfectly formed", this celebrated 10-seater is "run by a friendly and highly capable husband-and-wife team", and its cuisine shows "amazing attention to detail"; prices are necessarily high, though, and not all reporters this year were quite convinced that the premium was justified. / **Details:** on B1174 1m N of Grantham; 9.30 pm; closed Mon & Sun; no Amex; booking essential; children: 5+.

GREAT MILTON, OXFORDSHIRE 2–2D

Le Manoir aux Quat' Saisons £125 **H A ★ ★**
Church Rd OX44 7PD (01844) 278881

"Everything they say is true"; Raymond Blanc's "stunning" and "enchanted" manor house hotel (with rooms) offers simply "outstanding" Gallic cuisine ("in very classic style"); perhaps inevitably, though, even fans can find prices "anything but friendly".
/ **Details:** www.manoir.com; from M40, J7 take A329 towards Wallingford; 9.30 pm. **Accommodation:** 32 rooms, from £410.

GREAT MISSENDEN, BUCKINGHAMSHIRE 3–2A

The Nags Head £ 42 **★**
London Rd HP16 0DG (01494) 862200
"Improved hugely", this country inn attracts uniform praise for its "very high standard of cooking"; service is "friendly" too, if occasionally rather "slow". / **Details:** www.nagsheadbucks.com; Off the A413; 9.30 pm, Sun 8.30 pm. **Accommodation:** 5 rooms, from £90.

GREAT TEW, OXFORDSHIRE 2–1D

Falkland Arms £ 34 **T**
The Green OX7 4DB (01608) 683653
"A lovely village pub", in a "picturebook setting", tipped for its "simple" but "lovely" fare. / **Details:** www.falklandarms.org.uk; A361 between Banbury & Chipping Norton; 9.30 pm; children: +16 at D. **Accommodation:** 5 rooms, from £85.

GRINDLETON, LANCASHIRE 5–1B

The Duke Of York Inn £ 36 **★**
Brow Top BB7 4QR (01200) 441266
"Hearty meals with clever twists and elegant touches" are helping this "up-and-coming" gastropub make quite a reputation; don't be worried if you hear it's a Heathcote establishment – turns out to be nothing to do with the self-promoting Paul, but rather the unrelated Michael!
/ **Details:** www.dukeofyorkgrindleton.com; 9 pm, Sun 8 pm; closed Mon.

GRINSHILL, SHROPSHIRE 5–3A

The Inn at Grinshill £ 40
The High St SY4 3BL (01939) 220410
A "rural" inn that's made a bit of a name for food that's of "urban quality"; the chef changed in late-2009 however, so we'll have to wait till next year for a full assessment of the new régime.
/ **Details:** www.theinnatgrinshill.co.uk; 9.30 pm; closed Mon & Sun D; no Amex. **Accommodation:** 7 rooms, from £90.

A ✮

Rumwong   £ 34
18-20 London Rd GU1 2AF   (01483) 536092
Over thirty years in business, a Thai restaurant that attracts impressively consistent reports on its "divine" cuisine, and on its "buzzy" ambience too. / Details: www.rumwong.co.uk; 10.30 pm; closed Mon; no Amex.

The Thai Terrace   £ 35
Castle Car Pk, Sydenham Rd GU1 3RT   (01483) 503350
"Fantastic views" result from the "most strange location" of this fashionable oriental (on top of a car park), known for its "good food, good service and good prices"; not all reporters are convinced, though, and the room can be quite "noisy" at times. / Details: opposite Guildford Castle in town centre; 11 pm; closed Sun.

T

Zinfandel   £ 34
4 Chapel St GU1 3UH   (01483) 455155
"A friendly, produce-driven local eatery", tipped for offering a menu that's "always well-executed". / Details: www.zinfandel.org.uk; 10 pm; closed Mon D & Sun D.

✮

La Potinière   £ 53
Main St EH31 2AA   (01620) 843214
"Beautifully presented and executed food" and an "extensive wine list" make this traditionally-styled restaurant a continuing hit with all who comment on it, usually as a "wonderful" lunch destination – for a meal that's "light and full of flavour", and "good value" too, you won't do much better than here. / Details: www.la-potiniere.co.uk; 20m E of Edinburgh, off A198; 8.30 pm; closed Mon & Tue; no jeans or trainers; booking essential.

✮

Horn of Plenty   £ 65
PL19 8JD   (01822) 832528
*"Spectacular views over the Tamar Valley" contribute to a "lovely experience" at this well-known restaurant with rooms; feedback on the food was more consistent this year, with praise for "passionate" cooking using "top-quality ingredients".
/ Details: www.thehornofplenty.co.uk; 3m W of Tavistock on A390; 9 pm; no jeans or trainers; children: 10+ at D. Accommodation: 10 rooms, from £120.*

✮

Tom Browns Brasserie   £ 43
The Old School Hs NG14 7FB   (0115) 966 3642
*A smart contemporary riverside brasserie, which attracts consistent praise for its "good food" and "pleasant service"; an "excellent" early-bird dinner menu is especially worth seeking out.
/ Details: www.tombrowns.co.uk; 10 pm.*

HALE, CHESHIRE 5–2B

Earle £ 33
4 Cecil Rd WA15 9PA (0161) 929 8869
*The new suburban venture by Simon Rimmer (of Green's fame) has
inspired contradictory views – for most reporters, it's a "down-to-
earth" place offering "interesting" cooking in "good portions",
but critics have found some dishes "woeful".*
/ **Details:** www.earlerestaurant.co.uk; 10.30 pm, Sun 9.30 pm; closed Mon.

HALIFAX, WEST YORKSHIRE 5–1C

1885 The Restaurant £ 34
Recreation Ground HX4 9AJ (01422) 373030
*Converted from a row of former cottages, overlooking the Pennines,
this "lovely" restaurant pleases all reporters, not only with its
"interesting" cuisine, but with its "cosy" and "friendly" style too.*
/ **Details:** www.1885therestaurant.co.uk; 9.30 pm; closed Mon, Tue–Sat D only,
closed Sun D; no Amex.

Shibden Mill Inn £ 35
Shibden Mill Fold HX3 7UL (01422) 365840
*"A rural gem", offering "a simple bar menu of pub classics,
all superbly executed, plus a more adventurous restaurant menu";
no rating is appropriate, however, as the chef changed towards the
end of the survey year.* / **Details:** www.shibdenmillinn.com; off the A58,
Leeds/Bradford road; 9.15 pm, Sun 7.30 pm. **Accommodation:** 11 rooms,
from £95.

HAMBLETON, RUTLAND 5–4D

Finch's Arms £ 32
Oakham Rd LE15 8TL (01572) 756575
*"A lovely location overlooking Rutland Water" makes this "cottagey
pub, with terrace and restaurant" very popular locally (and Sundays,
in particular, can be "very crowded"); the year which saw the
transition to a new chef, however, produced unsettled reports, hence
we've left it un-rated.* / **Details:** www.finchsarms.co.uk; 9.30 pm, Sun 8 pm.
Accommodation: 6 rooms, from £95.

Hambleton Hall £ 85
LE15 8TH (01572) 756991

*"Creative cooking as good as any in the capital" ("if with prices
to match"); Tim Hart's "stunningly located" country house hotel,
overlooking Rutland Water, remains one of England's most notable
culinary destinations – as is confirmed by a large number of reports,
"the level of consistency is extraordinary".*
/ **Details:** www.hambletonhall.com; near Rutland Water; 9.30 pm.
Accommodation: 17 rooms, from £205.

Maes y Neuadd   **£ 47**

Talsarnau LL47 6YA   (01766) 780200

"A real Welsh experience"; this traditionally-styled country-house hotel has a number of attractions, including views of Snowdon, and a dining room tipped for its "value-for-money" cuisine.
/ **Details:** *www.neuadd.com; 3m N of Harlech off B4573; 8.40 pm; no Amex; no shorts; children: 8+ in the main restaurant.* **Accommodation:** *15 rooms, from £119.*

The Star Inn   **£ 55**

YO62 5JE   (01439) 770397

"Just the best place in the North", Andrew and Jacquie Pern's "friendly", "relaxed" and "generous" gastropub legend has been "much improved by the recent extension", and the food (in particular) is often "impossible to fault"; for the dining room, "book well ahead".
/ **Details:** *www.thestaratharome.co.uk; 3m SE of Helmsley off A170; 9.30 pm, Sun 6 pm; closed Mon L & Sun D; no Amex.* **Accommodation:** *14 rooms, from £130.*

The Bean Tree   **£ 42**

20a Leyton Rd AL5 2HU   (01582) 460901

"Stands out in a gastronomic desert"/"totally underwhelming" – two comments representative of the bizarrely contradictory feedback on this former coach house, in the town-centre; all you can really say in such circumstances is that it would seem to fall some way short of being a 'safe bet'! / **Details:** *www.thebeantree.co.uk; 9.30 pm; closed Mon, Sat L & Sun D; no trainers.*

The Fox   **£ 36**

469 Luton Rd AL5 3QE   (01582) 713817

"A good and reliable local gastropub", tipped for offering "better value than some of the more expensive restaurants" in this under-served part of the world. / **Details:** *www.thefoxharpenden.co.uk; 10 pm.*

Bettys   **£ 30**

1 Parliament St HG1 2QU   (01423) 502746

Considering that it is undoubtedly a "tourist trap", this "quintessential tearoom" manages to maintain surprisingly "high standards"; it may be "pricey", and the queues can be "awful", but – for most reporters – a visit here remains "an indulgent treat".
/ **Details:** *www.bettysandtaylors.co.uk; 9 pm; no Amex; no booking.*

The Boar's Head £ 53
Ripley Castle Estate HG3 3AY   (01423) 771888
*A grand village inn, sometimes tipped for "wonderful" food; reports are not entirely consistent, though, and the overall style is a little "stuffy" for some tastes. / **Details:** www.boarsheadripley.co.uk; off A61 between Ripon & Harrogate; 9 pm. **Accommodation:** 25 rooms, from £125.*

Brio £ 33
Hornbeam Pk, The Lenz HG2 8RE   (01423) 870005
*It may be located in a business park, but this laid-back Italian is again tipped for its "reliable" pizzas, pastas and the like. / **Details:** www.brios.co.uk; 10 pm; closed Sun; no Amex.*

Clocktower Restaurant
Rudding Park Hotel £ 60
HG3 1JH   (01423) 871350

*Reports on dining at this country house hotel are not numerous, but the terrace is particularly recommended as a "beautiful" destination on sunny days; more generally, the hotel is of particular interest to golfers. / **Details:** www.ruddingpark.co.uk; 9.30 pm.*
***Accommodation:** 49 rooms, from £195.*

Drum & Monkey £ 37
5 Montpellier Gdns HG1 2TF   (01423) 502650
*"Small, cluttered and noisy", this "characterful" and "popular" fish institution is getting back on top form, and remains extremely popular for its "simple, fresh and excellent" dishes. / **Details:** www.drumandmonkey.co.uk; 10 pm, Sun 6 pm; no Amex; booking: max 10.*

Graveley's Fish & Chip Restaurant £ 30
8-12 Cheltenham Pde HG1 1DB   (01423) 507093
*"More than just a glorified chippy", this smart and "pleasant" town-centre spot is not only "an excellent place for fish 'n' chips" – it offers a broad-ranging fish (and more) menu, with "everything of a high standard". / **Details:** www.graveleysofharrogate.com; 9 pm, Fri & Sat 10 pm, Sun 8 pm.*

Hotel du Vin et Bistro £ 45
Prospect Pl HG1 1LB   (01423) 856800
*Lots of reports on this outpost of the famous wine-led group; sadly, they mainly tend to support the reporter who says the place has "gone so far downhill that it's under water". / **Details:** www.hotelduvin.com; 9.45 pm, Fri & Sat 10.15 pm. **Accommodation:** 43 rooms, from £95.*

Orchid **£ 35**
28 Swan Rd HG1 2SE (01423) 560425
"Highly recommended" in almost all reports, this elegant oriental offers *"beautifully presented"* dishes, and service that's *"second to none"*. / **Details:** www.orchidrestaurant.co.uk; 10 pm; closed Sat L.
Accommodation: 36 rooms, from £99.

Quantro **£ 37**
3 Royal Pde HG1 2SZ (01423) 503034
This elegant, city-centre spot is tipped for *"good value, uncomplicated and wholesome cooking"*, from a menu that's *"constantly updated"*.
/ **Details:** www.quantro.co.uk; 10 pm, Sat 10.30 pm; closed Sun.

Rajput **£ 29**
11 Cheltenham Pde HG1 1DD (01423) 562113
"An authentic family-run town-centre Indian", tipped for its sometimes surprisingly *"innovative"* cuisine – *"the owner makes regular trips to India for new ideas"*. / **Details:** www.rajput.co.uk; midnight; D only; no Amex.

Royal Baths **£ 35**
Central Hall, Crescent Rd HG1 2WJ (01423) 536888
"Lovingly converted from the amazing Royal Baths", this year-old restaurant offers a *"stunning"* setting in which to enjoy Chinese cuisine that invariably satisfies; service, however, can be *"erratic"*.
/ **Details:** www.royalbathschineserestaurant.com; 10.30 pm; no Amex.

HARROW, GREATER LONDON 3–3A

Golden Palace **£ 32**
146-150 Station Rd HA1 2RH (020) 8863 2333
A reputation for *"probably the best dim sum outside Hong Kong"* helps inspire much feedback on this *"bland"* but *"heaving"* Cantonese establishment, and the dinnertime fare is often *"amazing"* too; a number of unhappy recent reports, however, support the suggestion that it has gone *"downhill"* a bit of late. / **Details:** 11.30 pm.

Incanto **£ 41**
41 High St, Harrow On The Hill HA1 3HT (0208) 426 6767
"A solitary spark of life in an otherwise desolate landscape", this *"excellent local restaurant"* impresses almost all reporters with its *"inventive"* Italian menu, and its overall *"value for money"*.
/ **Details:** www.incanto.co.uk; 10.30 pm; closed Mon & Sun D.

Skipjacks **£ 31**
268-270 Streatfield Rd HA3 9BY (020) 8204 7554
"Well worth a trip" and *"always packed"*, this *"friendly"* chippy is of note for its *"consistently excellent"* fish (and *"the best chips ever"*).
/ **Details:** 10.30 pm; closed Sun.

HARWICH, ESSEX 3–2D

The Pier at Harwich £ 48
The Quay CO12 3HH (01255) 241212
*A waterside hotel, whose first-floor restaurant offers "glorious" sea-views ("as long as you can regard container-ships being unloaded as 'entertainment'"); if you're looking for the sort of place which does "a very good old-fashioned lobster Thermidor", this is it.
/ Details: www.milsomhotels.com; 9.30 pm; no jeans. **Accommodation:** 14 rooms, from £105.*

HATFIELD PEVEREL, ESSEX 3–2C

The Blue Strawberry £ 37 ⭐
The Street CM3 2DW (01245) 381333
"Going from strength to strength", this "cramped" but "reliable" local restaurant almost invariably impresses with the "very good quality" of its cuisine. / Details: www.bluestrawberrybistro.co.uk; 3m E of Chelmsford; 10 pm; closed Sat L & Sun D.

HATFIELD, HERTFORDSHIRE 3–2B

Nolita £ 53
Great North Rd AL9 6NA (01707) 644858
The wittily-named NOrtherly outpost of Little ITAly (Soho) is decked out in "London style"; like its parent, it's a "happy" sort of place that sometimes seems a little pricey for what it is, and "unsure whether it's a restaurant or a nightclub" – it becomes "party central" later in the evening. / Details: www.nolitarestaurant.co.uk; midnight, Thu-Sat 2 am; no shorts.

HATHERSAGE, DERBYSHIRE 5–2C

The Plough Inn £ 39 Ⓣ
Leadmill Bridge S32 1BA (01433) 650319
*Located by the River Derwent, a "welcoming" and "friendly" country inn tipped for its "good" and sometimes "interesting" dishes.
/ Details: www.theploughinn-hathersage.co.uk; 9.30 pm, Sun 8 pm; no Amex; booking: max 10. **Accommodation:** 6 rooms, from £90.*

The Walnut Club £ 46 Ⓣ
Unit 6, The Sq, Main Rd S32 1BB (01433) 651155
A brasserie mainly tipped as a "pleasant lunch spot", but jazz evenings have also been enjoyed by reporters; vegan and gluten-free dishes are something of a speciality. / Details: www.thewalnutclub.com; 9 pm, Sun 6 pm; closed Mon & Sun D; no Amex.

HAWORTH, WEST YORKSHIRE 5–1C

Weaver's £ 34 ⭐
15 West Ln BD22 8DU (01535) 643822
*In Bronteland, the Rushworth family's restaurant-with-rooms makes a "buzzing and quirky" destination, of a consistently "high standard"; the food is "superb" and "wholesome", and service is notably "friendly" too. / Details: www.weaverssmallhotel.co.uk; 1.5m W on B6142 from A629, near Parsonage; 9 pm; closed Mon, Tue L, Sat L & Sun D; children: 5+ on Sat. **Accommodation:** 3 rooms, from £99.*

The Half Moon   £ 37
The St RH17 5TR   (01444) 461227
*Recent expansion has not particularly benefited the atmosphere
at this "attractive village pub"; on most accounts, however,
the "very good food" seems to have survived the transition reasonably
well. / Details: www.thehalfmoonwarninglid.co.uk; 9.30 pm; closed Sun D;
no Amex; no booking; children: 14+.*

Jeremy's at Borde Hill   £ 49
Balcombe Rd RH16 1XP   (01444) 441102
*"Tantalising" cooking and a "truly beautiful" terrace for hot summer
days have helped build a big following for Jeremy Ashpool's
"delightful" restaurant; most reports still hail the place as a "hidden
gem", but there's also a minority view that it's becoming just a little bit
"pleased with itself". / Details: www.jeremysrestaurant.com; Exit 10A from
the A23; 10 pm; closed Mon & Sun D.*

Sky Apple Cafe   £ 21
182 Heaton Rd NE6 5HP   (01912) 092571
*The atmosphere may be "somewhat chaotic and undistinguished",
but no one doubts the quality of the "interesting and delicious" fare
on offer at this well-established Heaton veggie.
/ Details: www.skyapple.co.uk; 9 pm; closed Mon, Tue D & Sun D; no credit cards.*

The Feathers Inn   £ 33
Hedley-on-the-Hill NE43 7SW   (01661) 843607
*"Really good Northumbrian cooking in a part of the world where
good pub food is rare" – all of the many reports on this "crowded" inn
are to pretty much the same upbeat effect; you "always need to book
nowadays". / Details: www.thefeathers.net; 8.30 pm; closed Mon; no Amex.*

Feversham Arms Hotel & Verbana Spa £ 54
YO62 5AG   (01439) 770766
*An ancient inn (now a 'Small Luxury Hotel of the World'), sometimes
tipped for its "tasty" cuisine; fans like the "relaxing" contemporary
interior too (as befits an establishment with a spa), but it rarely seems
to raise the spirits much, and critics find it a touch "pretentious".
/ Details: www.fevershamarmshotel.com; 9.30 pm; no trainers; children: 12+ after
8 pm. Accommodation: 33 rooms, from £210.*

Cochin   £ 28
61 High St HP1 3AF   (01442) 233777
*"Brilliantly different" South Indian cuisine – with "real wow-factor" –
has won quite a following for this "friendly spot"; it is also of note
as "just about the only decent restaurant in Hemel Hampstead".
/ Details: www.thecochincuisine.com; 10.45 pm, Fri & Sat 11.30 pm.*

HEMINGFORD GREY, CAMBRIDGESHIRE 3–1B

The Cock £ 38
High St PE28 9BJ (01480) 463609
"A wonderful pub serving creative food and great beer near the banks of the River Ouse"; all feedback concurs that this is an *"excellent"* place which simply *"never disappoints"*. / **Details:** www.cambscuisine.com; 9 pm, Fri & Sat 9.30 pm, Sun 8.30 pm; no Amex; children: 5+ at D.

HENLEY ON THAMES, OXFORDSHIRE 3–3A

Cherry Tree Inn £ 38
RG9 5QA (01491) 680430
A *"great find"* in an *"idyllic"* location – all reports concur that this village gastropub *"never fails to deliver good fresh food"*. / **Details:** www.thecherrytreeinn.com; 10 pm; closed Sun D; no Amex. **Accommodation:** 4 rooms, from £95.

Hotel du Vin et Bistro £ 48
New St RG9 2BP (01491) 848400
OK, we all know about the *"huge"* wine list (and some reporters have found a *"fantastic"* cheeseboard too), but this recent addition to the hotel/brasserie chain contributes to the impression that the group is losing its way – *"inadequate"* service is a particular bugbear, and the food is often *"very average"*. / **Details:** www.hotelduvin.com; 10.30 pm. **Accommodation:** 43 rooms, from £145.

Luscombes at The Golden Ball £ 40
Lower Assendon RG9 6AH (01491) 574157
A two-year-old contemporary-style inn hailed by reporters as a *"real find"*; it offers *"cooking of a very high order"*, and the dining experience in particular is *"fabulous"*. / **Details:** www.luscombes.co.uk; 10.30 pm, Sun 9 pm; no Amex.

Spice Merchant £ 47
Thameside RG9 2LJ (01491) 636118
A top local tip for those in search of *"modern Indian food in a modern setting"*; it's *"pretty pricey"*, though, and the rear dining room *"lacks atmosphere"*. / **Details:** www.spicemerchantgroup.com; 11 pm.

HEPWORTH, WEST YORKSHIRE 5–2C

The Butchers Arms £ 30
38 Towngate HD9 1TE (01484) 682361
"Top-quality" locally-sourced ingredients are turned into sometimes *"excellent"* food – including a novel Yorkshire take on tapas – at this recently revamped boozer, in a *"picturesque village, high in the Pennines"*. / **Details:** www.thebutchersarmshepworth.co.uk; 10 pm, Sun 9 pm; no Amex.

HEREFORD, HEREFORDSHIRE 2–1B

Café at All Saints £ 22
All Saints Church, High St HR4 9AA (01432) 370415
"A good city stop-off", tipped for its *"unusual"* setting, in a former church, and its *"lovely veggie fare"* (in particular). / **Details:** www.cafeallsaints.co.uk; near Cathedral; L only; closed Sun; no Amex; no booking; children: 6+ upstairs.

HERNE BAY, KENT   3–3D

Le Petit Poisson   £ 32   ⭐
Pier Approach, Central Parade CT6 5JN   (01227) 361199
*A "typically old-fashioned" French seafood restaurant, on the prom,
complete with ocean-views; it's a "friendly" place that's "cosy" too…
but will perhaps be less so when the expansion programme has
concluded. / **Details:** www.lepetitpoisson.co.uk; 9 pm, 9.30 pm ; closed Mon &
Sun D; no Amex.*

HERSHAM, SURREY   3–3A

The Dining Room   £ 38   ⭐
10 Queens Rd KT12 5LS   (01932) 231686
*"British comfort food, with some Med' and Asian touches, served in a
series of cottage rooms" – that's the rather "unusual" formula that's
made this "eclectic" but "not too fancy" spot popular for over
a quarter of a century. / **Details:** www.thediningroom.co.uk; 10.30 pm; closed
Sat L & Sun D.*

HERTFORD, HERTFORDSHIRE   3–2B

The Merchant House   £ 30
51 St Andrew St SG14 1HZ   (01992) 504504
*A village-restaurant yearling where some reporters already profess
themselves to be "loyal and happy customers"; views do vary, though,
and doubters have found the cuisine "poorly executed".
/ **Details:** www.themerchanthouse.co.uk.*

HETTON, NORTH YORKSHIRE   5–1B

The Angel   £ 42   🅗🅐⭐
BD23 6LT   (01756) 730263
*With over 25-years under Juliet (and the late Denis) Watkins,
this famous inn still offers "top-notch food" (particularly seafood),
"professional" service and "first-class" wines; it justifiably attracts
a huge volume of reports, which include praise for its elegant
bedrooms (and a cottage to stay in too). / **Details:** www.angelhetton.co.uk;
5m N of Skipton off B6265 at Rylstone; 9 pm; D only, ex Sun open L only.
Accommodation: 5 rooms, from £130.*

HEXHAM, NORTHUMBERLAND   8–2A

Bouchon Bistrot   £ 34   🅐⭐
4-6 Gilesgate NE46 3NJ   (01434) 609943
*"A wonderful touch of rural France" adds charm to this "superb"
bistro, which is almost universally described as a "really good" all-
rounder (and in a town that's otherwise "poorly served" too).
/ **Details:** www.bouchonbistrot.co.uk; 9.30 pm; closed Mon & Sun.*

HIGH WYCOMBE, BUCKINGHAMSHIRE   3–2A

The Old Queens Head   £ 36   🅐⭐
Hammersley Ln HP10 8EY   (01494) 813371
*Housed in an "outstanding ancient, vaulted, timber-framed barn",
this is a boozer offering a "fairly standard formula"; the menu
includes some "interesting" dishes, though, and service
is "knowledgeable" too. / **Details:** www.oldqueensheadpenn.co.uk; 9.30 pm,
Fri & Sat 10 pm.*

HINCKLEY, LEICESTERSHIRE   5–4C

Barnacles   **£ 39**
Watling St LE10 3JA   (01455) 633220
Under its former chef, this top-class restaurant, overlooking a lake, inspired unanimous raves for "seafood of the highest quality"; as the chef moved on in the summer of 2009, however, we'll sadly have to wait until next year for a proper assessment of the new régime. / **Details:** www.barnaclesrestaurant.co.uk; 9.30 pm; closed Mon L, Sat L & Sun D; no Amex.

HINDON, WILTSHIRE   2–3C

The Lamb Inn   **£ 35**
High St SP3 6DP   (01747) 820573
Particularly tipped as a "great Sunday lunch venue", this "olde-worlde" inn, just off the A303, attracts consistent praise for offering a "most enjoyable" overall experience. / **Details:** www.lambathindon.co.uk; 2 minutes from the A350, 5 minutes from the A303; 9.30 pm, Sun 9 pm. **Accommodation:** 17 rooms, from £90.

HINTON ST GEORGE, SOMERSET   2–3A

Lord Poulett Arms   **£ 37**
TA17 8SE   (01460) 73149
"Delicious, well prepared" food and very good service too keep fans coming back to this "lovely" old rural pub; prices, though, give nothing away. / **Details:** www.lordpoulettarms.com; 9 pm; no Amex. **Accommodation:** 4 rooms, from £88.

HOLKHAM, NORFOLK   6–3C

Victoria Hotel   **£ 42**
Park Rd NR23 1RG   (01328) 711008
The "lovely" atmosphere of this "Chelsea set" beach-side hotel has not been matched by its "run-of-the-mill" cuisine of late; perhaps new chef Roger Hickman can put the place to rights? / **Details:** www.victoriaatholkham.co.uk; on the main coast road, between Wells-next-the Sea and Burnham Overy Staithe ; 9 pm; no Amex; booking essential. **Accommodation:** 10 rooms, from £120.

HOLT, NORFOLK   6–3C

Byfords   **£ 34**
1 Shirehall Plain NR25 6BG   (01263) 711400
"Homely and unique", this "higgledy piggledy" cafe/restaurant is tipped for its "top-quality snacks", using "decent local produce" (much of which is also available at the adjacent deli). / **Details:** www.byfords.org.uk; 9.30 pm. **Accommodation:** 16 rooms, from £130.

The Pigs   **£ 32**
Norwich Rd NR24 2RL   (01263) 587634
"A firm favourite"; huge portions of "gutsy British food" – or, if you prefer, 'iffits', or Norfolk tapas – have quickly made this "quirky" gastroboozer very popular. / **Details:** www.thepigs.org.uk; 9 pm; closed Mon & Sun D; no Amex.

A ✪

Combe House
Combe House Hotel £ 45
Gittisham EX14 3AD (01404) 540400
This "sumptuous" and "lovely" Elizabethan country house hotel,
"beautifully situated" in a large estate, is one of those rare
destinations that's an "all-round wow" destinations; attractions include
"quite adventurous" cooking, and an "extensive" wine list.
/ **Details:** www.thishotel.com; 9 pm; no Amex. **Accommodation:** 15 rooms,
from £175.

T

The Holt £ 33
178 High St EX14 1LA (01404) 47707
It may look just like any old "small-town pub", but this multi-level
gastroboozer is tipped for "locally-sourced food" that's both
"imaginative" and "competently prepared"; "good wine list and great
beer" too. / **Details:** www.theholt-honiton.com; 9 pm, Fri & Sat 9.30 pm; closed
Mon & Sun.

T

Oak Room Restaurant
Tylney Hall £ 60
Rotherwick RG27 9AZ (01256) 764881
It's a top tip for a "grand occasion in traditional surroundings",
but sadly this "very classy" (and "expensive") country hotel attracts
too few reports for a more formal commendation.
/ **Details:** www.tylneyhall.com; 10 pm, Sun 9.30 pm. **Accommodation:** 112
rooms, from £170.

A ✪

The Bell Inn £ 41
High Rd SS17 8LD (01375) 642463
"This is a lovely historic Essex village, and The Bell is the jewel in its
crown" – a "lively" place, this 15th-century coaching inn attracts
an awful lot of feedback, and almost all of it confirms that its "really
good and varied menu" maintains a "very high standard".
/ **Details:** www.bell-inn.co.uk; signposted off B1007, off A13; 9.45 pm; booking:
max 12. **Accommodation:** 15 rooms, from £60.

T

Camellia Restaurant
South Lodge Hotel £ 80
Brighton Rd RH13 6PS (01403) 891711
Not much excitement in reports on the cuisine at this nicely-located
country house hotel, which is tipped mainly for its "huge and very
good wine list"; the only report, however, on the new open-kitchen
tasting-menu restaurant (The Pass) was of a "memorable" experience
all-round. / **Details:** www.southlodgehotel.co.uk; opposite the Crabtree pub
1 mile up road from Leonards Lee gardens; 9.30 pm. **Accommodation:** 89
rooms, from £230.

Restaurant Tristan £ 45

3 Stans Way, East St RH12 1HU   (01403) 255688

Tristan Mason has quite a cv, and his "first-class, imaginative cooking" is securing a big reputation for this charming restaurant in an old beamed building, and – if you go for lunch – it's "incredible value" too; "very popular, so book ahead". / **Details:** www.restauranttristan.co.uk; 9.30 pm; closed Mon & Sun.

HOUGH ON THE HILL, LINCOLNSHIRE 6–3A

Brownlow Arms £ 44

High Rd NG32 2AZ   (01400) 250234

A village boozer tipped for its "solid" cooking and a "good ambience"; "if you book, make sure you ask for the main room". / **Details:** www.brownlowarms.com; 11 pm; closed Mon, Tue–Sat D only, closed Sun D; no Amex; children: 12+. **Accommodation:** 4 rooms, from £96.

HOUNSLOW, GREATER LONDON 3–3A

Plane Food £ 42

Heathrow Airport, Terminal 5 TW6 2GA   (020) 8897 4545

"A cut above the usual airport terminal eateries", Gordon Ramsay's Terminal 5 restaurant is tipped as "a fairly quiet and peaceful corner of arguably the worst airport experience in the Western hemisphere". / **Details:** www.gordonramsay.com; 9.30 pm.

HOVE, EAST SUSSEX 3–4B

The Foragers £ 35

3 Stirling Pl BN3 3YU   (01273) 733134

"You don't go for the ambience", so it's clear why this "noisy" Hove gastropub is "always busy" – it's all down to the "fabulous" cooking ("using local line-caught fish and organic veg and meat from a local farm"). / **Details:** www.theforagerpub.co.uk; 10 pm; closed Sun D; children: 12+ after 8 pm.

HOYLAKE, MERSEYSIDE 5–2A

Lino's £ 37

122 Market St CH47 3BH   (0151) 632 1408

Recently revamped in a somewhat more "relaxed" style, this long-established restaurant still pleases all reporters with its "very good food at reasonable prices"; although the owners are Italian in origin, the menu is really more 'international'. / **Details:** www.linosrestaurant.co.uk; 3m from M53, J2; 10 pm; closed Sun, Mon and Sat L; no Amex.

HUDDERSFIELD, WEST YORKSHIRE 5–1C

Bradley's £ 37

84 Fitzwilliam St HD1 5BB   (01484) 516773

This "noisy" bistro offers "honest" cooking that's "good value for money" in a town "not renowned for culinary excellence"; the menu "changes frequently" too, and the wine list is "reasonable"; "a good night out". / **Details:** www.bradleys-restaurant.co.uk; 10 pm; closed Sat L & Sun; no Amex.

🆃

Artisan
£ 57

22 The Weir HU13 0RU   (01482) 644906
In a Georgian townhouse, the Johns family's restaurant is tipped is an "absolute gem" – only a small establishment (16 seats), it doesn't inspire a huge amount of commentary… but all 'raves'.
/ **Details:** www.artisanrestaurant.com; 8.30 pm; D only, closed Mon & Sun; children: 10+ D.

🆃

Fudge
£ 25

93 Princes Ave HU5 3QP   (01482) 441019
"A small neighbourhood restaurant" tipped "for living up to its strap line: 'Fresh Food, Great Tastes, No Fuss'"; the menu is "interesting" (and the fudge is "fantastic" too). / **Details:** www.fudgecafe-restaurant.com.

🅰

The Fox And Hounds
£ 38

2 High St SG12 8NH   (01279) 843999
The food has its ups and downs, but more reporters are won over by the "good range of dishes", and the "great ales on tap" at this "relaxed" inn, which is located in a "beautiful" village.
/ **Details:** www.foxandhounds-hunsdon.co.uk; situated just off the A414, 10 min from Hertford; 10 pm; closed Mon & Sun D.

🅰

Old Bridge Hotel
£ 43

1 High St PE29 3TQ   (01480) 424300
John Hoskins, proprietor and Master of Wine, has invested much care into putting together the "best wine list outside London" (well, nearly), at this ivy-clad, riverside hotel (which has a "delightful" terrace); up-and-down food reports average out somewhere round "OK".
/ **Details:** www.huntsbridge.com; off A1, off A14; 10 pm. **Accommodation:** 24 rooms, from £135.

⭐

Black Boys Inn
£ 44

Henley Rd SL6 5NQ   (01628) 824212
"Excellent game dishes" and a "good selection of fish" are among the strengths of the "down-to-earth" cuisine on offer at this "very enjoyable" country inn. / **Details:** www.blackboysinn.co.uk; 9 pm; closed Sun D; no Amex; children: 12+. **Accommodation:** 8 rooms, from £75.

🆃

The Olde Bell
£ 43

High St SL6 5LX   (01628) 825881
Its origins may go back as far as the 12th century, but this "proper old coaching inn" has been given a make-over with some notably contemporary touches; not many reports as yet, but it is tipped as an "excellent" gastropub all-round. / **Details:** www.theoldebell.co.uk; 10 pm; closed Sun D. **Accommodation:** 47 rooms, from £280.

HYTHE, KENT

Hythe Bay **£ 35**
Marine Pde CT21 6AW (01303) 267024
Under the same ownership as Eastwell Manor, a seaside fish
restaurant that's tipped for its "brilliant views" and "very good
the chef, however, changed just as our survey for the year was dr
to a close. / **Details:** *www.thehythebay.co.uk; 9.30 pm.*

ILFRACOMBE, DEVON 1–2C

The Quay **£ 48**
11 The Quay EX34 9EQ (01271) 868090
Overlooking the harbour, Damien Hirst's (surprisingly?) "delightful"
restaurant – decorated with his own works – is hailed by reporters
as a "valuable" asset to the area; "fantastic" seafood is a highlight,
with lunch offering particularly "good value".
/ **Details:** *www.11thequay.co.uk; 9 pm; closed Mon, Tue & Wed.*

ILKLEY, WEST YORKSHIRE 5–1C

Bettys **£ 30**
32-34 The Grove LS29 9EE (01943) 608029
Even having braved "the inevitable queue", many reporters still praise
the breakfast and lunch at this Yorkshire "staple" teahouse, which
boasts a "charm" that somehow transcends its tourist-trap status.
/ **Details:** *www.bettysandtaylors.com; 5.30 pm; no Amex; no booking.*

The Box Tree **£ 61**
35-37 Church St LS29 9DR (01943) 608484
"Improved" and "less stuffy" – but still "having problems with
consistency" – this famous Northern star is still something of a
curate's egg; fans insist that, thanks to the effort of chef Simon
Gueller, the food is "as good as ever, if not better", but "disappointing"
experiences are still reported too often for comfort.
/ **Details:** *www.theboxtree.co.uk; on A65 near town centre; 9.30 pm; closed*
Mon & Sun D; no Amex; children: 10+ at D.

The Far Syde **£ 34**
1-3 New Brook St LS29 8DQ (01943) 602030
"A restaurant that goes on improving, year after year" – after
15 years in business, chef-patron Gavin Beedhan is still "constantly
making an effort", and it shows through in all reports; "fish specials"
are particularly good. / **Details:** *www.thefarsyde.co.uk; 10 pm; closed Mon &*
Sun; no Amex.

ILMINGTON, WARWICKSHIRE 2–1C

The Howard Arms **£ 38**
Lower Grn CV36 4LT (01608) 682226
"An excellent example of a country pub serving above-average food";
its standards may be marginally lower since it moved into group
ownership, but its "consistency" still impress most reporters.
/ **Details:** *www.howardarms.com; 8m SW of Stratford-upon-Avon off A4300;*
9.30 pm, Fri & Sat 10 pm, Sun 9 pm; no Amex. **Accommodation:** *8 rooms,*
from £115.

⭐⭐

...on Townhouse Hotel £ 62

...V2 4SF (01463) 223777

...ous riverside dining room continues to impress reporters
...e board "both for the tasting menus, and à la carte" with its
..."top quality and good value"; if you feel like a wee dram
...wards, there are "several hundred whiskies to choose from".
...Details: www.abstractrestaurant.com; 10 pm; D only, closed Mon & Sun.
...Accommodation: 30 rooms, from £130.

Mustard Seed £ 34

16 Fraser St IV1 1DW (01463) 220220
Tipped for its "wonderful views", across the River Ness – a restaurant
in a Georgian church building where the food is "competent" ("if not
inventive"). / Details: www.themustardseedrestaurant.co.uk; On the bank of the
Ness river, 30 yards from steeple; 9.45 pm.

🅐⭐

Rocpool £ 39

1 Ness Walk IV3 5NE (01463) 717274
"Great for a special occasion"; this riverside hotel dining room
is unanimously applauded for its "gorgeous" and "slightly different"
cuisine, and its "amazingly good" service too.
/ Details: www.rocpoolrestaurant.com; 10 pm; closed Sun L; no Amex.

IPSWICH, SUFFOLK 3–1D

⭐⭐

Baipo £ 31

63 Upper Orwell St IP4 1HP (01473) 218402
"This really is first-class food" – even a reporter who regularly goes
East, for example, opines that this "traditional" establishment
is "just as good as many restaurants in Thailand" ("even though there
they have rather easier access to the ingredients!").
/ Details: www.baipo.co.uk; 10.45 pm; closed Mon L & Sun; no Amex.

Bistro on the Quay £ 32

3 Wherry Quay IP4 1AS (01473) 286677
"A good find in an otherwise poorly-served city", tipped for its
"good food and service" and its "very reasonably-priced set menu".
/ Details: www.bistroonthequay.co.uk; 9.30 pm; closed Sun D.

Hintlesham Hall £ 66

Dodge St IP8 3NS (01473) 652334
We include this famous country house hotel primarily for
completeness – though tipped as being "nice to visit", reporters also
tend to feel that it has been "trading on its name" of late
(and, according to one critic, "desperately needs a kick into the
21st century"). / Details: www.hintleshamhall.com; 4m W of Ipswich
on A1071; 9.30 pm; jacket at D; children: 12. Accommodation: 33 rooms,
from £150.

Mariners at Ill Punto £ 36

Neptune Quay IP4 1AX (01473) 289748
"A competent enough French-style restaurant, on a boat on Ipswich
dock", tipped as the "best place in town"; for somewhere owned
by the Crépy family (of Great House, Lavenham, fame), however,
feedback overall is a little muted. / Details: www.ilpunto.co.uk; 9.30 pm;
closed Mon & Sun; no Amex.

The Ship Inn £ 35 ⭐⭐

Church Ln IP10 0LQ (01473) 659573

*In the village of Levington, a few miles SW of the city-centre, "a terrific pub which always has an interesting and exciting menu"; it inspires impressively consistent feedback, all of which tends to confirm that: "the only drawback is its popularity". / **Details:** 9.30 pm, Sun 9 pm; no Amex; children: 14+.*

Trongs £ 31 ⭐

23 St Nicholas St IP1 1TW (01473) 256833

*"By far and away the best Chinese restaurant locally", this (Vietnamese) family-run joint is a place "where you are always treated as a special guest", and where the food "never disappoints"; it is "very busy" – book "weeks in advance". / **Details:** 10.30 pm; closed Sun; booking essential.*

IRELAND, BEDFORDSHIRE 3–1A

Black Horse at Ireland £ 42

SG17 5QL (01462) 811398

*A "stylish" and "welcoming" family-run rural gastroboozer that wins almost universal support from reporters for its "reliable" and "consistent" fare; "it's getting busier all the time, so book ahead". / **Details:** www.blackhorseireland.com; 10 pm; closed Sun D.*
Accommodation: 2 rooms, from £55.

ITTERINGHAM, NORFOLK 6–4C

The Walpole Arms £ 39

The Common, Itteringham NR11 7AR (01263) 587258

*All the more worth knowing about in a thin area, an 18th-century inn tipped for its "interesting" food, with "cheerful" service and "good wines" too. / **Details:** www.thewalpolearms.co.uk; from Norwich take A140, through Aylesham towards Blickling, 1m after Blickling Hall take first right to Itteringham; 9 pm; closed Sun D; no Amex.*

JERSEY, CHANNEL ISLANDS

Bohemia 🄷⭐⭐

The Club Hotel & Spa £ 70

Green St, St Helier JE2 4UH (01534) 876550

"A great experience"; this "smart" dining room – of a smart small hotel (and spa) near St Helier's 'central business district' – is worth seeking out for Shaun Rankin's "original" cuisine ("luxury, with a hint of something more rustic") at simply "astonishing" prices – the set lunch, in particular, offers "unbelievable value".
*/ **Details:** www.bohemiajersey.com; 10 pm; closed Sun; no trainers.*
Accommodation: 46 rooms, from £215.

Green Island Restaurant £ 46

St Clement JE2 6LS (01534) 857787

The 'most southerly restaurant in the British Isles' is a notably informal but ambitious (and surprisingly pricey) waterside spot, with terrace, tipped for its "fantastic" cuisine. / **Details:** *www.greenislandrestaurant.com; 9.30 pm; closed Mon & Sun D; no Amex.*

Longueville Manor £ 75

Longueville Rd, St Saviour JE2 7WF (01534) 725501

The island's grandest country house hotel, on the fringe of St Helier, is generally a consistent all-rounder, and benefits from particularly "delightful" service; "simpler dishes are best", though, and prices strike some reporters as "crazy, even for Jersey".

/ **Details:** *www.longuevillemanor.com; Head from St. Helier on the A3 towards Gorey; less than 1 mile from St. Helier; 10 pm; no jeans or trainers.*
Accommodation: *31 rooms, from £210.*

Ocean Restaurant
Atlantic Hotel £ 68

Le Mont de la Pulente, St Brelade JE3 (01534) 744101

For some reporters, the "very professional" dining room of this smart sea-view hotel is "by far the best in Jersey"; even a local who praises the "excellent local produce, cooked with a light touch", however, finds the establishment's Michelin star "hard to understand"; "good breakfasts". / **Details:** *www.theatlantichotel.com; 10 pm.*
Accommodation: *50 rooms, from £.*

Oyster Box £ 42

St Brelade's Bay JE3 8EF (01534) 743311

"Incredibly fresh fish" is just one of the attractions of this large, informal yearling, on beautiful St Brelade's Bay – a top all-round destination, good for adults and children (and veggies too). / **Details:** *www.oysterbox.co.uk; 9.30 pm; closed Mon L.*

Suma's £ 32

Gorey Hill, Gorey JE3 6ET (01534) 853291

Under the same ownership as Longueville Manor, this first-floor bistro offers "good local produce, competently prepared" – "the real point", however, is "sitting at a table on the balcony, watching the comings and goings at Gorey Harbour". / **Details:** *www.sumasrestaurant.com; underneath castle in Gorey Harbour; 9.30 pm; closed Sun D; booking: max 12.*

JEVINGTON, EAST SUSSEX 3–4B

Hungry Monk £ 52

Long Jevington Rd BN26 5QF (01323) 482178

A very pretty village restaurant of over 40 years' standing, and allegedly the home of Banoffi Pie, offering "good-quality plain cooking", and "quite interesting" puddings; there is a slight feeling, though, that the cuisine is "not as special as the pretensions suggest". / **Details:** *www.hungrymonk.co.uk; 5m W of Eastbourne; 9.30 pm; closed Sat L; children: 3+.*

KENILWORTH, WARWICKSHIRE 5–4C

Bosquet £ 50
97a, Warwick Rd CV8 1HP (01926) 852463
*The décor may be stuck in something of a "time warp", but Bernard and Jane Ligniers' "long-term favourite" continues to please most reporters with its "first-class" fare ("as good as anything in the South of France"); this year's reports, however, were a little more up-and-down than usual. / **Details:** www.restaurantbosquet.co.uk; on the main road through Kenilworth; 9 pm; closed Mon, Sat L & Sun; closed Aug.*

Petit Gourmand £ 37
101-103 Warwick Rd CV8 1HP (01926) 864567
*"No complaints to date"; the site which was for many years known as Simply Simpsons has proved itself a solid all-rounder under its new management, offering cooking that's "good" and "fresh", as well as "friendly and welcoming" service. / **Details:** www.petit-gourmand.co.uk; 9.45 pm; closed Sun D.*

KESWICK, CUMBRIA 7–3D

The Cottage In The Wood £ 31
Whinlatter Forest CA12 5TW (01768) 778409
*"Literally out in the woods", this "welcoming" family-run establishment attracts universal praise from reporters for its "interesting" and "tasty" menus; "lovely" rooms are available for those who wish to stay. / **Details:** www.thecottageinthewood.co.uk; 9 pm; closed Mon; no Amex.*
Accommodation: *9 rooms, from £90.*

Morrels £ 32
34 Lake Rd CA12 5DQ (01768) 772666
*"If you're going to the Theatre by the Lake, eat here first!" – this airy and "modern" restaurant, not far from the market square, is praised by all reporters for its "careful" and "interesting" cuisine. / **Details:** www.morrels.co.uk; 9 pm, Fri-Sat 9.30 pm; D only, closed Mon; children: +5.* **Accommodation:** *2 apartments rooms, from £.*

KETTLESHULME, CHESHIRE 5–2B

The Swan Inn £ 32
Macclesfield Rd SK23 7QU (01663) 732943
*"A gastronomic haven in the Cheshire peak district", this 15th century inn attracts consistent praise for "wonderful food, especially fish"; "book ahead, or you're unlikely to get a table". / **Details:** www.the-swan-inn-kettleshulme.co.uk; 8.30 pm, Thu-Fri 7 pm, Sat 9 pm, Sun 4 pm; closed Mon L; no Amex.*

KEYSTON, CAMBRIDGESHIRE 3–1A

The Pheasant £ 42
Loop Rd PE28 0RE (01832) 710241
*If you're looking for a "good option in a poorly-served part of the world", this pub-cum-restaurant is tipped as now getting "back on top form", after its sale by the former Huntsbridge group of gastropubs. / **Details:** www.thepheasant-keyston.co.uk; 1m S of A14 between Huntingdon & Kettering, J15; 9.30 pm, Sun 8.30 pm.*

273

Firenze   £ 42
9 Station St   LE8 0LN   (0116) 279 6260
"Some of the most authentic Tuscan cooking I have tasted outside of Tuscany" – the Poli family's decade-old venture still offers accomplished food at "very good value" prices, and is often "very busy". / **Details:** www.firenze.co.uk; 10 pm; closed Sun; no Amex.

KILLIN, STIRLING   9–3C

Ardeonaig Hotel & Restaurant   £ 73
South Road Loch Tay   FK21 8SU   (01567) 820400
"Not a Scottish restaurant, but a very good South African-themed dining room", in a "beautiful" and remote setting (seven miles from the nearest village); a recent revamp has really "raised its game", the only possible source of disenchantment most reporters can now find being the "high prices" of the "best ever" SA wine list.
/ **Details:** www.ardeonaighotel.co.uk; 8.30 pm; no Amex; children: 12+.
Accommodation: 27 rooms, from £100.

KINGHAM, OXFORDSHIRE   2–1C

The Kingham Plough   £ 42
The Grn   OX7 6YD   (01608) 658327
An ex-Fat Duck chef arrived at this "comfortable" inn with some "fanfare", but the overall package here is not a universal success with reporters – food varies from "innovative" (the majority view) to "indifferent", service "sometimes disappoints", and the atmosphere is "too Farrow & Ball" for some tastes.
/ **Details:** www.thekinghamplough.co.uk; 8.45 pm, Sun 8 pm; no Amex.
Accommodation: 7 rooms, from £85.

KINGSTON UPON THAMES, SURREY   3–3A

Byron   £ 27
4 Jerome Pl   KT1 1HX   (020) 8541 4757
An outpost of the smart (sibling to PizzaExpress) hamburger chain; this particular branch is a top tip in an under-served part of the world. / **Details:** www.byronhamburgers.com; 10 pm.

The Canbury Arms   £ 37
49 Canbury Park Rd   KT2 6LQ   (020) 8255 9129
Cooking that's "in the upper bracket of real pub food" makes this "buzzy" gastroboozer a popular destination with reporters; for what it is, however, it can seem "on the expensive side", and not all reporters are convinced that it's quite worth it; no children in the evening. / **Details:** www.thecanburyarms.com; 10 pm, Sun 9 pm.

Deea   £ 20
145-147 Richmond Rd   KT2 5BX   (020) 8974 5388
"Fantastic food, well-presented in a restaurant with light and fresh decor" – that's the (relatively rare) all-round formula that's won this "authentic" Bangladeshi spot a consistent fan club among reporters.

Frère Jacques £ 40
10-12 Riverside Walk KT1 1QN   (020) 8546 1332
A riverside brasserie oft-tipped for its "charming location" –
the "reasonable" Gallic cooking plays rather a supporting rôle.
*/ **Details:** www.frerejacques.co.uk; next to Kingston Bridge and market place;*
10.30 pm; no Amex.

Jamie's Italian £ 34 ⭐
19-23 High St   (020) 8912 0110
"A smart addition to the Jamie Oliver money-making machine";
for people "who can't be bothered to open up their Jamie books and
cook these dishes at home" – most people, that is – this early-days
member of his casual Italian chain is a "good-value" alternative that's
*"worth the wait". / **Details:** www.jamiesitalian.com; 11 pm, Sun 10.30 pm.*

KINGUSSIE, HIGHLAND 9–2C

The Cross £ 68 🅐⭐
Tweed Mill Brae, Ardbroilach Rd PH21 1LB   (01540) 661166
This "Highland-hideaway restaurant-with-rooms" continues to attract
praise for its "amazing" food, and a "great-value wine list" too;
*it's "always worth the effort to get there!" / **Details:** www.thecross.co.uk;*
*8.30 pm; D only, closed Mon & Sun; children: 9+. **Accommodation:** 8 rooms,*
from £100.

KIRK DEIGHTON, WEST YORKSHIRE 5–1C

The Bay Horse £ 36 ⓣ
Main St LS22 4DZ   (01937) 580058
It's still tipped as a "handy lunch spot", not far from the A1, but this
"great local pub" seems slightly to have lost its way since a recent
*change of ownership. / **Details:** 9 pm; no Amex.*

KIRKBURTON, WEST YORKSHIRE 5–2C

The Woodman Inn £ 30 ⓣ
Thunderbridge HD8 0PX   (01484) 605778
A "cosy" and "buzzy" pub, tipped for serving "good portions of hearty
traditional dishes"; "the food seems better in the restaurant".
*/ **Details:** www.woodman-inn.co.uk.*

KIRKBY LONSDALE, CUMBRIA 7–4D

Avanti £ 34 ⓣ
57 Main St LA6 2AH   (01524) 273500
"A cheery family-friendly café/restaurant, open long hours";
its atmosphere can sometimes seem a bit "twee", but it's a "pleasant"
place whose standards overall impress most reporters.
*/ **Details:** www.baravanti.com; 10 pm, Sun 9 pm; no Amex.*

£ 60

A ⭐⭐

g Hall
Bridge LA6 2JJ   (01524) 271187

"Top-quality food, service and surroundings" figure in almost all
reports on this "relaxed" country house hotel, which appears to have
emerged unscathed from the recent change of chef; the dining room –
15th century – is "particularly beautiful". / **Details:** www.hippinghall.com;
9.30 pm; Mon-Thu D only, Fri-Sun open L & D; no Amex; children: 10+.
Accommodation: 9 rooms rooms, from £165.

KNIGHTWICK, WORCESTERSHIRE   2–1B

The Talbot   £ 43

WR6 5PH   (01886) 821235
A "rustic" pub, where "all dishes are home-made" ("even bread
& preserves") – it impresses with the "quality and variety" of its
dishes too, but feedback is not entirely consistent.
/ **Details:** www.the-talbot.co.uk; 9m from Worcester on A44; 9 pm; no Amex.
Accommodation: 11 rooms, from £90.

KNUTSFORD, CHESHIRE   5–2B

T

Belle Époque   £ 45

King St WA16 6DT   (01565) 633060
This beautiful Art Nouveau restaurant – over 30 years in its current
ownership – is tipped as "having improved somewhat" from the
"depths" to which it has fallen in recent years; even if it's still
somewhat "resting on its laurels", it's undoubtedly "a nice place
to dine". / **Details:** www.thebelleepoque.com; 1.5m from M6, J19; 9.30 pm;
closed Sat L & Sun D; booking: max 6, Sat. **Accommodation:** 7 rooms,
from £115.

LANCASTER, LANCASHIRE   5–1A

The Bay Horse   £ 37   ⭐

Bay Horse Ln LA2 0HR   (01524) 791204
Since long before it became fashionable, "seriously locally-sourced
food" was the stock-in-trade of this handily-located gastropub just off
the M6 (J33), and the cooking here is still "uncomplicated" and
"delicious"; the dining room can seem "sterile", though.
/ **Details:** www.bayhorseinn.com; 0.75m S of A6, J33 M6; 9 pm; closed Mon &
Sun D. **Accommodation:** 3 rooms, from £89.

A ⭐

The Borough   £ 30

3 Dalton Sq LA1 1PP   (01524) 64170
An elegantly-housed city-centre gastropub "gem" – which is "where
Gordon Ramsay eats when he's in town", apparently – which offers
plenty of real ales. / **Details:** www.theboroughlancaster.co.uk; 9 pm.

Pizza Margherita

2 Moor Ln, LA1 1QD (01524…

Owned for three decades by the sa…

this "old favourite" has recently been …

a "buzzy" and "welcoming" spot to enjo…

pizza". / **Details:** www.pizza-margherita.co.uk; …

Simply French

£ 3…

27a St Georges Quay, LA1 1RD (01524) 843199

A city-centre bistro, tipped for "good value for money"; the …

quayside offshoot, Quite Simply French, is also popular – "book…

if you don't want to share" – offering "deli-type bistro food in a sm…

but pretty setting". / **Details:** www.quitesimplyfrench.co.uk; 9.30 pm, Sun &

Mon 9 pm; D only, ex Sun open L & D; no Amex.

Sultan of Lancaster

£ 23

Old Church, Brock St, LA1 1UU (01524) 61188

"Wonderfully fresh-tasting and authentic dishes" have made quite

a name for this intriguingly-housed subcontinental; "the only downside

is the no-alcohol rule – instead try the staggeringly gorgeous mango

lassi"; downstairs, the café/gallery is a "brilliant and very cheap lunch-

time venue". / **Details:** www.sultanoflancaster.com; 11 pm; D only, no Amex.

Langar Hall

£ 48

Church Ln, NG13 9HG (01949) 860559

Imogen Skirving's "lovely" if "slightly eccentric" country house hotel

is a very popular local rendezvous, especially for lunch; the "locally-

sourced" cuisine is generally "delicious" but less consistently rated than

it was this year. / **Details:** www.langarhall.com; off A52 between Nottingham &

Grantham; 9 pm; no Amex; no trainers. **Accommodation:** 12 rooms, from £95.

Northcote

Northcote Rd, BB6 8BE (01254) 240555

£ 65

Messrs Haworth and Bancroft were promoting the use of local

ingredients long before it became fashionable, and the "faultless"

cooking at their "sublime" country house restaurant-with-rooms is still

as good as ever – this is not just "Lancashire's best", but one of the

best in the UK too. / **Details:** www.northcote.com; M6, J31 then A59;

9.30 pm. **Accommodation:** 14 rooms, from £200.

3–4B

£ 32

...) 862419

...Details: www.hare-tunbridgewells.co.uk; on A264
...ri & Sat 10 pm, Sun 9 pm; no Amex; children: 18+
...h care is taken over ingredients and

5–4C

£ 35

...H, WARWICKSHIRE

...Boot

...Warwick Rd B94 6JU   (01564) 782464
...is a pub "for walkers" ("they don't mind muddy boots") and
...this is a pub "for walkers" ("they don't mind muddy boots") and
...for the latter, though, the food is tipped
..."for foodies" – even for the latter, though, the food is tipped
...as "well worth a detour". / Details: www.thebootinnlapworth.co.uk; 10 pm,
Sun 9 pm.

LASTINGHAM, NORTH YORKSHIRE

8–4C

The Blacksmiths Arms

£ 28

Front St YO62 6TL   (01751) 417247
A simple pub-with-rooms, in a "delightful village"; it's tipped as offering
"great food" (including a "very good Sunday lunch").
/ Details: www.blacksmithslastingham.co.uk; 3m north of the A170, between
Pickering and Kirkbymoorside; 8.45 pm, Sun 5 pm; no Amex. **Accommodation:** 3
rooms, from £70.

LAVANT, WEST SUSSEX

3–4A

The Earl Of March

£ 44

Lavant Rd P018 0BQ   (01243) 533993
This "nicely renovated" gastropub is the work of ex-Ritz executive chef
Giles Thompson, and his "innovative" and "wide-ranging" menu
pleases most reporters; service is far from consistent, though,
and critics find "something missing" on the atmosphere front too.
/ Details: www.theearlofmarch.com; 9.30 pm; closed Sun D; no Amex.

LAVENHAM, SUFFOLK

3–1C

Great House

£ 41

Market Pl CO10 9QZ   (01787) 247431

"A wonderful place", the Crépy family's market square restaurant-
with-rooms continues to enchant almost all reporters, not least with
"the best food in East Anglia" ("which comes complete with
a "stunning cheeseboard" and "superb wines"); "we make
a pilgrimage every three months", says one reporter, "and it never
fails". / **Details:** www.greathouse.co.uk; follow directions to Guildhall; 9.30 pm;
closed Mon & Sun D; no Amex. **Accommodation:** 5 rooms, from £96.

With *Anthony's* – one of the UK's most innovative restaurants
– as its flagship, it is not surprising that Leeds offers
an interesting range of dining-out possibilities. But while
there's quite a range of decent traditional Anglo/French/Italian
establishments, it's becoming ever more the case that the
best dining possibilities in the city are, by and large, Indian
or Thai – all but two of the 'stars' we've awarded (on the
basis of survey feedback) are to restaurants offering those
two eastern cuisines.

Aagrah   £ 29   Ⓐ✪✪
Aberford Rd LS25 2HF   (0113) 287 6606
A "brilliant branch" of a chain that's always creditable; it offers
a "wonderful wide-ranging menu" of "well-spiced" subcontinental
cooking at "welcoming" prices; located in the city-centre, it's "always
busy". / **Details:** www.aagrah.com; from A1 take A642 Aberford Rd to Garforth;
11.30 pm, 11 pm Sun; D only.

Akbar's   £ 27   ✪
16 Greek St LS1 5RU   (0113) 242 5426
"Just very good"; this "busy, busy, busy" city-centre Indian pleases
almost all reporters with its "superb all-round" dining experience –
fortunately, this includes service that's generally "incredibly efficient".
/ **Details:** www.akbars.co.uk; midnight; D only.

Anthony's   £ 60   ✪
19 Boar Ln LS1 6EA   (0113) 245 5922
"We live in London, but this is our favourite restaurant!" – fans of
Anthony Flinn's "exciting and interesting" cuisine (in 'molecular
gastronomy' style) "just can't fault the food, service or ambience"
of this ambitious city-centre spot; oddly, for a Northern star, desserts
seem something of a weakness. / **Details:** www.anthonysrestaurant.co.uk;
9.30 pm; closed Mon & Sun; no Amex.

Anthony's at Flannels   £ 30
68-78 Vicar Ln LS1 7JH   (0113) 242 8732
Are the Flinns trying to do too much? – half of reports still praise this
fashion-store restaurant for the "creative" touch for which parent
establishment Anthony's is renowned, but there's a growing feeling
in other quarters that standards here are "slightly disappointing".
/ **Details:** www.anthonysrestaurant.co.uk; closed Mon, L only; no Amex.

Art's   £ 35
42 Call Ln LS1 6DT   (0113) 243 8243
"Leeds's original bistro" is, say its supporters, "still the best", and they
still love its rather Bohemian atmosphere; "slow" and "distracted"
service, however, can take the edge off the experience.
/ **Details:** www.artscafebar.co.uk; near Corn Exchange; 10 pm, 2 am Sat;
no booking, Sat L.

Bibis   £ 40   Ⓐ
Criterion Pl, Swinegate LS1 4AG   (0113) 243 0905
OTT decoration in Art Deco style distinguishes this glitzy Italian
institution; the food tends to be "ordinary" and "overpriced" though,
so make sure you go on a cabaret night – "they're always worth
seeing, sometimes because they're so good, other times because
they're so terrible!" / **Details:** www.bibisrestaurant.com; 11.30 pm; no shorts;
no booking, Sat.

Brasserie Forty 4
£ 40
44 The Calls LS2 7EW (0113) 234 3232
A "buzzing" canal-side brasserie which seems to have found greater favour of late; it is strongly tipped as a "lovely" space, where the food is sometimes "startlingly good"; more reports please!
/ **Details:** www.brasserie44.com; 10 pm, Sat 10.30 pm; closed Sun L.

Bryan's
£ 32
9 Weetwood Ln LS16 5LT (0113) 278 5679
"Good fish 'n' chips, but pricey"; the famous Headingley chippy remains a destination of some note, but reports are variable, tending to confirm the suspicions of those who say that "Bryan's crown has slipped". / **Details:** www.bryansfishrestaurant.co.uk; off Otterley Rd; 9.30 pm, Sun 7 pm; no Amex; need 6+ to book.

Café Guru
£ 25
6 Brewery Pl LS10 1NE (0113) 244 2255
A "posh" canalside Indian restaurant – decorated rather like a smart modern nightclub – tipped as a very impressive all-rounder; more reports please. / **Details:** 11 pm; D only.

La Cantina 44
£ 34
1A, Austhorpe Rd LS15 8QR (0113) 368 0066
An unpretentious Cross Gates Italian, consistently tipped for "outstanding food and service" by its ardent local fan club.
/ **Details:** www.lacantina44.co.uk; 11.30 pm, Sun 10 pm; D only, closed Mon.

Casa Mia Grande
£ 36
33-37 Harrogate Rd LS7 3PD (0870) 444 5154
Though still sometimes tipped as a "top city-centre destination", this handy Italian stand-by also attracts quite a lot of flak nowadays, especially from reporters who say that it's "not as good as it used to be". / **Details:** www.casamiaonline.co.uk; 10.30 pm, Fri & Sat 11 pm, Sun 9.30 pm.

Chaophraya
£ 34
20a, First Floor, Blayds Ct LS2 4AG (0113) 244 9339
This is "the best Thai restaurant outside London", says a fan of this OTT city-centre operation; it does have the occasional detractor, but the more general view is that it offers "excellent value-for-money". / **Details:** www.chaophraya.co.uk; in Swinegate; 10.30 pm.

Flying Pizza
£ 32
60 Street Ln LS8 2DQ (0113) 266 6501
Fans still insist that this "full-of-life", see-and-be-seen Roundhay institution does "the best pizza outside Italy"; those who say its "halcyon days are now past", however, are becoming quite vociferous.
/ **Details:** www.theflyingpizza.co.uk; just off A61, 3m N of city centre; 11 pm, Sun 10 pm ; no shorts.

The Foundry Wine Bar
£ 39
1 Saw Mill Yd LS11 5WH (0113) 245 0390
"A bit tucked-away, but word seems to have got out and it's always busy" – this self-explanatory establishment is tipped as a "superb" all-rounder, with "good steaks" and "fantastic-value lunch menus" among its particular attractions. / **Details:** www.thefoundrywinebar.co.uk; 10 pm; closed Sat L & Sun; no Amex.

Fourth Floor Café
Harvey Nichols   **£ 39**

107-111 Briggate LS1 6AZ   (0113) 204 8000

*If you're looking for both "people-watching and food", this elevated
department store dining room (and terrace) is hard to beat;
"especially in good weather, it's a good lunch venue" – dinner inspires
little feedback. / Details: www.harveynichols.com; 10 pm; L only, ex Thu-Sat
open L & D; no booking, Sat L.*

Fuji Hiro   **£ 22**

45 Wade Ln LS2 8NJ   (0113) 243 9184

*Tipped as a "good pre-theatre or opera place", a Japanese bar that
specialises in "excellent soups and noodle dishes". / Details: 10 pm,
Fri & Sat 11 pm; no Amex; need 5+ to book.*

La Grillade   **£ 39**

Wellington St LS1 4HJ   (0113) 245 9707

*"Still going strong", this "top-notch" bistro of long standing (1981)
is "always full", thanks to its "varied" menu and its "top-notch" Gallic
styling; it offers "one of the best steaks in Leeds" too.
/ Details: www.lagrillade.co.uk; 10 pm; closed Sat L & Sun.*

Hansa's   **£ 26**

72-74 North St LS2 7PN   (0113) 244 4408

*"Awesome" Gujarati cuisine – "refreshingly different from the meat-
laden curries of the local competition" – maintains the very high
repute of Mrs Hansa-Dabhi's "friendly" city-centre veteran.
/ Details: www.hansasrestaurant.com; 10.30 mon-sat 11; D only, ex Sun L only;
no Amex.*

Kendells Bistro   **£ 35**

St Peters Sq LS9 8AH   (0113) 243 6553

*"An authentic French bistro, offering Yorkshire portions" –
this unbeatable cultural synthesis has speedily made this "friendly and
somewhat chaotic" city-centre spot (near the BBC) popular with all
who comment on it. / Details: www.kendellsbistro.co.uk; 10.30 pm; closed
Mon, Sat L & Sun; no Amex.*

Little Tokyo   **£ 31**

24 Central Rd LS1 6DE   (0113) 243 9090

*"A great entry-point to Japanese cuisine"; this small-scale outfit,
behind Debenhams, attracts almost invariable praise for its
"good selection of sushi, bento boxes and noodles", all "reasonably
priced". / Details: 10 pm, Fri & Sat 11 pm; need 8+ to book.*

No 3 York Place   **£ 45**

3 York Pl LS1 2DR   (0113) 245 9922

*Once very well-known, this rather serious city-centre restaurant
is characterised as something of a "hidden gem" nowadays, and fans
insist it offers "amazing food" at notably "reasonable" prices.
/ Details: www.no3yorkplace.co.uk; 9.30 pm; closed Sat L & Sun.*

The Olive Tree £ 30
74-76 Otley Road LS6 4BA (0113) 274 8282
A Headingley stand-by, tipped for its "consistent and pleasant Greek-style food", including "amazing moussaka" and "notable mixed dips".
/ **Details:** *www.olivetreegreekrestaurant.co.uk; 10.30 pm; no Amex.*

**The Piazza By Anthony
The Corn Exchange** £ 34
Corn Exchange, Call Ln LS1 6DT (0113) 247 0995
"Well done to the Victorians for building it, and even more well done to Anthony Flinn for such a convincing conversion" – most reporters much approve of the vast (and somewhat "cavernous") dining space in the "revitalised" Corn Exchange, where the food is sometimes (if not quite always) "of really excellent quality".
/ **Details:** *www.anthonysrestaurant.co.uk; 10 pm; no Amex.*

The Reliance £ 32
76-78 North St LS2 7PN (0113) 295 6060
*Not many reports on this gastropub a few minutes from the city-centre, but it's strongly tipped for its "good food and good value", and in a "lovely buzzy atmosphere" too. / **Details:** www.the-reliance.co.uk; 10, Thu-Sat 10.30 pm, Sun 9.30 pm; no booking.*

Sala Thai £ 28 ⭐
13-17 Shaw Ln LS6 4DH (0113) 278 8400
"Food and service great, décor needs updating" – seven words which tell you all you need to know about this Headingley Thai.
/ **Details:** *www.salathaileeds.co.uk; just off Otley Rd, near Arndale Centre; 11 pm; closed Sat L & Sun.* **Accommodation:** *rooms, from £-.*

Salvo's £ 38
115 Otley Rd LS6 3PX (0113) 275 5017
*"As popular as ever", this '70s-veteran is still, for some reporters, "the best Italian in Leeds"; "noisy" and "crowded", it certainly has "a bit of a buzz". / **Details:** www.salvos.co.uk; 2m N of University on A660; 10.30 pm, Sun 9 pm; no booking at D.*

Sous le Nez en Ville £ 38
Quebec Hs, Quebec St LS1 2HA (0113) 244 0108
*"A long-established eatery which never fails to satisfy"; this city-centre basement offers "good French wine and food", and is of particular note for its "decent" business lunches, and its "imaginative" early-bird dinners. / **Details:** www.souslenez.com; 10 pm, Sat 11 pm; closed Sun.*

Sukhothai £ 27 ⭐
8 Regent St LS7 4PE (0113) 237 0141

*A Chapel Allerton Thai, where the often-"excellent" food has drawn a real following - so much so that booking is "essential"; there's also a branch in Headingley. / **Details:** www.thaifood4u.co.uk; 11 pm; closed Mon L; no Amex.*

Tampopo   **£ 28**

15 South Pde LS1 5QS   (0113) 245 1816

In the style of Wagamama, this "cheap and cheerful" chain outlet is tipped as a stand-by that "never fails to satisfy"; the Express menu offers "excellent value" too. / **Details:** *www.tampopo.co.uk; 11 pm, Sun 10 pm; need 7+ to book.*

LEICESTER, LEICESTERSHIRE   5–4D

Bobby's   **£ 23**

154-156 Belgrave Rd LE4 5AT   (0116) 266 0106

"In spite of all the local competition", this grungy-looking Indian veteran "still has the edge", and – fortunately – "its appearance belies the quality of the food"; its range of sweets is a particular "delight". / **Details:** *www.eatatbobbys.com; 10 pm; no Amex.*

The Case   **£ 40**

4-6 Hotel St LE1 5AW   (0116) 251 7675

If you're looking for "a bit of London style", this attractive factory conversion is the closest approximation Leicester has to offer – even a reporter who notes that the food "can occasionally disappoint" says "guests are always impressed". / **Details:** *www.thecase.co.uk; near the Cathedral, and St Martins Square; 10.30 pm; closed Sun.*

Watsons   **£ 47**

5-9 Upper Brown St LE1 5TE   (0116) 255 1928

Not many reports yet on this relaunched – and much glammed-up – city-centre restaurant, but it's already tipped as a very good all-rounder; indeed, the transformation is so profound that one reporter found it "odd they didn't just find a new name". / **Details:** *www.watsons-restaurant.com; next to Phoenix Art Theatre; 10 pm; closed Mon & Sun.*

LEINTWARDINE, SHROPSHIRE   5–4A

Jolly Frog   **£ 35**

The Todden SY7 0LX   (01547) 540298

Bizarrely, "a French-style bistro in the middle of Herefordshire"; as the name suggests, this is quite a "relaxed" destination, and is of particular note for "a fantastic choice of fish dishes, beautifully presented". / **Details:** *www.jollyfrogpub.co.uk; 9.30 pm; closed Mon & Sun D.*

LEWDOWN, DEVON   1–3C

Lewtrenchard Manor   **£ 65**

EX20 4PN   (01566) 783256

This "wonderfully secluded Jacobean manor house", now a Von Essen hotel, is tipped for its "relaxing" location; reports on the food and service, however, are surprisingly mixed. / **Details:** *www.lewtrenchard.co.uk; off A30 between Okehampton & Launceston; 9 pm; no jeans or trainers; children: 8+ at D.* **Accommodation:** *14 rooms, from £150.*

LEWES, EAST SUSSEX

Bill's Produce Store **£ 25** ⭐
56 Cliffe High St BN7 2AN   (01273) 476918
"Piled high with delicious-looking produce", this "bustling" and "lively"
("chaotic") deli/café is a "family-friendly" operation with quite a name
as a breakfast destination; beware the queues.
/ **Details:** www.billsproducestore.co.uk; 6 pm; no Amex.

LINCOLN, LINCOLNSHIRE

Browns Pie Shop **£ 30**
33 Steep Hill LN2 1LU   (01522) 527330
"The food is returning to its former high standards", says a supporter
of this celebrated pie (and more) house, which is located in a "lovely
old building"; consistency, however, still has a way to go.
/ **Details:** www.brownspieshop.co.uk; near the Cathedral; 10 pm, Sun 8 pm;
no Amex.

Fourteen **£ 32** Ⓣ
14 Bailgate LN1 3AE   (01522) 576556
A handy city-centre restaurant with a "pleasant" modern interior;
the food is tipped as "interesting" (veggie options, especially),
but reports (few) aren't entirely consistent.
/ **Details:** www.fourteenrestaurant.co.uk; 10 pm.

The Old Bakery **£ 44** ⭐
26-28 Burton Rd LN1 3LB   (01522) 576057
In the shadow of the Castle, a restaurant-with-rooms whose "quirky"
and "imaginative" Anglo-Italian menu is executed with considerable
panache; "the word is spreading – book ahead".
/ **Details:** www.theold-bakery.co.uk; 9 pm; closed Mon; no jeans.
Accommodation: 4 rooms, from £63.

The Wig & Mitre **£ 37**
30-32 Steep Hill LN2 1TL   (01522) 535190
Housed in a medieval, stone-clad building, a large gastropub that's
had its ups and downs of late, but where the downstairs bar
is currently recommended for its "interesting" and "varied" menu
(including "chalkboard specials"); the "snug rooms" are great for
winter evenings. / **Details:** www.wigandmitre.com; between Cathedral & Castle;
10.30 pm.

LINLITHGOW, WEST LOTHIAN

Champany Inn **£ 82** Ⓣ
EH49 7LU   (01506) 834532
This celebrated inn attracts little survey commentary nowadays,
and it's rather mixed too – it's still tipped for its "succulent" steak and
its "fantastic" wine list, but prices are undoubtedly very high.
/ **Details:** www.champany.com; 2m NE of Linlithgow on junction of A904 & A803;
10 pm; closed Sat L & Sun; no jeans or trainers; children: 8+.
Accommodation: 16 rooms, from £135.

LITTLEHAMPTON, WEST SUSSEX

East Beach Cafe **£ 39**
Sea Rd, The Promenade BN17 5GB   (01903) 731903
In its second year of operation, it's not just the "ultra-modern" building
or the "unbeatable view" that's made this seaside café of note –
the "good regular menu" has also pleased most reporters (although
some dishes have seemed "over-ambitious" too).
/ **Details:** www.eastbeachcafe.co.uk; 8.30 pm, Sat & Sun 9 pm.

Just when it all seemed pretty hopeless for Liverpool, green shoots seem to be breaking out in the local restaurant world. The city's original fine dining restaurant of recent times, *Hope Street*, is having something of a renaissance, and the same team has launched a well regarded new venture *Host*. There are also some other pleasing mid-priced newcomers such as the *Italian Fish Club* and *Delifonseca*. The city's most-cherished all-rounder, however, is still the no-nonsense *Everyman Bistro*, now entering its fifth decade!

Alma De Cuba
St Peter's Church £ 39
Seel St L1 4AZ (0151) 702 7394
Tipped for its "amazing" setting, in a former church, this South American-themed outfit can otherwise seem "very ordinary" (and, for hardcore critics, simply "all hype"). / Details: www.alma-de-cuba.com; 11 pm, midnight Fri & Sat; no shorts; children: 18+ in bar.

Delifonseca £ 30
12 Stanley St L1 6AF (0151) 255 0808
The rarity-value of this "friendly" and "relaxed" city-centre dining room – "above an excellent deli" and serving "hearty" comfort food – have made it a very popular local destination; it's a "smallish" place with a "great atmosphere" (including "for romance"). / Details: www.delifonseca.co.uk; 9 pm, Fri & Sat 9.30 pm; closed Sun; no Amex.

Everyman Bistro £ 23
5-9 Hope St L1 9BH (0151) 708 9545
"A Liverpool institution"; this "cheap and cheerful" theatre-basement canteen continues to serve up the "hearty portions of home-made food" that have made it so popular for four decades; puddings in particular are "a special treat". / Details: www.everyman.co.uk; midnight, Fri & Sat 2 am; closed Sun.

Il Forno £ 33
132 Duke St, East Village L1 5AG (0151) 709 4002
"A better-than-average Italian" (with pizza a speciality) that's "handy for the Everyman Theatre and the Philharmonic"; it's "always bustling", but reporters have a slight feeling it "doesn't always hit the heights the ambitious pricing suggests". / Details: www.ilforno.co.uk; 11 pm, Fri-Sun 10.30 pm.

Gusto Restaurant & Bar £ 32
Edward Pavillon, Albert Dock L3 4AF (0151) 708 6969
Tipped as a "lively" Albert Dock destination, the former Est! Est! Est! premises aren't radically different under their new guise – this is still a large and "noisy" place, serving "standard Italian fare". / Details: www.gustorestaurants.uk.com; 10.30 pm, Fri & Sat 11 pm, Sun 10 pm.

Host £ 25
31 Hope St L1 9HX (0151) 708 5831
This new opening – from the same people as nearby 60 Hope Street – is likened to "a more adventurous take on Wagamama"; its "decent Asian-fusion fare" finds favour with all early-days reporters. / Details: www.ho-st.co.uk.

Italian Fish Club £ 30

85 Bold St L1 4HF (0151) 708 5508

"Simple Italo-Scottish fishy classics" – and at *"very fair prices"* too – have helped make this *"smart"* and *"buzzy"* new café/restaurant instantly popular; this is a cross-border incursion from the family behind Edinburgh's famous 'Valvona & Crolla', so it's perhaps no surprise they do *"the best coffee in Liverpool"* too. / **Details:** www.theitalianclubliverpool.co.uk.

The London Carriage Works
Hope Street Hotel £ 50

40 Hope St L1 9DA (0151) 705 2222

This locally-celebrated boutique hotel dining room started off so well, but has sadly totally lost its way; it still attracts many reports, but half of these are now very negative – service, in particular, is too often *"slow"* and *"obsequious"*, and prices for the *"mediocre"* cuisine can seem *"outrageous"*. / **Details:** www.tlcw.co.uk; Opposite the Philharmonic Hall; 10 pm, Sun 9 pm; no shorts. **Accommodation:** 48 rooms, from £140.

Mayur £ 35

130 Duke St L1 5AG (0151) 709 9955

"An Indian restaurant with a bit of class!" – this *"pleasant"* city-centre two-year-old receives a warm welcome from all who comment on it, and it's already hailed as *"probably the best subcontinental in town"*. / **Details:** www.mayurrestaurant.co.uk; 10.30 pm, Fri & Sat 11.30 pm.

Mei Mei £ 32

9-13 Berry St L1 9DF (0151) 707 2888

A *"friendly"* spot that's *"very popular with Chinatown residents"*. / **Details:** 11.30 pm, Fri & Sat midnight, Sun 10 pm; no Amex.

The Monro £ 31

92-94 Duke St L1 5AG (0151) 707 9933

"Popular all-round", this *"lively"* but upmarket city-centre gastropub pub offers *"restaurant-quality"* British fare that's *"well-presented"* and *"flavoursome"*. / **Details:** www.themonro.com; 9.45 pm, Sun 7.30 pm.

Panoramic
Beetham West Tower £ 58

Brook St L3 9PJ (0151) 236 5534

"Fantastic views" make this 34th-floor yearling *"great for a romantic evening"* (and not a bad place for business either); to no one's great surprise, though, the food is sometimes *"not quite up to its pretensions"*. / **Details:** www.panoramicliverpool.com; 9.30 pm; no trainers.

Puschka £ 43

16 Rodney St L1 2TE (0151) 708 8698

A *"hidden gem"*; there's the odd hint of variable standards, but this *"intimate"* restaurant pleases almost all reporters with its *"imaginative"* food, and its *"excellent"* service too. / **Details:** www.puschka.co.uk; 10 pm; D only, closed Mon.

The Quarter £ 28

7-11 Falkner St L8 7PU (0151) 707 1965

A *"popular'"* and *"casual"* bistro, just off Hope Street, which serves *"an eclectic range of salads, pastas and pizzas"* – results are *"a bit variable"*, but are sometimes *"memorable"*. / **Details:** www.thequarteruk.com; 11 pm.

60 Hope Street £ 46 ⭐

60 Hope St L1 9BZ (0151) 707 6060

Once again "best in the city" (at the grander end of the market, anyway), this "popular" and "pleasant" townhouse-restaurant – with a "bustling" brasserie downstairs – impresses almost all reporters with the "good quality" of its cuisine, and its wines too.

/ Details: www.60hopestreet.com; 10.30 pm; closed Sat L & Sun.

Spire £ 31

1 Church Rd L15 9EA (0151) 734 5040

"Possibly the best in Liverpool at the moment", say supporters, this Wavertree spot is praised for its "interesting menu, high-quality cooking, excellent wine list and friendly service"; one or two reporters, though, encountered a "bad night". / Details: www.spirerestaurant.co.uk; 9 pm, Fri & Sat 9.30 pm; closed Mon L & Sun.

Tapas Tapas £ 20 Ⓣ

14 Back Colquitt St L1 4DE (0151) 709 0999

A Waterloo (North Liverpool) tapas bar tipped as a place that "feels and smells and tastes authentic" – "like stepping into Barcelona"; the new city-centre offshoot, however, "doesn't hit the mark in the same way". / Details: www.tapastapas.co.uk.

Yuet Ben £ 29

1 Upper Duke St L1 9DU (0151) 709 5772

Terry Lim's Chinatown veteran is a "basic" sort of place; supporters find it "authentic", but there's also a slight feeling that it's "living on its reputation". / Details: www.yuetben.co.uk; 11 pm; D only, closed Mon.

Ziba £ 43 Ⓣ

Hargreaves Building, 5 Chapel St L3 9AG (0151) 236 6676

Better (but still few) reports of late on this grandly-housed city-centre dining room, which is tipped as a "relaxed" place, where "simply-cooked steaks" and so on are served in a "beautiful" period setting.

/ Details: www.racquetclub.org.uk; 9.30 pm, Fri & Sat 10 pm; closed Sat L & Sun.

Accommodation: *8 rooms, from £110.*

LLANDENNY, MONMOUTHSHIRE 2–2A

Raglan Arms £ 40 Ⓐ⭐

NP15 1DL (01291) 690800

With its "friendly service, good food and a good-value wine list", this "gem" of a gastropub would be worth knowing about anywhere – in this neck of the woods, its existence is something near miraculous!

/ Details: www.raglanarms.com; 9.30 pm; closed Mon & Sun D.

LLANDRILLO, DENBIGHSHIRE   4–2D

Tyddyn Llan   £ 60
LL21 0ST   (01490) 440264

"Outstanding local produce" is lovingly crafted into "outstanding dishes" ("best in Wales", say some) at the Webbs' "lovely" country restaurant-with-rooms, and the wine list is "comprehensive" too; for the style of place that it is, however, service can sometimes seem a little "remote". / **Details:** www.tyddynllan.co.uk; on B4401 between Corwen and Bala; 9 pm; closed Mon (Tue-Thu L by prior arrangement only); no Amex; booking essential Tue L-Thu L. **Accommodation:** 13 rooms, from £130.

LLANDUDNO, CONWY   4–1D

Bodysgallen Hall   £ 52
LL30 1RS   (01492) 584466
This grand country house hotel, 13th century in origin, is perhaps of most note for its "tranquil" location, "glorious views", and its "very good set lunches" too; otherwise, reports don't always hit quite the level of excitement that should go with such high prices.
/ **Details:** www.bodysgallen.com; 2m off A55 on A470; 9.15 pm, Fri 9.30 pm; closed Mon & Sun D; no jeans or trainers; booking: max 10; children: 6+.
Accommodation: 31 rooms, from £175.

Osborne's Café and Grill
Osborne House Hotel   £ 31
Promenade, 17 North Parade LL30 2LP   (01492) 860330
"Good brasserie food in rich fin-de-siècle surroundings" – the formula that makes this "classy" establishment well worth seeking; leave space for a "divine" bread 'n' butter pud". / **Details:** www.osbornehouse.com; 9.45 pm, Sun 8.45 pm. **Accommodation:** 6 rooms, from £145.

St Tudno Hotel
& Terrace Restaurant   £ 48
Promenade LL30 2LP   (01492) 874411
Reports on this once-celebrated hotel have been unsettled of late; under a new chef, it's tipped as "getting back to its old standard", but reports are still fewer than we would like.
/ **Details:** www.st-tudno.co.uk; 9.30 pm; no shorts; children: 6+ after 6.30 pm. **Accommodation:** 18 rooms, from £100.

LLANGAMMARCH WELLS, POWYS   4–4D

Lake Country House   £ 54
LD4 4BS   (01591) 620202
"Comfortable and well run", this country house hotel is tipped as something of a culinary "oasis" in these parts; its unfussy cuisine is "really very good". / **Details:** www.lakecountryhouse.co.uk; off A483 at Garth, follow signs; 9.15 pm; no jeans or trainers; children: 8+ at D. **Accommodation:** 30 rooms, from £175.

LLANGOLLEN, DENBIGHSHIRE 5–3A

Corn Mill £ 33
Dee Ln LL20 8PN (01978) 869555
*Tipped for its "fantastic situation" – dramatically posed above the
turbulent waters of the Dee – this is a gastropub whose standards are
otherwise somewhere between "good" and "adequate".
/ **Details:** www.cornmill-llangollen.co.uk; 9.30 pm, Sun 9 pm .*

LLANWRTYD WELLS, POWYS 4–4D

Carlton Riverside £ 49
Irfon Cr LD5 4ST (01591) 610248
*A riverside restaurant-with-rooms, tipped for its "great location",
its "personal and friendly" service, and its use of "fine local
ingredients". / **Details:** www.carltonriverside.com; 8.30 pm; closed Mon L &
Sun; no Amex; booking: max 10. **Accommodation:** 5 rooms, from £65.*

LLYSWEN, POWYS 2–1A

Llangoed Hall £ 64
LD3 0YP (01874) 754525
*"A nearly faultless dining room in the most beautiful setting";
this elegant country house hotel – formerly owned by the 'Laura
Ashley' family – is a "formal" sort of operation, where everything
remains "just so". / **Details:** www.llangoedhall.com; 11m NW of Brecon
on A470; 9.30 pm; no Amex; jacket required at D. **Accommodation:** 23 rooms,
from £210.*

LOCH LOMOND, WEST DUNBARTONSHIRE 9–4B

Lomonds
Cameron House £ 50
G83 8QZ (01389) 755565
*A grand lochside hotel, owned by De Vere, and tipped for its "great
location"; fans find the food "delightful" too, but the service can be a
"let-down", and prices sometimes seem excessive.
/ **Details:** www.cameronhouse.co.uk; over Erskine Bridge to A82, follow signs
to Loch Lomond; 9.45 pm; D only, closed Sun & Mon; jacket & tie required;
children: 14+. **Accommodation:** 129 rooms, from £208.*

LOCHINVER, HIGHLAND 9–1B

The Albannach £ 69
IV27 4LP (01571) 844407
*"A special small hotel where dinner is anticipated all day"; attractions
include "charming" hosts, an "excellent" wine list, and "great views"
from the darkly-panelled dining room; "I hope that heaven is like
this…" / **Details:** www.thealbannach.co.uk; D only, closed Mon; no Amex;
children: 12+. **Accommodation:** 5 rooms, from £250.*

LOCKSBOTTOM, KENT 3–3B

Chapter One £ 45
Farnborough Common BR6 8NF (01689) 854848
*"Beautiful" dishes with "complex flavours" continue to win a huge
following for this well-established "suburban oasis"; almost all of the
many reports speak of "consistently high standards" and "excellent
attention to detail". / **Details:** www.chaptersrestaurants.com; just before
Princess Royal Hospital; 10.30 pm; booking: max 12.*

LONG CRENDON, BUCKINGHAMSHIRE 2–2D

The Angel £ 46
47 Bicester Rd HP18 9EE (01844) 208268
*"Improved" under its new management, this "reliable" old inn
is unanimously hailed as a "good" and "traditional" operation,
and fans say it offers "the most reliable mid-price food in the area".
/ Details: www.angelrestaurant.co.uk; 2m NW of Thames, off B4011; 9.30 pm;
closed Sun D; no Amex; booking: max 12, Fri & Sat. Accommodation: 4 rooms,
from £95.*

The Mole & Chicken £ 35
Easington HP18 9EY (01844) 208387
*A pretty country inn, updated in contemporary style, with a "stunning
setting and views"; since its 2008 relaunch, it has inspired consistently
upbeat feedback. / Details: www.themoleandchicken.co.uk; follow signs from
B4011 at Long Crendon; 9.30 pm, Sun 9 pm. Accommodation: 5 rooms,
from £95.*

LONG MELFORD, SUFFOLK 3–1C

Scutchers £ 44
Westgate St CO10 9DP (01787) 310200
*"Fantastic" standards all-round are proclaimed by fans of this
"friendly" village bistro, which offers a "flexible" menu, on which
highlights include some "great fish and seafood".
/ Details: www.scutchers.com; 9.30 pm; closed Mon & Sun.*

LONGRIDGE, LANCASHIRE 5–1B

The Longridge Restaurant £ 46
104-106 Higher Rd PR3 3SY (01772) 784969
*Given that Paul Heathcote's former flagship has had a chequered
year – placed on the market, then withdrawn – it has generated
surprisingly good feedback; a couple of basically upbeat reports,
however, noted a "lack of custom". / Details: www.heathcotes.co.uk; follow
signs for Jeffrey Hill; 9.30 pm, 8.30 pm Sun; closed Mon & Sat L.*

LONGSTOCK, HAMPSHIRE 2–3D

Peat Spade Inn £ 42
SO20 6DR (01264) 810612
*Mixed reviews of late on this charming-village inn; fans praise its
"good seasonal bistro food", but the space can feel "crowded",
and "interminable waits" for dishes seem to have become a real
problem. / Details: www.peatspadeinn.co.uk; 1.25m from Stockbridge; 9 pm;
no Amex. Accommodation: 6 rooms, from £110.*

LOUGHBOROUGH, LEICESTERSHIRE 5–3D

The Hammer And Pincers £ 48
5 East Rd LE12 6ST (01509) 880735
*"An extremely friendly husband-and-wife restaurant", where the
cooking has an "innovative way with local ingredients"; for top value,
seek out the "excellent" mid-week earlybird menu.
/ Details: www.hammerandpincers.co.uk; 9.30 pm, Sun 9 pm; no Amex.*

LOWER HARDRES, KENT
3–3D

The Granville £ 36 ⭐

Street End CT4 7AL   (01227) 700402
A newish gastropub, "related to the well regarded Sportsman in Seasalter"; all reports confirm that it "consistently delivers".
/ **Details:** *9 pm; closed Sun D; no Amex.*

LOWER ODDINGTON, GLOUCESTERSHIRE
2–1C

The Fox Inn £ 36 🅐

GL56 0UR   (01451) 870555
"A pretty little pub", with "wholesome" and "well-cooked" food, "friendly staff" and a "nice garden"; it inspires a lot of reports, and almost all of them positive across-the-board.
/ **Details:** *www.foxinn.net; on A436 near Stow-on-the-Wold; 9.30 pm, Fri & Sat 10 pm; no Amex.* **Accommodation:** *3 rooms, from £70.*

LOWER SLAUGHTER, GLOUCESTERSHIRE
2–1C

Lower Slaughter Manor £ 65 🆃

GL54 2HP   (01451) 820456
In a pretty Cotswold village, a grand hotel that's now part of the Von Essen empire; not many reports, but it is consistently tipped as "a special place for a special treat".
/ **Details:** *www.lowerslaughter.co.uk; 2m from Burton-on-the-Water on A429; 9 pm; no jeans or trainers.* **Accommodation:** *19 rooms, from £230.*

LOWER WIELD, HAMPSHIRE
2–3D

Yew Tree £ 30 🆃

Alresford SO24 9RX   (01256) 389224
It may be rather "out of the way", but this "friendly" inn is a "popular" destination, tipped for "classic (gastro)pub food that's always well done". / **Details:** *www.the-yewtree.org.uk; 9 pm, Sun 8.30 pm; closed Mon; no Amex.*

LUDLOW, SHROPSHIRE
5–4A

La Bécasse £ 75 ⭐⭐

17 Corve St SY8 1DA   (01584) 872325
"Now Ludlow's prime destination", say some reporters, the northern counterpart to L'Ortolan (Shinfield) offers William Holland's "immaculate and careful cuisine, with innovative twists"; the atmosphere, though, can sometimes seem "slightly intimidating".
/ **Details:** *www.labecasse.co.uk; 9 pm; closed Mon, Tue L & Sun; no Amex.*

Mr Underhill's £ 63 Ⓐ⭐⭐
Dinham Wier SY8 1EH (01584) 874431

WINNER 2010

✦ REMY MARTIN

Perhaps it's down to the arrival of La Bécasse, but Chris & Judy Bradley's veteran, weir-side restaurant-with-rooms — sole long-term survivor of the so-called 'Ludlow phenomenon' — is now better than ever, and even more notable for the "sheer perfection" of its offer across the board. / **Details:** *www.mr-underhills.co.uk; 8.15 pm; D only, closed Mon & Tue; no Amex; children: 8+.* **Accommodation:** *8 rooms, from £140.*

LUND, NORTH YORKSHIRE   6–1A

Wellington Inn £ 42 Ⓣ
19 The Green YO25 9TE (01377) 217294
"The best pub food in this part of Yorkshire" — the Jeffreys' village boozer is tipped as an all-round crowd-pleaser. / **Details:** *9 pm; closed Mon & Sun D; no Amex; children: 14+.*

LUXBOROUGH, SOMERSET   1–2D

The Royal Oak Inn £ 37 Ⓐ⭐
TA23 0SH (01984) 640319
An Exmoor gastropub that's hailed as "wonderful inside and out", and with "excellent", locally-sourced food.
/ **Details:** *www.theroyaloakinnluxborough.co.uk; 9 pm; no Amex.*
Accommodation: *11 rooms, from £65.*

LYDFORD, DEVON   1–3C

The Dartmoor Inn £ 41 Ⓣ
Moorside EX20 4AY (01822) 820221
One of those inns that's "really more a restaurant-with-a-bar-attached", this pretty New England/Swedish-style spot is tipped for its "interesting pub meals". / **Details:** *www.dartmoorinn.com; on the A386 Tavistock to Okehampton road; 9.30 pm; closed Mon L & Sun D.*
Accommodation: *3 rooms, from £110.*

LYME REGIS, DORSET   2–4A

Harbour Inn £ 36 Ⓣ
Marine Pde DT7 3JF (01297) 442299
A "buzzy and fun" bistro, with a "winning" location "right on the beach"; one or two doubters fear, however, that this very advantage can lead to sometimes "apathetic" standards. / **Details:** *9 pm.*

Hix Oyster and Fish House £ 50

Cobb Rd DT7 3JP (01297) 446910

"What a lovely place!"; all reporters are blown away by ex-Caprice supremo Mark Hix's "beautifully positioned" seaside yearling (in gardens, "perched above the cliffs"), where the views are "amazing", and the seafood is usually "magnificent".
/ **Details:** www.restaurantsetcltd.co.uk; 10 pm; closed Mon.

LYMINGTON, HAMPSHIRE 2–4C

Egan's £ 41

Gosport St SO41 9BE (01590) 676165

"Much frequented by Lymington yachties", this "dependable" ten-year-old bistro, a couple of minutes walk from the waterfront, offers "interesting" food, and "amazingly good value" too – the "unbelievable" lunchtime menu attracts particular praise.
/ **Details:** 10 pm; closed Mon & Sun; no Amex; booking: max 6, Sat.

The Mill at Gordleton £ 44

Silver St SO41 6DJ (01590) 682219

"A converted New Forest mill, offering an imaginative menu and nice wine list in an amazing country setting"; even the establishment's sternest critic – who says the food is "good, not exceptional" – admits that the overall dining experience is "very pleasant indeed".
/ **Details:** www.themillatgordleton.co.uk; on the A337, off the M27; 9 pm, Sun 8.15 pm. **Accommodation:** 7 rooms, from £130.

MADINGLEY, CAMBRIDGESHIRE 3–1B

Three Horseshoes £ 37

CB23 8AB (01954) 210221

"One of the few places in or near Cambridge where you can get a reliably good meal", this long-established, thatched gastropub inspires many positive reports with its "high-quality, carefully sourced, Italianate food"; it can, however, seem a bit "pricey" for what it is.
/ **Details:** www.threehorseshoesmadingley.co.uk; 2m W of Cambridge, off A14 or M11; 9 pm, Fri & Sat 9.30 pm, Sun 8.30 pm; no Amex.

MAIDENHEAD, BERKSHIRE 3–3A

Boulters Lock £ 55

Boulters Island SL6 8PE (01628) 621291

With its "beautiful location on the Thames", this "splendid new venture" (a relaunched landmark right on the river) can offer some "very good" food; portions are "small", though, which is perhaps why the occasional reporter finds prices excessive.
/ **Details:** www.boultersrestaurant.co.uk; 10 pm; closed Mon & Sun D; no Amex.

MALVERN WELLS, WORCESTERSHIRE 2–1B

Outlook at The Cottage in the Wood
The Cottage in the Wood £ 47

Holywell Road WR14 4LG (01684) 588860

A "long and eclectic" wine list (with "reasonable mark-ups") and "spectacular" views (30 miles, they say) are the features which particularly impress visitors to this family-run hotel, but, on most accounts, the food measures up too.
/ **Details:** www.cottageinthewood.co.uk; 9.30 pm, Sun 9 pm.
Accommodation: 30 rooms, from £99.

Manchester has what is perhaps the oddest restaurant scene in the UK. On the one hand, with the help of a vast student population, it supports more restaurants that our survey suggests are worthy of listing than any other city outside the capital. Many of these are even worth a star.

Impressive, in their own terms, as many of the establishments are, however, the city – and particularly the city-centre – manages totally to lack any non-ethnic retaurants of real note. In this respect, the contrast with Birmingham – where the restaurant scene is otherwise of much less interest – is particularly stark. In fact, Manchester's perennial favourite non-ethnic restaurant is some miles from the city-centre – the *Lime Tree* in the affluent suburb of Didsbury.

In the city centre itself, we find that this is perhaps the only place in England where one of the most obvious non-ethnic cuisines to eat is... English! Popular local institutions *Sam's Chop House* and *Mr Thomas's Chop House*, are defiantly 'English'. The best city-centre option, however, is probably to eat Chinese, in which cuisine Manchester is pre-eminent outside London. The best-established name is the long-celebrated *Yang Sing*, but it currently risks being eclipsed by the more fashionable *Wings*.

Down at Castlefield, a mile or so from the city-centre, there are some pleasant – but not especially ambitious – waterside restaurants, among which, in quality terms, *Choice* lives up to its name.

Akbar's **£ 27** ⭐
73-83 Liverpool Rd M3 4NQ (0161) 834 8444
"Noisy, boisterous, good food, fast service" – six words which summarise pretty much all of the feedback on this very popular Castlefield Indian. / **Details:** *www.akbars.co.uk; 11 pm, Fri & Sat 11.30 pm; D only; need 10+ to book.*

Albert's Shed **£ 32** 🅐⭐
20 Castle St M3 4LZ (0161) 839 9818
"They could perhaps change the menu more often", but otherwise reporters really like this "consistently good" Castlefield "restaurant of character"; the food is "always well cooked", and comes "reasonably priced" too. / **Details:** *www.albertsshed.com; 10 pm, Fri 10.30 pm, Sat 11 pm, Sun 9.30 pm; no Amex.*

The Angel **£ 33** ⭐
6 Angel St M4 4BQ (0161) 833 4786
"The gastropub they forgot to renovate?"; it doesn't have a great location either (just off the Rochdale Road), but supporters find ample consolation in its "robust and well executed gastropub grub"; "good beer too". / **Details:** *www.theangelmanchester.co.uk; 10 pm; closed Sun D; no credit cards.*

Armenian Taverna £ 32 ⭐
3-5 Princess St M2 4DF (0161) 834 9025
After over 40 years in business, this "one-off" family-run city-centre basement restaurant is just getting "better and better", offering "outstanding" mezze as the centrepiece of its "authentic" Middle Eastern cuisine. / **Details:** www.armeniantaverna.co.uk; 11.30 pm; closed Mon, Sat L & Sun L; children: 3+.

Azzurro £ 30 ⭐
242 Burton Rd M20 2LW (0161) 448 0099
A "brilliant" West Didsbury Italian; it's especially praised for its "good range of daily seafood specials", but also offers "great meat and pasta too". / **Details:** www.azzurrorestaurant.com; 10 pm, Fri & Sat 11 pm; D only, closed Mon & Sun; no Amex.

Chaophraya Thai Restaurant & Bar £ 36 Ⓐ
Chapel Walks M2 1HN (0161) 832 8342
"Wonderful Thai food" quickly made a very big name for this "spacious" city-centre yearling; most reports remain very positive, but there's a slight feeling – perhaps the result of excessive popularity – that standards aren't quite being maintained. / **Details:** www.chaophraya.co.uk; 10.30 pm.

Choice £ 41 ⭐⭐
Castle Quay M15 4NT (0161) 833 3400
"A lovely quayside eatery that serves up seasonal offerings as tasty as they are inventive" – this Castlefield establishment may not have a huge 'profile' locally, but reporters offer notably strong and consistent support for its "locally-sourced" cuisine; service is "top-notch" too. / **Details:** www.choicebarandrestaurant.co.uk; 9.30 pm, Fri & Sat 10 pm.

Croma £ 28
1-3 Clarence St M2 4DE (0161) 237 9799
"Busy, informal, and offering great pizza too"; this rather PizzaExpress-style spot, near the Town Hall, remains a "trendy" central rendezvous, though reporter enthusiasm is not quite what it once was; the Chorlton branch also has quite a following. / **Details:** www.croma.biz; off Albert Square; 11 pm, Sun 10.30.

Dimitri's £ 34 Ⓐ
Campfield Arc M3 4FN (0161) 839 3319
"Even in the middle of the week, with a recession going on, you'll need to book in advance" to get a table at this intriguingly-sited "tapas/Greek/Mediterranean" restaurant, in a Victorian arcade just off Deansgate; it's not that the food's anything remarkable, but this is "a good place for a lively night out". / **Details:** www.dimitris.co.uk; near Museum of Science & Industry; 11.30 pm.

East Z East £ 29 ⭐
Princess St M1 7DL (0161) 244 5353
If you're looking for an Indian of the "trendy"/more central variety, this "packed", "buzzy and shiny" Punjabi establishment is "the best in Manchester by far"; there's also a 'Riverside' branch, near the Cathedral. / **Details:** www.eastzeast.com; midnight; D only.

Evuna £ 37
Deansgate M3 4EW (0161) 819 2752
*Near the Beetham Tower, an upmarket Spanish bar; it's tipped for its
"superb wine list", but the tapas impress too.* / **Details:** *www.evuna.com;
11 pm, Sun 9 pm.*

**French Restaurant
Midland Hotel** £ 48
Peter St M60 2DS (0161) 236 3333
*The (London) Ritz-style dining room of the city's grandest traditional
hotel is still tipped, in a "bygone age" sort of way, as being "perfect for
business"; the food, though, is not much more than "OK".*
/ **Details:** *www.themidland.co.uk; 10.30 pm, Fri & Sat 11 pm; D only, closed
Mon & Sun; no jeans or trainers.* **Accommodation:** *311 rooms, from £145.*

Gaucho £ 50
2a St Mary's St M3 2LB (0161) 833 4333
*"Very good, and the steak is excellent… but the prices are very,
very steep" – the almost invariable flavour of commentary on this
"sexy" chain-steakhouse, by House of Fraser.*
/ **Details:** *www.gauchorestaurants.com; 10.30 pm, Fri & Sat 11 pm.*

Grado £ 44
Piccadilly M1 4BD (0161) 238 9790
*Ooops!; after such a promising start, this ambitious city-centre
Spaniard has ended up being "another Heathcote disappointment" –
it has its fans, but "minute portions" and "overpricing" now head up a
litany of complaints from reporters.* / **Details:** *www.heathcotes.co.uk;
10 pm, Sat 11 pm; closed Sun.*

Great Kathmandu £ 24
140 Burton Rd M20 1JQ (0161) 434 6413
*A West Didsbury stalwart, which continues to attract a huge volume
of commentary, almost all of which is to the same effect – "despite
the shabby-looking interior, this is one of the finest places to go for
a curry".* / **Details:** *www.greatkathmandu.com; near Withington hospital;
midnight.*

Green's £ 33
43 Lapwing Ln M20 2NT (0161) 434 4259
*The recent expansion of this celebrated, 20-year-old Didsbury veggie
has not been to its advantage – some "fantastic" meals are still
recorded, but others have seemed "overspiced", and "overpriced" too.*
/ **Details:** *www.greensdidsbury.co.uk; 4m S of city centre; 10.30 pm; closed Mon L;
no Amex.*

Grill on the Alley £ 34
5 Ridgefield M2 6EG (0161) 833 3465
*Under the same ownership (Blackhouse) as London's Smithfield Bar
& Grill, this "lively" and "upmarket" city-centre steakhouse
is becoming a notably "reliable" all-round destination; the meat
is "excellent" (and veggies are well catered for too).*
/ **Details:** *www.blackhouse.uk.com; 11 pm, Thu-Sat 1 am.*

Grinch £ 29
5-7 Chapel Walks, off Cross St M2 1HN (0161) 907 3210
*Tipped as "a bit of a find for a pre-theatre meal", this Bohemian
café/bistro, just off St Anne's Square, makes "a solid choice for
a pizza"; "good 'deals'" too.* / **Details:** *www.grinch.co.uk; 10 pm.*

Gurkha Grill
£ 26

194-198 Burton Rd M20 1LH (0161) 445 3461
"All the better after the recent refurbishment", this West Didsbury Nepalese continues to offer food that's consistently *"tasty"* and *"interesting"*. / **Details:** www.gurkhagrill.com; midnight, Fri & Sat 1 pm; D only.

Gusto Restaurant & Bar
£ 32

756 Wilmslow Road M20 2DW (0161) 445 8209
Part of a northern chain, an *"upmarket Italian"*, in Didsbury, tipped as a good all-rounder – it even attracts *"a good spattering of local celebrities"*. / **Details:** www.gustorestaurants.uk.com; 10.30 pm; no Amex.

Ithaca
£ 39

36 John Dalton St M2 6LE (0870) 740 4000
It may offer *"more style than substance"*, but this lavish (*"pretentious"*) and *"hugely expensive"* city-centre Japanese yearling has the occasional fan among reporters, and is sometimes tipped for its romantic potential. / **Details:** www.ithacamanchester.com; 10 pm, Thu & Fri 10.30 pm, Sat 11 pm.

Jem and I
£ 39

1c School Ln M20 6RD (0161) 445 3996
Jem O'Sullivan's informal restaurant is now challenging the celebrated Lime Tree as Didsbury's top all-rounder – in fact, his *"reliably high-quality"* cuisine now pips the rating of this longer-established rival, but the (improving) service and ambience still have a little way to go. / **Details:** www.jemandirestaurant.co.uk; 10 pm, Fri-Sat 10.30 pm Sun 10 pm; closed Mon L.

Katsouris Deli
£ 8

113 Deansgate M3 2BQ (0161) 819 1260
An impressively-housed delicatessen, tipped for *"great soups, carvery sandwiches and Greek specialities"* (served in *"huge portions"*). / **Details:** L only; no Amex.

Koh Samui
£ 31

16 Princess St M1 4NB (0161) 237 9511
"Fantastic flavours every time" secure reporters' affections for this decade-old Thai restaurant, on the fringe of Chinatown; a *"well-priced business lunch"* is a highlight. / **Details:** www.kohsamuirestaurant.co.uk; opp City Art Gallery; 11.30 pm; closed Sat L & Sun L.

Kro Piccadilly
£ 27

1 Piccadilly Gdns, Unit A & B M1 1RG (0161) 244 5765
The large scale may make it *"impersonal"*, but – between Piccadilly Gardens and Station – this Danish-owned café is tipped as *"an excellent meeting place"*, for breakfast, coffee or a cake. / **Details:** www.kro.co.uk; 10 pm; children: 18+ after 8.30 pm.

The Lime Tree
£ 38

8 Lapwing Ln M20 2WS (0161) 445 1217
"Consistent, reliable, informal, dependable and above all fun: may it continue for ever!" – feedback on this West Didsbury brasserie of two decades' standing remains characterised by its enthusiastically upbeat nature, and it's still often acclaimed as *"number one in Manchester"*. / **Details:** www.thelimetreerestaurant.co.uk; 10 pm; closed Mon L & Sat L.

Little Yang Sing £ 35

17 George St M1 4HE   (0161) 228 7722

On some accounts, this Chinatown basement is "the best Chinese in town"; overall however, reporters currently tend to rate it a little way behind its more famous big brother. / Details: www.littleyangsing.co.uk; 11.30 pm.

Livebait £ 41

22 Lloyd St M2 5WA   (0161) 817 4110

In a city with no real competition, this city-centre outlet of a London-based chain is "famed for fish" – it's pretty "uninspiring", though, and many reporters see "scope for improvement". / Details: www.livebaitrestaurant.co.uk; 10.15 pm, 10.45 pm Sat, 8.45 pm Sun.

Lounge 10 £ 45

10 Tib Ln M2 4JB   (0161) 834 1331

A vibe-y city-centre venue tipped as "the most romantic, and sexiest, restaurant in the North West" ("and possibly the rest of the UK too!"); it's sometimes claimed that the food is "very good" too. / Details: www.loungeten.co.uk; 10.30 pm, Fri & Sat 11 pm, Sun 9 pm; closed Sat L & Sun.

Luso £ 45

63 Bridge St M3 3BQ   (0161) 839 5550

Handily located near House of Fraser (formerly Kendals), this "small 'modern Portuguese' restaurant" is a "relaxed" and "likeable" rendezvous that leaves some reporters "mystified why it doesn't draw the crowds" – those who find the performance a "curate's egg" perhaps provide the answer. / Details: www.lusorestaurant.co.uk; 10.30 pm; closed Sun; children: 12+.

Metropolitan £ 37

2 Lapwing Ln M20 2WS   (0161) 438 2332

Tipped as a "good, reliable local gastropub", this very popular (and sometimes "noisy") West Didsbury rendezvous attracts praise from reporters of all ages. / Details: www.the-metropolitan.co.uk; near Withington hospital; 9.30 pm, Fri & Sat 10 pm, Sun 9 pm .

Michael Caines at ABode
ABode Hotel £ 51

107 Piccadilly M1 2DB   (0161) 200 5678

"Unbelievable value" from the lunchtime grazing menu (especially if you go for the wine-matching option) inspires many happy reports at this Gidleigh Park-chef-branded outfit, near Piccadilly Station; the setting is a touch "dingy", though, and – especially at dinner – some reporters find the experience too "chain"-like. / Details: www.michaelcaines.com; 10 pm; closed Sun; no shorts; children: D 5+.
Accommodation: *61 rooms, from £79.*

The Modern £ 35

Urbis, Cathedral Gdns M4 3BG   (0161) 605 8282

Offering both a "great view" and "good regionally-inspired food", this 8th-floor city-centre restaurant is indeed a rare sort of beast; even more remarkably, it is "reasonably priced", and offers a wine list that's "always interesting" too. / Details: www.themodernmcr.co.uk; 10 pm; closed Sun D.

Moss Nook £ 59
Ringway Rd M22 5NA   (0161) 437 4778
Though modestly updated of late, the style of this grand and long-established (1973) restaurant near the Airport may still seem bizarrely Victorian for some tastes; fans insist the place offers a "lovely all-round experience", though, including "high-quality" cuisine, and notably "friendly" service. / Details: www.mossnookrestaurant.co.uk; on B5166, 1m from Manchester airport; 9.30 pm; closed Mon, Sat L & Sun; children: 12+. Accommodation: 1 room, at about £120.

Mr Thomas's Chop House £ 38
52 Cross St M2 7AR   (0161) 832 2245
Still a top choice for "delicious, if calorific, British food", this Victorian institution remains a "special" place for many Mancunians, not least for business – perhaps not entirely coincidentally, however, there's a slight feeling among sceptical reporters that it's "living off its reputation". / Details: www.tomschophouse.com; 9.30 pm, Sun 8 pm.

Pacific £ 31
58-60 George St M1 4HF   (0161) 228 6668
This two-floor Chinatown oriental is of particular note for its "awesome" dim sum and its "superb-value" lunchtime offers (which include a Thai buffet, upstairs); it remains very popular, but even the occasional fan may feel that it's "slipping" a bit. / Details: www.pacificrestaurant.co.uk; 11.30 pm.

Palmiro £ 36
197 Upper Chorlton Rd M16 0BH   (0161) 860 7330
Shame that what is perhaps the 'foodiest' of Manchester's Italians, in Whalley Range, is so erratic – even a supporter describes it as only "occasionally sublime", whilst another admits that standards are plain "unpredictable". / Details: www.palmiro.net; 10.30 pm; D only, ex Sun open L & D; no Amex.

Piccolino £ 36
8 Clarence St M2 4DW   (0161) 835 9860
This "reliable" chain Italian attracts many reports, and is still often recommended as "one of the few good places to eat in central Manchester"; it's certainly "busy", but some reports also tend to support the view that it's fallen into "a bit of a rut". / Details: www.individualrestaurantcompanyplc.co.uk; 11 pm, Sun 10 pm.

Punjab Tandoori £ 28
177 Wilmslow Rd M14 5AP   (0161) 225 2960
"The best South Indian cooking on the Curry Mile" makes this Rusholme stalwart well worth seeking out. / Details: midnight; closed Mon L.

Red Chilli £ 29
70-72 Portland St M1 4GU   (0161) 236 2888
Of most note for its "sublime" and "unusual" Sichuanese dishes, this Chinatown spot is something a "spicy food heaven", and it inspires a considerable number of upbeat reports (even if the odd "poor night" is not totally unknown); there's also a branch near the University. / Details: www.redchillirestaurant.co.uk; 11 pm; need 6+ to book.

The Restaurant Bar & Grill £ 47
14 John Dalton St M2 6JR   (0161) 839 1999
"A doyen of the Manchester business dining scene", this city-centre spot offers "reliable" food (with an Asian twist), and is "good for people-watching"; a couple of reporters, though, noted that it's "not as good as its Leeds offshoot". / Details: www.therestaurantbarandgrill.co.uk; 11 pm, Sun 10.30 pm; booking: max 8 at weekends.

El Rincon £ 26

Longworth St, off St John's St M3 4BQ (0161) 839 8819
"Great atmosphere, terrible food" – there's a feeling that the place is "resting on its laurels", but "you do genuinely feel you are in Spain" at this 15-year-old tapas bar, just off Deansgate. / **Details:** *off Deansgate; 11 pm.*

Sam's Chop House £ 40

Back Pool Fold, Chapel Walks M2 1HN (0161) 834 3210
With its "traditional" (rather "pubby") style, and its menu of "very English staples", this "friendly" city-centre basement seems a rather "male" destination (and it's "good with overseas visitors" too); standards are impressively consistent. / **Details:** *www.samschophouse.com; 9.30 pm, Sun 7 pm .*

San Carlo £ 43

40 King Street West M3 2WY (0161) 834 6226
If you're looking for a really "vibrant" restaurant, it's hard to beat this "above-average" Italian, near House of Fraser; admittedly, it's on the "pricey" side, but "glimpses of actors and minor football stars" offer some compensation. / **Details:** *www.sancarlo.co.uk; 11 pm.*

Second Floor Restaurant
Harvey Nichols £ 53

21 New Cathedral St M1 1AD (0161) 828 8898
This "calm" department store restaurant (with brasserie adjoining) is certainly of interest for a "good-value" lunch, and there are reports of "excellent value-for-money" dinners too – as the former (highly-regarded) chef left during our survey year, however, conclusions need to be regarded as tentative. / **Details:** *www.harveynichols.com; 10.30 pm; closed Mon D & Sun D.*

Shimla Pinks £ 31

Dolefield, Crown Sq M3 3EN (0161) 831 7099
A grand modern Indian in Spinningfields, which inspires very consistent feedback on its "good food and location" ("especially for business") and its general "attention to detail".
/ **Details:** *www.shimlapinksmanchester.com; opp Crown Courts; 11.30 pm, Sat & Sun 11 pm; closed Sat L & Sun L.*

Stock £ 45

4 Norfolk St M2 1DW (0161) 839 6644
"Spectacularly-located", in the impressive, old Stock Exchange, this 10-year-old all-rounder offers "high-class classic cooking", from "high-quality ingredients" and usually (if not invariably) "excellent" service; it is, however, "not cheap". / **Details:** *www.stockrestaurant.co.uk; 10 pm; closed Sun.*

Tai Pan £ 33

81-97 Upper Brook St M13 9TX (0161) 273 2798
It helps if you like "crazy Chinese-style chaos", but this "aircraft hangar"-sized Longsight operation has a particular name as a Sunday destination for dim sum. / **Details:** *11 pm, Sun 9.30 pm.*

Tai Wu £ 27

44 Oxford Rd M1 5EJ (0161) 236 6557
A "hangar-like" city-centre Chinese, with a ground-floor restaurant (where dishes "are always freshly cooked") and a "remarkably acceptable" all-you-can-eat basement buffet. / **Details:** *www.tai-wu.co.uk; 2.45 am.*

Tampopo £ 27

16 Albert Sq M2 5PF (0161) 819 1966

"The best noodle bar in the city-centre" (and also in the Triangle) –
"functional" it may be, but it's a "great destination at any time for
healthy fast food". / ***Details:*** *www.tampopo.co.uk; 11pm, Sun 10 pm; need 7+*
to book.

This & That £ 10

3 Soap St M4 1EW (0161) 832 4971

"Staggeringly good value" – with its "three curries and rice for
a fiver", this Northern Quarter "workers' caff" really is impossible
to beat; "now open later in the evenings".
/ ***Details:*** *www.thisandthatcafe.com; 4 pm, Fri & Sat 8 pm; no credit cards.*

Vermilion £ 42 Ⓐ

Lord North St M40 8AD (0161) 202 0055

For an adventure, leave your pre-conceptions behind, and visit this
"superbly-designed" behemoth (conceived to complement the
Manchester super-casino that was never built); the oriental food
generally comes at "high prices", but some impressive 'deals' –
most notably the Sunday lunch buffet – are available.
/ ***Details:*** *www.vermilioncinnabar.com; 10 pm, Sat 11 pm; no trainers.*

Wing's £ 44

1 Lincoln Sq M2 5LN (0161) 834 9000

"Impeccable" Chinese cuisine (and "authentic" too, says a reporter
just back from Beijing) makes this smart city-centre spot "better than
the Yang Sing" nowadays; service is generally very good too… "though
it can suffer when they have the footballers in"!
/ ***Details:*** *www.wingsrestaurant.co.uk; midnight, Sun 11 pm; closed Sat L;*
no trainers; children: 11+ after 8 pm Mon-Fri, 21+ at D .

Yakisoba £ 25

360 Barlow Moor Rd M21 8AZ (0161) 862 0888

"Great-value fast oriental food" – served, though not all-Japanese,
in bento boxes – makes this "brilliant" Chorlton destination popular
with all who comment on it. / ***Details:*** *www.yakisoba.co.uk; 11 pm, Fri & Sat*
midnight; closed weekday L.

Yang Sing £ 35

34 Princess St M1 4JY (0161) 236 2200

"Still setting the standard for Chinese restaurants", Manchester's
Cantonese veteran remains, for many reporters, simply "unsurpassed"
(with dim sum, and banquets, particularly recommended); in the light
of the high visitor expectations, though, the occasional visit of late has
seemed rather "unexciting". / ***Details:*** *www.yang-sing.com; 11.30 pm.*

MANNINGTREE, ESSEX 3–2C

Lucca Enoteca £ 24

39-43 High St CO11 1AH (01206) 390044

"A pretty restaurant in a lovely setting"; this is a "pure Italian" affair,
with "good food and a proper Italian wine list" – "large" and "lovely"
pizzas a speciality. / ***Details:*** *www.luccafoods.co.uk; 9.30 pm, Fri & Sat*
10 pm.

Coles Bar & Restaurant £ 47

27 Kingsbury St SN8 1JA (01672) 515004

An impressively-housed bar/restaurant, nicely done up in contemporary style; it's tipped as a "warm" and "friendly" destination that's "always wonderful for lunch or dinner".
/ **Details:** www.colesrestaurant.co.uk; 10 pm; closed Sun; no Amex.

The Harrow at Little Bedwyn £ 64

Little Bedwyn SN8 3JP (01672) 870871

"Famous for its fantastic wine list", this "classy" inn also offers "very good" food and "quietly competent" service; since Michelin awarded a star, however, prices "seem to have risen", and one long-term fan now discerns a tendency to "over-elaboration".
/ **Details:** www.theharrowatlittlebedwyn.co.uk; 9 pm; closed Mon, Tue & Sun D; no Amex.

The Oak Room
Danesfield House Hotel £ 88

Henley Rd SL7 2EY (01628) 891010

"Improving on every visit", the dining room of this "Victorian folly" of a country house hotel is a "surprisingly unstuffy" destination, where Adam Simmonds's realisation of an "unusual" répertoire can be "stunning". / **Details:** www.danesfieldhouse.co.uk; 3m outside Marlow on the A4155; 9.30 pm; closed Mon, Tue L & Sun; no jeans or trainers.
Accommodation: 87 rooms, from £260.

Hand & Flowers £ 48

West St SL7 2BP (01628) 482277

Tom Kerridge's pretty and "popular" pub bears "the mark of Michelin" nowadays – food comes "in geometric parcels, arranged on vast and bizarre flatware"; results are still often "outstanding", but not as consistent as they were – service can be "very slow", and critics fear "complacency" may be setting in.
/ **Details:** www.thehandandflowers.co.uk; 9.30 pm; closed Sun D.
Accommodation: 4 rooms, from £140.

Marlow Bar & Grill £ 48

92-94 High St SL7 1AQ (01628) 488544

A "good buzzy bar and grill", handily located in the heart of the town, and with a charming courtyard to the rear; it attracts quite a lot of feedback, even though the food is arguably no better than "average". / **Details:** www.therestaurantbarandgrill.co.uk; Towards the river end of the High Street; 11 pm, Sun 10.30 pm; booking essential.

The Royal Oak £ 33

Frieth Rd, Bovingdon Grn SL7 2JF (01628) 488611

"Consistently good pub food" is but one of the charms of this "friendly" and "reliable" whitewashed inn, just outside the town, which inspires many survey reports. / **Details:** www.royaloakmarlow.co.uk; half mile up from Marlow High Street; 9.30 pm, Fri & Sat 10 pm.

The Vanilla Pod £ 58
31 West St SL7 2LS (01628) 898101

Michael Macdonald's "tiny dining room, tucked-away off the high street", pleases almost all reporters with his "innovative, exemplary and stylish" cuisine; most experiences are "very good" all round, but the odd quibble was also recorded this year, not least on the pricing front. / **Details:** www.thevanillapod.co.uk; 10 pm; closed Mon & Sun; no trainers.

MASHAM, NORTH YORKSHIRE 8–4B

Black Sheep Brewery Bistro £ 34
Wellgarth HG4 4EN (01765) 680101
Perhaps unsurprisingly, it's the beer which is tipped as the "highlight" of a visit to this rustic microbrewery, but the place also has its uses as a "family stopping-off point". / **Details:** www.blacksheep.co.uk; 9 pm; Sun-Wed L only, Thu-Sat L & D; no Amex.

Samuel's
Swinton Park Hotel & Spa £ 60
HG4 4JH (01765) 680900
Shame about the sometimes "intrusive" (or even "overwhelming") service at this grand Victorian country house hotel, as other aspects of the "formal" dining experience impress most (if not quite all) reporters. / **Details:** www.swintonpark.com; 9.30 pm; no jeans or trainers; children: 8+ at D. **Accommodation:** 30 rooms, from £160.

Vennells £ 40
7 Silver St HG4 4DX (01765) 689000

Run by a "delightful" husband-and-wife team, this is "a great find", offering "seasonal" menus which concentrate on "local produce", and offers "great value for money".
/ **Details:** www.vennellsrestaurant.co.uk; 9.30 pm; closed Mon, Tue–Sat D only, closed Sun D.

MEDBOURNE, LEICESTERSHIRE   5–4D

Horse & Trumpet   £ 47
12 Old Grn LE16 8DX   (01858) 565000
This "busy" pub/restaurant (with rooms) in a cute village is hailed both
as a handy lunchtime spot, and for its more ambitious evening tasting
menus, and pleased most (if not quite all) reporters this year.
/ **Details:** www.horseandtrumpet.com; 9.30 pm; closed Mon & Sun D; no Amex;
children: 12+ at D. **Accommodation:** 4 rooms, from £75.

MELBOURNE, DERBYSHIRE   5–3C

Bay Tree   £ 48
4 Potter St DE73 8HW   (01332) 863358
For most reporters, "absolutely reliable" cooking still makes Rex
Howell's restaurant, in an "out-of-the-way" village, "the best in the
area" – the occasional critic, though, still opines that it's "not quite
as good as they like to think it is". / **Details:** www.baytreerestaurant.co.uk;
9.30 pm; closed Mon & Sun D.

MELLOR, LANCASHIRE   5–1B

Cassis
Stanley House Hotel   £ 65
Off Preston New Rd BB2 7NP   (01254) 769200
This boutique hotel dining room – a "favourite special-occasion
restaurant", for some observers – offers Gallic cuisine which "never
disappoints"; critics warn of "hit-and–miss" service, though,
and complain of "OTT décor and presentation" ("as a result of which
the food can arrive tepid"). / **Details:** www.stanleyhouse.co.uk; 9.30 pm,
Fri & Sat 9.45 pm; closed Mon, Tue, Sat L & Sun D; no trainers.
Accommodation: 12 rooms, from £185.

MELMERBY, CUMBRIA   8–3A

Village Bakery   £ 24
CA10 1HE   (01768) 881811
"Great deterioration" is the theme of too many reports on this
celebrated café (whose products, notionally, are now available in many
supermarkets) – complaints included scones "like bricks" and
a surprising lack of bread ("in a bakery'!").
/ **Details:** www.village-bakery.com; 10m NE of Penrith on A686; L only; no Amex;
need 6+ to book.

MICKLEHAM, SURREY   3–3A

The Running Horses   £ 42
Old London Rd RH5 6DU   (01372) 372279
"A pub with a very smart restaurant, staffed by Italians"; it's tipped for
its "interesting" menu (even if it does sometimes seems rather pricey
for what it is). / **Details:** www.therunninghorses.co.uk; 9.30 pm, Sun 9 pm;
children: 14+ in bar. **Accommodation:** 5 rooms, from £110.

MILTON KEYNES, BUCKINGHAMSHIRE   3–2A

Brasserie Blanc   £ 37
Chelsea Hs, 301 Avebury Boulevard MK9 2GA
(01908) 546590
"Of the limited choices round here, this one stands out"; in the style
of this improving brasserie chain, it's tipped as a "consistent and
reliable" sort of place, with a "pleasant buzz". / **Details:** 9.45 pm.

Jaipur £ 35 A ⭐

599 Grafton Gate East MK9 1AT (01908) 669796

"A remarkable restaurant in a gastronomic desert"; this vast and "OTT" Indian offers a "true taste of the subcontinent", and the menu offers "some interesting dishes, especially the fish".
/ **Details:** www.jaipur.co.uk; near the train station roundabout; they are the big white building; 11.30 pm; no shorts.

MISTLEY, ESSEX   3–2D

The Mistley Thorn
The Mistley Thorn Hotel £ 34

High St CO11 1HE (01206) 392 821

A "friendly" and "well-run" riverside Georgian coaching inn, recently updated, that attracts impressively consistent commentary for its "fine pub food"; "good wine list" too. / **Details:** www.mistleythorn.com; 9.30 pm; no Amex. **Accommodation:** 5 rooms, from £80.

MOLD, FLINTSHIRE   5–2A

56 High St. £ 35 Ⓣ

56 High St CH7 1BD (01352) 759225

Still no great volume of commentary on this "local-favourite" town-centre restaurant, which has a bit of a name for its fish and seafood; all positive, though. / **Details:** www.56highst.com; 9.30 pm, Fri & Sat 10.30 pm; closed Mon & Sun; no Amex.

Glasfryn £ 32 Ⓣ

Raikes Ln CH7 6LR (01352) 750500

"Good rather than exciting", this "shabby-chic" operation is a tip worth knowing of in a thin area; with its "predictable" dishes, it's a classic example of the (locally pre-eminent) Brunning & Price group of gastropubs. / **Details:** www.glasfryn-mold.co.uk; 9.30 pm, Sun 9 pm.

MORETON-IN-MARSH, GLOUCESTERSHIRE 2–1C

Horse & Groom £ 33 Ⓣ

GL56 0XH (01451) 830584

"A minimalist take on a Cotswold gastropub", tipped for a menu that "if not gastronomique, is always interesting" (and in particular for a sticky toffee meringue which is "in a league of its own").
/ **Details:** www.horseandgroom.uk.com; 11 pm; no Amex.

MORPETH, NORTHUMBERLAND   8–2B

Black Door Bar & Dining Rooms £ 39 Ⓣ

59 Bridge St NE61 1PQ (01670) 516200

A "good all-rounder" tipped for its "reasonable prices" (and "good early-evening offers" in particular); there's a growing feeling, however, that the cuisine "lacks ambition".
/ **Details:** www.blackdoorbaranddiningrooms.co.uk; 9.30 pm; closed Sun D.

Morston Hall   **£ 68**
Main Coast Rd NR25 7AA   (01263) 741041
*TV celebrity is so often a curse, and so it is proving with Galton
Blackiston's country house hotel – there are reporters who still speak
of the "faultless simplicity" and "unbelievable value" of the cuisine,
but almost as many who complain of overpricing and a lack of choice,
and of a pretty "dull" ambience too.* / **Details:** www.morstonhall.com;
between Blakeney & Wells on A149; 8 pm; D only, ex Sun open L &
D. **Accommodation:** 13 rooms, from £145.

Ⓐ ✪

The Beetle & Wedge Boathouse   **£ 43**
Ferry Ln OX10 9JF   (01491) 651381
*"A most delightful setting", by the river, has long been the main selling
point of this "beautifully converted boathouse" (also notable for its
literary associations, with Jerome K Jerome and 'The Wind in the
Willows'); on the cooking front, however, the new chef seems to have
made great improvements to the (largely) rôtisserie fare.*
/ **Details:** www.beetleandwedge.co.uk; on A329 between Streatley & Wallingford,
take Ferry Lane at crossroads; 9.45 pm. **Accommodation:** 3 rooms, from £90.

Ⓐ ✪

Black Bull   **£ 50**
DL10 6QJ   (01325) 377289
*The new owner of this long-popular fish restaurant "has really got his
act together" – the food is "sublime", the staff ("some ex-Sharrow
Bay"!) are "very good", and the unusual setting (a former Pullman
railway carriage) is very "intimate".* / **Details:** www.blackbullmoulton.com;
1m S of Scotch Corner; 9.30 pm, Fri & Sat 10 pm; closed Sun D; no Amex.

✪

Cornish Range   **£ 39**
6 Chapel St TR19 6SB   (01736) 731488
*"Local art on the walls" sets an attractive tone at this "well-run"
"small" restaurant "down a side street", praised for its "really
imaginative" cuisine by all who comment on it.*
/ **Details:** www.cornishrange.co.uk; on coast road between Penzance & Lands End;
9.30 pm, 9 pm in Winter; no Amex. **Accommodation:** 3 rooms, from £80.

✪

2 Fore Street Restaurant   **£ 38**
2 Fore St TR19 6QU   (01736) 731164
*A bistro near the waterfront, where the "imaginative" and "good-
value" cooking includes some "superb fish dishes" ("we were
so impressed we went on two consecutive nights!"); during the day,
lunches and cream teas are served in the garden.*
/ **Details:** www.2forestreet.co.uk; 9.30 pm.

The Nut Tree Inn   **£ 47**
Main St OX5 2RE   (01865) 331253
*This guide's endorsement last year – and possibly the subsequent one
from Michelin too! – risks going straight to the head of this "stunning"
thatched pub; there are still reports of "sublime" cooking in a
"relaxed" setting, but also rather too many of meals that have seemed
"very average".* / **Details:** www.nuttreeinn.co.uk; 9 pm, Sun 8.30 pm.

Barley Bree £ 35
6 Willoughby St PH5 2AB (01764) 681451
"What a find!"; this two-year-old restaurant-with-rooms – "hidden-away between Crieff and the A9" – is hailed by all reporters as a "surprise", and one that's simply "excellent" all round too.
/ **Details:** www.barleybree.com; 9pm Wed-Sat, 7.30pm Sun; closed Mon & Tue.
Accommodation: 6 rooms, from £45.

Calcot Manor (Gumstool Inn) £ 50
GL8 8YJ (01666) 890391

It's tipped as a "great option with kids", but the gastropub adjoining this famously family-friendly hotel can really be recommended generally; service, though, can be very up-and-down.
/ **Details:** www.calcotmanor.co.uk; cross roads of a46 & A41345; 9.30 pm, Sun 9 pm; no jeans or trainers; no booking; children: 12+ at dinner in Conservatory.
Accommodation: 35 rooms, from £230.

Boath House Hotel £ 88
IV12 5TE (01667) 454896
"Delightful", "welcoming" and "charming" – the sort of adjectives reporters invariably apply to the dining experience at this grand Georgian country house hotel. / **Details:** www.boath-house.com; 0; no Amex; no jeans or trainers. **Accommodation:** 8 rooms, from £300.

The Foxhunter £ 47
Abergavenny NP7 9DN (01873) 881101
A "tucked-away" boozer – in a former stationmaster's house – with quite a name for its "excellent" cuisine, and good wine too; "since they started winning awards", though, there's a feeling amongst reporters that it's "not as good as it used to be".
/ **Details:** www.thefoxhunter.com; 9.30 pm; closed Mon & Sun D; no Amex.
Accommodation: 2 cottages rooms, from £145.

Y Polyn Bar & Restaurant £ 40
SA32 7LH (01267) 290000

*This "first-class" family-run restaurant may be somewhat "rustic", but its "great cooking from local ingredients" pleases most reporters; service is "friendly" too, "leaving no doubt about professionalism or the desire to please". / **Details:** www.ypolyn.co.uk; 9 pm; closed Mon & Sun D; no Amex.*

Rookery Hall Hotel & Spa
Hand Picked Hotels £ 56
Main Rd CW5 6DQ (01270) 610016
*Fans really like the "grand" dining hall of this flamboyant country house hotel, which "absorbs you and coddles you, and then tempts you with great food" (which is generally "beautifully presented" too). / **Details:** www.handpicked.co.uk; 9.30 pm; D only, ex Sun open L & D; no jeans or trainers. **Accommodation:** 70 rooms, from £135.*

The Wizard £ 32
Macclesfield Rd SK10 4UB (01625) 584000
*"An ancient inn with numerous small rooms", tipped as "an excellent destination for a satisfying pub meal"; the food has perhaps been a little "predictable" of late, but it's still "well prepared". / **Details:** www.ainscoughs.co.uk; from A34, take B5087; 9.30 pm, Sat 10 pm, Sun 8 pm.*

The Highwayman £ 35
LA6 2RJ (01524) 273338
*"Proper British food" that's "executed with finesse" is part of the "winning formula" that's won a very big following for this "bright, modern and friendly" gastropub offshoot of Northcote (Langho); it's a large-scale operation, though, and critics can find the style slightly "corporate". / **Details:** www.highwaymaninn.co.uk; 9 pm, Sun 8.30 pm.*

White Hart £ 36
High St RG9 5DD (01491) 641245
*"A great fixed price Sunday lunch" is a particular feature of this country boozer, which specialises in seafood dishes that can be "very good indeed"; there's a "decent" wine list too, at "ungreedy" prices. / **Details:** www.whitehartnettlebed.com; Between Wallingford & Henley-on-Thames on the A430; 9.30 pm; closed Sun D. **Accommodation:** 12 rooms, from £125.*

NEW MILTON, HAMPSHIRE 2–4C

H

Chewton Glen £ 82
Christchurch Rd BH25 6QS (01425) 275341

"The real attraction is the spa, the hotel and the nearby walks" at this famous hotel, which is not perhaps the culinary destination it once was; for true fans, however, it's still an *"effortlessly perfect"* all-rounder, and the *"good value set lunch"* attracts consistent praise.
/ **Details:** www.chewtonglen.com; on A337 between New Milton & Highcliffe; 9.30 pm; no jeans; children: 5+ at D. **Accommodation:** 58 rooms, from £299.

NEWARK, NOTTINGHAMSHIRE 5–3D

A

Café Bleu £ 37
14 Castle Gate NG24 1BG (01636) 610141
This *"charming"* bistro has long had a lofty reputation; *"erratic"* service, however, seems to be contributing to a growing feeling among reporters that overall standards are merely *"satisfactory"* nowadays, rather than anything more. / **Details:** www.cafebleu.co.uk; 9.30 pm; closed Sun D; no Amex.

T

New King Wah £ 25
5 Kirk Gate NG24 1AD (01636) 703114
Opposite the Castle, a Cantonese restaurant tipped for its very high all-round standards; well, they must be doing something right to have lasted for nearly half a century! / **Details:** www.newkingwah.co.uk.

NEWBURY, BERKSHIRE 2–2D

The Crab at Chieveley £ 58
Wantage Rd RG20 8UE (01635) 247550
With quite a reputation as a *"memorable"* fish restaurant, this rural spot is *"usually extremely busy"*; since last year's change of ownership, however, standards have slipped quite noticeably.
/ **Details:** www.crabatchieveley.com; M4 J13 to B4494 – 0.5 mile on right; 9 pm, Sat & Sun 9.30 pm. **Accommodation:** 14 rooms, from £160.

Yew Tree Inn £ 51
Hollington Cross, Andover Rd RG20 9SE (01635) 253360
Celebrity-chef branding is as often a warning as an encouragement, but the *"traditional British fare with a French influence"* at this Marco Pierre White-branded boozer can be *"excellent"*; perhaps inevitably, though, it can also seem *"surprisingly average"*.
/ **Details:** www.yewtree.tablesir.com; Off the A343, near Highclere Castle; 9.30 pm, Sun 9 pm. **Accommodation:** 6 rooms, from £100.

Most visitors would probably be surprised by the decent range of eating possibilities available in a city that's perhaps more famous for its bars and pubs than its restaurants. With the possible exception of *Café 21*, there are admittedly no real culinary 'stand-outs', but the city offers a pleasing range of quality restaurants of which a good number are also of note for their pleasant ambience. The range of cuisines available to a good standard – both European and 'ethnic' – is impressive too.

Barn Asia £ 39 ★
Waterloo Sq, St James Boulevard NE1 4DN (0191) 221 1000
For "an enjoyable night out, with interesting food", it's hard to beat this "friendly", "eclectic" and "adventurous" spot, where the "mix of European and oriental dishes" offers some "fantastic original flavours". / **Details:** www.barnasia.com; 9.45 pm; closed Mon L, Tue L, Wed L, Thu L, Sat L & Sun.

Blackfriars Restaurant £ 40 Ⓐ
Friars St NE1 4XN (0191) 261 5945
"Hidden-away in the heart of Newcastle", this "real gem of a restaurant" is located in an "ancient monastic cloister, overlooking the gardens"; most reporters are very pleased by the "locally sourced" food too. / **Details:** www.blackfriarsrestaurant.co.uk; 10 pm; closed Sun D.

Brasserie Black Door £ 42
Biscuit Factory, Stoddard St NE2 1AN (0191) 260 5411
"Safe for steak and chips", but "not in the same class as the original Black Door" (a fine-dining restaurant) – that's the verdict on this brasserie in a former biscuit factory, which benefits from service that's particularly "prompt" and "friendly". / **Details:** www.blackdoorgroup.co.uk; 10 pm; closed Sun D.

Café 21 £ 49 ★
Trinity Gdns NE1 2HH (0191) 222 0755
"A real treat"; this "steadfast fixture" – the "honest" and "unpretentious" flagship of the North East's leading chef/restaurateur, Terry Laybourne – is a "very good all-rounder" that remains "at the top of its game"; it still attracts more feedback than anywhere else in town. / **Details:** www.cafetwentyone.co.uk; 10.30 pm, Sun 10 pm.

Café 21
Fenwick £ 35
39 Northumberland St, First Floor NE1 7DE (0191) 384 9969
A department store offshoot of the famous Café 21; with its "good standards all round", it "does nothing to let the name down". / **Details:** www.cafetwentyone.co.uk; 0; L only.

Café Royal £ 35
8 Nelson St NE1 5AW (0191) 231 3000
Newcastle's 'Wolseley'! – this grand café is "excellent for coffee, cakes and sandwiches" and does some "good fresh bistro-style dishes too"; a "crowded" and "noisy" place, it's also "good for people-watching". / **Details:** www.sjf.co.uk; 6 pm, Sun 4 pm; L only, ex Thu open L & D; no booking, Sat.

Caffè Vivo £ 34
29 Broad Chare NE1 3DQ (0191) 232 1331
*Local hero Terry Laybourne's "new Italian café-style establishment",
on the Quayside, may be something of a "barn", but its "interesting
and reasonably-priced" food makes it very popular; "good 'express'
menus in the early-evening". / Details: www.caffevivo.co.uk; 10 pm; closed
Mon & Sun.*

Caffe Z £ 29
87-89 Goldspink Ln NE2 1NQ (0191) 230 4981
*"A proper southern Italian restaurant in a residential street, offering
hearty rustic food at reasonable prices"; a "busy" and "friendly" place,
it's "ideal with children". / Details: www.caffezonzo.com; 9.30 pm; closed
Sun; no Amex.*

The Cherry Tree £ 32
9 Osborne Rd NE2 2AE (0191) 239 9924
*This smartly-furnished two-tier yearling, in Jesmond Dene, is a "busy"
and "bustling" sort of place, offering generally "interesting" food,
and "attentive" service too ("sometimes to excess").
/ Details: www.thecherrytreejesmond.co.uk; 9.30 pm, Sat 10 pm, Sun 9 pm;
no Amex.*

Fisherman's Lodge £ 56
Jesmond Dene NE7 7BQ (0191) 281 3281
*This grand local restaurant, which for many years offered the leading
'destination' dining locally, moved into new ownership shortly before
this guide went to press; a prime aim of the the new régime,
we understand, is to rid it of its rather "snobby" former image.
/ Details: www.fishermanslodge.co.uk; 2m from city centre on A1058, follow
signposts to Jesmond Dene; 10 pm; closed Mon & Sun.*

The Flatbread Cafe £ 28
69-75 High Bridge NE1 6BX (0191) 241 5184
*An "interesting" concept – "Middle Eastern/Asian tapas" – that's
"going from strength to strength"; staff who are "always pleasant"
play no small part. / Details: www.flatbreadcafe.com; 11 pm; closed Sun.*

Francesca's £ 21
Manor House Rd NE2 2NE (0191) 281 6586
*"The very definition of 'cheap and cheerful' – this "Geordie-Italian"
cantina delivers "great atmosphere" and the odd flash of inspiration
on the food front"; the queues outside say it all. / Details: 9.30 pm;
closed Sun; no Amex; no booking.*

Grainger Rooms £ 41
7 Highham Pl NE1 8AF (0191) 232 4949
*In a Georgian townhouse "in the heart of the city", a restaurant
offering "interesting menus with a modern twist", and that's "well-
priced" too. / Details: www.graingerrooms.co.uk; 9.30 pm; closed Sun.*

Jesmond Dene House £ 64
Jesmond Dene Rd NE2 2EY (0191) 212 3000
*"Terry Laybourne's city country house venture" (in a fine Arts & Crafts
house), is "Newcastle's finest", offering "delicious food in a lovely
setting"; there is, however, a small but vocal dissident camp – "I keep
being told this is top-drawer, but whenever I go I just can't see it".
/ Details: www.jesmonddenehouse.co.uk; out of the city centre, towards Jesmond,
which is clearly signposted; 10 pm. Accommodation: 40 rooms, from £210.*

311

Pan Haggerty £ 35

21 Queen St NE1 3UG   (0191) 221 0904

Fans say the original Cafe 21 space has been "spectacularly brought to life" by a new team, but its "hearty" local fare ("not for the faint-hearted") has attracted rather mixed early reports.
/ ***Details:*** *www.panhaggerty.com; 10 pm; closed Sun D.*

Pani's £ 27

61-65 High Bridge NE1 6BX   (0191) 232 4366

"As lively and authentically Italian as ever", this "cheap", "very cheerful" and "popular" spot, just off Grey Street, is "a great place for a quick pasta, panini or salad". / ***Details:*** *www.paniscafe.co.uk; off Gray Street; 10 pm; closed Sun; no Amex; no booking at L.*

Paradiso £ 34

1 Market Ln NE1 6QQ   (0191) 221 1240

"Fantastic" service helps make this "cheery" Italian a very popular destination... for everything from "an informal business event" to "dinner with the kids". / ***Details:*** *www.paradiso.co.uk; opp fire station; 10.30 pm, Fri & Sat 10.45 pm; closed Sun D.*

Rasa £ 31

27 Queen St NE1 3UG   (0191) 232 7799

"The most rewarding Indian in the town"; this outpost of a legendary London group attracts nothing but praise for its "wonderful" and "authentic" Kerala dishes. / ***Details:*** *www.rasarestaurants.com; 11 pm; closed Sun.*

Sachins £ 31

Forth Banks NE1 3SG   (0191) 261 9035

This long-established Punjabi spot, five minutes from the Central railway station, is still generally praised for offering a "top-quality dining experience". / ***Details:*** *www.sachins.co.uk; behind Central Station; 11.15 pm; closed Sun.*

Secco Ristorante Salentino £ 38

86 Pilgrim St NE1 6SG   (0191) 230 0444

"Interesting" and "authentic" fare makes this "eclectic" ("kitsch to Koons") and "noisy" townhouse-Italian a very popular destination; for top value, seek out the set lunch. / ***Details:*** *www.seccouk.com; 10 pm; closed Sun.*

Six
BALTIC Centre for Contemporary Art £ 40

Gateshead Quays, South Shore Rd NE8 3BA   (0191) 440 4948

Fans say this new venture – a "unique space" on the top floor of a riverside cultural centre – is a "joyful" replacement for its predecessor McCoy's, lauding its "great" food and "good" service too; it's a "noisy" and "tightly-packed" place, though, whose performance doesn't please all reporters. / ***Details:*** *www.sixbaltic.com; 9.30 pm, Fri & Sat 10 pm; closed Sun D; no Amex.*

A Taste of Persia £ 24

14 Marlborough Cr NE1 4EE   (0191) 221 0088

It "looks basic and nondescript", but this "Persian family restaurant" in the city-centre attracts a lot of praise for its "authentic" food at "amazing" prices; it's "really friendly" too (if "not the place for a wild night out"). / ***Details:*** *www.atasteofpersia.com; 10 pm; closed Sun.*

Tyneside Coffee Rooms
Tyneside Cinema　　　　　£ 23
10 Pilgrim St NE1 6QG　(0191) 227 5520
Tipped for "unbeatable '30s decor and comfort food", these Art Deco
coffee rooms are a popular local rendezvous; paradoxically, however,
the actual coffee is said to be better in the (separate) café
downstairs! / **Details:** *www.tynecine.org; 9 pm; no Amex.*

Valley Junction 397　　　　£ 30
Old Jesmond Stn, Archbold Ter NE2 1DB　(0191) 281 6397
Reporters find simply nothing to fault with "the best Indian
in Newcastle" – "even the venue (a railway carriage) is diverting".
/ **Details:** *www.valleyrestaurants.co.uk; near Civic Centre, off Sandyford Rd;*
11.30 pm; closed Mon, Fri L & Sun L.

Vujon　　　　　£ 35
29 Queen St NE1 3UG　(0191) 221 0601
"The décor may need improvement, but the food is good" at this
Quayside spot, which is lauded by many as "the best Indian in town".
/ **Details:** *www.vujon.com; 11.30 pm; closed Sun L.*

NEWENT, GLOUCESTERSHIRE　　　2–1B

Three Choirs Vineyards　　　£ 45
GL18 1LS　(01531) 890223
As the name suggests, this is a dining room tipped for its "splendid"
vineyard view, and a wine list which includes some "delicious" English
vintages; the food, however, is somewhere between "average" and
"slightly disappointing". / **Details:** *www.threechoirs.com; 8.45 pm; no Amex.*
Accommodation: *8, & 3 lodges rooms, from £115.*

NEWICK, EAST SUSSEX　　　3–4B

Newick Park
Newick Park Hotel　　　　£ 61
BN8 4SB　(01825) 723633
A privately-owned country-house hotel, consistently praised for its
"wonderful" setting, "excellent" food and "exceptional" service.
/ **Details:** *www.newickpark.co.uk; off Church Rd; 9 pm; booking essential.*
Accommodation: *16 rooms, from £165.*

NEWLAND, GLOUCESTERSHIRE　　2–2B

The Ostrich Inn　　　　£ 36
GL16 8NP　(01594) 833260
"A lovely family- and dog-friendly pub in a beautiful setting, frequented
by locals and visitors to the area in equal number"; it's a "welcoming"
place, where the "home-cooked" fare is "generally very good".
/ **Details:** *www.theostrichinn.com; 2m SW of Coleford; 9.30 pm.*

NEWPORT, NEWPORT　　　2–2A

The Chandlery　　　　£ 41
77-78 Lower Dock St NP20 1EH　(01633) 256622
An hotel dining room tipped as "the best place to eat in Newport";
it's undoubtedly a "buzzy" sort of place, but reports on the food are
rather up-and-down. / **Details:** *www.thechandleryrestaurant.com; at the foot*
of George St bridge on the A48 (hospital side); 10 pm; closed Mon, Sat L & Sun D.

Cnapan Country House £ 40
East St SA42 0SY (01239) 820575

A real "home from home" – this restaurant-with-rooms is a notably "friendly" and "efficient" operation, where the "good family fare" is "always reliable". / **Details:** *www.cnapan.co.uk; on A487 between Fishguard and Cardigan; 8.45 pm; D only, closed Tue; no Amex.* **Accommodation:** *5 rooms, from £80.*

Llys Meddyg £ 48
East St SA42 0SY (01239) 820008

New chef Scott Davis "has worked with some of the UK's best chefs, and it shows" – this "very relaxing" Georgian townhouse restaurant-with-rooms attracts praise across the board, but in particular for its "wonderful" fish and seafood. / **Details:** *www.llysmeddyg.com; 9 pm; closed Mon L; no Amex.* **Accommodation:** *8 rooms, from £100.*

Fistral Blu £ 35
Fistral Beach, Headland Rd TR7 1HY (01637) 879444

"The place to enjoy good food in a romantic setting watching a wonderful sunset over the Atlantic"; this large and ever-evolving beach-side operation has a particular name for its "delicious fresh seafood". / **Details:** *www.fistral-blu.co.uk; 10 pm.*

Crooked Billet £ 40
2 Westbrook End MK17 0DF (01908) 373936

"Off the beaten track" it may be, but this "great" and "atmospheric" little pub – offering "hearty, if not gastronomic" fare in a "very picturesque location" – has a great following among reporters; "music evenings a speciality". / **Details:** *www.thebillet.co.uk; 11 pm, Sat 9.30 pm; D only, ex Sun open L only.*

Moore's £ 35
6, Greenbank, High St EX10 0EB (01395) 568100

"An outstanding small restaurant-with-rooms, of the family-run type"; its straightforward charms – not least its "reliable" and "interesting" cuisine – commend it to all who comment on it. / **Details:** *www.mooresrestaurant.co.uk; on the A3052, Exeter to Lyme Regis road; 9.30 pm; closed Mon & Sun D.* **Accommodation:** *3 rooms, from £50.*

Cook & Barker £ 33
NE65 9JY (01665) 575234

A pub-with-rooms that attracts a lot of (mostly upbeat) commentary from reporters, with praise for its "good and reasonably-priced" food; arguably it's main advantage, however, is "proximity to the A1", which is why we've included it only as a 'tip'. / **Details:** *www.cookandbarkerinn.co.uk; 12m N of Morpeth, just off A1; 9 pm.* **Accommodation:** *19 rooms, from £75.*

NOMANSLAND, WILTSHIRE 2–3C

Les Mirabelles £ 39

Forest Edge Rd SP5 2BN   (01794) 390205

*"A very French restaurant in the New Forest, notable for its rich and
adventurous food and elaborate puddings"; it really pleases
most reporters, but it can also hit a "pretentious" note ("a mixture
of the very good, and the oh, dear!")"* / **Details:** *www.lesmirabelles.co.uk;
off A36 between Southampton & Salisbury; 9.30 pm; closed Mon & Sun.*

NORDEN, LANCASHIRE 5–1B

Nutter's £ 45

Edenfield Rd OL12 7TT   (01706) 650167

*"The best restaurant in the Rochdale area" is a true family affair,
with Mr and Mrs N doing front-of-house, and Master N in the kitchen
– rather unusually, the year's reviews included a couple of real let-
downs, but the more general view is that this is a "relaxed" and
"welcoming" place, where the food is "superb".*
/ **Details:** *www.nuttersrestaurant.com; between Edenfield & Norden on A680;
9.30 pm; closed Mon.*

NORTH BOVEY, DEVON 1–3C

Bovey Castle £ 30

TQ13 8RE   (01647) 445016

*These "wonderful building and grounds", on the edge of Dartmoor,
house both a restaurant and a bistro; most reporters are "pleasantly
surprised" by the standards of both (but the odd "truly grim" and
"horribly overpriced" experience is reported too).*

NORTH KILWORTH, LEICESTERSHIRE 5–4D

Kilworth House Hotel £ 48

Lutterworth Road North LE17 6JE   (01858) 880058

*This privately-owned country house hotel has a "superb" setting,
and an airy and pleasant dining room; the "inventive" cuisine is often
"lovely" too, but standards are not entirely consistent.*
/ **Details:** *www.kilworthhouse.co.uk; 9.30 pm; no jeans or trainers.*
Accommodation: *44 rooms, from £140.*

NORTH SHIELDS, TYNE & WEAR 8–2B

Kristian Fish Restaurant £ 15

3-9 Union Quay NE30 1HJ   (0191) 258 5155

*"A brilliant chippy, 10 yards from where the fish are landed!" –
if you're looking for fish that's simply "as fresh as can be", this is the
place.* / **Details:** *9 pm; closed Sun D; no credit cards.*

Sambuca £ 20

10-11 Union Quay NE30 1HJ   (0191) 270 8891

*A popular, family eatery, tipped for its "cheap, cheerful and always-
good" Italian fare; it's usually "packed to the gunnels".*
/ **Details:** *10.30 pm, Sun 9 pm ; no credit cards.*

McCoys at the Tontine   £ 48
DL6 3JB   (01609) 882 671

"It's the quirkiness that appeals, coupled with the very competent cooking" at the McCoy brothers' *"one-of-a-kind"* local institution; if you stay, *"the breakfast is particularly good"*.
/ **Details:** www.mccoystontine.co.uk; junction of A19 & A172; 9.30 pm; bistro L & D every day, restaurant Sat D only. **Accommodation:** 6 rooms, from £120.

NORTON, WILTSHIRE   2–2B

The Vine Tree   £ 37
Foxley Rd SN16 0JP   (01666) 837654

"Off the beaten track", this *"true country classic"* inn is a *"very welcoming"* sort of place, offering *"well prepared"* and *"unfussy"* fare, much of which truly is *"local"* (*"try the wonderful steak from the farm next door"*). / **Details:** www.thevinetree.co.uk; 9.30 pm, Fri & Sat 9.45 pm.

NORWICH, NORFOLK   6–4C

Brummells   £ 50
7 Magdalen St NR3 1LE   (01603) 625555

"Local fish and seafood, well cooked, in a lovely old house" – that's the formula that has sustained this city-centre restaurant for over three decades. / **Details:** www.brummells.co.uk; 10.30 pm.

By Appointment   £ 50
25-29 St George's St NR3 1AB   (01603) 630730

"A real find"; *"quirky, small and full of character"*, this *"lovely old house"* offers an experience that's both *"fun"* and *"unique"* – service is *"very personal"*, and the food is *"fresh"* and *"beautifully cooked"*.
/ **Details:** www.byappointmentnorwich.co.uk; in a courtyard off Colegate; 9 pm; D only, closed Mon & Sun; no Amex; children: 12+. **Accommodation:** 6 rooms, from £110.

Delia's Restaurant & Bar   £ 42
Norwich City Football Ground, Carrow Rd NR1 1JE
(01603) 218705

Much improved in recent times, the TV chef's eatery at the football club of which she is a director is now unanimously tipped as *"a real treat on all fronts"*. / **Details:** www.deliasrestaurantandbar.com; 9.30 pm; open Sat D only; no Amex; no jeans or trainers.

Shiki £ 35
6 Tombland NR3 1HE (01603) 619262
*"Fantastic" food and "very helpful" service are among the features
which especially commend this Japanese five-year-old to reporters;
"good-value lunchtime bento boxes" are especially worth seeking out.*
/ **Details:** www.shikirestaurant.co.uk; 10.30 pm; closed Sun; no Amex.

Waffle House £ 22
39 St Giles St NR2 1JN (01603) 612790
*"Been around for ever, but still consistently good" – this coffee house-
cum-restaurant is tipped as a destination offering "fantastic value for
money"; "don't go if you don't like waffles though!"*
/ **Details:** www.wafflehouse.co.uk; 10 pm; no Amex; need 6+ to book.

NOSS MAYO, DEVON 1–4C

Ship Inn £ 40
PL8 1EW (01752) 872387
*Tipped for its "enviable position by the Yealm Estuary" this "friendly"
pub has quite a following; the food, though, can seem "inconsistent".*
/ **Details:** www.nossmayo.com; 9.30 pm; no Amex.

NOTTINGHAM, NOTTINGHAMSHIRE 5–3D

For a city which is not widely seen as a major dining
destination, Nottingham harbours a surprisingly impressive
core of good-quality restaurants in the middle and upper
range, including the long-standing *Hart's* and – at the top end
of the market – *Restaurant Sat Bains*. These are
complemented by a good range of other quality operations,
both European and 'ethnic'.

Atlas £ 10
9 Pelham St NG1 2EH (0115) 950 1295
*"Fantastic" sandwiches – and the "strongest" coffee too – make it
worth seeking out this long-established deli/café, near the Council
House; although in business since 1995, "it just seems to get better
and better".* / **Details:** L only.

Chino Latino
Park Plaza Hotel £ 51
41 Maid Marian Way NG1 6GD (0115) 947 7444
*An "exotic" oriental-fusion menu is realised to sometimes "stunning"
effect at this "pricey" hotel dining room; the would-be trendy
surroundings, however, seem rather "unimpressive" nowadays,
and service likewise.* / **Details:** www.chinolatino.co.uk; 10.30 pm; closed Sun.
Accommodation: 178 rooms, from £-.

4550 Miles From Delhi £ 25
Maid Marian Way NG1 6HE (0115) 947 5111
*A trendy city-centre subcontinental; it doesn't raise reporters to great
heights of eloquence, but all are impressed by the quality of the
cuisine.*

French Living £ 30
27 King St NG1 2AY (0115) 958 5885
"As French as you can get in a basement in the centre of Nottingham", this is *"a friendly bistro just like you went to on holiday"* – it *"may not be inspiring"*, but the *"rustic"* cuisine is *"reliable"* and *"reasonably-priced"*. / **Details:** www.frenchliving.co.uk; near Market Square; 10 pm; closed Mon & Sun; no Amex; booking: max 10.

Hart's £ 46
Standard Ct, Park Row NG1 6GN (0115) 911 0666
Tim Hart's *"top-class"* eatery, near the Castle, is a perennial city-centre success-story of a type that's still rather rare; the new toque's style is a bit *"cheffy"* for some tastes, though, and reporter satisfaction slipped a little this year. / **Details:** www.hartsnottingham.co.uk; near Castle; 10.30 pm, Sun 9 pm. **Accommodation:** 32 rooms, from £120.

Iberico £ 34
The Shire Hall, High Pavement NG1 1HN (01159) 410410
In part of the large crypt beneath the Shire Hall, this *"upmarket"* two-year-old tapas bar retains a considerable reporter following, thanks not least to the *"consistent high quality"* of its dishes (*"both classic and unusual"*). / **Details:** www.ibericotapas.com; 10 pm; closed Mon & Sun; no Amex; children: 16+ D.

Kayal £ 25
8 Broad St NG1 3AL (0115) 941 4733
"A breath of fresh air"; *"imaginative"* South Indian fare – prepared with a view to healthy eating – has won a big following for this city-centre two-year-old.

Laguna Tandoori £ 34
43 Mount St NG1 6HE (0115) 941 1632
A lavish town-centre Indian of over three decades' standing, still tipped as *"one of the best and most consistent in town"*.
/ **Details:** www.lagunatandoori.co.uk; nr Nottingham Castle; 11 pm; closed Sat L & Sun L.

The Larder on Goosegate £ 34
1st Floor, 16 -22 Goosegate NG1 1FE (01159) 500111
On an intriguing first-floor Hockley site (home to the original branch of Boots, apparently), a restaurant tipped for those in search of *"quality locally-sourced"* cooking, and *"friendly personal service"*, in a *"relatively quiet"* ambience. / **Details:** www.thelarderongoosegate.co.uk; 9 pm, Thu-Sat 10 pm; closed Mon & Sun D.

The Library Bar Kitchen £ 30
61 Wollaton Rd NG9 2NG (0115) 922 2268
All dishes arrive *"in taster-size portions"* at this (non-Spanish) Beeston 'tapas' bar, and the results are sometimes *"outstanding"*; staff, though, *"are not always very good at explaining the system"*. / **Details:** 10 pm; closed Sun; no shorts.

Loch Fyne £ 35
15-17 King St NG1 2AY (0115) 988 6840
Yes, we all know this city-centre spot is a chain outlet, but reports tend to suggest that its standards have *"markedly improved"* of late, and – for seafood-lovers – it makes a *"reliable"* destination.
/ **Details:** www.lochfyne.com; 10 pm, Fri & Sat 10.30 pm.

MemSaab   **£ 38** ⭐
12-14 Maid Marian Way NG1 6HS   (0115) 957 0009
*"No ordinary curry house"; this "upmarket", central subcontinental
offers "interesting" and "subtle" cuisine (sometimes using "unusual"
ingredients) that has won it quite a fan club.
/ **Details:** www.mem-saab.co.uk; near Castle, opposite Park Plaza Hotel;
10.30 pm, Fri & Sat 11 pm, Sun 10 pm; D only; no shorts.*

Merchants
Lace Market Hotel   **£ 46** ⓣ
29-31 High Pavement NG1 1HE   (0115) 958 9898
*Disappointingly little commentary on the "formal" dining room of this
smart and handily-located boutique hotel – such as it is, however, is all
positive. / **Details:** www.lacemarkethotel.co.uk; 10.30 pm; D only, closed Mon &
Sun. **Accommodation:** 42 rooms, from £169.*

Petit Paris   **£ 29** ⓣ
2 Kings Walk NG1 2AE   (0115) 947 3767
*A "popular" city-centre Gallic bistro, tipped for its "exceptional-value
lunch and pre-theatre menus". / **Details:** www.petitparisrestaurant.co.uk;
near Theatre Royal; 10.15 pm.*

Restaurant Sat Bains   **£ 95** ⭐
Old Lenton Ln NG7 2SA   (0115) 986 6566
*The location is "unpromising" ("between a huge flyover and
an industrial estate"), but Sat Bains's "inspirational" cooking can
be "absolutely stunning"; even fans ("best meal ever!") can find prices
"shocking", though, and the whole experience sometimes seems too
"up-tight" to really sing. / **Details:** www.restaurantsatbains.com; 9 pm; D only,
closed Mon & Sun; children: 8+. **Accommodation:** 7 rooms, from £90.*

Tarn Thai   **£ 29** ⓣ
9 George St NG1 3BH   (0115) 959 9454
*A tip "for those looking for something a little classier and more
expensive than your usual Thai restaurant"; it's quite a lavish affair
(with no fewer than five water features), and some, if not quite all,
reporters say it's "wonderful in every way". / **Details:** www.tarnthai.co.uk;
10.30 pm, Fri & Sat 11 pm.*

Victoria Hotel   **£ 29**
Dovecote Ln NG9 1JG   (0115) 925 4049
*A real-ale pub, by Beeston station, where the food is "reliably good"
(with "plenty of excellent vegetarian options"), and served
in "huge portions"; space is tight, though, and you "often end up in the
marquee in the back yard". / **Details:** www.victoriabeeston.co.uk; by Beeston
railway station; 9.30 pm, Sun-Tue 8.45 pm; no Amex; no booking, Sun; children: 18+
after 8 pm.*

World Service   **£ 49** ⭐
Newdigate Hs, Castle Gate NG1 6AF   (0115) 847 5587
*With its "imaginative" cuisine and "interesting" décor, this locally-
renowned hotspot (with cute courtyard) "out-performs all others
in Nottingham", for its many fans; of late, however, the food has
seemed a touch more "variable" than usual.
/ **Details:** www.worldservicerestaurant.com; 10 pm; children: 12+ at D.*

The Three Mariners £ 32
2 Church Rd ME13 0QA (01795) 533633
A "lovely" and "relaxed" (but "cramped") country pub, just "100 yards
from an oyster bed"; most reports find its "wholesome food at good
prices" simply "amazing". / *Details:* www.thethreemarinersoare.co.uk;
11 pm, Fri & Sat midnight, Sun 9 pm; closed Mon; no Amex.

Ee-Usk (Seafood Restaurant) £ 40
North Pier PA35 5QD (01631) 565666

"Quality seafood in a quality setting"; you can "watch the comings
and goings in the harbour" as you enjoy some "terrific fresh fish"
at this "lovely" waterside spot. / *Details:* www.eeusk.com; 9.30 pm;
no Amex; children: children 10+ at L, not welcome at dinner .

Bryce's at the Old School House £ 42
RH5 5TH (01306) 627430
In the Surrey Hills, a rather unexpected "fish restaurant in a pub";
the "imaginatively prepared" dishes please almost all of the many
reporters who comment on it. / *Details:* www.bryces.co.uk; 8m S of Dorking
on A29; 9 pm; no Amex.

The Neptune £ 50
85 Old Hunstanton Rd PE36 6HZ (01485) 532122
"A great addition to Norfolk fine dining", where – all reports confirm
– the cuisine is "good going-on exceptional"; this is an "unpretentious"
place too, with notably "reasonable" prices.
/ *Details:* www.theneptune.co.uk; 9 pm; closed Mon, Tue–Sat D only, Sun open
L & D; no Amex; children: 10. **Accommodation:** 7 rooms, from £110.

Smiths Brasserie £ 51
Fyfield Rd CM5 0AL (01277) 365578
An "out of town gem"; this brick-lined and leather-boothed restaurant
serves "consistently good" food – notably "a good selection of diverse
fish dishes" – in a "buzzy" (verging on "noisy") setting.
/ *Details:* www.smithsbrasserie.com; left off A414 towards Fyfield; 10.30 pm;
closed Mon; no Amex; children: 12+.

ORFORD, SUFFOLK 3–1D

Butley Orford Oysterage £ 34
Market Hill IP12 2LH (01394) 450277
Service and surroundings may be "iffy", but it's the "simple, honest fish" and "wonderfully fresh seafood" which draw many reporters to the Pinney family's "school-cafeteria-type" joint, in business since 1963. / Details: www.butleyorfordoysterage.co.uk; on the B1078, off the A12 from Ipswich; 9 pm; no Amex.

The Crown & Castle £ 45
IP12 2LJ (01394) 450205
Slightly mixed reviews on this popular coastal hotel – the food is generally hailed as "good and reliable" (and the "quirky" wine list has its fans too), but some reporters find the ambience a touch "uninspiring". / Details: www.crownandcastle.co.uk; on main road to Orford; 9.15 pm; closed Sun D in winter; no Amex; booking: max 8; children: 9+ at D. Accommodation: 19 rooms, from £115.

ORPINGTON, KENT 3–3B

Xian £ 29
324 High St BR6 0NG (01689) 871881
"Very busy, every night of the week" - this "cramped" spot is sometimes claimed to be "by far the best Chinese restaurant outside central London"; the cooking is "not particularly fancy", but its "fresh" and "authentic" style wins many fans… including, it is claimed, Gary Rhodes! / Details: Near the war memorial; 11 pm; closed Sun L.

OVINGTON, HAMPSHIRE 2–3D

The Bush Inn £ 36
SO24 0RE (01962) 732764
"It's worth the wait to eat (just)", say fans of this notably pretty pub; at weekends, though, it can be far too popular, and service can "really struggle". / Details: www.wadworth.co.uk; just off A31 between Winchester & Alresford; 9 pm, Sun 8.30 pm.

OXFORD, OXFORDSHIRE 2–2D

So many restaurants… (almost) all so dull! The rich and beautiful city remains a deplorable place to eat. Even on the ambience front, few places – most notably *Gees* and *Cherwell Boathouse* – stand out. And when it comes to cuisine, the place is something approaching a write-off, the Thai *Chaing Mai* being the only central restaurant of any real note.

Al Shami £ 26
25 Walton Cr OX1 2JG (01865) 310066
Thanks to its "reliable" charms, this Jericho Lebanese attracts a lot of feedback from reporters – pretty much all of it is to the effect that this is a "genuine" spot offering "flavoursome" food; the wine list offers some surprisingly "affordable" Château Musar too. / Details: www.al-shami.co.uk; midnight. Accommodation: 12 rooms, from £50.

Al-Salam £ 22
6 Park End St OX1 1HH (01865) 245710
"Fresh and good-value" Lebanese fare ("to eat in or take-away") makes this "friendly" and "good-value" spot, near the railway station, very popular; it "can be noisy".

Aziz
£ 33

228-230 Cowley Rd OX4 1UH (01865) 794945

A Cowley Road veteran, often rated as the "best Oxford Indian"; while the food is "consistently good", though, service "can be chaotic".
/ **Details:** www.aziz.uk.com; 11.15 pm; closed Fri L.

Bangkok House
£ 29

42a, Hythe Bridge St OX1 2EP (01865) 200705

Fans still tip this "trusty old Thai", handily-located near the station.
/ **Details:** 11 pm; closed Sun.

Bombay
£ 22

82 Walton St OX2 6EA (01865) 511188

In business for more than half a century, a "straightforward" and "dependable" Jericho spot still sometimes tipped as "Oxford's best Indian". / **Details:** 11 pm; closed Fri L; no Amex.

Branca
£ 39

111 Walton St OX2 6AJ (01865) 556111

"Generally very reliable food, at a good price point, in a space that works very well" – the gist of all of the many comments on this "all-purpose" Jericho Italian; portions can be large – "a half-serving of pizza or pasta will usually do". / **Details:** www.branca-restaurants.com; 11 pm.

Brasserie Blanc
£ 37

71-72 Walton St OX2 6AG (01865) 510999

It's been a long haul, but it does seem that this Jericho chain-brasserie – branded with the name of the great chef from nearby Great Milton – has at last got its act together again; its fare of steak/frites and so on was never rated less than "dependable" this year, and the set menus are "hard to beat". / **Details:** www.brasserieblanc.com; 10 pm, Sat 10.30 pm, Sun 9.30 pm.

Browns
£ 34

5-11 Woodstock Rd OX2 6HA (01865) 511995

"How the mighty are fallen!"; even when it was "trendy", 30 years ago, this famous English brasserie "was always a formula restaurant" – nowadays, it's just "well past the sell-by date".
/ **Details:** www.browns-restaurants.com; 11 pm, Fri & Sat 11.30 pm, Sun 10.30 pm; need 5+ to book.

Cherwell Boathouse
£ 39

Bardwell Rd OX2 6ST (01865) 552746

The "legendary" wine list (the long-time owner is a merchant) and an "excellent" setting by the water are still the main reasons to seek out this "genial" spot; the food remains something of a supporting attraction, but it has generally been at least "pretty good" of late.
/ **Details:** www.cherwellboathouse.co.uk; 9.30 pm.

Chiang Mai
£ 35

Kemp Hall Pas, 130a High St OX1 4DH (01865) 202233

"Still Oxford's finest" (and by quite a margin too); it's the "sheer consistency" of "beautifully-flavoured" Thai food that makes this "cosy" spot stand out – popularity is such that the dining rooms, in a quirky Tudor building off The High, can sometimes be "noisy", and even "frenetic". / **Details:** www.chiangmaikitchen.co.uk; 10.30 pm.

Chutney's Indian Brasserie £ 29
36 St Michael's St OX1 2EB (01865) 724241
*"It's a cut above the average curry house, and the specials (especially
the veggie ones) are good" at this "friendly", "popular" and "hectic"
city-centre Indian highly recommended, particularly for its
"less common" dishes.* / **Details:** *www.chutneysoxford.co.uk; 11 pm, Fri & Sat
11.30 pm.*

La Cucina £ 34
39-40 St Clements OX4 1AB (01865) 793811
*This "very welcoming proper Italian", in St Clement's, continues "to do
what it says on the tin", serving up "staples of solid quality",
plus "a range of interesting specials".* / **Details:** *www.lacucinaoxford.co.uk;
10.30 pm.*

Edamame £ 17
15 Holywell St OX1 3SA (01865) 246916
*A "basic", "tiny" and "cramped" Japanese café, tipped as "a delightful
stop for a quick lunch"; it can be "fun with kids" too.*
/ **Details:** *www.edamame.co.uk; opp New College; 8.30 pm; L only, ex Fri & Sat
open L & D, closed Mon; no Amex; no booking.*

Fishers Seafood Restaurant £ 37
36-37 St Clements OX4 1AJ (01865) 243003
*Renewed support of late for "the best fish restaurant in Oxford";
a "cramped" but "friendly" establishment of long standing, it was
consistently praised for its "unpretentious good value".*
/ **Details:** *www.fishers-restaurant.com; by Magdalen Bridge; 10.30 pm; closed
Mon L.*

The Fishes £ 35
North Hinksey OX2 0NA (01865) 249796

Tipped for its "pleasant situation unexpectedly near the A34",
in North Hinksey village, a gastropub with a "nice garden"; fans laud
"perfect" cooking too, but to critics it's "the location that makes the
place of interest". / **Details:** *www.fishesoxford.co.uk; just off the A34; 10 pm;
no Amex.*

Gee's £ 46
61 Banbury Rd OX2 6PE (01865) 553540
*With its "lovely greenhouse dining room", this is almost certainly
"the most beautiful restaurant in Oxford", well suited to a "special
occasion" (especially of a romantic variety); the food is generally
"good", but naturally it's "pricey" for what it is.*
/ **Details:** *www.gees-restaurant.co.uk; 10 pm Fri & Sat.*

Jamie's Italian £ 34
24-26 George St OX1 2AE (01865) 838383
*"Definitely Oxford's best Italian… but then there's not much
competition!" – the "loud" original branch of J Oliver's "pseudo-rustic"
chain comes as a "pleasant surprise" to some reporters; this is the
weakest member of the group, though, and some reporters find
standards "very ordinary". / Details: www.jamiesitalian.com; 11 pm,
Sun 10.30 pm.*

Malmaison £ 44
3 Oxford Circle OX1 1AY (01865) 268400
*Mixed reactions to this hotel brasserie, intriguingly housed in the city's
(unusually centrally-located) former prison; fans say it's "more than
a novelty venue" and "worth a trip", whereas critics would rate
it anything from "pretty average" to "really disappointing".
/ Details: www.malmaison.com; 10.30 pm. **Accommodation:** 94 rooms,
from £160.*

The Old Parsonage £ 49
1 Banbury Rd OX2 6NN (01865) 292305
*A medieval building, just north of the city-centre, tipped for its
"charming" ambience; up-and-down reports, however, make it more
recommendable for a "good English breakfast" or a "leisurely Sunday
lunch" than for anything more ambitious.
/ Details: www.oldparsonage-hotel.co.uk; 0.5m N of city centre; 10.30 pm.
Accommodation: 30 rooms, from £190.*

The Perch £ 39
Binsey Ln OX2 0NG (01865) 728891
*This "fabulous" French-owned pub, with large garden – "a rural idyll,
within Oxford" – is universally hailed by reporters for its "heavenly"
(and substantial) fare, and its "pleasant" service and ambience.
/ Details: www.the-perch.co.uk; 9.30 pm, Sun 8.30 pm; no Amex.*

Pierre Victoire £ 32
Little Clarendon St OX1 2HP (01865) 316616
*"Possibly the only survivor of the long-established PV bistro chain",
this Jericho spot is tipped for "good-value basic dishes, served in a
cheerful and bustling atmosphere". / Details: www.pierrevictoire.co.uk;
11 pm, 10 pm Sun; no Amex.*

Quod
Old Bank Hotel £ 37
91-94 High St OX1 4BN (01865) 799599
*Many fans praise this Italianate city-centre brasserie for its "decent"
food, its "buzzy" atmosphere, and its "fast and efficient" service; there
are almost as many critics, though, for whom it is decidedly "nothing
special". / Details: www.oldbank-hotel.co.uk; opp All Souls College; 11 pm,
Sun 10.30 pm; no booking at D. **Accommodation:** 42 rooms, from £175.*

Shanghai 30s £ 33
82 St Aldates OX1 1RA (01865) 242230
*Views on this "elegant", "mysterious" and "romantic" city-centre
Chinese have become unsettled; many reporters do still find the food
"delicious" and "different", but others find it only "superficially
interesting" nowadays (and "overpriced" too).
/ Details: www.shanghai30s.com; 11 pm; closed Mon L.*

OXTED, SURREY
3–3B

The Gurkha Kitchen £ 28 ⭐

111 Station Road East RH8 0AX (01883) 722621

*A self-explanatory joint, praised for its "lovely, varied Nepalese menu" ("for both meat and seafood lovers"), and "pleasant" service too. / **Details:** www.moolirestaurant.co.uk; 11 pm, Sun 10 pm; no Amex.*

OXTON, WIRRAL
5–2A

Fraiche £ 52 ⭐⭐

11 Rose Mount CH43 5SG (0151) 652 2914

*"An unlikely location for such quality" (and one highlighted by Harden's as a destination of note long before Michelin ever got there); Mark Wilkinson is a "superb" chef, and he can devote all his energies to cooking at this tiny "gourmet haven". / **Details:** www.restaurantfraiche.com; 9 pm; closed Mon, Tue, Wed L, Thu L & Sun L; no Amex.*

PADSTOW, CORNWALL
1–3B

Custard £ 32

1A, The Strand PL28 8AJ (0870) 170 0740

*"A real find, away from all the Stein eateries", this "hidden-away" Cornish diner is a handy stand-by, serving "modern bistro food" in a "jazzy" (but sometimes "noisy") setting. / **Details:** www.custarddiner.com; 9.30 pm, Fri & Sat 10 pm; no Amex.*

Margot's £ 37 ⭐

11 Duke St PL28 8AB (01841) 533441

*"Just as good as the Seafood, but only half the price!"; this "Padstein gem" is a "tiny" (22-seat) bistro, with one sitting nightly, allowing you "to sit and enjoy Adrian Oliver's fabulous food for as long as you want"; for an evening table, "book weeks ahead". / **Details:** www.margots.co.uk; On the back street behind the Inner Harbour, on the same road as the Post Office; 9.30 pm; closed Mon & Sun; booking: max 10.*

No 6 Café £ 40 ⭐

6 Middle St PL28 8AP (01841) 532093

*A small restaurant that fans have traditionally insisted is "better than the Seafood"; recent reports have been a bit more inconsistent than usual however, but the majority view remains that this is a "fun" place offering "sophisticated" and "carefully prepared" dishes. / **Details:** www.number6inpadstow.co.uk; Off the main square in Padstow, next door to Rick Stein's; 10.30 pm; D only Fri- Sun, ex for residents; no Amex.*

Rick Stein's Café £ 35 ⭐

10 Middle St PL28 8AP (01841) 532700

*"Can't get in to the Seafood Restaurant, who cares?" – "top-quality food" (including "the most delicious fish 'n' chips") helps make this all-hours bistro a worthy alternative to Rick Stein's flagship establishment; most – but not all – reporters find prices "reasonable" too. / **Details:** www.rickstein.com; 9.30 pm; no Amex. **Accommodation:** 3 rooms, from £90.*

St Petroc's Hotel & Bistro   £ 48

4 New St PL28 8EA   (01841) 532700
*"A 'celebrity' restaurant that really does live up to expectations" –
this Rick Stein bistro may be "noisy", but all reports acclaim it as
a "good–value" destination (and a "family-friendly" one too).
/ Details: www.rickstein.com; 9.30 pm; no Amex. Accommodation: 10 rooms,
from £135.*

Seafood Restaurant   £ 75

Riverside PL28 8BY   (01841) 532700
*"Still (almost) perfect", says one of the many fans of the "stunning
piscatorial experience" on offer on this 'barn' of a place, by the
'Padstein' waterfront; critics complain of a lack of inspiration, though,
and there have been resurgent concerns of late about "ridiculous"
prices. / Details: www.rickstein.com; opp harbourmaster's car park; 10 pm;
no Amex; booking: max 14; children: 3+. Accommodation: 16 rooms, from £135.*

Stein's Fish & Chips   £ 29
South Quay PL28 8BL   (01841) 532700
*Mixed reports on this "plain" and "unglamorous" chippy; the majority
view is that it "does what it says on the can", offering "smashing" fish
'n' chips… but critics say "you do just as well elsewhere for half the
price, and without having to queue for the privilege".
/ Details: www.rickstein.com; 10 pm; no Amex.*

PARK GATE, HAMPSHIRE   2–4D

Kam's Palace   £ 36

1 Bridge Rd SO31 7GD   (01489) 583328
*"So Chinese I could imagine I was in Shanghai" – this popular
establishment is an "excellent" all-rounder, offering a "very varied and
interesting menu". / Details: www.kamspalace.co.uk; 10.30 pm.*

PARKGATE, CHESHIRE   5–2A

Marsh Cat   £ 32
1 Mostyn Sq CH64 6SL   (0151) 336 1963
*"Cheap 'n' cheerful, and imaginative too" – this "cramped" bistro
is also of note for offering "beautiful views over the Dee Estuary";
"great wine tasting nights". / Details: www.marshcat.com; 10 pm,
Mon, Tue & Sun 9 pm.*

PEEBLES, SCOTTISH BORDERS   9–4C

Cringletie House   £ 68
Edinburgh Rd EH45 8PL   (01721) 725750
*A "stunning" Borders hotel, where the frescoed dining room offers
"innovative" cuisine that's often (if not quite invariably) "very good".
/ Details: www.cringletie.com; between Peebles and Eddleston on A703, 20m S
of Edinburgh; 9 pm; D only, ex Sun open L & D. Accommodation: 13 rooms,
from £220.*

PENSHURST, KENT

3–3B

Spotted Dog   £ 33

Smarts Hill TN11 8EE   (01892) 870253

"Overlooking Penshurst Place", this 15th century inn is tipped not only for its view, but also for "very good traditional pub food using all-local produce"; "winter visits are best – it's too busy otherwise". / **Details:** *www.spotteddogpub.co.uk; near Penshurst Place; 9 pm, Fri & Sat 9.30 pm, Sun 7 pm.*

PENZANCE, CORNWALL

1–4A

The Honey Pot   £ 13

5 Parade St TR18 4BU   (01736) 368686

"A lovely café", and with "real buzz", tipped for "amazing" cakes, and "very tasty main meals" too (for which it's safest to book). / **Details:** *L only, closed Sun; no credit cards.*

PERTH, PERTH & KINROSS

9–3C

Cafe Tabou   £ 33

4 St John's Pl PH1 5SZ   (01738) 446698

A "true French bistro" so "popular" that "booking is always advisable, even for lunch" – given the all-round hymn of praise in the reports, one can easily understand why! / **Details:** *www.cafetabou.com; 9 pm, Wed & Thu 9.30 pm, Fri & Sat 10 pm; closed Mon D & Sun; no Amex.*

PETERSFIELD, HAMPSHIRE

2–3D

JSW   £ 56

20 Dragon St GU31 4JJ   (01730) 262030

Roughly two thirds of reporters are still thrilled with the "careful and well-presented" cuisine ("best-in-the-area") on offer at Jake Watkins's converted coaching inn (and it benefits from a "great outdoor eating area" too); the other third, however, tend to support those who say it's "not as good as it used to be". / **Details:** *www.jswrestaurant.com; On the old A3; 8 min walk from the railway station; 9.30 pm; closed Mon & Sun; no Amex; children: 8+.* **Accommodation:** *3 rooms, from £85.*

PETWORTH, WEST SUSSEX

3–4A

The Noahs Ark Inn   £ 38

Lurgashall GU28 9ET   (01428) 707346

"Charmingly-located" on the green, this village boozer is tipped for offering a "short" menu of dishes that are "invariably well prepared". / **Details:** *www.noahsarkinn.co.uk; 9.30 pm; closed Sun D.*

Well Diggers Arms   £ 25

Lowheath GU28 0HG   (01798) 342287

A "very popular" and "congenial" family-run pub which induces wide-ranging satisfaction in all who comment on it; it's "nothing fancy, but the meals are good and interesting". / **Details:** *1m out of town on Pulborough Road; 9 pm; closed Mon, Tue D, Wed D & Sun D.*

PICKERING, NORTH YORKSHIRE 8–4C

The White Swan £ 44
Market Pl YO18 7AA (01751) 472288
*An old inn with a "lovely cosy bar" (in which you can eat), and a
"chilled out" restaurant; it serves "straightforward" cuisine –
with "delicious puds". / **Details:** www.white-swan.co.uk; 9 pm.
Accommodation: 21 rooms, from £145.*

PINNER, GREATER LONDON 3–3A

Friends £ 46
11 High St HA5 5PJ (020) 8866 0286
*"In an area lacking almost any decent restaurants this one stands out
a mile"; Terry Farr's "fine local" – in a "quaint" black-and-white house
– is almost invariably praised by reporters for its "solid" and "reliable"
cuisine. / **Details:** www.friendsrestaurant.co.uk; near Pinner Underground station;
9.30 pm; closed Mon & Sun D; no shorts.*

PLOCKTON, HIGHLAND 9–2B

Plockton Inn £ 33 **T**
Innes St IV52 8TW (01599) 544222
*An inn (with its own smokery), tipped for "fish straight from sea
to plate, at most reasonable prices" (and "the best prawns anywhere"
too). / **Details:** www.plocktoninn.co.uk; 9 pm, Winter 8.30 pm; no Amex.
Accommodation: 14 rooms, from £94.*

PLUMTREE, NOTTINGHAMSHIRE 5–3D

Perkins £ 37
Old Railway Station NG12 5NA (0115) 937 3695
*"A reliable, good-quality bistro-style eaterie"; run by the second
generation of the same family, it's a notably "friendly" sort of place
where set menus, in particular, can offer "excellent value".
/ **Details:** www.perkinsrestaurant.co.uk; off A606 between Nottingham & Melton
Mowbray; 9.30 pm; closed Sun D.*

PLYMOUTH, DEVON 1–3C

The Barbican Kitchen Brasserie £ 30 **★**
60 Southside St, The Barbican PL1 2LA (01752) 604448
*Intriguingly located in the Plymouth Gin Distillery, this "lively" brasserie
certainly has a handy location; its "comprehensive" menus offer
"high standards", and "good value" too.
/ **Details:** www.barbicankitchen.com; 10 pm, Sun 9 pm.*

Chloe's
Gill Akaster House £ 52 **T**
Princess St PL1 2EX (01752) 201523
*Near the Theatre Royal, a Gallic-owned brasserie that comes
especially tipped for its "particularly good-value prix-fixe menus" –
both for lunch and pre-show. / **Details:** www.chloesrestaurant.co.uk; 10 pm;
closed Mon & Sun.*

Platters £ 36 **★**
12 The Barbican PL1 2LS (01752) 227262
*"The best fish restaurant in Plymouth, and possibly all of Devon too" –
it's tempting to describe the place as an upmarket chippy, but its aims
nowadays are rather more exalted.
/ **Details:** www.platters-restaurant.co.uk; 10.30 pm.*

Tanners Restaurant   **£ 46**   ⭐

Prysten Hs, Finewell St PL1 2AE   (01752) 252001

"Plymouth's best restaurant by a mile"; the "youthful and well-run" restaurant – operated by the eponymous brothers – is quite a "charming" destination, whose "outstanding food and great service" can come as something of a "surprise" to first-time visitors.
/ **Details:** www.tannersrestaurant.com; 9.30 pm; closed Mon & Sun.

POOLE, DORSET   2–4C

Guildhall Tavern   **£ 38**   ⭐

15 Market St BH15 1NB   (01202) 671717

"Welcoming, well-organised, and totally French in style", this former boozer not only offers "the best service for miles around", but also some "truly excellent" fish and seafood.
/ **Details:** www.guildhalltavern.co.uk; 9.30 pm; closed Mon; no Amex.

Harbour Heights Hotel   **£ 46**

73 Haven Rd, Haven Rd BH13 7LW   (01202) 707272

This elevated (in every sense) hotel has always offered "great views", especially from its expansive terrace, as well as "your chance to mix with the Sandbanks set"; nowadays, however, it boasts an important additional advantage: "a chef who can cook"!
/ **Details:** www.harbourheights.net; 9.15 pm. **Accommodation:** 38 rooms, from £100.

Loch Fyne   **£ 37**   🅣

47 Haven Road, Canford Cliffs BH13 7LH   (01202) 609000

A "reliable" chain "stand-by", tipped for well-executed seafood dishes at "competitive" prices – it "does what it says on the tin".
/ **Details:** www.lochfyne.com; 10.30 am. **Accommodation:** 8 rooms, from £95.

Storm   **£ 46**   🅐⭐

16 High St BH15 1BP   (01202) 674970

"The freshest of fish" is served on "rickety tables", at this town-centre restaurant, run by a fisherman who boasts of serving only his own catch; the "charming" staff and "far-reaching" wine list attract equal praise – "you won't find better for miles". / **Details:** www.stormfish.co.uk; 9.30 pm, Fri & Sat 10 pm; closed Mon L, Tue L & Sun L.

PORT APPIN, ARGYLL & BUTE   9–3B

Airds Hotel   **£ 65**   🅗🅐⭐⭐

PA38 4DF   (01631) 730236

"Cooking of the highest standard" figures in all reports on this "wonderfully-situated" lochside hotel – for his most OTT fans, chef Paul Burns "could walk on those very waters that yield some of his finest ingredients!" / **Details:** www.airds-hotel.com; 20m N of Oban; 9.30 pm; no Amex; no jeans or trainers; children: 8+ at D. **Accommodation:** 11 rooms, from £245.

Pierhouse Hotel   **£ 42**

PA38 4DE (01631) 730302

In a "heavenly" location on the shore of Loch Linnhe, and with "excellent views", a dining room which attracts particular praise for its "fresh and excellent" seafood. / **Details:** www.pierhousehotel.co.uk; just off A828, follow signs for Port Appin & Lismore Ferry; 9.30 pm.

Accommodation: 12 rooms, from £95.

PORTHGAIN, PEMBROKESHIRE   4–4B

The Shed   **£ 47**

SA62 5BN (01348) 831518

"Imaginative fish dishes in a rustic and cosy setting" have made a big name for this "quirky" and "lively" seaside spot; it's "not cheap", though, and – on a bad day – service can be "amateur and chaotic". / **Details:** www.theshedporthgain.co.uk; 9 pm; closed Tue D & Sun D; no Amex.

PORTHLEVEN, CORNWALL   1–4A

Kota   **£ 38**

Harbour Head TR13 9AQ (01326) 562407

On the harbour, a restaurant that's beginning to make quite a name, thanks to its production of "superb seafood dishes, with a Pacific slant" to a standard that's sometimes "simply extraordinary"; "good wine list" too. / **Details:** www.kotarestaurant.co.uk; 9.30 pm; closed Mon L, Tue L, Wed L, Thu L & Sun; no Amex. **Accommodation:** 2 rooms, from £55.

PORTHMADOG, GWYNEDD   4–2C

Yr Hen Fecws   **£ 35**

16 Lombard St LL49 9AP (01766) 514625

A Snowdonia restaurant-with-rooms, tipped for its "honest" fare ("lamb, of course, is always a favourite"), and a "wonderful" atmosphere. / **Details:** www.henfecws.com; 10 pm; D only, closed Sun.

Accommodation: 7 rooms, from £67.

PORTMAHOMACK, HIGHLAND   9–2C

The Oystercatcher   **£ 42**

Main St IV20 1YB (01862) 871560

"Right by the sea, a relaxed and friendly café with superb food"; it's tipped as "the best place in the world to have breakfast", but the "sea-based" cuisine is good at other times too. / **Details:** www.the-oystercatcher.co.uk; 11 pm; closed Mon & Tue; no Amex.

Accommodation: 3 rooms, from £70.

PORTMEIRION, GWYNEDD   4–2C

Portmeirion Hotel   **£ 46**

LL48 6ET (01766) 770000

"An excellent weekend break destination"; the hotel at the heart of Sir Clough Williams-Ellis's famous Italianate village certainly has a "stunning" setting… but although lunch is generally held to offer "fantastic value", the food otherwise only intermittently lives up. / **Details:** www.portmeirion-village.com; off A487 at Minffordd; 9 pm.

Accommodation: 14 rooms, from £188.

Knockinaam Lodge   £ 66
DG9 9AD   (01776) 810471
*A remote hunting lodge (with views) that really is "historic" – Churchill
and Eisenhower plotted D Day here; on the culinary front, it's still
quite a "find" too, and its "simple but sublime cuisine", from "superb"
ingredients, makes it "well worth a long journey".*
/ **Details:** *www.knockinaamlodge.com; off A77 at Colfin Smokehouse, follow signs
to lodge; 9 pm; no jeans or trainers; children: 12+ after 7 pm.*
Accommodation: *10 rooms, from £240.*

abarbistro   £ 33
58 White Hart Rd PO1 2JA   (02392) 811585
*Right on the harbour, with views of Spinnaker Tower, this former bar
has been revamped as a "pleasant", "buzzy" and "family-friendly"
bistro, offering a "varied" menu that's generally realised to a high
standard; there's also an "extensive" wine selection.*
/ **Details:** *www.abarbistro.co.uk; 2 min walk from Portsmouth Cathedral; midnight,
Sun 11 pm.*

Le Café Parisien   £ 24
1 Lord Montgomery Way PO1 2AH   (023) 9283 1234

*"Always buzzing with people from all walks of life", this "university
eatery" – which recently moved into new ownership – is a top tip for
those in search of "paninis, salads, baguettes and breakfasts".*
/ **Details:** *www.lecafeparisien.com; 8 pm; closed Sun; no Amex.*

Rosie's Vineyard   £ 31
87 Elm Grove PO5 1JF   (02392) 755944
*A "gorgeous little wine bar", in the town centre, which is tipped as a
"cosy" sort of place that's "perfect for a romantic night out"; on the
menu, "fresh, seasonal food", and jazz too (if you're lucky).*
/ **Details:** *www.rosies-vineyard.co.uk; South from M275 towards Southsea.
At roundabout turn left into King's Rd, leading to Elm Grv; 11 pm; D only, ex Sun
open L & D.*

The Hat Shop   £ 32
7 High St LD8 2BA   (01544) 260017
*Tipped as "great value, at lunchtime in particular", this "relaxed"
café/bistro is celebrating 20 years in business – "delicious soups,
salads and specials of the day".* / **Details:** *9 pm; closed Sun.*

PRESTON BAGOT, WARWICKSHIRE 5–4C

The Crabmill £ 39
B95 5EE (01926) 843342
*"Surprisingly good food for a pub" (and "excellent beer" too) win
pretty consistent reviews for this "busy" and "inviting" gastroboozer,
not far from the M40. / Details: www.thecrabmill.co.uk; on main road
between Warwick & Henley-in-Arden; 9.30 pm; closed Sun D; no Amex.*

PRESTON, LANCASHIRE 5–1A

Bukhara £ 18
154 Preston New Rd PR5 0UP (01772) 877710
*With its "consistently good" and "authentic" cuisine, this smart and
"efficient" Samlesbury spot is claimed as "the best Indian in Central
Lancashire"… even if it does have a no-booze policy.
/ Details: www.bukharasamlesbury.co.uk; 11pm; D only; no Maestro.*

PRIORS HARDWICK, WARWICKSHIRE 2–1D

The Butchers Arms £ 46
Church End CV47 7SN (01327) 260504
*"In the middle of nowhere", this "fantastic spit and sawdust pub" can
seem rather a "surreal" find; most reports are essentially positive,
but feedback does span the whole range from "excellent in every
way" to "massively over-rated and overpriced".
/ Details: www.thebutchersarms.com; off J11/12 of the M40; 9.30 pm; closed
Sat L & Sun D.*

PURTON, WILTSHIRE 2–2C

Pear Tree at Purton £ 51
Church End SN5 4ED (01793) 772100
*In a "lovely location", on the fringe of the village, this former rectory –
now an hotel – attracts consistent praise for its "high-quality" cooking;
service is "excellent" too. / Details: www.peartreepurton.co.uk; 9.15 pm.*
Accommodation: *17 rooms, from £110.*

PWLLHELI, GWYNEDD 4–2C

Plas Bodegroes £ 58
Nefyn Rd LL53 5TH (01758) 612363

*"An oasis of real style and panache"; this "idyllically located"
restaurant-with-rooms pleases all with cooking that
is almost invariably "very good indeed", and the wine
list "has bargains to shame any London restaurant".
/ Details: www.bodegroes.co.uk; on A497 1m W of Pwllheli; 9.30 pm; closed Mon,
Tue-Sat D only, closed Sun D; no Amex; children: .* **Accommodation:** *11 rooms,
from £110.*

QUEENSFERRY, CITY OF EDINBURGH   9–4C

Dakota Forth Bridge   £ 34   Ⓐ ✪
EH30 9QZ (0870) 423 4293
*The setting – "a large black glass box, in a business park by the Forth
Bridge" – may not sound impressive, but this "chic" and
"sophisticated" hotel dining room is consistently praised for its
"simple" dishes from "excellent ingredients"; fish and seafood
a highlight. / Details: www.dakotaforthbridge.co.uk; 10 pm.*

RAMSBOTTOM, LANCASHIRE   5–1B

Ramsons   £ 60   ✪
18 Market Pl BL0 9HT (01706) 825070
*Chris Johnson's "intimate" restaurant in a picturesque village offers
"meticulously-sourced" cuisine of an "incredibly high standard", plus a
"fabulous" all-Italian wine list to go with it; the place has acquired
a very large local following, though, and doubters do fear it's becoming
rather "over-rated". / Details: www.ramsons-restaurant.com; 9.30 pm; closed
Mon & Tue L; no Amex; booking: max 10.*

RAMSGILL-IN-NIDDERDALE, NORTH YORKSHIRE
8–4B

Yorke Arms   £ 75   Ⓐ ✪ ✪
HG3 5RL (01423) 755243
*"Sublime food in the most picturesque village in the Yorkshire Dales"
– Frances & Gerald Atkins's famous inn really is an all-round crowd-
pleaser, if you stay the night, you can enjoy a "great" breakfast too.
/ Details: www.yorke-arms.co.uk; 4m W of Pateley Bridge; 9 pm; no Amex.*
Accommodation: *12 rooms, from £150.*

RAWTENSTALL, LANCASHIRE   5–1B

The Dining Room   £ 47   ✪ ✪
8-12 Burnley Rd BB4 8EW (01706) 210567
*"Deserving of wider-ranging recognition", this "intimate modern
restaurant" is consistently hailed for the exceptional quality of Andrew
Robinshaw's "inventive" cuisine; service is notably "attentive" too.
/ Details: www.thediningroomrestaurant.co.uk; 9.30 pm; closed Tue, Wed L &
Thu L.*

READING, BERKSHIRE   2–2D

Forbury's Restaurant & Wine Bar   £ 42
1 Forbury Sq RG1 3BB (0118) 957 4044
*Chef Gavin Young seems to be settling in nicely at this "formal" but
"friendly" town-centre restaurant, and his Gallic cuisine is generally
(if not quite invariably) held to be "something special"; the "great-
value market menu" attracts particular praise.
/ Details: www.forburys.com; 10 pm; closed Sun.*

London Street Brasserie   £ 46   ✪
2-4 London St RG1 4SE (0118) 950 5036
*"Great to find a good Reading restaurant, and so close to the centre!";
this "perennial favourite", by the River Kennet, is notable for the
consistency of reports it attracts – indeed, its sole critic finds
it "disappointingly predictable"! / Details: www.londonstbrasserie.co.uk;
On the corner of the Oracle shoping centre; 10.30 pm.*

Mya Lacarte £ 34
5 Prospect St, Caversham RG4 8JB (0118) 946 3400
*There's a big focus on "local, seasonal and sustainable" ingredients
at this "buzzy" Caversham bistro, where the cuisine is often "original"
and "interesting". /* **Details:** *www.myalacarte.co.uk; 10 pm; closed Sun D.*

REETH, NORTH YORKSHIRE 8–4B

Overton House Café £ 34
High Row DL11 6SY (01748) 884332
*"A café overlooking the village green, serving lunch daily and evening
meals Thu-Sat; it's tipped as a "firm favourite" by those who live
in these parts. /* **Details:** *www.overtonhousecafe.co.uk; 9 pm; closed Mon,
Tue & Sun; no Amex.*

REIGATE, SURREY 3–3B

La Barbe £ 45
71 Bell St RH2 7AN (01737) 241966
*"A great night out" draws many reporters to this "very French"
suburban bistro (which gets notably "noisy at weekends with small
parties and celebrations"); the chef – who has been in situ for
a quarter of a century – still achieves impressively "consistent"
standards. /* **Details:** *www.labarbe.co.uk; 9.30 pm; closed Sat L & Sun D.*

Tony Tobin @ The Dining Room £ 58

59a High St RH2 9AE (01737) 226650
*"Fantastic attention to detail" helps makes TV Chef Tony Tobin's
"simple" town-centre operation popular with all reporters who
comment on it; even fans, though, sometimes sense a "lack of
excitement". /* **Details:** *www.tonytobinrestaurants.co.uk; 10 pm; closed Sat L &
Sun D; booking: max 8, Fri & Sat.*

The Westerly £ 41
2-4 London Rd RH2 9AN (01737) 222733
*You need to book "further and further ahead" for a table at this
"first-rate" town-centre restaurant – testament indeed to the "superb"
and "interesting" cuisine, as reporters do not see the rather "austere"
(and "noisy") dining room as any great attraction in itself.
/* **Details:** *www.thewesterly.co.uk; 10 pm; closed Mon, Tue L, Sat L & Sun.*

REYNOLDSTON, SWANSEA 1–1C

Fairyhill £ 56
SA3 1BS (01792) 390139
*"Peaceful" and "relaxed" are the sort of words that crop up a lot
in reports on this remote, but well-known country house hotel;
the food is sometimes (but not invariably) "stunning" too, and is
complemented by a "varied and extensive" wine list.
/* **Details:** *www.fairyhill.net; 20 mins from M4, J47 off B4295; 9 pm; no Amex;
children: 8+ at D.* **Accommodation:** *8 rooms, from £175.*

RHIWBINA, CARDIFF 2–2A

Juboraj £ 29
11 Heol-y-deri CF14 6HA (029) 2062 8894
*Tipped by its fans as "the best Indian in South Wales", this HQ of a
small local chain is praised for its "very wide-ranging menu",
and "excellent specials". /* **Details:** *www.juborajgroup.com; 10.30 pm;
closed Sun.*

RICHMOND, SURREY   3–3A

The Dysart Arms   £ 36
135 Petersham Rd TW10 7AA   (020) 8940 8005
"An ideal spot for lunch after walking in Richmond Park", this "child-friendly" Petersham boozer almost invariably pleases reporters with its "good food and nice atmosphere". / **Details:** www.thedysartarms.co.uk; 9.30 pm; closed Sun D; no Amex; children: 12+ after 8 pm.

Pizzeria Rustica   £ 30
32 The Quadrant TW9 1DN   (020) 8332 6262
A restaurant by the railway station, tipped for offering "the best pizzas in Richmond" – it's "excellent value" too and is "always busy". / **Details:** www.pizzeriarustica.co.uk; 11.15 pm.

Richmond Café   £ 22
58 Hill Rise TW10   (020) 8940 9561
In the town-centre, an "intimate, but not too cramped" establishment, tipped for "cheap and excellent Thai food".

RIDGEWAY, SOUTH YORKSHIRE   5–2C

The Old Vicarage   £ 79
Ridgeway Moor S12 3XW   (0114) 247 5814
Few, but much more consistent, reports of late on this ambitious restaurant in a grand Victorian house – they all tend to agree that, while the cuisine is "very good", the wine list is "outstanding".
/ **Details:** www.theoldvicarage.co.uk; 10 mins SE of city centre; 9.30 pm; closed Mon, Sat L & Sun; no Amex.

RIPLEY, SURREY   3–3A

Drakes   £ 63
The Clock Hs, High St GU23 6AQ   (01483) 224777
Quite possibly offering "the best cooking in Surrey", Steve Drake's restaurant is almost invariably hailed for the "outstanding" quality of its food and service; there's no getting away from it, though – the interior often strikes reporters as "drab".
/ **Details:** www.drakesrestaurant.co.uk; just beyond the intersection of A3 and M25 (J10) heading towards Guildford; 9.30 pm; closed Mon, Sat L & Sun; no Amex; booking: max 6; children: 12+.

RIPON, NORTH YORKSHIRE   8–4B

Lockwoods   £ 37
83 North St HG4 1DP   (01765) 607555
A city-centre café/restaurant, tipped for its "something-for-everyone" menu, created from "very high quality local ingredients"; pizzas and burgers both attract particular praise.
/ **Details:** www.lockwoodsrestaurant.co.uk; 9.30 pm, Sat 10 pm; closed Mon & Sun.

The Old Deanery   £ 32
Minster Rd HG4 1QS   (01765) 600003
"A jewel in the North Yorkshire crown"; this restaurant-with-rooms, nicely located near the Cathedral, has been "refurbished with smart modern decor, but without detracting from the building's olde worlde charm"; the food – "different, imaginative and very tasty" – is "always of the same high standard". / **Details:** www.theolddeanery.co.uk; 9 pm, Fri & Sat 9.30 pm; closed Sun D; no Amex. **Accommodation:** 11 rooms, from £120.

RIPPONDEN, WEST YORKSHIRE 5–1C

El Gato Negro Tapas £ 31
1 Oldham Rd HX6 4DN (01422) 823070
*"Quite simply the best tapas I have ever had outside Spain!";
this "cheery and well-managed" former boozer with its "high quality"
Hispanic cuisine makes an unexpected find "in the middle of scenic
Yorkshire". / **Details:** www.elgatonegrotapas.com; 9.30 pm, 10 pm Sat; closed
Mon, Tue, Wed L, Thu L, Fri L & Sun D; no Amex.*

RISHWORTH, WEST YORKSHIRE 5–1C

Old Bore £ 34
Oldham Rd HX6 4QU (01422) 822291
*A "cosy" country pub, not far from the M62, which retains a "friendly
and rural feel", and where the "honest and rustic" food pleases
most reporters. / **Details:** www.oldbore.co.uk; 9.30 pm, Sun 8 pm; no Amex.*

ROADE, NORTHAMPTONSHIRE 3–1A

Roade House £ 46
16 High St NN7 2NW (01604) 863372
*In the "culinary desert" which is Northampton, a "friendly" restaurant
that remains a "bastion of good food"; themed gastronomic evenings
attract particular praise. / **Details:** www.roadehousehotel.co.uk; 9 pm; closed
Sat L & Sun D; no shorts; booking essential. **Accommodation:** 10 rooms,
from £75.*

ROCK, CORNWALL 1–3B

L'Estuaire £ 45
Rock Rd PL27 6JS (01208) 862622
*Nothing 'estuaire' about any of the accents here! – "first-class",
"creative" cooking ("from a French chef who married a local girl,
who does the front-of-house") makes this a seaside restaurant
of more-than-usual note. / **Details:** www.lestuairerestaurant.com; 9 pm; closed
Mon & Tue; no Amex.*

ROCKBEARE, DEVON 1–3D

Jack in the Green Inn £ 44
London Rd EX5 2EE (01404) 822240
*For most reporters, this "welcoming" pub-cum-restaurant, handily
situated just off the A303, is still "an oasis on the road to Cornwall";
standards appear to be in decline, though, with some reporters now
finding visits here simply "disappointing".
/ **Details:** www.jackinthegreen.uk.com; 2 miles from Exeter airport on the old A30;
9.30 pm; no Amex.*

ROMALDKIRK, COUNTY DURHAM 8–3B

The Rose & Crown £ 42
DL12 9EB (01833) 650213
*A "very friendly" Georgian inn – set amongst no fewer than three
village greens – where the food is always "satisfying", and service
is "excellent"; puddings a highlight. / **Details:** www.rose-and-crown.co.uk;
6m NW of Barnard Castle on B6277; 8.45 pm; D only, ex Sun open L &
D; no Amex; children: 6+ in restaurant. **Accommodation:** 12 rooms, from £140.*

ROSEVINE, CORNWALL
1–4B

Driftwood
Driftwood Hotel   **£ 56**
TR2 5EW   (01872) 580644

It's not just the *"great sea views"* and the *"mellow music"* which make
this trendy seaside hotel dining room of note; the menu
is *"imaginative"*, and the cuisine *"shows care and attention to detail
at every every stage"*. / **Details:** www.driftwoodhotel.co.uk; Off the A30
to Truro, towards St Maees; 9.30 pm; D only; booking: max 6; children: 8+.
Accommodation: 15 rooms, from £195.

ROWDE, WILTSHIRE
2–2C

George & Dragon   **£ 44**
High St SN10 2PN   (01380) 723053
This rural *"favourite"* continues to attract much praise for its
"consistently excellent" dishes (not least fish, which arrives daily from
St Mawes); perhaps no bargain, but *"well worth a visit"*.
/ **Details:** www.thegeorgeanddragonrowde.co.uk; on A342 between Devizes &
Chippenham; 10 pm; closed Sun D; no Amex; booking: max 8.
Accommodation: 3 rooms, from £85.

ROWSLEY, DERBYSHIRE
5–2C

The Peacock   **£ 60**
DE4 2EB   (01629) 733518
"A beautiful modern country hotel with attentive staff" that provides
a *"tranquil"* environment; reviews, though often positive, tend to come
with a 'catch', notably about over-blown pricing.
/ **Details:** www.thepeacockatrowsley.com; 9 pm, Sun 8.30 pm; children: 10+ at D.
Accommodation: 16 rooms, from £145.

ROYAL LEAMINGTON SPA, WARWICKSHIRE
5–4C

Emperors   **£ 32**
Bath Pl CV31 3BP   (01926) 313666
"Offering some dishes rarely found in the UK", this well-established
Chinese establishment is unanimously hailed by reporters for its
"consistently good" fare. / **Details:** 11 pm; closed Sun.

RYE, EAST SUSSEX
3–4C

Webbes at the Fish Café   **£ 40**
17 Tower St TN31 7AT   (01797) 222210
A fish restaurant still tipped by supporters as *"giving J Sheekey a run
for its money!"*; *"inconsistency"*, however, seems to have become quite
a problem of late, and – if you're unlucky – neither service nor
ambience offer any particular compensation.
/ **Details:** www.thefishcafe.com; 9 pm; children: 10+ at D.

SALCOMBE, DEVON 1–4C

Oyster Shack £ 30
10-13 Island St TQ8 8FE (01548) 843596
*A seasonal outpost of the year-round Bigbury stalwart tipped for
"fresh fish, cooked simply"; critics, though, sense standards reflect
"a lack of local competition". / Details: www.oystershack.co.uk; 9 pm.*

SALISBURY, WILTSHIRE 2–3C

Anokaa £ 36
60 Fisherton St SP2 7RB (01722) 414142
*"Still Salisbury's best restaurant of any kind"; this side-street
subcontinental serves up "imaginative" and "superbly well-flavoured"
food (with Gallic influences evident on the presentation front);
for "fantastic value", seek out the lunchtime buffet.
/ Details: www.anokaa.com; 10.30 pm; no shorts.*

SALTAIRE, WEST YORKSHIRE 5–1C

Salts Diner £ 30
Salts Mill, Victoria Rd BD18 3LB (01274) 530533
*It can seem "a touch pricey for what it is", but all reporters approve
of the "great food" on offer at this mill-turned-arts centre;
("the upstairs fish/champagne bar is even pricier, but it offers well-
cooked crustaceans, and there you eat surrounded by flowers and
David Hockney prints"). / Details: www.saltsmill.org.uk; 2m from Bradford
on A650; L & afternoon tea only; no Amex.*

SALTHOUSE, NORFOLK 6–3C

Cookies Crab Shop £ 15
The Grn, Coast Rd NR25 7AJ (01263) 740352
*"Ridiculously good value for very fresh fish and seafood platters,
all served cold, and the location is great too; BYO, and also a cork
screw" – one reporter speaks for all on this "famous" local institution,
"in a garden shed". / Details: www.salthouse.org.uk; on A149; 7.30 pm;
no credit cards.*

SANDSEND, NORTH YORKSHIRE 8–3D

Estbek House £ 50
East Row YO21 3SU (01947) 893424
*"An excellent and welcoming fish-based restaurant-with-rooms, on the
seashore, just outside Whitby"; all reports attest to its quality, and it
offers "a terrific selection of good wines" too, many available by the
glass. / Details: www.estbekhouse.co.uk; 9 pm; D only; no Amex.*
Accommodation: *4 rooms, from £110.*

SAPPERTON, GLOUCESTERSHIRE 2–2C

The Bell at Sapperton £ 40
GL7 6LE (01285) 760298
*A "beautiful, old-fashioned pub", "immaculately restored and
maintained", where fans say the "imaginative, locally-sourced food"
is an "absolute revelation"; reporters differ on whether to opt for
basics like burgers or "fancier fare". / Details: www.foodatthebell.co.uk;
from Cirencester take the A419 towards Stroud, turn right to Sapperton; 9.30 pm;
no Amex; no booking at L; children: 10+ at D.*

The Straw Hat Oriental £ 41
Harrow Rd CM21 0AJ (01279) 722434
*"Everyone must try it!" say fans of Mr & Mrs Li's exceptional oriental
in a thatched cottage, which inspires rave reviews for its "top Asian-
fusion" food including "the finest sushi" (for which "beware a possible
long wait"). / Details: www.strawhat-oriental.co.uk; On the A1184, 1m south
of Sawbridgeworth; 11 pm, Sun 9.30 pm; no shorts; children: no children after
9 pm.*

The Spread Eagle £ 36
BB7 4NH (01200) 441202
*This ancient pub – with its "beautiful picture window, overlooking the
River Ribble" – has undergone an "amazing transformation" under its
new owners; the "unusual" cuisine, however, induces rather mixed
reports. / Details: www.spreadeaglesawley.co.uk; 9 pm, Sun 7.30 pm.*

Jade Fountain £ 26
42-46 High St CB2 4BG (01223) 836100
*A "family favourite" Chinese, with "charming" staff and "tasteful"
décor, and within easy reach of Cambridge too; the food is "well above
average". / Details: 1m from M11, J10; 11 pm; closed Mon.*

Bell Hotel £ 35
31 High St IP17 1AF (01728) 602331
*Most reporters find the dining room of this 17th-century coaching inn
a useful and "good-value" destination – with "more panache",
however, not least on the service front, it could so easily be rather
more. / Details: www.bellhotel-saxmundham.co.uk; 9 pm; closed Mon & Sun.*
Accommodation: *10 rooms, from £80.*

Lanterna £ 52
33 Queen St YO11 1HQ (01723) 363616

*Not only a "first-class" Italian operation, but one that's "haunted
by celebrities"! – fortunately, "the only place in town worth visiting"
keeps most reporters well satisfied. / Details: www.giorgioalessio.co.uk;
near the Old Town; 9.30 pm; D only, closed Sun; no Amex.*

Pepper's **£ 44**
Stephen Joseph Theatre YO11 1JW (01723) 500642
*Tipped as a "surprisingly good haven in Scarborough's culinary
desert", this "unpretentious family-run restaurant" now has a new
location, on the first floor of a theatre.*
*/ **Details:** www.peppersrestaurant.co.uk; 10 pm; closed for L Mon-Fri & Sun.*

SCAWTON, NORTH YORKSHIRE 8–4C

Hare Inn **£ 35**
YO7 2HG (01845) 597769
*A "remote" inn (parts of which go back as far as the 13th century),
tipped for its "tasty" local fare; service, however, can sometimes
be rather "slow". / **Details:** www.thehareinn.co.uk; off A170; 9 pm; closed
Mon & Sun D.*

SEAHAM, COUNTY DURHAM 8–3C

The White Room
Seaham Hall **£ 85**
Lord Byron's Walk SR7 7AG (0191) 516 1400
*"A restaurant of which the North East can be proud, showing
amazing attention to detail in both flavours and presentation" –
almost all reporters reckon that the new (Von Essen) régime at this
ambitious hotel-cum-spa has got off to a very good start.*
*/ **Details:** www.seaham-hall.co.uk; 10 pm; closed Mon L & Tue L; no trainers;
booking: max 8. **Accommodation:** 20 rooms, from £200.*

SEVENOAKS, KENT 3–3B

The Vine **£ 34**
11 Pound Ln TN13 3TB (01732) 469510
*In the heart of the town, a light and bright restaurant praised for its
"honest" and "good-value" cuisine; set lunch menus (including
on Sunday) come particularly highly recommended.*
*/ **Details:** www.vinerestaurant.co.uk; 11 pm; closed Sun D; no Amex.*

SHALDON, DEVON 1–3D

Ode **£ 52**
Fore St TQ14 0DE (01626) 873977
*Tim Bouget is a chef with quite a cv, and it shows in the standards
of the "lovely fresh organic fare" on offer at this townhouse-
restaurant, set in an "attractive" village; for top value, lunch and
brunch are particularly recommended. / **Details:** www.odetruefood.co.uk;
9.30 pm; closed Mon, Tue, Wed L, Sat L & Sun; no Amex.*

SHEFFIELD, SOUTH YORKSHIRE 5–2C

Aagrah **£ 27**
Unit 1 Leopold Sq, Leopold St S1 2JG (0114) 279 5577
*"One of the few places one can actually eat with any confidence
in the centre of Sheffield!" – this "excellent modern Indian" maintains
the exemplary standards for which this Yorkshire chain is rightly
renowned (including "stern but efficient" service).*
*/ **Details:** www.aagrah.com; 11.30 pm, Fri & Sat midnight, Sun 10.30 pm; D only;
no Amex.*

Artisan £ 37
32-34 Sandygate Rd S10 5RY (0114) 266 6096

Tipped as a "recession-beater", Richard Smith's "friendly" bistro (with even cheaper diner attached) where reports unanimously confirm that the food is "always of good quality"; the menu "changes often" too. / **Details:** *www.relaxeatanddrink.com; 10 pm.*

Kashmir Curry Centre £ 15
123 Spital Hill S4 7LD (0114) 272 6253

The setting may "break new boundaries of plainness" – "I like to imagine this is what a Kashmiri transport caff feels like" – but this "excellent curry house" attracts more reports than anywhere else in town; "efficient" service "with real personality" plays no small part in its success. / **Details:** *midnight; D only, closed Sun; no credit cards.*

Nirmals £ 25
189-193 Glossop Rd S10 2GW (0114) 272 4054

"Nirmal's hasn't changed much in 30 years" ("it's the only restaurant I know where the blackboard specials are actually painted on"), but reporters' enthusiasm for its "great" Indian food is – by and large – undimmed. / **Details:** *near West St; midnight; closed Sun L.*

Nonna's £ 38
539-541 Eccleshall Rd S11 8PR (0114) 268 6166

There is always a "real Italian experience" to be had at this Eccleshall spot, which "manages the almost impossible trick of growing larger while maintaining its 'village' touch"; for really "phenomenal" value, visit before 7pm. / **Details:** *www.nonnas.co.uk; M1, J33 towards Bakewell; 9.45 pm; no Amex.*

Rafters £ 42
220 Oakbrook Rd, Nether Grn S11 7ED (0114) 230 4819

In Ranmoor, up a narrow staircase, a "local stalwart" with a "well-deserved reputation"; there's no doubt that it remains a "civilised" destination, but concerns are also expressed that it has "taken its eye off the ball". / **Details:** *www.raftersrestaurant.co.uk; 10 pm; D only, closed Tue & Sun.*

Silversmiths £ 32
111 Arundel St S1 2NT (0114) 270 6160

"The Kitchen Nightmare treatment seems to have worked!"; this restaurant in the city's newly-named 'Cultural Quarter' is praised by all reporters for offering "good-value" cuisine from a "short but nicely thought-out menu". / **Details:** *www.silversmiths-restaurant.com; 11.30 pm, Fri & Sat midnight; D only, closed Sun; no Amex.*

Wasabisabi £ 32
227A, London Rd S2 4NF (0114) 258 5838

A "good and popular" restaurant, consistently praised for "sushi that's second to none", and "impeccable" service too.
/ **Details:** *www.wasabisabi.co.uk; 11 pm; no Amex.*

Three Acres £ 49
Roydhouse HD8 8LR (01484) 602606

It may be "off the beaten track" out on Emlyn Moor, but this well-known rural inn "ticks all the boxes for quality of food, service and location", and it has a huge following (so book); the recent extension, however, doesn't seem to have done anything to boost the place's charm-quotient. / *Details:* www.3acres.com; near Emley Moor TV tower; 9.30 pm; no Amex. **Accommodation:** 16 rooms, from £120.

Charlton House £ 33
Charlton Rd BA4 4PR (01749) 342008
Occupying a "splendid" rambling country house, a dining room tipped for its "lovely" cuisine, which makes good use of "wonderful locally-sourced meat and vegetables". / *Details:* www.charltonhouse.com; on A361 towards Frome; 9.30 pm, Fri & Sat 10 pm. **Accommodation:** 26 rooms, from £180.

The Green £ 43
The Green DT9 3HY (01935) 813821
Tipped as "the best restaurant round here by a country mile", this is an establishment still generating slightly up-and-down reports; "the cheaper midweek menu is better value, and attracts a younger and more boisterous crowd". / *Details:* 9 pm; closed Mon & Sun; no Amex.

Kinghams £ 47
Gomshall Ln GU5 9HE (01483) 202168
A long-standing cottage-restaurant which has gathered quite a following with its "wholesome and well prepared" food; not all reporters succumb to the place's "grey pound" charms, though, and doubters complain of food stuck in a "time warp". / *Details:* www.kinghams-restaurant.co.uk; off A25 between Dorking & Guildford; 9 pm; closed Mon & Sun D.

SHINFIELD, BERKSHIRE   2–2D

L'Ortolan   £ 81
Church Ln RG2 9BY   (0118) 988 8500
*Alan Murchison's celebrated restaurant, in a former rectory, can still
offer a "superb" dining experience overall; of late, however,
it's impossible to avoid the impression that "for the price, everything
should be just a bit better", with the atmosphere, in particular, found
"lacking in warmth and intimacy".*
/ **Details:** www.alanmurchisonrestaurants.co.uk; J11, take first exit left on all three
roundabouts, then follow sign posts; 9.30 pm; closed Mon & Sun.

SHIPBOURNE, KENT   3–3B

The Chaser Inn   £ 35
Stumble Hill TN11 9PE   (01732) 810360
*This family-friendly gastroboozer has a very large SE London following
as a "lovely out-in-the-country sort of restaurant"; there's quite
a feeling that it's "gone downhill" of late, though, with "having to place
your order at the under-staffed bar" a particular source of irritation.*
/ **Details:** www.thechaser.co.uk; 9.30 pm, Sun 9 pm; no Amex.

SHIPLEY, WEST YORKSHIRE   5–1C

Aagrah   £ 28
4 Saltaire Rd BD18 3HN   (01274) 530880
*"Busy every day of the week, and deservedly so" – it will come as no
surprise to anyone who knows this Yorkshire chain that this is a curry
house which is simply "excellent".* / **Details:** www.aagrah.com; 11.30 pm;
closed Sat L & Sun L.

SKELWITH BRIDGE, CUMBRIA   7–3D

Chesters   £ 23
LA22 9NN   (01539) 432553
*"A busy café with good food and cheerful staff", tipped for its
"stunning and stylish river-edge setting".*
/ **Details:** www.chesters-cafebytheriver.co.uk; 5 pm, Sat & Sun 5.30 pm; L only;
no Amex.

SKENFRITH, MONMOUTHSHIRE   2–1B

The Bell at Skenfrith   £ 41
NP7 8UH   (01600) 750235
*More consistent reviews of late on this "improved" riverside
"gastropub-with-rooms" – the "eclectic" wine list is still the stand-out
attraction, but the "carefully sourced" cuisine now generally attracts
praise too.* / **Details:** www.skenfrith.co.uk; on B4521, 10m E of Abergavenny;
9.30 pm, Sun 9 pm; no Amex; children: 8+ at D. **Accommodation:** 11 rooms,
from £110.

SLEAT, HIGHLAND   9–2B

Kinloch Lodge   £ 73
IV43 8QY   (01471) 833333
*"What a pity it's such a long, long way away!"; almost all reporters
are swept away by the experience of staying at the Macdonald
of Macdonalds' ancestral house, overlooking the loch, where "new chef
Marcello Tully has been a great success".*
/ **Details:** www.kinloch-lodge.co.uk; 9 pm; no Amex. **Accommodation:** 14
rooms, from £150.

SMALL HYTHE, KENT 3–4C

Richard Phillips at Chapel Down £ 41
Tenterden Vineyard TN30 7NG (01580) 761616
*"It's bringing London-quality dining to deepest Kent", say fans,
who insist this celebrated vineyard's restaurant is a
"vast improvement" on its previous incarnations; it's undoubtedly
"a good place for lunch on a summer's day", but reports are
otherwise rather up-and-down.*
/ **Details:** www.richardphillipsatchapeldown.co.uk; 10.30 pm; closed Mon D,
Tue D, Wed D & Sun D.

SNAPE, SUFFOLK 3–1D

The Crown Inn £ 35
Bridge Rd IP17 1SL (01728) 688324
*A cosy town-centre inn, now settling into its new ownership, and tipped
for "a short menu of fresh, mainly local fare".* / **Details:** off A12 towards
Aldeburgh; 9.30 pm, Sat 10 pm; no Amex.

SNETTISHAM, NORFOLK 6–4B

Rose & Crown £ 32
Old Church Rd PE31 7LX (01485) 541382
*"A moorland pub, with good traditional food"; it's tipped as a "gem" –
perhaps that's why it's sometimes "overcrowded", with consistency
suffering as a result.* / **Details:** www.roseandcrownsnettisham.co.uk; 9 pm;
no Amex. **Accommodation:** 16 rooms, from £90.

SONNING-ON-THAMES, WOKINGHAM 2–2D

The French Horn £ 78
RG4 6TN (0118) 969 2204
*"Traditional old English fare" (most famously, duck) "beautifully
presented and served in a welcoming ambience" – a formula that's
winning ever-warmer praise for this "perfect" riverside spot, which,
as its 40th year approaches, seems to have found new life under the
second generation of its founding family.*
/ **Details:** www.thefrenchhorn.co.uk; M4, J8 or J9, then A4; 9.30 pm; booking:
max 10. **Accommodation:** 21 rooms, from £160.

SOUTH SHIELDS, TYNE & WEAR 8–2B

Colman's £ 15
182-186 Ocean Rd NE33 2JQ (0191) 456 1202
*A fourth-generation chippy tipped for "the most perfect fish 'n' chips"
– since 1926, they've certainly gathered an impressive collection
of awards.* / **Details:** www.colmansfishandchips.com; L only; no Amex.

SOUTHAMPTON, HAMPSHIRE 2–3D

Kuti's £ 34
37-39 Oxford St SO14 3DP (023) 8022 1585
*An Indian restaurant often tipped as "the best in Southampton"
(of any type), and with quite a fan club; doubters, though, "struggle
to see how it's different from any other high street subcontinental".*
/ **Details:** www.kutis.co.uk; near Stanley Casino; 11 pm.

Vatika **£ 57**
Botley Rd S032 2HL (01329) 830 405
*"Fascinating combinations and truly inventive ideas" make Atul
Kochhar's "outstanding" (and not inexpensive) Indian yearling
a surprise find in a Hampshire vineyard; not everyone, though,
is convinced it's quite up to the standards of his Mayfair flagship,
Benares.* / **Details:** *www.vatikarestaurant.com; 9.30 pm; closed Mon & Tue.*

SOUTHEND-ON-SEA, ESSEX 3–3C

The Pipe of Port **£ 33**
84 High St SS1 1JN (01702) 614606
*A "traditional" restaurant of long standing, tipped for food that's
"never overcomplicated, but always beautifully cooked and seasoned
to perfection", and served by "knowledgeable" and "welcoming" staff
too.* / **Details:** *www.pipeofport.com; basement just off High Street; 10.30 pm;
closed Sun; no Amex; children: 16+.*

SOUTHPORT, MERSEYSIDE 5–1A

Auberge Brasserie **£ 35**
1b Seabank Rd PR9 0EW (01704) 530671
*Expansions don't seem to have done a great deal for the food
or ambience of this town-centre brasserie, but this is still described
as an "ever-popular" destination, tipped for offering good-value menus
all day.* / **Details:** *www.auberge-brasserie.com; 10.30 pm; no Amex.*

Michael's **£ 37**
47 Liverpool Rd PR8 4AG (01704) 550886
*"A very cosy and intimate restaurant, with friendly staff and fabulous
food" – the tenor of all reports on this "proper independent",
in Birkdale Village, which offers "quality home cooking"
at "very reasonable prices".* / **Details:** *www.michaelsbirkdale.co.uk;
2 minutes walk from Birkdale train station; 10 pm; D only, closed Mon & Sun.*

Warehouse Brasserie **£ 41**
30 West St PR8 1QN (01704) 544662
*"Modern and stylish, and with a lively atmosphere", this "reliable"
brasserie certainly stands out in this part of the world; let's hope that
new chef Darren Smith is maintaining – or perhaps gently improving
– standards.* / **Details:** *www.warehousebrasserie.co.uk; 10.30 pm; closed Sun;
no Amex.*

SOUTHROP, GLOUCESTERSHIRE 2–2C

The Swan at Southrop **£ 40**
GL7 3NU (01367) 850205
*"A gem of a gastropub in a beautiful Cotswold village"; its "good and
imaginative" food really impresses most reporters, but the odd let-
down is not unknown.* / **Details:** *www.theswanatsouthrop.co.uk; 9 pm; closed
Sun D; no Amex.*

SOUTHSEA, HAMPSHIRE 2–4D

No 8 Kings Road **£ 33**
8 Kings Rd PO5 3AH (08451) 303234
*"A good watering hole in a desert" – this "beautifully-converted
former banking hall" is tipped for its "consistently excellent food and
service".* / **Details:** *www.8kingsroad.co.uk; midnight; D only, ex Sun L only;
no Amex.*

The Crown
Adnams Hotel   **£ 39**
High St IP18 6DP (01502) 722275
*This famous, "crowded" Adnams inn offers the "excellent" wine list for
which the brewer is, paradoxically, famous, and also (improving) food
that's often hailed as "delicious" and "unpretentious"; "get there early
– you can't book and the locals grab the best tables".*
/ **Details:** www.adnamshotels.co.uk; 9 pm, Fri & Sat 9.30 pm.
Accommodation: 14 rooms, from £138.

Sutherland House   **£ 39**
56 High St IP18 6DN (01502) 724544
*Only positive reports on this "beautifully decorated" contemporary-
styled restaurant in a 15th-century building; the "well-presented"
dishes really are "locally sourced" – "they show the food miles on the
menu!"* / **Details:** www.sutherlandhouse.co.uk; 9.30 pm. **Accommodation:** 3
rooms, from £140.

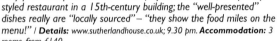

Gimbals   **£ 36**
Wharf St HX6 2AF (01422) 839329
*A "buzzy little bistro" where the owners "always seem pleased to see
you", and "really care about food" too – it attracts only complimentary
reports.* / **Details:** www.gimbals.co.uk; 9.15 pm; D only, closed Sun; no Amex.

The Millbank   **£ 36**
Millbank Rd HX6 3DY (01422) 825588

*"Sweeping hill views from the conservatory" add drama to a visit
to this "beautifully located" inn, where the "tasty" fare is "always of a
very good standard".* / **Details:** www.themillbank.com; The M62, between
junctions 22 and 23; 9.30 pm, Sun 8 pm; closed Mon; no Amex.

The Plough Inn   **£ 40**
SO21 2NW (01962) 776353
*A "busy" but "friendly" gastropub that's tipped as a "well above-
average" destination; of late, however, there's a slight feeling among
reporters that it has become "over-ambitious" and "overpriced".*
/ **Details:** www.theploughsparsholt.co.uk; 9 pm, Sun & Mon 8.30 pm, Fri & Sat
9.30 pm; no Amex.

The Old Plow   **£ 40**   ⭐

Flowers Bottom Ln HP27 0PZ   (01494) 488300

In a converted Chilterns pub, a bistro and (marginally preferred) restaurant, distinguished by the consistent "high standards" of its cooking and its "friendly" service; "the daily specials are always interesting". / Details: www.yeoldplow.co.uk; 20 mins from M40, J4 towards Princes Risborough; 9 pm; closed Mon, Sat L & Sun D.

ST ALBANS, HERTFORDSHIRE   3–2A

The Albany   **£ 35**

7 George St AL3 4ER   (01727) 730888

*Already hailed as a "gem" by some reporters, this new establishment – handily sited on the continuation of the High Street – offers some "outstanding-value" set menus of "well-cooked" fare, in rather intriguing medieval surroundings; there are sceptics, but even some of them admit "it has a certain charm".
/ Details: www.albanyrestaurant.co.uk; 10.30 pm; closed Mon & Sun D.*

Asia   **£ 33**

2 Beaconsfield Rd AL1 3RD   (01727) 800002

*An "interesting and wide-ranging menu" – mixing dishes from various Asian countries – helps make this former post office a "good-value" destination, so far as most reporters are concerned; inevitably, though, purists may feel that "the concept doesn't quite work".
/ Details: www.asia-dining.co.uk; in front of Trinity Church; 11 pm, 11.30 pm Fri & Sat.*

Barissimo   **£ 13**   ⓣ

28 St Peters St AL1 3NA   (01727) 869999

A bustling café which attracts a number of reports; it's a "warm" and "friendly" sort of place, tipped for "excellent coffee and a range of light meals made with fresh ingredients". / Details: L only; no credit cards.

La Cosa Nostra   **£ 33**   ⭐

62 Lattimore Rd AL1 3XR   (01727) 832658

*"A small family-friendly Italian", with quite a name locally for its "top-quality pizzas"; "it's worth the premium over PizzaExpress".
/ Details: near railway station; 10.30 pm; closed Sat L & Sun; no Amex.*

Darcy's   **£ 42**

2 Hatfield Rd AL1 3RP   (01727) 730777

"Still good, but its crown is slipping in the direction of Lussmans" – this "buzzy" city-centre restaurant still often offers food that's "interesting" and "well-prepared"; a "lack of consistency", however, continues to gnaw away at support. / Details: www.darcysrestaurant.co.uk; 9 pm, Fri & Sat 10 pm.

Lussmanns   **£ 37**

Waxhouse Gate, High Street AL3 4EW   (01727) 851941

A "great location, opposite the Abbey" is perhaps one of the reasons explaining the large volume of reports on this "bright", "airy" and "relaxed" contemporary restaurant (which is part of a small chain) – the food, however, is "not infallible". / Details: www.lussmans.com; Off the High Street, close to the cathedral; 10 pm, 10.30 pm Fri & Sat, 9 pm Sun.

Mumtaj £ 26

⭐

115 London Rd AL1 1LR (01727) 843691
*Near the Old Cinema Hall, a stalwart Indian still of note for its
"delightful" food and "buzzing" atmosphere... albeit in a venue
described as "a converted sitting room". / Details: midnight.*

St Michael's Manor £ 48

Ⓣ

Fishpool St AL3 4RY (01727) 864444
*The new chef is tipped as "shaking things up" at this country house
hotel, whose "beautiful location" has traditionally rather outshone the
food and service. / Details: www.stmichaelsmanor.com; near the Cathedral;
9 pm. Accommodation: 30 rooms, from £180.*

**The Waffle House
Kingsbury Water Mill** £ 22

Ⓣ

St Michael's St AL3 4SJ (01727) 853502
*As the "weekend queues" attest, this is a top tip for "the best family
lunch out in St Albans", and some reporters are "surprised by how
delicious waffles can be". / Details: www.wafflehouse.co.uk; near Roman
Museum; 6 pm; L only; no Amex; no booking.*

ST ANDREWS, FIFE 9–3D

**Road Hole Grill
Old Course Hotel** £ 77

Ⓣ

KY16 9SP (01134) 474371
*Still relatively early days for the dining room of this grand modern golf-
hotel, but it's already tipped for offering a tasting menu that's
"inventive, exciting and just superb".
/ Details: www.oldcoursehotel.kohler.com.*

Seafood Restaurant £ 61

Ⓐ⭐

The Scores KY16 9AB (01334) 479475
*"Don't be put off by the glass walls – it's surprisingly cosy within";
this "stunningly-located" cliff-side restaurant is widely acclaimed for
"imaginative" fish and seafood dishes, cooked to "perfection"
(plus "one of the best white wine lists in Scotland").
/ Details: www.theseafoodrestaurant.com; 9.30 pm; no shorts; children: 12+ at D.*

Vine Leaf £ 41

⭐⭐

131 South St KY16 9UN (01334) 477497
*"Much love and experience" is evident in the "excellent choice
of dishes" on offer at the Hamiltons' veteran bistro, which continues
to impress all who comment on it. / Details: www.vineleafstandrews.co.uk;
9.30 pm; D only, closed Mon & Sun. Accommodation: 3 guest apartments
rooms, from £80.*

ST DAVIDS, PEMBROKESHIRE 4–4A

Cwtch £ 40

⭐

22 High St SA62 6SD (01437) 720491
*A "cosy", "friendly" and "buzzing" restaurant which "uses local
produce to great effect"; it can sometimes get a little "crowded".
/ Details: www.cwtchrestaurant.co.uk; 9.30 pm; D only.*

ST GEORGE, CONWY 4–1D

The Kinmel Arms £ 42

The Village LL22 9BP (01745) 832207

A former inn that's now tipped as a "buzzing" destination of the sort that's still quite rare in these parts; the food can be "a bit mixed", but generally seems to satisfy. / Details: www.thekinmelarms.co.uk; From Chester, J24a on A55, turn left into village; 9.30 pm; closed Mon & Sun; no Amex. Accommodation: 4 rooms, from £115.

ST IVES, CORNWALL 1–4A

Alba Restaurant £ 41

The Old Lifeboat Hs, Wharf Rd TR26 1LF (01736) 797222

The "beautiful location" above the harbour is the same as ever, but transition to new ownership has upset feedback on this popular waterside restaurant, which some reporters feel has "slipped" under the new régime. / Details: www.thealbarestaurant.com; 9.30 pm.

Porthgwidden Beach Café £ 35

Porthgwidden Beach TR26 1SL (01736) 796791

"Not to be confused with the much more upmarket Porthminster Café", this is a "real beach-side café"; if you're looking for the likes of "an excellent crab sandwich" or "good cakes and coffee", it's nevertheless tipped as quite a "trendy" destination. / Details: www.porthgwiddencafe.co.uk; 10 pm; no Amex; booking: max 10.

Porthminster Café £ 44

Porthminster Beach TR26 2EB (01736) 795352

"The worlds best beach view, with food to match" – this "friendly" and "relaxed" café/bistro almost invariably inspires reports of "a wonderful total experience", in which "great seafood" often plays a part. / Details: www.porthminstercafe.co.uk; near railway station; 10 pm; no Amex.

The Seafood Café £ 36

45 Fore St TR26 1HE (01736) 794004

An "exceptional range" of fish is on offer at this high street spot, which looks "rather like a fish shop"; you choose your own fish, and the sauce to go with it – a formula that means "booking is essential, regardless of the time of year!" / Details: www.seafoodcafe.co.uk; map on website; 10.30 pm; no Amex.

Tate Cafe
Tate Gallery £ 29

Porthmeor Beach TR26 1TG (01736) 791122

"On the top floor of the gallery", a "busy" café, tipped for "great views and great cakes"; "good fresh fish" too. / Details: www.tate.org.uk; L only; no Amex.

St Kew Inn   £ 31   ⭐

PL30 3HB   (01208) 841259

Local celeb-chef Paul Ripley is now in charge at this "rambling" gastroboozer; its "good" food ("without frills") at "sensible prices" ensures that it is often "busy". / Details: www.stkewinn.co.uk; just off the A39, between Wadebridge and Camelford; 11 pm; no Amex; children: no children in bar.

The Well House   £ 53   ⭐

PL14 4RN   (01579) 342001

"Delicious seafood" is a highlight of the "beautiful" cuisine on offer at this Looe Valley country house restaurant-with-rooms. / Details: www.wellhouse.co.uk; half way between Liskeard & Looe off the B3254; 9 pm; no Amex; children: 8+. Accommodation: 9 rooms, from £125.

St Clement's   £ 34

3 Mercatoria   TN38 0EB   (01424) 200355

All the more worth knowing about in an area "with few alternatives", "a compact but excellent restaurant in a thoroughly unassuming location", where ex-Caprice chef Nick Hale takes "fish straight off the boats in Hastings" to produce some "imaginative" dishes. / Details: stclementsrestaurant.co.uk; 10.30 pm; closed Mon & Sun D; no Amex.

Walletts Court   £ 55   Ⓣ

Westcliffe   CT15 6EW   (01304) 852424

Tipped as a "haven for cross-Channel travellers", a country house hotel – in the ownership of the same family for 30 years – that still makes a "welcome" find; realisation of its locally-based menu is sometimes hailed as "above-average" too. / Details: www.wallettscourt.com; on A258 towards Deal, 3m NE of Dover; 9 pm; D only, ex Sun open L & D; children: 8+ at D. Accommodation: 17 rooms, from £129.

The Galley   £ 10   Ⓐ⭐

The Pde   TR21 0LP   (01720) 422602

A chippy-cum-bistro which attracts consistent praise for its "wide range of very fresh and imaginatively cooked local fish" (all, apparently, caught by the proprietor's extended family); "book early".

Juliet's Garden   £ 37

Seaways Flower Farm   TR21 0NF   (01720) 422228

"Superb views, especially at sunset" are not the only attraction of this Scillies "institution" – a café/restaurant tipped for "good snack food during the day", and "evening meals" of quality. / Details: www.julietsgardenrestaurant.co.uk; 8.30 pm; closed Tue D; no Amex.

Hotel Tresanton   **£ 54**
27 Lower Castle Rd TR2 5DR   (01326) 270055

"A spectacular setting in which to enjoy well-executed dishes,
beautifully presented" – Olga Polizzi's harbourside hotel is decidedly
"not cheap", but otherwise "ticks all the boxes" for a great meal
either in the "delightful" dining room, or on the lovely outside terrace.
/ **Details:** www.tresanton.com; near Castle; 9.30 pm; booking: max 10; children:
6+ at dinner. **Accommodation:** 29 rooms, from £230.

ST MONANS, FIFE   9–4D

The Seafood Restaurant   **£ 56**
16 West End KY10 2BX   (01333) 730327
Not many words wasted on this bright dining room in a fishing village,
but all of the (few) reports agree that it's simply "excellent".
/ **Details:** www.theseafoodrestaurant.com; 9.30 pm; closed Mon & Tue;
children: 5+.

STADHAMPTON, OXFORDSHIRE   2–2D

The Crazy Bear   **£ 51**
Bear Ln OX44 7UR   (01865) 890714
"The most eclectic place you can imagine!"; this "wacky" and
"decadent" gastropub is certainly a "sexy" destination, with food that's
pretty "reasonable" too – the Thai menu being sometimes preferred
to the English one. / **Details:** www.crazybeargroup.co.uk; 10 pm.
Accommodation: 17 rooms, from £115.

STAMFORD, LINCOLNSHIRE   6–4A

The George Hotel   **£ 53**
71 St Martins PE9 2LB   (01780) 750750
"Grand, but not too formal", this famous coaching inn is a bastion
of "traditional English food" (including a "huge dessert trolley and
cheese board") and "good old-style service"; more budget-conscious
options include the Garden Room brasserie and the summer BBQ
in the courtyard. / **Details:** www.georgehotelofstamford.com; off A1, 14m N
of Peterborough, onto B1081; 10 pm; jacket and/or tie; children: 8+ at
D. **Accommodation:** 47 rooms, from £132.

Jim's Yard   **£ 38**
3 Ironmonger St PE9 1PL   (01780) 756080
An intriguing conservatory restaurant, in the centre of town, tipped
as a "consistent performer", and one with a "decent wine list" too.
/ **Details:** www.jimsyard.biz; 9.30 pm; closed Mon & Sun; no Amex.

STANTON, SUFFOLK   3–1C

Leaping Hare Vineyard   **£ 39**
Wyken Vineyards IP31 2DW   (01359) 250287
A "beautiful" old barn where the food, "using lots of local produce",
is almost invariably "good"; the wines — including, of course, their own
— are "interesting" too. / **Details:** www.wykenvineyards.co.uk; 9m NE of Bury
St Edmunds; follow tourist signs off A143; 9 pm; L only, ex Fri & Sat open L &
D; no Amex.

STATHERN, LEICESTERSHIRE   5–3D

Red Lion Inn   **£ 33**
2 Red Lion St LE14 4HS   (01949) 860868
Notably consistent reports on the "cheerful welcome" and
"good value" on offer at this "very good gastropub", in a "pretty
village near Belvoir Castle". / **Details:** www.theredlioninn.co.uk; 9.30 pm;
closed Sun D; no Amex.

STOCKBRIDGE, HAMPSHIRE   2–3D

Clos du Marquis   **£ 47**
London Rd SO20 6DE   (01264) 810738
"Totally unexpected", this rural "oasis" has a very big reputation for its
"hearty Gallic fare, and the wines to go with it" — all of the many
reports confirm that standards are "consistently good".
/ **Details:** www.closdumarquis.co.uk; 2m E on A30 from Stockbridge; 9 pm; closed
Mon & Sun D.

STOCKCROSS, BERKSHIRE   2–2D

The Vineyard at Stockcross   **£ 94**
RG20 8JU   (01635) 528770
"First-class cuisine married to an enormous Californian-oriented wine
list" have forged a growing reputation for this "elegant, if rather
impersonal" contemporary country house hotel dining room; we don't
think a rating is appropriate though, as new chef Daniel Galmiche
takes over as this guide goes to press. / **Details:** www.the-vineyard.co.uk;
from M4, J13 take A34 towards Hungerford; 9.30 pm; no jeans or trainers.
Accommodation: 49 rooms, from £199.

STOKE HOLY CROSS, NORFOLK   6–4C

The Wildebeest Arms   **£ 36**
82-86 Norwich Rd NR14 8QJ   (01508) 492497
"A bright spot for food in an area which lacks anything exciting",
sometimes tipped for its "good, seasonal and locally-sourced" menu;
feedback, however, is not entirely consistent.
/ **Details:** www.animalinns.co.uk; from A140, turn left at Dunston Hall, left at
T-junction; 9 pm.

STOKE ROW, OXFORDSHIRE   2–2D

The Crooked Billet   **£ 45**
Newlands Ln RG9 5PU   (01491) 681048
"Wonderful food in a very picturesque location"; if you're looking for
food that's "hearty and tasty, as opposed to gastronomic", it's hard
to beat this "friendly" inn, which has a huge following among
reporters. / **Details:** www.thecrookedbillet.co.uk; off the A4130; 10 pm;
no Amex.

STOKE-BY-NAYLAND, SUFFOLK   3–2C

The Angel Inn   **£ 32**
Polstead St CO6 4SA   (01206) 263245
*It's perhaps less ambitious than it once was, but this pretty 16th-century coaching inn is still tipped for its "nicely cooked" grub, which comes at "excellent prices" too. / **Details:** www.theangelinn.net; 5m W of A12, on B1068; 9.30 pm, Sun 8.30 pm. **Accommodation:** 6 rooms, from £50.*

The Crown   **£ 40**
CO6 4SE   (01206) 262346
*"The best gastropub for miles"; on the food front, "fresh fish" is a highlight of a cuisine that's sometimes "surprisingly good", but it's the "comprehensive" wine list that tends to attract particular interest. / **Details:** www.eoinns.co.uk; on B1068; 9.30 pm, Fri & Sat 10 pm, Sun 9 pm; no Amex.*

STOKESLEY, NORTH YORKSHIRE   8–3C

Howards   **£ 18**
30 College Sq TS9 5DN   (01642) 713391
*Already "busy", this recently-established bistro pleases all reporters with its "superb mix of dishes"; for nice days, there's a "sun trap terrace" too. / **Details:** www.howards-eatery.co.uk.*

STONEHAVEN, ABERDEENSHIRE   9–3D

Marine Hotel   **£ 37**
9-10 Shore Head AB39 2JY   (01569) 762155
*The chef changed at this attractive harbourside pub just as this guide was going to press – let's hope the new man is offering a cuisine to match up to the "stunning range of beers". / **Details:** www.britnett-carver.co.uk/marine; 9 pm. **Accommodation:** 6 rooms, from £110.*

STOW ON THE WOLD, GLOUCESTERSHIRE   2–1C

The Old Butchers   **£ 38**
7 Park St GL54 1AQ   (01451) 831700
*"Delicious food and very attentive service" make this main-street Mediterranean bistro very popular with reporters; it can, however, be a little "noisy". / **Details:** www.theoldbutchers.com; 9.30 pm; closed Mon.*

STRATFORD UPON AVON, WARWICKSHIRE   2–1C

Lambs   **£ 38**
12 Sheep St CV37 6EF   (01789) 292554
*A "cosy" but "contemporary" restaurant, housed in an attractive Tudor house, tipped as an "excellent" destination for pre-theatre deals. / **Details:** www.lambsrestaurant.co.uk; 9.30 pm; closed Mon L & Sun D; no Amex; booking: max 12.*

The Oppo   **£ 34**
13 Sheep St CV37 6EF   (01789) 269980
*A cosy restaurant of two decades' standing – in a nicely modernised beamed building near the Courtyard Theatre – tipped as a "consistently good" option. / **Details:** www.theoppo.co.uk; 10 pm, Sun 9.30 pm; closed Sun L; no Amex; booking: max 12.*

The Vintner £ 34

4-5 Sheep St CV37 6EF (01789) 297259

Similar in feel to the The Oppo and Lambs (same ownership), and "offering much the same food", this rather charming town-centre restaurant – in a building five centuries old – is tipped as the best of the three. / **Details:** *www.the-vintner.co.uk; 10 pm, Sun 9 pm; no Amex.*

STRATHCARRON, ROSS-SHIRE 9–2B

Kishorn Seafood Bar £ 26

Kishorn IV54 8XA (01520) 733240

A sparse and rustic dining room with wooden benches outside, all with sea-views to the Isle of Skye, tipped for the quality of its seafood, and in particular the "squatties" (squat lobster tails). / **Details:** *www.kishornseafoodbar.co.uk.*

STUCKTON, HAMPSHIRE 2–3C

Three Lions £ 51

Stuckton Rd SP6 2HF (01425) 652489

Michael Womersley's "delicious" use of "local ingredients" ("not too fussily presented") and wife Jayne's "warm welcome" make a compelling combination at this "intimate" New Forest inn, which inspires reports of impressive consistency. / **Details:** *www.thethreelionsrestaurant.co.uk; 1m E of Fordingbridge off B3078; 9 pm, Fri & Sat 9.30 pm; closed Mon & Sun D; no Amex.* **Accommodation:** *7 rooms, from £80.*

STUDLAND, DORSET 2–4C

Shell Bay Seafood £ 37

Ferry Rd BH19 3BA (01929) 450363

"Location, location and location… " – it's the "stunning" view, across Poole Harbour, which really makes this bistro a destination, though, as its fish dishes can "lack imagination". / **Details:** *www.shellbay.net; just near the Sandbanks to Swanage ferry; 9 pm.*

STURMINSTER NEWTON, DORSET 2–3B

Plumber Manor £ 44

DT10 2AF (01258) 472507

Run by the three Prideaux brothers since 1972, this "welcoming" country house hotel is a "professional" venture that pleases all who report on it; it's the sweet trolley, though, which is "the real star". / **Details:** *www.plumbermanor.com; off A357 towards Hazelbury Bryan; 9.30 pm; D only, ex Sun open L & D.* **Accommodation:** *16 rooms, from £110.*

SUDBURY, SUFFOLK 3–2C

Ballingdon Valley Tandoori £ 25

57 Ballingdon St CO10 2DA (01787) 376777

A smart contemporary-style joint that's always "buzzing", thanks to its "consistently good" and "interesting" Bangladeshi cuisine, and its "crisp" service too. / **Details:** *www.ballingdonvalley.co.uk; 11.30 pm, Fri & Sat midnight.*

Ⓐ

ThrowingStones
National Glass Centre   £ 22
Liberty Way SR6 0GL   (0191) 565 3939
It's "the setting that strikes you first" – "acres of glass and a view
of the river and the quays" – at this intriguing industrial museum;
the cooking is "predictable" ("in the best sense of the word"), which
does nothing to stop this being "a great place for lunch".
/ **Details:** www.nationalglasscentre.com; A19 to Sunderland, follow signs for
National Glass Centre; L only; no Amex.

★

The French Table   £ 45
85 Maple Rd KT6 4AW   (020) 8399 2365
"One of the best 'locals' I have ever visited"; the dining room may
be "noisy" and "cramped", but this "consistent" spot offers the
"superb" cooking of an "accomplished" chef (Eric Guignard); the wine
list "continues to add surprises" too. / **Details:** www.thefrenchtable.co.uk;
10.30 pm; closed Mon & Sun D; booking: max 10, Fri & Sat.

★

Joy   £ 29
37 Brighton Rd KT6 5LR   (020) 8390 3988
"A very good new wave Indian restaurant with friendly service,
chic décor and inventive dishes of high quality"; reporters don't seem
to mind that it's "relatively pricey". / **Details:** www.joy-restaurant.co.uk;
11.30 pm.

Ⓐ

The Anchor   £ 40
Bury Ln CB6 2BD   (01353) 778537
"A kitchen that really knows what it's doing" is a bit of a rarity in this
obscure part of the Fens, so this "beautifully located" and
"unpretentious" inn is generally worth seeking out – as ever, though,
the occasional off-day is far from unknown.
/ **Details:** www.anchorsuttongault.co.uk; 7m W of Ely, signposted off B1381
in Sutton; 9pm, Sat 9.30 pm. **Accommodation:** 4 rooms, from £79.5.

Ⓣ

Olive Tree   £ 46
Sutton Green Rd GU4 7QD   (01483) 729999
It perhaps looks "ordinary", but this "continually improving" spot
is tipped for "clever, simple and tasty" fare, including some "very good
fish". / **Details:** 9.30 pm; closed Mon D & Sun D; no Amex.

Ⓣ

The Wheatsheaf at Swinton   £ 43
Main St TD11 3JJ   (01890) 860257
In a former pub, a restaurant all the more worth knowing about in a
very thin area, tipped for its "outstanding" food.
/ **Details:** www.wheatsheaf-swinton.co.uk; between Kelso & Berwick-upon-Tweed,
by village green; 9 pm; Closed Sun D Jan & Feb; no Amex; children: 10+ at D.
Accommodation: 10 rooms, from £112.

Aagrah   £ 28   ⭐

York Rd LS24 8EG   (01937) 530888

An outpost of the exemplary Yorkshire subcontinental chain which maintains the group's usual high standards – "it may look like a curry barn, but it's worth a visit if you're in the area".

/ **Details:** www.aagrah.com; 7m from York on A64; 11.30 pm, 11 pm Sun; D only.

Terrace

Cliveden House   £ 75

Cliveden Rd SL6 0JF   (01628) 668561

Presumably it's all to do with the arrival of Chris Horridge (ex-Bath Priory) as executive chef, but standards at this grand room-with-a-view have shot up this year – "enthusiastic" service sets the tone for an all-round experience which is, on most accounts, simply "unbeatable".

/ **Details:** www.clivedenhouse.co.uk; 9.30 pm; no trainers. **Accommodation:** 39 rooms, from £240.

🅣

Brazz

Castle Hotel   £ 37

Castle Bow TA1 1NF   (01823) 252000

A "cheerful" brasserie that's been attracting much more consistent commentary of late, and is particularly tipped as a venue for a "fine informal lunch". / **Details:** www.brazz.co.uk; 10 pm. **Accommodation:** 44 rooms, from £230.

The Castle Hotel   £ 59   🅐⭐

Castle Grn TA1 1NF   (01823) 272671

"Very good food and knowledgeable staff make it the best place for fifty miles"; it's had its ups and downs in recent times, but the Chapman family's landmark hotel (since 1950) is currently a real "class act". / **Details:** www.the-castle-hotel.com; follow tourist information signs; 9.30 pm; closed Sun D. **Accommodation:** 44 rooms, from £230.

The Willow Tree   £ 37   🅐⭐

3 Tower Ln TA1 4AR   (01823) 352835

"A long-term favourite which keeps getting better" – a "real trier", it offers "outstanding food" in "charming surroundings".

/ **Details:** www.willowtreerestaurant.co.uk; 10 pm; D only, closed Sun & Mon; no Amex.

TAVISTOCK, DEVON

Hotel Endsleigh   **£ 58**
PL19 0PQ   (01822) 870 000
Set in over 100 acres, a "gem" of a country house hotel, offering
"lots of cosy nooks" and "great food" too, and where all-round high
standards impress most reporters. / *Details: www.hotelendsleigh.com;*
10.30 pm. **Accommodation:** *16 rooms, from £200.*

TEFFONT EVIAS, WILTSHIRE

Howards House Hotel   **£ 60**
SP3 5RJ   (01722) 716392
A 'country hotel and restaurant' that was consistently tipped under its
former management; the chef has survived a change of régime,
so let's hope the "usual high standards" carry on too.
/ Details: www.howardshousehotel.co.uk; 9m W of Stonehenge off A303; 9 pm.
Accommodation: *9 rooms, from £165.*

TENTERDEN, KENT

The Raja Of Kent   **£ 25**
Bibbenden Rd   TN30 6SX   (01233) 851191
The leading branch of a trio of Kentish Indians, tipped as offering
"some of the best subcontinental food in the country",
with "many unusual and original dishes"; can it really be so good? –
more reports next year please! / *Details: www.therajaofkent.com; midnight.*

TETBURY, GLOUCESTERSHIRE

Calcot Manor   **£ 55**
GL8 8YJ   (01666) 890391
The main dining room of this Cotswold hotel is generally quite
a crowd-pleaser ("not cheap, but good") but it's main attraction is as
part of an establishment which offers much for all the family –
children's facilities are excellent, and there's an impressive spa for
grown-ups too. / *Details: www.calcotmanor.co.uk; junction of A46 & A4135;*
9.30 pm, Sun 9 pm. **Accommodation:** *35 rooms, from £230.*

THAMES DITTON, SURREY

The Albany   **£ 34**
Queens Rd   KT7 0QY   (020) 8972 9163
"A delightful spot overlooking the Thames at Hampton Court";
all reports confirm it as a "great family restaurant, with lovely food".
/ Details: www.the-albany.co.uk; 10 pm.

THORNBURY, GLOUCESTERSHIRE

Thornbury Castle   **£ 67**
Castle St   BS35 1HH   (01454) 281182
"Perfect in every way!"; this is a "real historic castle complete with its
own vineyard!", and one of those Von Essen hotels where "the food
matches the wonderful atmosphere" (not invariably the case...)
/ Details: www.thornburycastle.co.uk; near intersection of M4 & M5; 9.30 pm;
no jeans or trainers. **Accommodation:** *27 rooms, from £190.*

THORPE LANGTON, LEICESTERSHIRE   5–4D

Bakers Arms   £ 38
Main St LE16 7TS (01858) 545201
"A dream pub in a thatched cottage in a village
amidst quintessentially rolling English countryside, offering high-quality,
non-faddish food" – under its current owners for over a decade and
a half, and still "as good as ever". / **Details:** www.thebakersarms.co.uk;
near Market Harborough off A6; 9.30 pm; D only, ex Sat open L & D & Sun open
L only, closed Mon; no Amex; children: 12+.

TIGHNABRUAICH, ARGYLL & BUTE   9–4B

An Lochan
An Lochan Hotel   £ 40
PA21 2BE (01700) 811239
"A beautiful lochside restaurant", with "one of the best views of the
Isle of Bute"; its "ambitious" cuisine uses "fresh local produce",
generally to "very good" effect. / **Details:** www.anlochan.co.uk; 8.30 pm;
no Amex. **Accommodation:** 11 rooms, from £110.

TITLEY, HEREFORDSHIRE   2–1A

Stagg Inn   £ 41
HR5 3RL (01544) 230221
"A complete surprise in the middle of nowhere"; this "stylish
gastropub" is hailed as a "supremely enjoyable" destination all-round,
offering "excellent value for money"… and, even more remarkably,
it has so far failed to succumb to the 'curse' of its Michelin star!
/ **Details:** www.thestagg.co.uk; on B4355, NE of Kington; 9 pm; closed Mon &
Sun D; no Amex. **Accommodation:** 6 rooms, from £85.

TOPSHAM, DEVON   1–3D

Darts Farm Café   £ 30
Clyst St George EX3 0QH (01392) 875587
Tipped for its "good nursery food", this largely al fresco café (part of
a rural retail complex) attracts particular praise as a
breakfast destination. / **Details:** www.dartsfarm.co.uk; M5 Junction 30,
A376 towards Exmouth; L only; no Amex.

The Galley   £ 52
41 Fore St EX3 0HU (01392) 876078
A "friendly" nautically-themed restaurant, tipped for its "outstanding"
fish dishes. / **Details:** www.galleyrestaurant.co.uk; 9.30 pm; closed Mon & Sun;
booking essential; children: 12+.

La Petite Maison   £ 48
35 Fore St EX3 0HR (01392) 873660
"A real winner"; a "good family-run restaurant", whose cuisine
is "full of flavour", and offers "value for money" too.
/ **Details:** www.lapetitemaison.co.uk; Next to The Globe Hotel; 10 pm; closed
Mon & Sun; no Amex; booking essential at L.

Cafe Fish £ 31

The Pier PA75 6NU (01688) 301253

This particular 'end-of-the-pier show' (which debuted in 2006) is a "relaxed" and "unpretentious" sort of place, where the fish – "caught on the restaurant's own boat" – is tipped as "truly incredible".
*/ **Details:** www.thecafefish.com; 30-40 min drive north from the ferry pier at Criagnure; 9 pm; no Amex.*

TORCROSS, DEVON 1–4D

Start Bay Inn £ 28

TQ7 2TQ (01548) 580553

"Huge portions of fish 'n' chips" are just the highlight of the "fresh and well-cooked" dishes on offer at this coastal boozer; "good range of wines and ciders", too, and even a "decent local vintage"!
*/ **Details:** www.startbayinn.co.uk; on beach front (take A379 coastal road to Dartmouth); 10 pm; no Amex; no booking.*

TORQUAY, DEVON 1–3D

Elephant Bar & Restaurant £ 45

3-4 Beacon Ter, Harbourside TQ1 2BH (01803) 200044

*Often "stunning" fine dining makes this "elegant" and "professional" first-floor restaurant (with harbour-view) a popular destination for all who comment on it; the brasserie, below, is similarly a "good-value" destination. / **Details:** www.elephantrestaurant.co.uk; 9.30 pm; closed Mon & Sun D; children: 14+ at bar.*

No 7 Fish Bistro £ 47

Beacon Ter TQ1 2BH (01803) 295055

*A popular harbourside bistro, offering locally-caught fish cooked in a "simple" style; fans insist that this is "the place to eat in Torquay", but some reporters do wonder if it isn't beginning to get rather "pricey". / **Details:** www.no7-fish.com; 9.30 pm; D only Sun-Tue.*

TOTNES, DEVON 1–3D

Kingsbridge Inn £ 38

9 Leechwell St TQ9 5SY (01803) 863324

*"A surprise find"; this recently-refurbished inn attracts only modest commentary, but is consistently tipped for its "good meat and fish". / **Details:** www.thekingsbridgeinn.com; 11 pm, Sun 10.30 pm.*

TREEN, CORNWALL 1–4A

Gurnards Head £ 35

TR26 3DE (01736) 796928

"A surprise find in a beautiful and isolated location", this "gem" of a pub pleases all reporters with the "perfect simplicity" of its cuisine; service, however, doesn't quite measure up.
*/ **Details:** www.gurnardshead.co.uk; on coastal road between Land's End & St Ives, near Zennor B3306; 9.30 pm; no Amex. **Accommodation:** 7 rooms, from £85.*

TROUTBECK, CUMBRIA 7–3D

Queen's Head £ 36
Townhead LA23 1PW (01539) 432174
*Located high on a Lakeland pass, this "delightful" country inn,
with "lovely" views, is tipped for its "very good food" – "a bit pricey,
but worth it".* / **Details:** *www.queensheadhotel.com; A592 on Kirkstone Pass;
9 pm; no Amex; booking: max 8, Fri & Sat.* **Accommodation:** *15 rooms,
from £110.*

TUNBRIDGE WELLS, KENT 3–4B

The Black Pig £ 34
18 Grove Hill Rd TN1 1RZ (01892) 523030
*A "good new gastropub" hailed by fans as a "versatile" destination
offering a "sensibly simple menu"; not all reporters, however,
are convinced that early-days standards are being maintained.*
/ **Details:** *www.theblackpig.net; 11 pm, Sat 10 pm, Sun 9.30 pm; no Amex.*

Hotel du Vin et Bistro £ 45
Crescent Rd TN1 2LY (01892) 526455
*Even the "really lovely setting" of this early-days member of the wine-
driven hotel/bistro chain can't save it from the general impression
of mediocrity that now hangs over the HduV brand – the "really
varied" wine selection is now its only sure-fire attraction.*
/ **Details:** *www.hotelduvin.com; Opposite the Assembly Hall; 10 pm, Fri & Sat
10.30 pm; booking: max 10.* **Accommodation:** *34 rooms, from £95.*

Thackeray's £ 52
85 London Rd TN1 1EA (01892) 511921
*The "best-value set lunch ever" on offer at Richard Phillips' elegant
restaurant in a Regency villa wins hearty praise from reporters;
it's usually a "solid" dinner destination too, although its critics find
it "overpriced".* / **Details:** *www.thackerays-restaurant.co.uk; near Kent and
Sussex hospital; 10.30 pm; closed Mon & Sun D.*

TUNSTALL, LANCASHIRE 7–4D

Lunesdale Arms £ 33
LA6 2QN (01524) 274203
*"Not really a pub any more, more a restaurant with a bar in the
middle" – this "friendly" establishment is almost invariably hailed
by reporters as a "reliable" destination, offering cuisine that's "varied"
and "enjoyable".* / **Details:** *www.thelunesdale.co.uk; 15 min from J34 on M6
onto A683; 11 pm; closed Mon.*

TURNERS HILL, WEST SUSSEX 3–4B

Alexander House Hotel £ 64
East St RH10 4QD (01342) 714914
*In its "ideal setting", this trendified country house hotel (and spa)
is tipped as a "dependable" destination for "special occasion dining";
the food, though, is somewhat outshone by the notably "attentive"
service.* / **Details:** *www.alexanderhouse.co.uk; off M23 J10, follow signs to E.
Grinstead and Turners Hill, on B2110; 10 pm; closed Mon -Thu, Fri & Sat L &
Sun D; no jeans or trainers; children: 14+ except Sun L in restaurant.*
Accommodation: *38 rooms, from £185.*

Groes Inn   **£ 38**   Ⓐ
LL32 8TN   (01492) 650545
The "isolated" location of this tastefully updated ancient inn impresses
all who comment on it, and most (but not all) reporters think the food
measures up. / **Details:** www.groesinn.co.uk; on B5106 between Conwy &
Betws-y-coed, 2m from Conwy; 9 pm; children: 10+ in restaurant.
Accommodation: 14 rooms, from £103.

The Three Crowns Inn   **£ 40**   Ⓐ
HR1 3JQ   (01432) 820279
A half-timbered inn has a "lovely feel"; results can be "hit or miss",
but most reports are of "diligent" cooking of "great ingredients",
and "very friendly" service too. / **Details:** www.threecrownsinn.com;
1.5m from A417; 9.30 pm; closed Mon; no Amex. **Accommodation:** 1 room,
at about £95.

Sharrow Bay   **£ 71**   Ⓐ✪
CA10 2LZ   (01768) 486301
Inevitably, critics say England's original country house hotel "isn't
as good since it was taken over by a group" (Von Essen); they're
surprisingly few in number, though, and this "charming" destination
(with its "amazing lakeside setting") still offers those of an "old-
fashioned" bent the "ultimate gourmet treat".
/ **Details:** www.sharrowbay.co.uk; on Pooley Bridge Rd towards Howtown; 8 pm;
children: 10+. **Accommodation:** 24 rooms, from £350.

The Bay Horse   **£ 46**   Ⓐ
Canal Foot LA12 9EL   (01229) 583972
On most (if not quite all) reports, something of a "hidden gem",
this "quirky" coaching inn (with impressive bay-view conservatory)
offers a "regularly-changing" menu, on which "local fish" is a highlight.
/ **Details:** www.thebayhorsehotel.co.uk; after Canal Foot sign, turn left & pass
Glaxo factory; 8 pm; closed Mon L; children: 9+ at D. **Accommodation:** 9 rooms,
from £100.

Lords of the Manor   **£ 76**
GL54 2JD   (01451) 820243
The food can be "very good", but there's a strong feeling among
reporters that this "lovely" Cotswold country house risks becoming
"a fashion statement rather than a place to enjoy".
/ **Details:** www.lordsofthemanor.com; 4m W of Stow on the Wold; 9.30 pm;
D only, ex Sun open L & D; no jeans or trainers; children: 7+ at D in restaurant.
Accommodation: 26 rooms, from £191.

UPPINGHAM, RUTLAND   5–4D

The Lake Isle   **£ 42**
16 High Street East LE15 9PZ   (01572) 822951
An elegant, small restaurant with rooms sometimes tipped as "worth
a detour", thanks to its good all-round standards, even if arguably its
"good wine" and attractive setting outshine the cooking.
/ **Details:** www.lakeisle.co.uk; past the Market place, down the High Street; 9 pm,
Fri & Sat 9.30 pm; closed Mon L & Sun D. **Accommodation:** 12 rooms,
from £75.

URMSTON, GREATER MANCHESTER   5–2B

Isinglass   **£ 38**
46 Flixton Rd M41 5AB   (0161) 749 8400
A "friendly" and "intimate" bistro, in Urmston, which comes over
as something of a "labour of love"; its British cuisine is invariably "top-
notch", and the wines are "interesting" too.
/ **Details:** www.isinglassrestaurant.co.uk; 10 pm; closed Mon, Tue-Fri D only, Sat &
Sun open L & D.

USK, MONMOUTHSHIRE   2–2A

Nags Head   **£ 32**
6-8 Twyn Sq NP15 1BH   (01291) 672820
An attractive old coaching inn, in traditional style, tipped for its very
high standards all-round. / **Details:** 9.30 pm.

UTTOXETER, STAFFORDSHIRE   5–3C

Restaurant Gilmore   **£ 57**
Strine's Farm ST14 5DZ   (01889) 507100
"Staffs' only 'gastronomic' destination" – this farmhouse-restaurant
is a "charming" place offering very thoughtful cuisine ("we were given
a note about the food's relation to Escoffier"); it's an "excellent" but
"unpretentious" experience (compared by one misty-eyed reporter
to London's Connaught… before the vandals got there).
/ **Details:** www.restaurantgilmore.com; 9 pm; closed Mon, Tue, Wed L, Sat L &
Sun D; no Amex.

VENTNOR, ISLE OF WIGHT   2–4D

The Hambrough   **£ 64**
PO38 1SQ   (01983) 856333

Robert Thompson is undoubtedly a "clever young chef", and his
"very serious cooking" ("excelling in both presentation and flavours")
has made an instant name for this contemporary-style restaurant-
with-rooms. / **Details:** www.thehambrough.com; 9.30 pm; closed Mon & Sun;
no Amex; children: 5+ at D. **Accommodation:** 7 rooms, from £150.

The Royal Hotel **£ 38**
Belgrave Rd PO38 1JJ (01983) 852186

An "elegant" traditional family-run hotel (of the grander sort), where the food is "surprisingly good" – "way above average", and "really interesting" too. / **Details:** www.royalhoteliow.co.uk; 9 pm; children: 3+. **Accommodation:** 54 rooms, from £170.

VIRGINSTOW, DEVON 1–3C

Percy's **£ 58**
EX21 5EA (01409) 211236
"Superb local food from the estate" provides the basis for the cuisine at this "beautifully-located" country house hotel; the wine list is "poor", though, and the welcome of late has not always been as warm as hoped for. / **Details:** www.percys.co.uk; 9.30 pm; D only; no Amex; children: 12+. **Accommodation:** 7 rooms, from £150.

WADDESDON, BUCKINGHAMSHIRE 3–2A

The Five Arrows **£ 45**
High St HP18 0JE (01296) 651727
As you'd expect from an imposing inn with 'Rothschild' written all over it (it being on their estate), this is a rather superior venture, which offers "lovely food in lovely surroundings", and "wonderful" wine. / **Details:** www.thefivearrows.co.uk; on A41; 9.15 pm. **Accommodation:** 11 rooms, from £95.

WADEBRIDGE, CORNWALL 1–3B

Relish **£ 13**
Foundry Ct PL27 7QN (01208) 814214
A "café-cum-deli", in a "sunny courtyard", which is tipped specifically for its coffee (from a champion barista) and also for its all-round charm. / **Details:** www.relishwadebridge.co.uk; closed Sun; no Amex.

WALBERSWICK, SUFFOLK 3–1D

The Anchor **£ 35**
Main St IP18 6UA (01502) 722112
A seaside pub popular with the "yachtie crowd", and where "everything is good" – from the fish-and-chips to the choice of beers; fans say this country cousin of Fulham's White Horse is the "best place in the area", too ("outperforming anything in nearby Southwold"). / **Details:** www.anchoratwalberswick.com; 9 pm. **Accommodation:** 7 rooms, from £45/person.

Bell Inn £ 34
Ferry Rd IP18 6TN (01502) 723109
Tipped for its "superb location" and "friendly staff", a pub offering fare of the standard of "reliable home cooking".
/ **Details:** www.adnams.co.uk; off A12 on B1387 (no access from Southwold); 9 pm; no booking. **Accommodation:** 6 rooms, from £80.

WARWICK, WARWICKSHIRE 5–4C

The Art Kitchen £ 38
7 Swan St CV34 4BJ (01926) 494303
"Unfailingly delivering the finest Thai food", this "welcoming" and "reasonably-priced" establishment is also of note for its "excellent" wine list – it even offers a good range by the glass!
/ **Details:** www.theartkitchen.com; 10 pm.

Saffron £ 22
Unit 1 Westgate Hs, Market St CV34 4DE (01926) 402061
An establishment tipped (but not quite invariably) as "the best Indian for miles around" ("and that includes Brum!"); perhaps the occasional dissenter is put off by the location – "a concrete shopping mall overlooking the bus station". / **Details:** www.saffronwarwick.co.uk; 11.30 pm; D only.

Saxon Mill £ 40
Coventry Rd, Guys Cliffe CV34 5YN (01926) 492255
A "bustling village pub" tipped for its "stunning" waterside location, and "great views"; the food is "generally good" too.
/ **Details:** www.saxonmill.co.uk; 9.30 pm, Sun 9 pm.

WATERGATE BAY, CORNWALL 1–3B

Fifteen Cornwall £ 60

Watergate Bay Hotel TR8 4AA (01637) 861000
No one doubts that Jamie Oliver's "vibey" beach-side training operation has a "stunning" location with "fantastic" views; the food, like the service, can be "variable", but, of late, standards overall have shown signs of improvement. / **Details:** www.fifteencornwall.co.uk; on the Atlantic coast between Padstow and Newquay; 9.15 pm; children: 7+ before 7 pm only.

WATERMILLOCK, CUMBRIA 7–3D

Leeming House Hotel £ 56
CA11 0JJ (01768) 486674
One of the better Macdonald Hotels outfits, this lake-view country house is tipped as a useful place to know about if you should find yourself in the area (but not really a destination in its own right).
/ **Details:** www.macdonald-hotels.co.uk; directly off A592; 9 pm; no jeans or trainers. **Accommodation:** 41 rooms, from £155.

WATH-IN-NIDDERDALE, NORTH YORKSHIRE 8–4B

Sportsman's Arms £ 42

HG3 5PP (01423) 711306
"Always a warm welcome, and good value for money too" – over three decades in the same ownership, this Dales inn is the epitome of a "reliable country pub/restaurant". / **Details:** take Wath Road from Pateley Bridge; 9 pm, Sun 8 pm; no Amex. **Accommodation:** 11 rooms, from £60/person.

WAVENDON, BUCKINGHAMSHIRE   3–2A

The Plough Wavendon   **£ 56** ⭐
72 Walton Rd MK17 8LW   (01908) 587576
"Fine dining comes to Milton Keynes!" – all reporters agree that this
is a destination offering *"truly outstanding"* food; there are quibbles,
though, not least the rather *"bland"* décor of the potentially
"beautiful" building, and service which is sometimes *"over-zealous"*.
/ **Details:** www.theploughwavendon.com; 10.30 pm; closed Mon & Sun D;
no Amex; no shorts.

WELLS, SOMERSET   2–3B

Goodfellows   **£ 45** ⭐⭐
5 Sadler St BA5 2RR   (01749) 673866

The setting may be Spartan, but *"the highest standard of creativity
and execution"* are evident in Adam Fellows's *"light and flavoursome"*
fish-based cuisine; there's a café too, particularly praised for its
"excellent snack lunches", where the fare is typically more
carnivorous. / **Details:** www.goodfellowswells.co.uk; Near the Cathedral and the
Market Square; 9.30 pm; closed Mon, Tue D & Sun. **Accommodation:** 0 rooms,
from £0.

Old Spot   **£ 35** 🅣
12 Sadler St BA5 2SE   (01749) 689099
*Run by an ex-Bibendum chef, a restaurant in the cathedral precincts,
tipped for its "very good" food.* / **Details:** 10.30 pm; closed Mon, Tue L &
Sun D.

WELSH HOOK, PEMBROKESHIRE   4–4B

Stone Hall Mansion   **£ 48** 🅣
SA62 5NS   (01348) 840212
*"A wonderful old house, in the depths of the countryside"; Gallic-run,
it is tipped for its "traditional" (perhaps "rather unrefined") Gallic
cuisine.* / **Details:** www.stonehall-mansion.co.uk; 9 pm; D only, closed Mon &
Sun. **Accommodation:** 4 rooms, from £100.

WELWYN, HERTFORDSHIRE   3–2B

**Auberge du Lac
Brocket Hall**   **£ 78**
AL8 7XG   (01707) 368888
*"The perfect venue for a smart summer lunch"; this "idyllically-
located" lakeside restaurant (with terrace) is the "ne plus ultra
of romantic locations", and supporters say Phil Thompson's "fabulous"
food "always excels"; for doubters, though, the food remains merely
"competent" ("rather than inspired").* / **Details:** www.brocket-hall.co.uk;
on B653 towards Harpenden; 9.30 pm; closed Mon & Sun; no jeans or trainers;
booking: max 10 in restaurant. **Accommodation:** 16 rooms, from £175.

The Wellington £ 38
1 High St AL6 9LZ (01438) 714036
For oenophiles, a special relationship with d'Arenberg wines (South Australia) adds to the interest of a visit to this "lovely Old Welwyn pub"; the food – "a good, robust selection of small or large plates" – is perhaps best regarded as a supporting attraction.
/ **Details:** www.wellingtonatwelwyn.co.uk; 10 pm.

WEST BYFLEET, SURREY 3–3A

Chu Chin Chow £ 34
63 Old Woking Rd KT14 6LF (01932) 349581
*"Excellent, for a local Chinese", serving "standard fare, and some more unusual items too"; "the interior is both larger and more welcoming than the exterior suggests". / **Details:** www.chuchinchow.com; 11 pm.*

WEST CLANDON, SURREY 3–3A

**L'Auberge
Onslow Arms** £ 41
The Street GU4 7TE (01483) 222447
*Part of a small chain of in-boozer brasseries, a "charming" establishment tipped for its "reliably great French food at reasonable prices". / **Details:** www.massivepub.com; 9.30 pm.*

WEST KIRBY, MERSEYSIDE 5–2A

La Paz £ 37
3 Banks Rd CH48 4HD (0151) 625 7200
Tipped for its simple but "scrupulously sourced" fare, an all-day bistro that all reporters rate as a perfect suburban stand-by.
/ **Details:** www.lapazrestaurants.co.uk; 9.30 pm, Sat 10 pm, Sun 8 pm; closed Mon & Sun D.

WEST MALLING, KENT 3–3C

The Swan £ 45
35 Swan St ME19 6JU (01732) 521910
A "buzzy" and "atmospheric" inn, where an "imaginative" menu is realised to sometimes "brilliant" effect; "haphazard" service, though, can sometimes take the edge off the experience.
/ **Details:** www.theswanwestmalling.co.uk; 11 pm, Sun 8 pm.

WEST MERSEA, ESSEX 3–2C

The Company Shed £ 16
129 Coast Rd CO5 8PA (01206) 382700
*"A real experience"; no one really minds about the "rough" ambience, and the "off-hand" service, of this "eccentric", ultra no-frills shack – it's "the freshest oysters and crab" that people go for; take your own Sancerre. / **Details:** L only, closed Mon; no credit cards; no booking.*

West Mersea Oyster Bar £ 24
Coast Rd CO5 8LT (01206) 381600
"Slightly more salubrious" than the famous Company Shed, nearby, this is an establishment tipped not only for "great oysters at give-away prices", but also for "cracking" fish 'n' chips.
/ **Details:** www.westmerseaoysterbar.co.uk; 5pm, Fri & Sat 10pm; Sun-Thu closed D.

The Wensleydale Heifer   £ 45 ⭐

Main St DL8 4LS (01969) 622322

"About as far from the sea as you can get but the best seafood we've had anywhere"; this decidedly land-locked Dales inn has quite a name for its cuisine, and – "in finest Yorkshire tradition" – the portions are "huge" too. / **Details:** www.wensleydaleheifer.co.uk; 9.30 pm.
Accommodation: *9 rooms, from £110.*

Oldhams   £ 24 ⭐

13 West Rd SS0 9AU (01702) 346736

For those in search of "old-fashioned fish 'n' chips", a town-centre establishment that's of note for its "good selection" of fare, and its "consistent" standards. / **Details:** *On the A13; no Amex.*

Kinara ⭐
Pitts Cottage   £ 33

High St TN16 1RQ (01959) 562125

A "lovely" beamed cottage is, perhaps, an unlikely location in which to sample Pakistani food that's "a cut above the usual"; at off-peak times, though, the atmosphere can seem "very quiet".
/ **Details:** www.pittscottage.co.uk; 11.30 pm.

Napoli E   £ 20 Ⓣ

18a-18b, Market Sq TN16 1AR (01959) 561688

A decade old, this prettily-housed pizzeria is tipped for its "delicious" pasta and pizza dishes, served in "plentiful" portions.

The Wild Mushroom   £ 42 ⭐

Westfield Ln TN35 4SB (01424) 751137

Cooking of a "very high standard" distinguishes this "chic" restaurant, housed in a converted Sussex farmhouse; a stream of canapés and inter-course tidbits from the chef increase an overall sense of "good value". / **Details:** www.webbesrestaurants.co.uk; 9.30 pm; closed Mon & Sun D; children: 8+ at D.

Perry's   £ 39 Ⓣ

4 Trinity Rd, The Old Harbour DT4 8TJ (01305) 785799

"A delightful restaurant with good views over the harbour", tipped for "the freshest fish" and a wine list that's "interesting" and "good value". / **Details:** www.perrysrestaurant.co.uk; 9.30 pm; no Amex; children: 7+.

Food by Breda Murphy £ 31 ⭐⭐
41 Station Rd BB7 9RH (01254) 823446
From the former head chef of the famous Inn at Whitewell, an "excellent eatery and delicatessen" which specialises in "simple things done brilliantly". / Details: www.foodbybredamurphy.com; closed Mon, Tue D, Wed D, Thu D, Fri D, Sat D & Sun.

Three Fishes £ 37 ⭐
Mitton Rd BB7 9PQ (01254) 826888
Off-shoot of Northcote (Langho), this "terrifically busy" (no-booking) gastropub makes good use of the "locally sourced" ingredients which are a trademark of the group; the setting, though, can sometimes seem a little "barn-like". / Details: www.thethreefishes.com; 9 pm, Sun 8.30 pm.

Greens £ 43 ⭐
13 Bridge St YO22 4BG (01947) 600284
"The tastiest and freshest fish you could ever wish to eat" is the highlight of the "imaginative use of great local produce" which makes makes the Greens' "friendly" bistro quite a "rave" for all who comment on it. / Details: www.greensofwhitby.com; 9.30 pm, Fri & Sat 10 pm.

Magpie Café £ 28 ⭐⭐
14 Pier Rd YO21 3PU (01947) 602058
"Just a pity it's so busy!"; "don't be put off by the queue", though (or by the somewhat "uncomfortable" interior) – if you're looking for "the fish 'n' chips of the gods", this legendary harbourside chippy remains the place to go. / Details: www.magpiecafe.co.uk; opp Fish Market; 9 pm; no Amex; no booking at L.

Trenchers £ 36 ⭐
New Quay Rd YO21 1DH (01947) 603212
"Forget the Magpie", say some reporters – this "modern" and "comfortable" chippy is "better than all the others in town", and a "refreshingly nice" place too. / Details: www.trenchersrestaurant.co.uk; opp railway station, near marina; 8.30 pm; need 7+ to book.

The White Horse & Griffin £ 48
Church St YO22 4BH (01947) 604857
A celebrated inn which rather divides opinion – fans say the food (especially the "superb" range of fish) is "stunning", but there's also quite a strong view that the place is "over-rated" and "overpriced". / Details: www.whitehorseandgriffin.co.uk; centre of old town, on Abbey side of river; 9 pm. Accommodation: 10 rooms, from £65.

Royal Oak £ 54 ⭐
Paley St SL6 3JN (01628) 620541
'Parkie's pub' – run by the son of the famous TV interviewer – is praised for a "delightfully enticing menu on which most dishes have a modern touch"; it is, though, perhaps "a bit self-conscious about its celebrity associations". / Details: www.theroyaloakpaleystreet.com; 9.30 pm, Fri & Sat 10 pm; closed Sun D.

WHITEBROOK, MONMOUTHSHIRE 2–2B

The Crown at Whitebrook £ 63

NP25 4TX (01600) 860254

*"A lovely hide-away in a stunning valley", this "delightful" restaurant-with-rooms pleases most reporters very much all-round; the style can sometimes seem a little "starchy", though, and the occasional "off-day" has been noted of late. / **Details:** www.crownatwhitebrook.co.uk; 2m W of A466, 5m S of Monmouth; 9 pm; closed Sun D; no Amex; children: 12+. **Accommodation:** 8 rooms, from £115.*

WHITLEY, WILTSHIRE 2–2B

The Pear Tree Inn £ 39

Top Ln SN12 8QX (01225) 709131

*"A terrific local pub that's more of a restaurant these days" – it's still relatively early days, but the signs are that it's being transformed (for the good) by a new chef. / **Details:** www.maypolehotels.com; 9.30 pm, Sun 9 pm; no Amex. **Accommodation:** 8 rooms, from £90.*

WHITSTABLE, KENT 3–3C

Crab & Winkle £ 44

South Quay, Whitstable Harbour CT5 1AB (01227) 779377

*"Lots of local seafood, served with aplomb", and at "reasonable prices" too – the attraction that makes the restaurant above the fish market "well worth a trip"; quality at the shop downstairs, though, is "surprisingly variable". / **Details:** www.crab-winkle.co.uk; 9.30 pm; no Amex.*

JoJo £ 24

209 Tankerton Rd CT5 2AT (01227) 274591

*You get "excellent food in unpretentious surroundings", and a "warm welcome" too at this open-kitchen operation, which has a big following for its tapas-style dishes; costs are kept low by the BYO policy too (modest corkage). / **Details:** www.jojosrestaurant.co.uk; 10.30 pm; closed Mon, Tue, Wed L, Thu L, Fri L & Sun D; no credit cards.*

The Pearson's Arms £ 32

The Horsebridge, Sea Wall CT5 1BT (01227) 272005

*"A modern harbour pub with a nice line in seafood, cocktails and mojitos", where the attractions include "some of the best fish 'n' chips ever"; "try to get a table upstairs for fantastic sea views". / **Details:** www.pearsonsarms.com; 9 pm, Fri & Sat 9.30 pm; no Amex.*

Samphire £ 34

4 High St CT5 1BQ (01227) 770075

*"Deco meets Boho" at this small three-year-old bistro on the High Street; service may be "erratic", but the food – if no bargain – is often "excellent". / **Details:** www.samphirerestaurant.co.uk; 9 pm; no Amex.*

Sportsman £ 43

Faversham Rd, Seasalter CT5 4BP (01227) 273370

*Located "on the salt marshes, just outside the town", this nowadays famous gastropub (of ten years standing) really is "pretty much faultless" – a "relaxing" place where the fish-based cuisine is simply "superb". / **Details:** www.thesportsmanseasalter.co.uk; 8.45 pm; closed Mon & Sun D; no Amex; children: 18+ in main bar.*

Wheeler's Oyster Bar £ 34

8 High St CT5 1BQ (01227) 273311

"Sublime and wonderful seafood" ("possibly the best in the UK") leads many reporters to this unlikely, tiny "hole in the wall", which simply "never disappoints"; "as it's unlicensed you can take your own wine… and then blow the budget on the most inventive and delicious food". / Details: www.seewhitstable.com; 7.30 pm, Sun 7 pm; closed Wed; no credit cards.

Whitstable Oyster Fishery Co. £ 50

Horsebridge CT5 1BU (01227) 276856

This "unusual, very busy and rather noisy restaurant" is a prime tourist destination on the beach, offering "great and simply prepared fish" that's generally "worth a detour"; given the slightly up-and-down standards, though, critics find it "too expensive". / Details: www.oysterfishery.co.uk; on the seafront; 9 pm, Fri 9.30 pm, Sat 9.45 pm, Sun 8.30 pm; closed Mon .

WHITTLESFORD, CAMBRIDGESHIRE   3–1B

The Tickell Arms £ 56

1 North Rd CB2 4NZ (01223) 833128

With its "opera, ducks, fountain and candles", this OTT inn has long been principally known as an "amazingly atmospheric" destination for Cambridge undergrads and their parents; it has recently acquired a new chef, though, and he is tipped as "outstanding". / Details: www.thetickellarms.co.uk; 9.30 pm; closed Mon & Sun D; no Amex; children: 3+.

WILLIAN, HERTFORDSHIRE   3–2B

The Fox £ 39

SG6 2AE (01462) 480233

"A gem for all occasions!"; this "wonderful gastropub" has won quite a following among reporters for its (generally) "spot-on" cuisine – "fresh seafood daily from Norfolk" is a highlight. / Details: www.foxatwillian.co.uk;/1 mile from junction 9 off A1M; 9.15 pm; closed Sun D; no Amex.

WINCHCOMBE, GLOUCESTERSHIRE   2–1C

5 North Street £ 59

5 North St GL54 5LH (01242) 604566

Marcus Ashenford's cuisine is "delicious" and "very accomplished", and most reporters warm to the "relaxing", "cosy" and "informal" restaurant he runs with his wife; it's "not cheap", though, and this year's reports were a fraction more variable than usual. / Details: just off the high street; 9 pm; closed Mon, Tue L & Sun D.

Wesley House £ 45   Ⓐ ✪
High St GL54 5LJ   (01242) 602366

In a beautiful Tudor building, a "charming" and "elegant" restaurant
that "never fails to impress with its excellent and inventive dishes".
/ *Details:* www.wesleyhouse.co.uk; next to Sudeley Castle; 9 pm; closed Sun D.
Accommodation: 5 rooms, from £80.

WINCHESTER, HAMPSHIRE   2–3D

The Black Rat £ 46   ✪
88 Chesil St SO23 0HX   (01962) 844465
Ignore the "strange name" and "unprepossessing location" of this
former boozer – this is an "innovative" restaurant whose
"high standard of cuisine" has survived the departure of its former
big-name chef surprisingly well; summer visitors may be able to bag
their own tropical hut to eat in… in the back yard.
/ *Details:* www.theblackrat.co.uk; 9.30 pm; closed weekday L.

The Chesil Rectory £ 40
1 Chesil St S023 0HU   (01962) 851555
Mixed reviews, since it re-opened in late-2008, on what's sometimes
hailed as "Winchester's best restaurant" – supporters say it's "under-
appreciated", but there is also support for those who find the food
here simply "uninspiring". / *Details:* www.chesilrectory.co.uk; 9.30 pm, Fri &
Sat 10 pm; closed Sun D; children: 12+ at D Sat & Sun.

The Chestnut Horse £ 42   Ⓐ
Easton Village SO21 1EG   (01962) 779257
"A very cosy ancient pub with well-presented food, a good wine
list and very friendly staff" – "popular, and for all the right reasons",
it generates impressively consistent reports.
/ *Details:* www.thechestnuthorse.com; 9.30 pm, Sun 8 pm; no Amex.

Hotel du Vin et Bistro £ 50
14 Southgate St SO23 9EF   (01962) 841414
Like most HduV properties, the "original and best" member of the
nationwide hotel/bistro chain is clearly drifting badly; in an under-
served city, however, it retains quite a following aided by its "informal"
style and "monumental" wine list. / *Details:* www.hotelduvin.com; Central
Winchester, top of high street, near the Cathedral; 9.45 pm; booking: max 10.
Accommodation: 24 rooms, from £140.

Avenue
Lainston House Hotel £ 75
SO21 2LT   (01962) 776088
What a shame that one single theme dominates most of the many
reports on this "classy" country house hotel dining room, which
is variously described as "incredibly expensive" and "grossly
overpriced" (and all points in-between). / *Details:* www.lainstonhouse.com;
9.30 pm, 10 pm Fri & Sat. *Accommodation:* 50 rooms, from £235.

371

The Old Vine £ 32

8 Great Minster St SO23 9HA (01962) 854616

"The best pub food in town"; this elegant and "friendly" operation, near the cathedral, is tipped for dishes that are sometimes "surprisingly novel and tasty". / Details: www.oldvinewinchester.com; 9.30 pm, Sun 9 pm; children: 6+. Accommodation: 5 rooms, from £130.

WINDERMERE, CUMBRIA 7–3D

First Floor Café
Lakeland Limited £ 28

Alexandra Buildings LA23 1BQ (015394) 47116

Steve Doherty (once of Le Gavroche) "continues to excel" in this unlikely venue – the "airy" dining room above a famous kitchenware shop. / Details: www.lakeland.co.uk; 6 pm, Sat 5pm, Sun 4 pm; no Amex.

Gilpin Lodge £ 68

Crook Rd LA23 3NE (01539) 488818

"All-round excellence" (including, perhaps surprisingly, a "fantastic vegetarian menu") is the theme of most commentary on this celebrated country house hotel, which comes complete with "fabulous views"; to some tastes, though, its traditional style can seem "stuffy". / Details: www.gilpinlodge.co.uk; 9.15 pm; no jeans; children: 7+. Accommodation: 20 rooms, from £290.

Holbeck Ghyll £ 68

Holbeck Ln LA23 1LU (01539) 432375

"Refined" cuisine of "simple brilliance", with "immaculate service" too, is making this long-established country house hotel – whose dining room enjoys "spectacular views" – of ever greater note; the "traditional" décor, though, risks becoming rather "jaded". / Details: www.holbeckghyll.com; 3m N of Windermere, towards Troutbeck; 9 pm; booking essential; children: 8+ at D. Accommodation: 23 rooms, from £220.

Jerichos at The Waverly £ 44

College Rd LA23 1BX (01539) 442522

Amongst "the best in the Lakes" – Chris & Jo Blaydes' enthusiastic, "reliable" and "reasonably priced" restaurant-with-rooms almost invariably impresses reporters with its "beautifully cooked" food, and wine. / Details: www.jerichos.co.uk; 9.30 pm; closed L; children: 12+. Accommodation: 10 rooms, from £80.

Linthwaite House £ 62

Crook Rd LA23 3JA (01539) 488600

More contemporary in style than most Lake District hotels, this country house establishment (with "great views") is hailed by most (if not quite all) reporters for offering "stunning food in a stunning atmosphere"; "wines to die for" too. / Details: www.linthwaite.com; near Windermere golf club; 9 pm; no jeans or trainers; children: 7+ at D. Accommodation: 32 rooms, from £180.

WINDSOR, BERKSHIRE 3–3A

Al Fassia £ 27

27 St Leonards Rd SL4 3BP (01753) 855370

A rough-around-the-edges Moroccan joint that's been an "impressively consistent performer" for over a decade; it's a "welcoming" sort of place, serving "blissful" food at "very reasonable" prices. / Details: 10.30 pm, Fri & Sat 11 pm.

The Greene Oak £ 37

SL4 5UW (01753) 864294

"A decent pub near Windsor!" (and "well positioned just off the M4" too); it has no great culinary ambitions but is tipped for its "good-quality food and wine", and its "convivial" atmosphere.
/ **Details:** *www.thegreeneoak.co.uk; 9.30 pm; no Amex.*

WINKFIELD, BERKSHIRE 3–3A

Cottage Inn £ 48

Winkfield St SL4 4SW (01344) 882242

Tipped as quite a "romantic" destination, a well-established gastropub, offering "reliable and well-cooked comfort food".
/ **Details:** *www.cottage-inn.co.uk; 10 pm; closed Sun D.* **Accommodation:** *10 rooms, from £100.*

WINTERINGHAM, LINCOLNSHIRE 5–1D

Winteringham Fields £ 88

DN15 9ND (01724) 733096

How are the mighty fallen!; to think that, until it changed hands in 2005, this quaint and charming restaurant-with-rooms was once among England's top establishments; many reporters note that, though still a pricey place, it's "not what it was" nowadays, and that service is sometimes "especially poor".
/ **Details:** *www.winteringhamfields.com; 4m SW of Humber Bridge; 9.30 pm; closed Mon & Sun; no Amex; booking: max 8.* **Accommodation:** *10 rooms, from £155.*

WITHAM, ESSEX 3–2C

Lian £ 39

5 Newland St CM8 2AF (01376) 510684

"One of the best Chinese restaurants I have been to, out-of-the-way location notwithstanding" – with its "fresh" and "wonderful" fare and its "attentive" service, this quarter-centenarian continues to please all who comment on it. / **Details:** *10 pm; closed Sun.*

WOBURN, BEDFORDSHIRE 3–2A

Birch £ 42

20 Newport Rd MK17 9HX (01525) 290295

Slightly mixed reviews on this "very popular dining pub"; fans insist it still offers a "delightful experience" all-round, but value of late has often seemed merely "OK". / **Details:** *www.birchwoburn.com; between Woburn and Woburn Sands on the Newport rd; 10 pm; closed Sun D; booking: max 12, Fri & Sat.*

Paris House £ 68

Woburn Pk MK17 9QP (01525) 290692

Still tipped as "a place to impress" (and for the quality of its soufflés), this long-established restaurant has a beautiful location within the Bedford Estate; for some tastes, though, this quarter-centenarian establishment is rather too much of a "time warp" for comfort.
/ **Details:** *www.parishouse.co.uk; on A4012; 9.30 pm; closed Mon & Sun D.*

WOKING, SURREY 3–3A

Inn @ West End £ 40
42 Guildford Rd GU24 9PW (01276) 858652
*"Worth the trek into deepest Surrey" (two miles from the M3 at J3),
this "friendly" dining pub gets "top marks for food and wine" from
almost all who comment on it. /* **Details:** *www.the-inn.co.uk; 9.30 pm,
Sun 9 pm; children: 5+.*

WOLTERTON, NORFOLK 6–4C

Saracen's Head £ 37
NR11 7LZ (01263) 768909
*A "friendly" inn, tipped for its "delicious food" – with seafood dishes
especially commended – and "atmospheric surroundings".
/* **Details:** *www.saracenshead-norfolk.co.uk; 2m W of A140 through Erpingham;
9 pm; closed Mon & Tue L; booking essential.* **Accommodation:** *6 rooms,
from £90.*

WOLVERCOTE, OXFORDSHIRE 2–2D

The Trout Inn £ 34
195 Godstow Rd OX2 8PN (01865) 510930
*As-seen-in-Inspector Morse, this often-"heaving" pub certainly has
a "stunning" riverside setting; the food is "inconsistent", though,
and service can be "very shoddy" on occasions.
/* **Details:** *www.thetroutoxford.co.uk; 2m from junction of A40 & A44; 10 pm,
Fri & Sat 10.30 pm, Sun 9.30 pm.*

WOLVERHAMPTON, WEST MIDLANDS 5–4B

Bilash £ 45
2 Cheapside WV1 1TU (01902) 427762
*Especially "for such a culinary wasteland", this well-established Indian
makes a phenomenal "find", and wins more-than-local praise for its
"top quality" cooking and "warm welcome".
/* **Details:** *www.thebilash.co.uk; opp Civic Centre; 10.30 pm; closed Sun.*

WOODBRIDGE, SUFFOLK 3–1D

The Riverside £ 40
Quayside IP12 1BH (01394) 382174
*Don't let the fact that there's also a theatre/cinema on site give you
the wrong impression – this long-established town-centre spot
is "worth a detour" for the food alone – "from the fantastic home-
made breads right through to the puds, every course is a winner".
/* **Details:** *www.theriverside.co.uk; next to Woodbridge train station; 9.30 pm;
closed Sun D.*

WOODLANDS, HAMPSHIRE 2–4C

Terravina
Hotel Terravina £ 47
174 Woodlands Rd SO40 7GL (023) 8029 3784
*Gerard Basset's "extensive, well chosen wine list" and service with
"great warmth" is helping carve a name for this small New
Forest hotel (a new venture from the co-founder of the Hotel du Vin
chain); the food in the "ultra-modern" dining room can be "very good"
too, but reports of late have been a little uneven.
/* **Details:** *www.hotelterravina.co.uk; 9.30 pm.* **Accommodation:** *11 rooms,
from £135.*

WOOKEY HOLE, SOMERSET 2–3B

The Wookey Hole Inn £ 36
BA5 1BP (01749) 676677
"A wonderfully quirky pub near the famous Caves", tipped for its
"interesting menu, friendly staff and laid-back interior".
/ **Details:** www.wookeyholeinn.com; 9.30 pm; closed Sun D. **Accommodation:** 5
rooms, from £80.

WORCESTER, WORCESTERSHIRE 2–1B

Brown's £ 50
24 Quay St WR1 2JJ (01905) 26263
"Outstanding" cooking and "obliging" service often figure in reports
on this interestingly-housed riverside restaurant; à la carte prices can
be "high", though, but a range of 'deals' help keep costs down.
/ **Details:** www.brownsrestaurant.co.uk; near the Cathedral on riverside; 9.30 pm;
closed Sun D.

Glasshouse £ 43
Danesbury Hs, Sidbury WR1 2HU (01905) 611120
A bright and attractive restaurant, tipped for food that's "generally
very good"; service, though, seems surprisingly "erratic".
/ **Details:** www.theglasshouse.co.uk; 9.30 pm; closed Sun.

WORTHING, WEST SUSSEX 3–4A

Bryce's Seafood Brasserie £ 31
The Steyne BN11 3DU (01903) 214317
"Good food, with a smile, served from the open kitchen" – after three
years in business, that's the formula that's making this "fresh fish"
specialist "deservedly popular". / **Details:** www.seafoodbrasserie.co.uk;
9.30 pm; no Amex.

The Fish Factory £ 22
51-53 Brighton Rd BN11 3EE (01903) 207123
"In a town lacking in good eating", our tip is this "decent" fish
restaurant, where service is noted as being particularly "prompt" and
efficient. / **Details:** www.protorestaurantgroup.com; 10 pm.

WRESSLE, NORTH YORKSHIRE 5–1D

Loftsome Bridge Coaching House £ 38
YO8 6EN (01757) 630070
By the River Derwent, a Georgian coaching inn – that subsequently
became a farm for much of its history – that's tipped for its "decent"
food, and a "wonderful-value" wine list too.
/ **Details:** www.loftsomebridge-hotel.co.uk; Off the A63, on the turning for
Wressle, Bubwith & Brighton; 9 pm; D only, ex Sun L only; no jeans.
Accommodation: 17 rooms, from £67.50.

WREXHAM, WREXHAM 5–3A

Pant-yr-Ochain £ 35
Old Wrexham Rd LL12 8TY (01978) 853525
Part of the Brunning & Price chain, a pretty former manor house pub
which maintains a strong name locally for "excellent food and ale";
it has a "lovely" garden, with a small lake, best enjoyed on a
"late summer evening". / **Details:** www.pantyrochain-gresford.co.uk; 1m N
of Wrexham; 9.30 pm, Sun 9 pm.

WRIGHTINGTON BAR, LANCASHIRE 5–1A

High Moor £ 30
High Moor Ln WN6 9QA (01257) 252364
*A "beautiful" former coaching inn (with good views), tipped for "high standards across the board"; the "traditional" menu is noted for its "very good value". / **Details:** www.highmoorrestaurantwigan.co.uk; J27 of the M6; 9.30 pm, Sun 8 pm; closed Mon & Sat L; no Amex.*

Mulberry Tree £ 44
9 Wood Ln WN6 9SE (01257) 451400
*"Always enjoyable, despite the invariable long wait", this former pub is tipped for its "vast range of dishes"; the bar is "better value" than the restaurant, and often preferred anyway. / **Details:** www.themulberrytree.info; 2m along Mossy Lea Rd, off M6, J27; 9.30 pm; no Amex.*

WYE, KENT 3–3C

The Wife of Bath £ 43
4 Upper Bridge St TN25 5AF (01233) 812232
*"A good-value restaurant-with-rooms", which maintains a "steady" standard – indeed, fans say it serves up "probably the best food in this part of Kent". / **Details:** www.thewifeofbath.com; off A28 between Ashford & Canterbury; 10 pm; closed Mon, Tue L & Sun D. **Accommodation:** 5 rooms, from £85.*

WYKE REGIS, DORSET 2–4B

Crab House Café £ 40
Ferrybridge Rd DT4 9YU (01305) 788867
*In a "very informal ramshackle location", a "great little hut-restaurant" with quite a name for its crabs ("fresh from the bay") and its "really imaginative fish cookery". / **Details:** www.crabhousecafe.co.uk; 9 pm, Sat 9.30; closed Tue; no Amex.*

YARMOUTH, ISLE OF WIGHT 2–4D

George Hotel £ 50
Quay St PO41 0PE (01983) 760331
*Quite a lot of feedback on this well-known waterside hotel-brasserie, where the food has a Mediterranean slant – sadly, rather too much of it was to the effect that it's "expensive, but not at all special". / **Details:** www.thegeorge.co.uk; 9.30 pm. **Accommodation:** 19 rooms, from £190.*

YARPOLE, HEREFORDSHIRE 2–1B

The Bell Inn £ 36
Green Ln HR6 0BD (01568) 780359
*Run by the brother of the proprietor of London's (and formerly nearby Ludlow's) famed Hibiscus, this is a "welcoming" and "friendly" gastropub, where "simple seasonal food" is "superbly prepared and beautifully presented". / **Details:** www.thebellinnyarpole.co.uk; 9.30 pm; closed Mon; no Amex.*

YATTENDON, BERKSHIRE   2–2D

Pot Kiln   £ 39
Frilsham RG18 0XX   (01635) 201366
"A bit out of the way", but "well worth the effort of finding",
this "rustic" gastropub has quite a name for its way with (often locally-
shot) game. / **Details:** *www.potkiln.org; between J12 and J13 of the M4; 9 pm;*
closed Sun D.

Royal Oak Hotel   £ 48
The Square RG18 0UG   (01635) 201325
"Worth the trip on a sunny day", this handsome coaching inn in a
picturesque village is tipped for its "imaginative" and "reliable"
cuisine. / **Details:** *www.royaloakyattendon.com; 5m W of Pangbourne,*
off B4009; 9.30 pm, Sun 9 pm. **Accommodation:** *5 rooms, from £130.*

YIEWSLEY, GREATER LONDON   3–3A

Water Palace   £ 20
131 High St VB7 7QL   (01895) 422464
"Oddly, near Heathrow", a Chinese whose food makes it a "winner",
as evidenced by its "large Asian following".
/ **Details:** *www.waterpalace.com.*

YORK, NORTH YORKSHIRE   5–1D

Bettys   £ 30
6-8 St Helen's Sq YO1 8QP   (01904) 659142
"A unique experience, if a little pricey" – this famous Edwardian
tearoom is generally hailed as a "good-quality" destination, where
"massive" queues are the main drawback; critics, though, insist it's
just "trading on its past". / **Details:** *www.bettysandtaylors.com; down Blake*
St from York Minster; 9 pm; no Amex; no booking.

The Blackwell Ox Inn   £ 37
Huby Rd YO61 1DT   (01347) 810328
A village boozer where the food is tipped as "always wonderful";
the "friendly" service, though, can sometimes be "amateurish".
/ **Details:** *www.blackwelloxinn.co.uk; 9.30 pm; closed Sun D; no Amex.*
Accommodation: *7 rooms, from £95.*

The Blue Bicycle   £ 48
34 Fossgate YO1 9TA   (01904) 673990
"Why do you still list this place?", thunders one reporter; our only
excuse is the considerable number of reports this "busy" local stand-
by attracts – of late, however, too many of these are, admittedly,
of experiences which are "really disappointing".
/ **Details:** *www.thebluebicycle.com; 9.30 pm, Sun 9 pm; closed Mon - Wed L;*
no Amex; booking: max 8 Sat D. **Accommodation:** *5 rooms, from £165.*

Café Concerto   £ 37
21 High Petergate YO1 7EN   (01904) 610478
Tipped as a "fantastic place for lunch", this café by the Minster is an
"old-reliable" sort of place, where the food is generally
of "good quality"; the queue, though, can take "ages".
/ **Details:** *www.cafeconcerto.biz; by the W entrance of York Minster; 9.30 pm;*
booking: max 6. **Accommodation:** *1 room, at about £-.*

Cafe No. 8 Bistro   £ 38

8 Gillygate YO31 7EQ   (01904) 653074

A small and "unpretentious" café, near the Minster, often tipped for "great sandwiches", and for other simple fare that's "much nicer than the understated setting would suggest"; there's a "pleasant courtyard at the back" too. / **Details:** *www.cafeno8.co.uk; 9.30 pm; closed Sun D; no Amex.*

City Screen Café Bar
City Screen Picturehouse   £ 30

Coney St YO1 9QL   (01904) 612940

"Popular, but worth the wait" – this riverside cinema café is tipped for its "good range of dishes" (including some "interesting salads and vegetarian platters"). / **Details:** *www.picturehouses.co.uk; 9 pm; no Amex; no booking.*

J Baker's Bistro Moderne   £ 40

7 Fossgate YO1 9TA   (01904) 622688

"The best food in York"; the "startlingly original" cuisine of Jeff Baker's two-year-old venture can come as something of a "surprise" to the uninitiated (to the extent that it is perhaps inevitable that the style will sometimes seem "pretentious"); atmosphere? – "bring your own". / **Details:** *www.jbakers.co.uk; 10 pm; closed Mon & Sun.*

Melton's   £ 42

7 Scarcroft Rd YO23 1ND   (01904) 634 341

For "unbelievably consistent" and "tasty" meals at "sensible prices", this long-established spot, in an unfashionable corner of the city, is well worth seeking out; the interior, though, can seem a little "dated" nowadays. / **Details:** *www.meltonsrestaurant.co.uk; 10 mins walk from Castle Museum; 10 pm; closed Mon L & Sun; no Amex.*

Melton's Too   £ 30

25 Walmgate YO1 9TX   (01904) 629 222

"Reformed and improved", this popular spot is tipped as an "all-round bistro" where tapas dishes in particular offer "good value". / **Details:** *www.meltonstoo.co.uk; 2 minutes from the City centre; 10.30 pm, Sun 9.30 pm; no Amex.*

Middlethorpe Hall   £ 66

Bishopthorpe Rd YO23 2GB   (01904) 641241

In "beautiful" gardens, on the fringe of the city, a "formal" country house hotel (in the style that's "going out of fashion"), which offers the visitor "a few hours of gracious living"; a regular reports "improved" food of late too. / **Details:** *www.middlethorpe.com; next to racecourse; 9.30 pm; no shorts; children: 4+.* **Accommodation:** *29 rooms, from £190.*

Oscar's Wine Bar & Bistro   £ 29

27 Swinegate YO1 8AZ   (01904) 652002

"A Great York institution"; this "buzzy" wine bar offers "good food" in "generous portions", and at "reasonable prices" too. / **Details:** *www.oscarswinebar.com; 10 pm; no Amex.*

UK MAPS

Overview

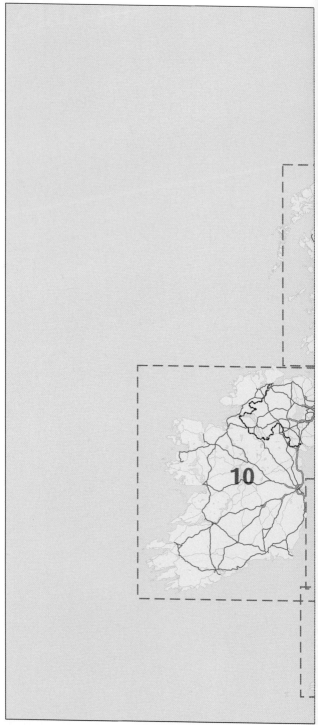

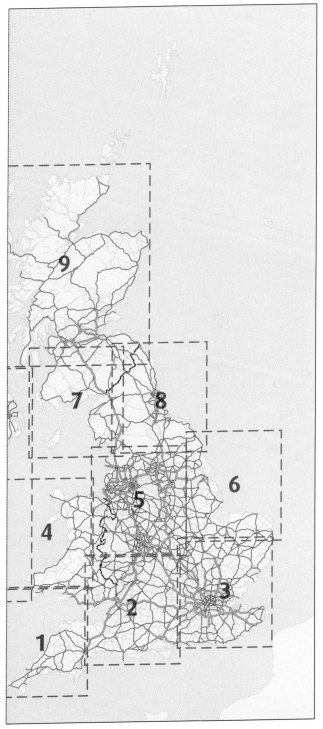

Map 1

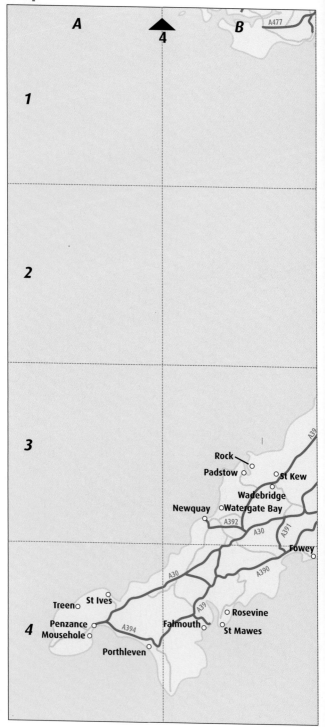

A   4   B   A477

1

2

3   Rock
     Padstow ○   ○ St Kew
          ○
          Wadebridge
     Newquay ○Watergate Bay
          ○   A392   A30   A391
                    A390   Fowey ○

     A30   A390

     Treen○ St Ives ○
     Penzance ○   A394   ○ Rosevine
     Mousehole ○   Falmouth ○ ○ St Mawes
4   Porthleven ○

Map 1

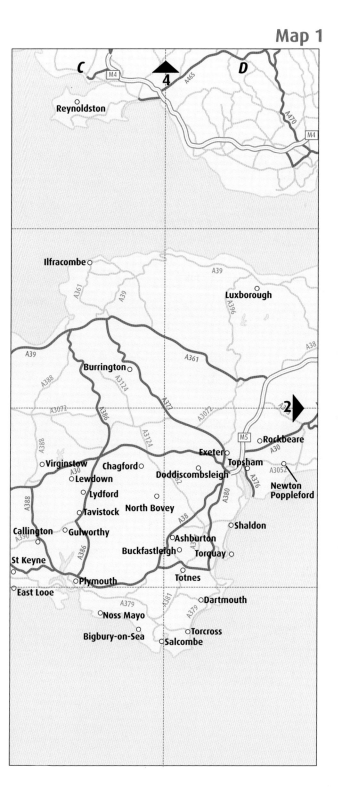

Map 2

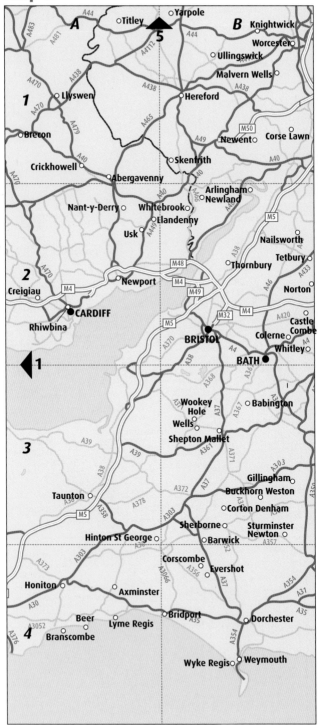

Map 2

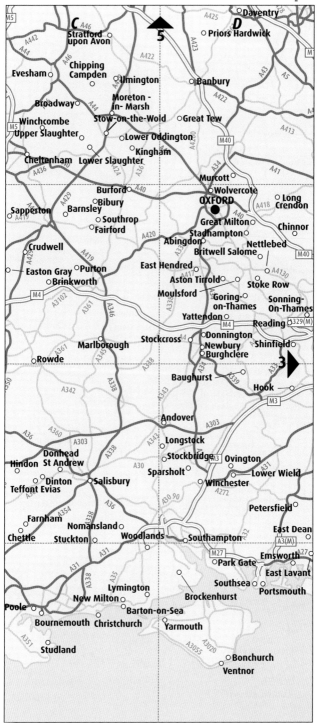

Map 3

Map 3

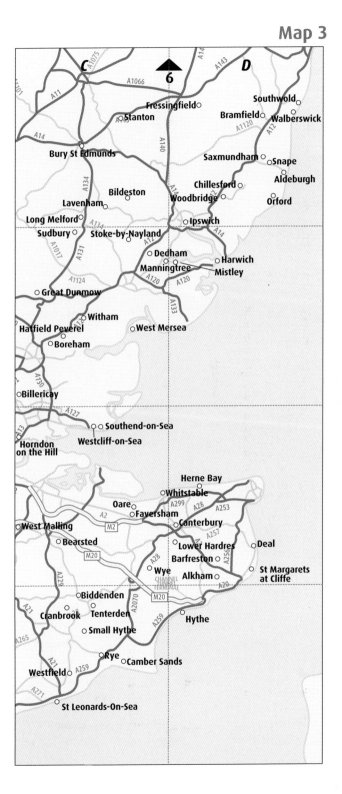

Map 4

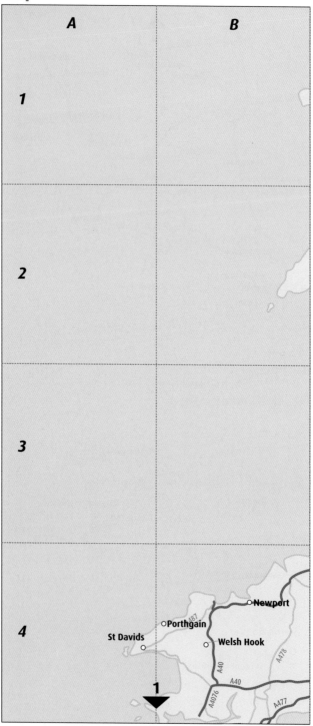

A   B

1

2

3

4

Newport

Porthgain

St Davids

Welsh Hook

Map 4

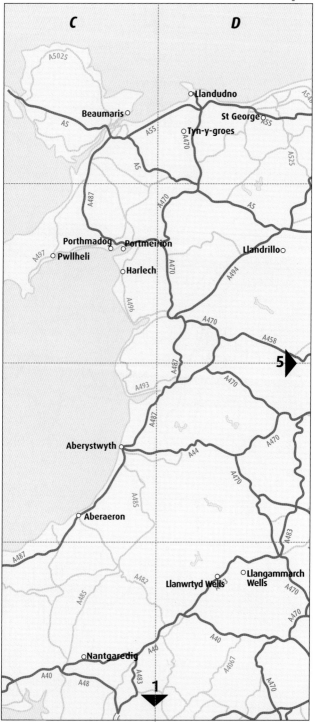

Map 5

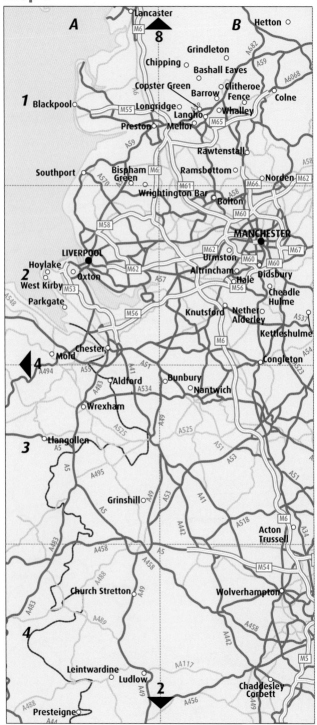

Map 5

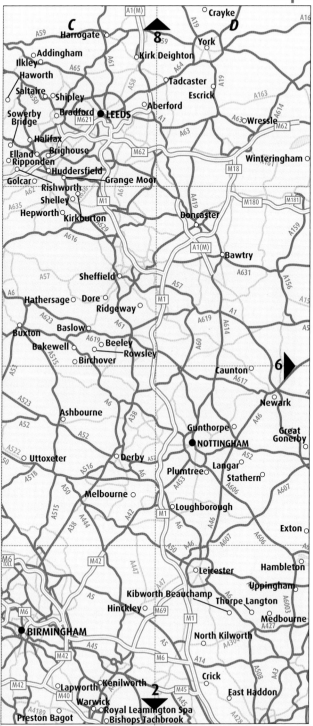

Map 6

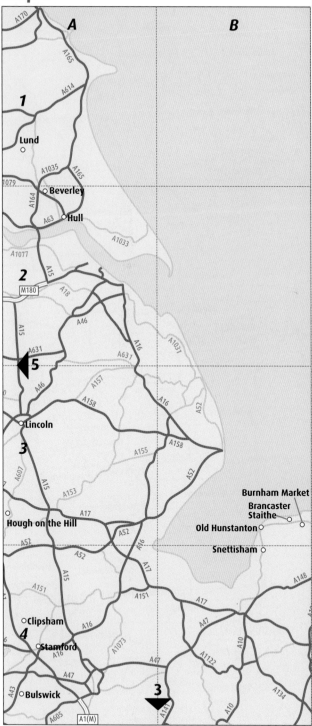

A

B

1

Lund

A170
A165
A614
A1035
A165
1079
A164
A63
Beverley
Hull
A1033

2

A1077
A15
M180
A18
A46
A15
A631
A16
A1031
A631
A46
A157
A16
A52
A158
A158

5

Lincoln

3

A607
A155
A52
A15
A153
A17
A52
A52
A16
A17

Hough on the Hill

Burnham Market
Brancaster
Staithe
Old Hunstanton
Snettisham

A52
A151
A148
A15
A151
A17
A47
A10
Clipsham
A16
A1073
A47
A1122
A10

4

Stamford

A43
A47
A134
Bulswick
A605
A1(M)
A14

3

Map 6

Map 7

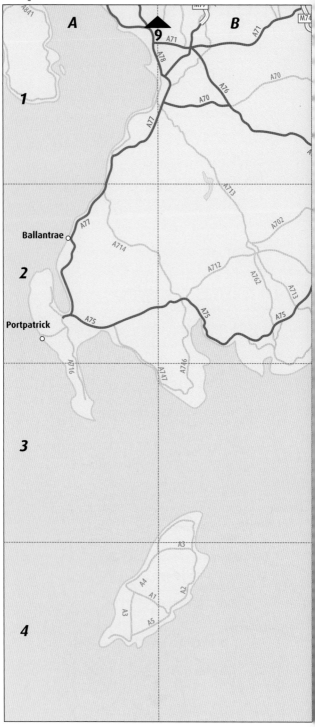

9

A

B

1

2

Ballantrae

Portpatrick

3

4

Map 7

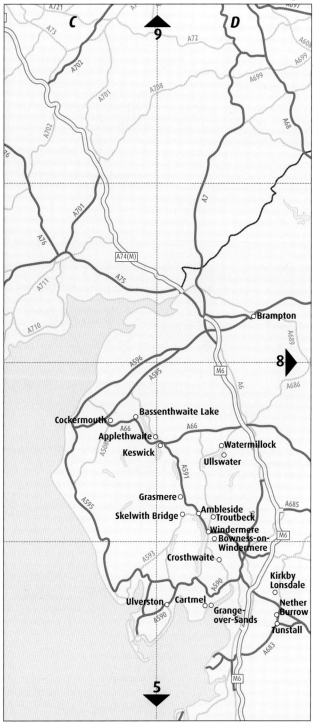

Map 8

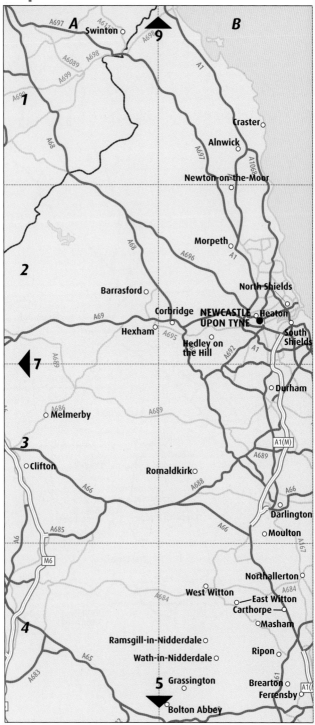

Map 8

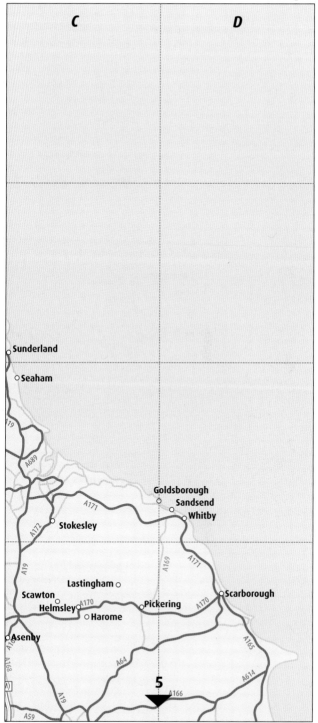

C

D

Sunderland

Seaham

A19

A689

Goldsborough

A171

Sandsend

Whitby

A172

Stokesley

A19

A169

A171

Lastingham

Scawton

A170

Helmsley

Pickering

A170

Scarborough

Harome

Asenby

A168

A165

A64

5

A166

A614

A19

A59

Map 9

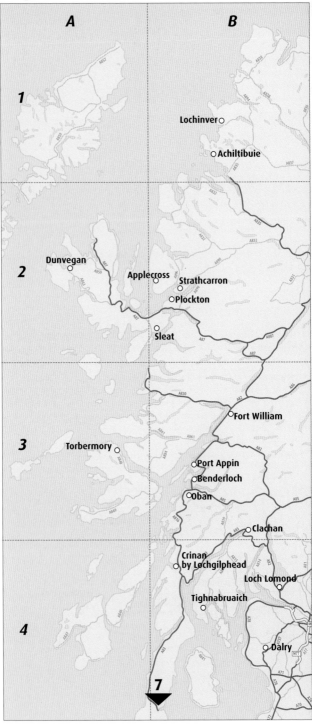

A   B

1

Lochinver ○

○ Achiltibuie

2

Dunvegan ○

Applecross ○   ○ Strathcarron
             ○ Plockton

○ Sleat

Fort William ●

3 Torbermory ○

Port Appin ○
Benderloch ○
Oban ○

Clachan ○

Crinan ○
by Lochgilphead

Loch Lomond ○

Tighnabruaich ○

4

○ Dalry

7

Map 9

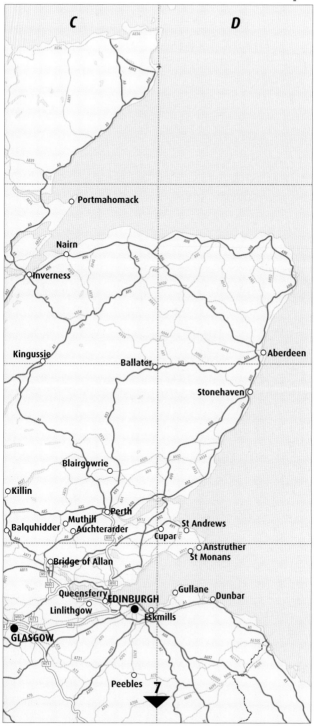

C

D

Portmahomack

Nairn

Inverness

Kingussie

Ballater

Aberdeen

Stonehaven

Blairgowrie

Killin

Perth

Muthill

Balquhidder Auchterarder

St Andrews

Cupar

Anstruther
St Monans

Bridge of Allan

Queensferry

Gullane Dunbar

EDINBURGH

Linlithgow

Eskmills

GLASGOW

Peebles

7

Map 10

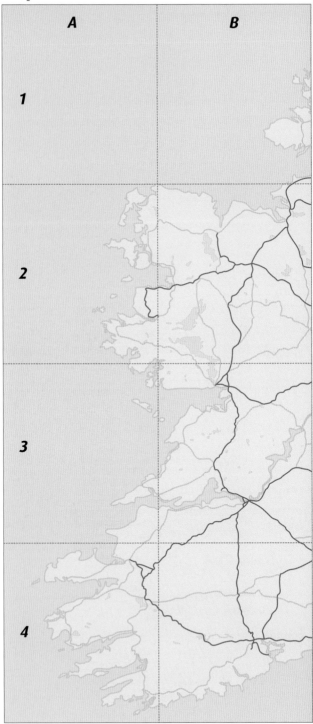

Map 10

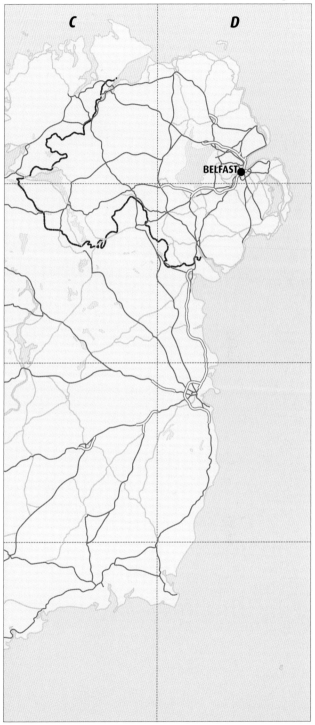

C

D

BELFAST

ALPHABETICAL
INDEX

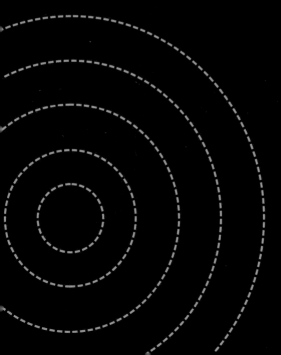

ALPHABETICAL INDEX

404

ALPHABETICAL INDEX

ALPHABETICAL INDEX

ALPHABETICAL INDEX

ALPHABETICAL INDEX

Printed in Italy
by Rotolito Lombarda S.p.A.